Ferdinand Bol, 1616-1680, Dutch, "The Woman with a Pear," etching,
1960.612. The Albert P. Strietmann Collection

From Palette to Palate

550 Favorite Recipes
from the Women's Committee of the
Cincinnati Art Museum

Published by
Cincinnati Art Museum
1985

Copyright 1985 by the Cincinnati Art Museum
Printed in the United States of America

All rights reserved, including the right
to reproduce this work in any form whatsoever
without permission in writing from
the publisher, except for brief passages
in connection with a review.

For information write:
Cincinnati Art Museum, Publications Department
Eden Park, Cincinnati, Ohio 45202

Library of Congress Cataloging Data in progress

Printer: The Hennegan Company
Typesetter: Cobb Typesetting Company
Designer: Noel Martin
Assistant: Dana Martin

ISBN 0-931537-01-0

Contents

Introduction 7

Acknowledgments 8

Appetizers and Party Foods 9

Soups, Salads, and Sauces 25

Meats 47

Poultry and Seafood 79

Eggs, Cheese, Rice, and Pasta 107

Fruits and Vegetables 123

Breads, Cakes, and Pastries 141

Desserts 165

Glossary 181

Index 185

Crispijn De Passe De Oude, ca. 1565-1637, Dutch, "September,"
series: "The Months," after Marten De Vos, 1532-1603,
Flemish, engraving. 1962.283 h. Bequest of Edmund Kerper

Introduction

From the establishment of the Women's Art Museum Association in 1877, the women of Cincinnati have provided support and leadership to the cultural institutions of the city. The Association was formed to continue the work of a committee that was responsible for the successful exhibition by the city's women art potters and craftswomen at the Women's Pavilion of the Centennial Exposition of 1876 in Philadelphia. The group wished to provide classes in art, to acquire and display collections of art, and to provide temporary exhibitions of art. In 1880, the Association opened an internationally publicized exhibition which prompted Mr. Charles West to provide a gift of $150,000 to establish a permanent art museum if a like amount could be provided from the community. The amount was quickly pledged, and in 1881, the Cincinnati Museum Association was formed.

So, throughout the years, the women of Cincinnati have been leaders in the support, guidance, and expansion of the Cincinnati Art Museum. This book is a continuation of that involvement. It is an additional means for the Women's Committee to enhance the Museum and to provide support to the institution that they have served so well and so faithfully.

This book, as all recipe anthologies of this type, is the result of the contributions and efforts of many. Recipes were solicited from members of the Women's Committee, the community, and friends near and far. The recipes have been edited, sometimes modified, and a diligent testing committee has spent many enjoyable hours cooking and tasting. The resulting book is a collection of recipes from throughout the world which reflects the culinary interests of the country and of Cincinnatians today. We have attempted to provide recipes that are not too difficult for the home chef to accomplish, yet which display a knowledge of world cuisine and its fascinating variations.

As with all cookbooks, this is intended to be only the beginning of your experimentation and readers will bring their own interpretations and individual approaches to the recipes. Cooking all over America is becoming more interesting and varied because of the growing availability of fresh and exotic ingredients and the influence of ethnic cultures in the fabric of society. Wherever possible, use the best and freshest of herbs, vegetables, and other ingredients. We hope that new and old friends throughout the country will enjoy the book, and through it and its illustrations become better acquainted with the Cincinnati Art Museum.

– Karen Rafuse, Editor

Acknowledgments

Our thanks to the Cincinnati Art Museum members and friends who contributed their recipes and to all the recipe collectors and testers whose efforts and talents have resulted in this collection of recipes. We also wish to thank those who gave of their talents and time but chose to be anonymous. The Committee regrets that similarity has prevented our using some of the recipes received. Special thanks to the late Betty L. Zimmerman for her encouragement and artistic talent; Robert B. Ott, President, The Hennegan Company, for his guidance and generosity; Millard F. Rogers, Jr., Director, for his support.

Committee

Editors	Margaret Minster
	Karen Rafuse
Associate Editor	Audrey McCafferty
Steering Committee	Mrs. J. Richard Andre
	Mrs. J. Gordon Dixon
	Mrs. Richard Thayer
Designer	Noel Martin
Marketing	Mrs. John L. Strubbe
Treasurer	Mrs. John E. Roth, Jr.
Art Advisor	Mrs. John Durrell
Promotional Events	Mrs. James Hader
	Mrs. Allen D. Lett
Publicity	Mrs. John C. Mueller
Volunteer Coordinator	Mrs. George R. Smith

The proceeds from the sale of this book will benefit the Cincinnati Art Museum

Attributed to Juriaen van Streeck, 1632-1687, Dutch,
"Still Life," late 17th century, oil on panel, 1954.117.
Gift of Dr. and Mrs. J. Louis Ransohoff.
This color reproduction donated by
Mrs. Witham Smith

Pleasures of the table were doubly enjoyed by the prosperous residents of the Netherlands of the 17th century, not only as they dined but also in the still life paintings which frequently decorated their homes and showed food and drink in beguiling detail. Many motifs had specific symbolic meaning.

This work, attributed to Juriaen van Streeck of Amsterdam, dates from the latter years of the century and combines favorite subjects: freshly washed fruit, a shallow bowl, a goblet and a wine glass catching the light. The thinness of the bowl suggests that it was a Chinese import rather than Delftware, the domestically manufactured imitation of Chinese porcelain. The elegant glasses were themselves luxury possessions in the Netherlands at that time.

Appetizers and Party Foods

» Anchovy Eggs «

¼ cup butter
¼ cup parsley, chopped
2 cloves garlic, minced
8 anchovies
6 oz. can tomato paste
Pepper
12 hard-cooked eggs, halved

Simmer together the butter, parsley, garlic, and anchovies. Add tomato paste and pepper; cook slowly for ½ hour. Serve over hard-cooked egg halves. Makes 12 servings.

– Eunice Gronauer (Mrs. Raymond)

» Brandied Braunschweiger «

1 lb. braunschweiger sausage
2 tablespoons mayonnaise
1 tablespoon prepared horseradish
1 teaspoon Worcestershire sauce
1 tablespoon brandy
3 oz. pkg. cream cheese, softened
2 tablespoons mayonnaise
Dash of Worcestershire sauce
2 tablespoons milk
1 tablespoon parsley, chopped
1 clove garlic, crushed
1 teaspoon chives, chopped
Sliced stuffed olives

Mix braunschweiger, mayonnaise, horseradish, Worcestershire sauce, and brandy. Put into a greased mold; chill overnight. Beat together cream cheese, mayonnaise, Worcestershire sauce, milk, parsley, garlic, and chives. Remove the braunschweiger from the mold; frost it with the cream cheese mixture and decorate with the sliced olives. Makes 9″ round mold.

– Rosemarie Culver

» Artichoke Dip «

14½ oz. can artichoke hearts, well drained
1 cup mayonnaise
1 cup grated Parmesan cheese
½ teaspoon garlic, minced
Paprika
Crackers

Cut artichoke hearts into eighths. Mix well with mayonnaise, Parmesan cheese, and garlic. Place in small casserole that can be used for serving; bake 20 minutes at 350°, or until heated through and lightly browned on top. Sprinkle paprika over top and serve as a dip with crackers. Makes 3 cups.

– Rosemary Munsen (Mrs. Robert)

» Camaron Rebosado «

As is done in this fried shrimp recipe, Philippine cooks often marinate shellfish in lemon or lime juice to tenderize and partially "cook" the flesh before the final cooking process takes place.

15 large raw shrimp, peeled and deveined
Juice of 4 lemons
Salt
3 tablespoons flour
4 eggs, beaten
Peanut oil for frying

Soak shrimp in lemon juice and salt to taste for at least 1 hour. Drain and roll in flour to cover and then in beaten eggs. Fry in 2″ deep hot oil until crisp and brown. Makes 3 first-course servings.

– Nellie Obial (Mrs. Guadencio)

» Caraway Spread «

1 lb. Cheddar cheese, grated or cut into small cubes
½ cup beer
2 tablespoons butter
½ teaspoon garlic salt
1 tablespoon caraway seeds
Rye bread or wheat thins

Heat cheese, beer, and butter in saucepan just until cheese melts – no more. Remove from heat. Add garlic salt and caraway seeds; beat with egg beater, blender, or food processor until thoroughly mixed. Pour into dish or mold. Refrigerate until ready to use. Serve with rye bread or wheat thins. Makes 1½ cups.

– Nan Strubbe (Mrs. John L.)

» Carpaccio «

Carne al Carpaccio is a dish from the Piedmont region of Italy, and Giuliano Bugialli says that the name probably has nothing to do with the Venetian Renaissance painter, Carpaccio, but probably means "beef in the style of the Carpathian Mountains."

1 egg yolk
½ cup Parmesan cheese, grated
6 tablespoons Dijon mustard
2 cloves garlic, peeled and crushed
2½ tablespoons Worcestershire sauce
10 tablespoons olive oil
Salt and pepper
1 lb. raw beef, sliced paper thin
1 cup Parmesan cheese, grated
1 loaf French bread, sliced

Mix egg yolk, Parmesan, Dijon mustard, garlic cloves, Worcestershire sauce, olive oil, salt, and pepper in a food processor or blender until smooth. Spread sauce over the bottom of a large, shallow platter and place the raw beef over the sauce like petals. In order to slice the beef into paper-thin slices, freeze it partially and use a very sharp knife to cut the stiffened beef. Sprinkle remaining Parmesan over beef and serve with crisp French bread. Makes 10 to 12 servings.

– Lawsie Coler (Mrs. Michael)

» Indian Cashews «

Miss Meuttman collected this recipe when she was a missionary in India.

½ lb. cashews, unsalted
4 tablespoons butter, melted
¼ teaspoon curry powder
1 teaspoon celery seed

Toss cashews lightly with melted butter. Sprinkle with spices and mix well.

– Antoinette Meuttman

» Caviar Appetizer «

6 hard-cooked eggs, mashed but not smooth
3 tablespoons butter, melted
8 oz. pkg. cream cheese, softened
1 cup sour cream
½ small onion, finely chopped
2 ozs. caviar
Melba toast

Mix mashed eggs and melted butter; press into a 9″ pie dish. Refrigerate for 20 minutes, or put in freezer for 10 minutes, long enough to set. Mix cream cheese, sour cream, and onions well. Spread on top of chopped eggs. Spread caviar on top of cheese mixture. Chill. Can be prepared several hours ahead. Serve with Melba toast. Makes 20 servings.

– Jane Sweeder (Mrs. Willard C.)

» Céleri Rémoulade «

This spicy French sauce which is often served with seafood here complements strips of celery root or celeriac for an intriguing appetizer or salad.

1 medium celery root, peeled and quartered
1 hard-cooked egg
1 egg yolk
2 teaspoons tarragon vinegar, or 2 teaspoons white wine vinegar plus a dash of dried or fresh tarragon
1½ teaspoons Dijon mustard
Salt and pepper
½ cup olive oil
2 tablespoons chives, minced
2 tablespoons parsley, minced
Bibb lettuce leaves

Blanch celery root in boiling water until tender; cut into long ⅛″ wide julienne strips. Mash together hard-cooked egg, raw egg yolk, vinegar, mustard, salt, and pepper. After making a smooth paste, add olive oil slowly, stirring constantly with a wire whisk, or in a blender or food processor, until mixture is the consistency of mayonnaise. Add chives and parsley and mix with julienne celery root. Serve as first course or salad on Bibb lettuce leaves. Makes 4 servings.

– Winnie Love (Mrs. Wesley)

» Chinese Chicken Fingers with Plum Sauce «

At the opening of the exhibit of Silk Roads/China Ships, which came to the Cincinnati Art Museum on loan from the Royal Ontario Museum of Toronto, this was one of the tasty appetizers served. A tangy plum sauce contrasts beautifully with crispy-coated strips of chicken breast.

1½ cups buttermilk
2 tablespoons lemon juice
2 teaspoons
    Worcestershire sauce
1 teaspoon soy sauce
1 teaspoon paprika
1 tablespoon Greek
    seasoning
1 teaspoon salt
1 teaspoon pepper
2 cloves garlic, minced
6 whole chicken breasts,

skinned, boned, and
    cut into ½″ strips
4 cups soft bread crumbs
½ cup sesame seeds
¼ cup butter, melted
¼ cup shortening, melted
1½ cups red plum jam
1½ tablespoons prepared
    mustard
1½ tablespoons prepared
    horseradish
1½ teaspoons lemon juice

Combine buttermilk, lemon juice, Worcestershire sauce, soy sauce, paprika, Greek seasoning, salt, pepper, and garlic in large bowl. Add chicken, mixing until well-coated. Cover and refrigerate overnight. Drain chicken thoroughly. Combine bread crumbs and sesame seeds, mixing well. Add chicken and toss to coat. Place chicken in 2 greased 9″x13″ baking dishes. Combine butter and shortening; brush on chicken. Bake in preheated 350° oven for 35 to 40 minutes. Meanwhile, mix well in small saucepan jam, mustard, horseradish, and lemon juice. Place over low heat just until warm, stirring constantly. Serve chicken with plum sauce. Makes 12 to 14 servings.

– Davis Catering

» Tangy Cheese Bread «

This cheese-topped bread is very easy and delicious, almost like a mock quiche. It may be assembled and refrigerated earlier in the day and baked immediately before serving, or baked earlier and reheated in the microwave. It can also be used as a hot luncheon bread, served with a fruit salad.

1 cup biscuit mix
2 eggs
⅓ cup milk
2 tablespoons instant
    minced onion, or ½ cup
    onions, finely minced
8 oz. pkg. cream cheese,
    softened

¼ cup blue cheese,
    crumbled
1 teaspoon fines herbes or
    dry parsley flakes, or 1
    tablespoon fresh
    parsley, chopped

Combine biscuit mix, 1 egg, milk, and 1 tablespoon minced onion in mixing bowl; beat well by hand. Turn into well-greased 8″ square pan and spread evenly. Beat cream cheese with remaining egg until softened; stir in remaining onion, blue cheese, and fines herbes or parsley. Spread evenly over biscuit mix layer. Bake in a preheated 425° oven for 20 to 25 minutes, until lightly browned on top. Cut into bite-size squares and serve hot as hors d'oeuvres. Makes 64-1″ hors d'oeuvres or 16-2″ luncheon bread squares.

– Audrey McCafferty

» Clams Casino «

16 medium clams
3 green peppers
3 pimientos
4 stalks celery
2 shallots, minced

Pinch thyme
¼ cup olive oil
Salt and pepper
8 slices bacon, cut in half
Lemon wedges

Open clams carefully. Discard top shell and place on baking sheet. Chop peppers, pimientos, and celery in a food processor or blender. Add shallots, thyme, oil, salt, and pepper. Add some of mixture to each shell and cover with uncooked bacon, large enough to cover shell. Bake in a preheated 350° oven until bacon is crisp. Serve with lemon wedges. Makes 4 servings.

– Chef Bruno Fatino
The Met Club, Tequesta, Florida

» Ceviche «

This delicious recipe is from La Ballera in Acapulco. The lime juice "cooks" the fish. Any tender-fleshed fish such as sole, red snapper, flounder, or scallops may be used.

5 cups raw fish fillets, cut in ¾" cubes, and/or scallops
1 cup lime juice
3 cups tomato juice
5 tablespoons olive oil
1 tablespoon oregano
1 teaspoon black pepper
½ teaspoon Tabasco sauce

½ cup orange juice
½ cup tomato puree
½ cup catsup
1 to 2 Jalapeno peppers, chopped
2 cups fresh tomatoes, chopped
1 cup onion, chopped
Salt

Soak cubed fish and/or scallops in lime juice for 20 minutes, stirring occasionally. Remove fish, drain, and rinse with cold water. Mix with remaining ingredients, cover, and marinate in refrigerator for at least 6 hours. Serve as an appetizer or first course. Makes 10 servings.

– Dottie Rockel (Mrs. Donald W.)

» Frick-a-dillers «

These light Danish meatballs have a delightful sweet-sour sauce that is unusual because of the apple flavor. They are easy to prepare and a grand addition to the cocktail table.

1 cup soft bread crumbs
1 egg, well beaten
1 cup applesauce
1 teaspoon salt
½ cup catsup

½ teaspoon nutmeg
⅛ teaspoon pepper
1 ½ lbs. ground beef
¼ cup onion, minced
¼ cup white wine

Mix bread crumbs, egg, half of applesauce, salt, half of catsup, and seasonings. Add ground beef and onion; mix lightly. Form into 1" balls, being careful not to pack mixture tightly. Arrange balls close together in a baking pan and bake in a preheated 425° oven for 15 minutes. Drain fat from pan. Combine remaining applesauce and catsup with wine. Spoon over the meatballs and bake for 10 minutes longer. Serve heated in a chafing dish. Makes 15 to 20 meatballs.

– Barbara Wagner (Mrs. James H.)

» Hot Clam Dip «

½ green pepper, seeded and chopped
1 small pimiento, chopped
1 onion, chopped
3 tablespoons butter
10½ oz. can minced clams
¼ lb. Cheddar cheese, cubed

¼ cup catsup
1 tablespoon Worcestershire sauce
1¼ tablespoons milk
¼ teaspoon cayenne pepper
Few drops Tabasco sauce
Corn chips or crackers

Sauté green pepper, pimiento, and onion in butter, until onions are light brown. Place in double boiler over boiling water. Add clams, Cheddar cheese, catsup, Worcestershire sauce, milk, cayenne pepper, and Tabasco. Stir until cheese melts. Serve hot, preferably in a chafing dish, for dipping with corn chips or crackers. Makes 2 cups.

– Nan Strubbe (Mrs. John L.)

» Ginger Cream Cheese Ball «

8 oz. box pitted dates
8 candied ginger bits
⅔ cup walnuts or pecans

2-8 oz. pkgs. cream cheese
½ cup coconut, flaked
Gingersnaps

Chop dates, ginger, and nuts in blender or food processor. Add cream cheese and blend. Chill; shape mixture into a ball. Sprinkle with coconut, and serve with gingersnaps. Makes 10" ball.

– Melissa Jacobs (Mrs. Daniel Lee)
Atlanta, Georgia

» Crispy Coconut Treats «

These make excellent hors d'oeuvres. Coconut recipes always remind me of the new bride I knew who bought her first fresh coconut when she moved to Florida and was astonished to find that it was not grated inside!

3 Fresh Coconuts

Make a hole in the coconuts with an ice pick or other sharp instrument. Drain milk out of coconuts. Put them in a preheated 350° oven until they crack open. If they do not crack enough, use a hammer to finish the job – after removing from oven. Peel coconut to remove brown inside covering. A swivel-bladed peeler works very well. Slice thinly. Line a shallow baking pan with aluminum foil and spread coconut slices evenly in pan. Heat in a 225° oven, stirring occasionally. Reduce oven temperature to about 200°; bake until coconut is slightly brown and crispy. Makes 1 quart.

– Margaret Minster (Mrs. Leonard)

» Marbled Tea Eggs «

Hard-cooked eggs with cracked shells are soaked in a solution of tea and star anise which gives them a beautiful marbled appearance. Star anise is a seed formation with eight pods which resembles a star; it is available in Oriental groceries.

6 large eggs	*2 buds star anise*
3 cups cold water	*½ tablespoon soy sauce*
2 tea bags	*1 tablespoon salt*

Place eggs and water in a heavy saucepan. Bring to a boil and simmer gently 10 minutes. Remove eggs and place in cold water to cool. Add tea bags, star anise, soy sauce, and salt to the simmering water. Using a teaspoon, crack each egg shell gently all around. Do not remove the shell. The cracks will admit the tea solution. Return eggs to tea water; simmer for an additional 30 minutes. Be sure that water covers eggs. Add more water if needed. Remove eggs, cool, and peel. Cut into halves or quarters, and serve as an appetizer. Makes 6 servings.

– Dora Ang (Mrs. Francis)

» Layered Guacamole Dip «

15 oz. can refried beans	*2 teaspoons chili powder*
8 oz. can chopped chili peppers	*Few drops Tabasco*
½ cup prepared Mexican salsa	*1 cup sour cream*
1 teaspoon salt	*2 cups sharp Cheddar cheese, grated*
1 clove garlic	*1 cup pitted black olives, sliced*
1 medium avocado	*Tortillas or corn chips*
1 teaspoon lemon juice	

In a blender or food processor fitted with steel blade, process refried beans until smooth. Place the beans in a layer in an attractive shallow dish. Add a layer of chili peppers and sprinkle with salsa; use only a portion of the peppers for a milder dish. Sprinkle salt in another shallow pan and rub well with garlic. Mash the avocado into the salt and add lemon juice, chili powder, and Tabasco to taste. Stir in sour cream and layer on top of beans and chili peppers. Sprinkle cheese over top and garnish with sliced olives. Chill, covered, until ready to serve. Serve with crisp tortillas or corn chips. Makes 10 servings.

– Jean Lehman (Mrs. Nat)

» Pete's Guacamole «

Traditionally, this mixture is blended with a molcajete and tejolote – a three-legged stone mortar and pestle. A potato masher and bowl are good substitutes if you do not have a blender or food processor. Cilantro is a variety of parsley and can be found in specialty stores.

3 ripe, medium avocados, peeled and pitted	*1 clove garlic, crushed*
½ onion, coarsely chopped	*2 pickled Jalapeno peppers, coarsely chopped*
2 teaspoons water	*1 tablespoon lemon juice*
2 sprigs cilantro, chopped	*Salt and pepper*

Blend avocados, onion, and water in a blender or food processor just enough to mix. Add cilantro, garlic, peppers, and lemon juice; mix well. Add salt and pepper to taste. Taste as you go along and alter proportions to suit your preference. If the peppers make it a bit too hot, add another avocado. Serve as a dip or as a topping for enchiladas, tostados, or frijoles. Makes about 3 cups.

– Lupe Gonzalez-Hoyt

» Hummous Dip «

Chick peas are found under various names in many countries. In Italy, they're ceci, in France pois chiches, and in Spain and Mexico, they're garbanzos. This Middle Eastern recipe uses native ingredients to create a unique Mediterranean flavor.

1 lb. can chick peas
2 heaping tablespoons
    tahini, or sesame seed
    paste
Juice of 1 lemon

1 teaspoon salt
1 large clove garlic, peeled
½ teaspoon cumin,
    optional
Pita bread

Drain chick peas; reserve liquid. Place all ingredients in blender or food processor; blend until smooth. Add reserved liquid from chick peas until desired dipping consistency is reached. Serve dip with bite-sized triangles of pita bread. Makes 2 cups dip.

– Vesta Kitchens Dajani (Mrs. Adnan)

» Herb Cheese «

8 oz. pkg. cream cheese,
    softened
3 tablespoons fresh
    chives, chopped, or 1
    teaspoon dried chives
3 tablespoons fresh basil,
    chopped, or 1 teaspoon
    dried basil

3 tablespoons fresh dill,
    chopped, or 1 teaspoon
    dried dill weed
1 teaspoon caraway seed
1 clove garlic, minced or
    pressed
Bread rounds or artichoke
    hearts

Combine first six ingredients in a food processor or blender; process until well blended. Chill and use as a spread or topping for hors d'oeuvres, such as bread rounds or artichoke hearts. Makes 1 cup.

– The Heritage Restaurant

» Florence Shullman's Famous Chopped Liver «

This is the best chopped liver you'll ever taste. The secret is in the chicken fat! Chicken fat may be rendered and liver cooked in advance, so that only final mixing is needed at the last minute. Do not use chicken livers or calves' livers – they're too soft for the proper texture.

2 lbs. baby beef liver,
    sliced
5 hard-cooked eggs
2 large onions, peeled and
    quartered

Salt and pepper
1 cup rendered chicken
    fat, at least
Rye rounds

Boil liver for 15 to 20 minutes. Rinse; remove skin and veins. Mash egg yolks in large bowl. Grind into this bowl liver, onions, and whites of eggs, using food chopper or grinder. Mix well. Season with salt and pepper. Add 1 cup or more of chicken fat to bring to proper consistency. If there's a question, add a little more chicken fat. Serve with small rye rounds. Makes about 25 servings.

How to Render Perfect Chicken Fat

1 lb. chicken fat
1 tablespoon salt

1 large onion, peeled and
    quartered

Wash and cube chicken fat. Place in a heavy saucepan with salt and onion. Cook slowly until rendered; strain. Keep refrigerated until ready to use.

– Audrey McCafferty

» Mushroom Roll with Pâté «

This is a delightful French addition to the cocktail table or a savory for the tea tray.

2 lbs. mushrooms,
    chopped
¼ cup butter
1 medium onion, minced
Salt and pepper
1½ cups bread crumbs
1 cup Parmesan cheese,
    freshly grated

6 large egg whites, stiffly
    beaten
16 oz. can imported pâté,
    diced
3 tablespoons Cognac
    brandy
¼ lb. sweet butter,
    softened
¼ cup whipping cream

Sauté mushrooms in the butter in a heavy pan until most of the moisture has evaporated. Add onion, salt, and pepper; continue cooking until onions are lightly browned and moisture has evaporated, leaving a thick vegetable purée. Fold in bread crumbs, Parmesan cheese, and egg whites. Line a 12"x18" pan with parchment or waxed paper; spread the mixture evenly in the pan. Bake in a preheated 350° oven for 20 to 25 minutes, or until mixture is firm to the touch but still slightly moist. Remove from oven and cool on a rack for 5 minutes. Turn out onto a clean towel and peel paper off. Meanwhile, in a blender or food processor, mix remaining ingredients until smooth. Spread over cooled mushroom layer and roll up as for a jelly roll. Refrigerate at least 4 hours. Cut into thin slices to serve. Makes 4 dozen slices.

— Carlene Martin (Mrs. Thomas)
Barrington, Illinois

» Stuffed Mushrooms «

This recipe is from Thornbury Castle, Gloucestershire, in the Southwest of England. The mushrooms are served with aperitifs.

48 large mushroom caps	*¾ cup bread crumbs*
Salt and pepper	*1 cup Swiss cheese, grated*
½ cup butter, melted	*1 cup Parmesan cheese,*
¾ cup onions, minced	*grated*
¼ cup olive oil	*¾ cup parsley, chopped*
¾ cup green onions,	*1 teaspoon tarragon*
chopped	*½ cup whipping cream*
1 cup dry sherry	*Swiss cheese, grated*

Wash and dry mushroom caps; sprinkle with salt and pepper. Brush with butter. Sauté onions in remaining butter, and olive oil in skillet. Add green onions; continue sautéing in same skillet. Add sherry and reduce until sherry is almost gone. Remove from heat; add bread crumbs and grated cheeses. Add parsley, tarragon, and whipping cream. Fill caps with mixture; top with additional grated Swiss cheese. Bake in preheated 325° oven for 15 to 20 minutes. Makes 48 appetizers.

» Snaffles Mousse «

The recipe for this delicious first course comes from the famous Dublin restaurant, where we have enjoyed many fine meals.

2-8 oz. pkgs. cream	*1 teaspoon garlic salt*
cheese, softened	*½ teaspoon curry powder*
2-10 oz. cans consommé	*Lemon wedges*
with gelatin	*Chopped parsley*

Blend cream cheese, consommé, garlic salt, and curry powder in a blender or food processor until smooth and creamy. Pour into individual ramekins, demi-tasse cups, or small cups. Refrigerate overnight and serve, garnished with lemon and parsley. Makes 8 servings.

— Anne Gebbie (Mrs. Douglas)

» Navarin de Coquilles St. Jacques «

This elegant navarin, or stew, is a feature of Cincinnati's Maisonette Restaurant, one of only 11 five-star restaurants in the United States.

1 lb. sea scallops	*¼ cup celery, finely*
1 cup strong fish stock	*chopped*
¼ cup dry white wine	*1 oz. truffles, chopped*
1 tablespoon fresh	*¼ cup whipping cream*
shallots, chopped	*Salt and pepper*
¼ cup carrots, finely	*¼ cup sweet butter*
chopped	*½ tablespoon fresh*
¼ cup white part of leeks,	*parsley, finely chopped*
finely chopped	*1 tablespoon fresh chives,*
	finely chopped

Cook the scallops very briefly in the fish stock and wine. Remove and keep warm. Add all the other ingredients except the parsley, chives, and butter. Reduce until the sauce is lightly thick. Correct seasoning, adding salt and pepper if necessary. At the last minute, add the butter and the herbs. Mix to incorporate – do not boil any more. Put the hot scallops in the sauce and transfer to a serving dish. Makes 4 appetizer servings.

— Chef de Cuisine George Haidon
Maisonette Restaurant

» Party Nuts «

6 tablespoons butter	*½ teaspoon chili powder*
1 clove garlic, minced	*1 teaspoon seasoned salt*
Dash of Tabasco sauce	*½ teaspoon salt*
1 lb. mixed nuts	

Melt butter and add garlic. Set aside for at least 1 hour. Add Tabasco and mix. Toss nuts in butter mixture to coat well, then spread evenly on a cookie sheet. Toast in a preheated 325° oven for 15 minutes. Toss or turn nuts every 5 minutes during the 15-minute period. Mix together the chili powder and salts; sprinkle over the nuts. Return to oven for 4 minutes. Toss nuts once more and return to oven for 3 minutes. Toss and let cool. Pack in an airtight container. Store in a cool, dry place. These nuts will easily keep for 6 weeks. Makes 2 cups.

» Pâté de Campagne «

This French classic may be served with cocktails, as a first course, or as a light meal with a crisp green salad and crusty bread. The use of veal and liver makes this a campagne, or country, pâté.

1 lb. fresh pork shoulder	½ cup Madeira wine
½ lb. veal	1 teaspoon salt
½ lb. pork or beef liver	½ teaspoon freshly ground
¼ lb. salt pork, diced and	black pepper
blanched in boiling	½ teaspoon thyme
water	⅛ teaspoon mace
½" thick slice cooked	⅛ teaspoon allspice
ham, diced	⅛ teaspoon rosemary
2 slices firm white bread	6 slices bacon
1 cup milk	Bay leaves
1 egg	French bread
½ cup whipping cream	Cornichons

Using a food processor or grinder, chop meats coarsely. Soak bread in milk, squeeze dry, and chop coarsely. Combine with meats, egg, cream, wine, salt, pepper, thyme, mace, allspice, and rosemary. Line a terrine or loaf pan with bacon and fill with pâté mixture. Top with bay leaves. Place in a larger, shallow pan and pour boiling water into larger pan until it reaches halfway up terrine pan. Bake in a preheated 350° oven for 1½ hours. Remove from oven and place weights on top of pâté – another loaf pan with canned goods inside serves very well. Refrigerate for 2 days; unmold, slice thinly, and serve with crusty French bread and cornichons. Makes 1 loaf.

– Carlene Martin (Mrs. Thomas)
Barrington, Illinois

Cruet Set, English, 1761-2, John Delmester, silver and glass. 1959.34, Bequest of Edmund C. Kerper

» Pâté aux Champignons «

This is a lighter, updated version of a French pâté, and is best when made a day ahead to allow the flavors to meld.

1 medium onion, minced	Mayonnaise
2 tablespoons butter	Salt
½ lb. fresh mushrooms	Freshly ground pepper
2 tablespoons lemon juice	Melba toast or plain
1 teaspoon	crackers
Worcestershire sauce	

Sauté onion in butter until golden. Chop mushrooms finely and add to onions; sauté for 5 minutes, stirring lightly to mix well. Add lemon juice and Worcestershire sauce, mix well, and remove from heat. Cool slightly and add enough mayonnaise (preferably homemade) to bind the mixture together. Pack pâté into a crock or mound on a plate and cover tightly. Chill well before serving with Melba toast or plain crackers. Makes 2 cups.

– Barbara Lauterbach (Mrs. Peter)

» Duck Pâté «

The French have devised a wonderful way to use the duck livers left from the birds used for roasting. Save a little of the leg or breast meat to combine with the livers and the result will be a delicious pâté.

¼ lb. raw duck livers	Juice from 1 orange
¼ lb. raw, lean duck meat	1 egg
¼ cup dry red wine	Salt and freshly ground
Zest of 1 orange, grated	pepper
1 tablespoon parsley,	2 tablespoons dry sherry
chopped	1 bay leaf, ground
¼ lb. pork sausage	Bacon slices
1 medium onion, minced	French bread
1 slice dark bread	Cornichons

In a blender or food processor, chop duck livers and duck meat finely. Combine with wine, orange zest, parsley, sausage, and onion; marinate 2 hours at room temperature. Meanwhile, soak the bread in orange juice. Blend or process the bread and orange juice; add to the duck mixture, along with egg, salt, pepper, sherry, and bay leaf. Line a terrine or loaf pan with bacon slices and fill with pâté mixture. Lay additional bacon slices across the top of the mixture. Place in a larger, shallow pan and pour boiling water into larger pan until it reaches halfway up terrine pan. Bake in a preheated 350° oven for 1½ hours. Remove from oven and place weights on top of pâté – another loaf pan with canned goods inside serves very well. Chill overnight; unmold pâté and serve thin slices with crisp French bread and cornichons. Makes 1 loaf.

– Carlene Martin (Mrs. Thomas)
Barrington, Illinois

» Liver Pâté «

This smooth and creamy spread is a recipe from London's famous Inn on the Park.

1 lb. chicken livers	½ teaspoon salt
4 tablespoons butter	Freshly ground black
3 tablespoons mayonnaise	pepper
2 tablespoons lemon juice	8 to 10 drops bottled hot
2 tablespoons butter,	pepper sauce
softened	2 eggs, hard-cooked and
1 tablespoon onion,	chopped, or parsley,
minced	optional
½ teaspoon dry mustard	Crackers or Melba toast

Sauté livers in butter in a covered pan, stirring occasionally, until livers are just done and no longer pink. Place in a blender, food mill, or food processor with the mayonnaise, lemon juice, butter, onion, dry mustard, salt, pepper, and pepper sauce. Blend thoroughly and pour into a decorative mold or small loaf pan. Chill overnight, unmold, garnish with chopped egg or parsley, if desired, and serve with crackers or Melba toast. Makes 1¾ cups.

– Ann Gebbie (Mrs. Douglas)

» Liver Pâté «

This smooth and creamy pâté is excellent served with pita bread or crusty French bread. Photographer Marie Cosindas was commissioned in 1980 to create the Cincinnati Art Museum's Centennial poster.

1 lb. chicken livers	Salt
2 onions, chopped	8 oz. pkg. cream cheese,
2 tablespoons butter	softened
1 teaspoon chili powder	Pita bread
1 teaspoon oregano	

Sauté chicken livers and onions in butter until browned. Add chili powder, oregano, and salt; let cool. Place in a blender or food processor with the cream cheese; blend well. Chill until ready to serve with pita bread triangles. Makes 3 cups.

– Marie Cosindas

» Spiced Pecans «

2 cups pecan halves
3 tablespoons butter,
    melted
3 tablespoons
    Worcestershire sauce
2 teaspoons salt
¼ teaspoon cayenne
    pepper
¼ teaspoon cinnamon
4 drops Tabasco sauce

Place pecans in a shallow baking pan. Mix other ingredients together and pour over pecans, coating as evenly as possible. Bake in preheated 300° oven for 30 minutes, stirring occasionally. Makes 2 cups. If you double or triple this recipe, cut back a little on the butter and Worcestershire sauce.

– Nancy Coith (Mrs. Robert)

» Peanut Chutney Spread «

This makes a different and tasty snack with cocktails. It can be made ahead and kept in a covered jar in the refrigerator for weeks.

3 oz. pkg. cream cheese
½ lb. chunky-style peanut
    butter
½ cup chutney, coarsely
    chopped
¼ teaspoon seasoned salt
¼ teaspoon
    Worcestershire sauce
Dry red wine
Shredded wheat crackers,
    cocktail rye bread, or
    saltines

Mix and blend above ingredients together with a tablespoon, using only enough wine to moisten the mixture so that it can be spread easily. This is best on shredded wheat crackers, but it is also good on cocktail rye bread or saltines. Makes 2 cups.

– Audrey McCafferty

» Hot Pepper Jelly with Cream Cheese «

1½ cups cider vinegar
1 cup green peppers,
    coarsely chopped
3 tablespoons hot pepper
    sauce
6½ cups sugar
3 oz. liquid fruit pectin
2 to 3 drops green food
    coloring
Paraffin
8 oz. pkg. cream cheese
Crackers

Mix vinegar, pepper, and hot pepper sauce in a blender until smooth. In a 6-quart saucepan, combine with sugar; cook and stir over medium heat, bringing mixture to just below boiling point. Continue stirring until sugar is dissolved, about 5 minutes. Do not boil. Remove from heat and immediately add liquid pectin and food coloring, mixing well. Skim off foam if necessary. Pour quickly into sterilized, ½-pint glasses or jars. Cover at once with ⅛" hot paraffin. Seal tightly. To serve, place cream cheese on serving plate and spoon jelly generously over the cheese. Serve with mild-flavored crackers. Makes 4½-pint glasses.

– Jane Sweeder (Mrs. Willard C.)

» Samosas «

These steak-filled turnovers from India are spicy morsels for the cocktail hour, or may be used as a main course with accompanying dishes. The recipe was provided by Nancy Mehta, the wife of Zubin Mehta, the music director of the New York Philharmonic Orchestra.

2 tablespoons butter
1 teaspoon ginger, minced
3 cloves garlic, minced
1 large onion, minced
1 lb. lean round steak,
    finely ground
1 teaspoon curry powder
¾ teaspoon cumin powder
¾ teaspoon turmeric
¼ teaspoon cayenne
¼ teaspoon pepper
1 cup water
3 whole green chilies,
    minced
1 large tomato, peeled,
    seeded, and diced
1 tablespoon catsup
3 tablespoons sugar
3 tablespoons vinegar
Salt
1 tablespoon fresh
    cilantro, chopped
1 lb. pkg. frozen phyllo
    dough, thawed
4 cups oil
1 large tomato, minced
1 small onion, minced
¼ cup cilantro, finely
    chopped
1 tablespoon vinegar
½ teaspoon dried red
    pepper flakes
½ teaspoon salt

Melt butter in 10" skillet. Add ginger and garlic and sauté 2 to 3 minutes. Add onion and cook over medium heat until soft. Add meat and cook until browned. Thoroughly blend in next 6 ingredients. Stir in water, chilies, tomato, and catsup. Cook over medium heat, stirring frequently, about 15 minutes, until most of the moisture has evaporated. Season with sugar, vinegar, and salt. Cook 5 minutes, stirring frequently. Add cilantro. Cut strips of phyllo dough about 1¼"x18". Keep phyllo dough wrapped in its own paper or a lightly dampened paper towel as you work so that it does not dry out. Place about 1 teaspoon of mixture at tip of dough. Make a triangle and fold over mixture. Continue folding triangle over and over to end of strip; trim excess. Continue until all of the mixture has been used, keeping triangles covered with a damp towel. Heat oil to 400° and add samosas, 4 to 6 at a time, and deep fry until rich golden brown, about 3 minutes per side. Drain on paper towels. Keep warm in oven until ready to serve. Combine remaining six ingredients and use as a dip with the samosas. Makes about 48 turnovers.

– Nancy Mehta (Mrs. Zubin)

» Popcorn-Nut Crunch «

2 quarts popcorn, freshly popped	*⅓ cup water*
2 cups whole almonds, walnuts, pecans, or peanuts	*⅓ cup honey*
	¼ cup butter
	1 tablespoon vanilla
1 cup sunflower seeds	*½ teaspoon salt*
1 cup sugar	*½ cup wheat germ*

In a large bowl, toss popcorn, nuts, and sunflower seeds; set aside. In a 2-quart pan, stir together sugar, water, and honey; cook over medium heat until syrup reaches 250° on a candy thermometer. Add butter and stir until melted. Stir in vanilla, salt, and wheat germ. Pour syrup over popcorn mixture and toss together until evenly coated. Spread into 2 buttered 10"x15" baking pans and bake, uncovered, in a preheated 300° oven for 30 minutes, stirring once after 15 minutes. Turn out of pan and spread on foil. Let cool completely. Store up to 2 weeks in an airtight container. Makes 3 quarts.

– Toni Eyrich (Mrs. David)

» Pirozhki «

These Russian meat turnovers may be served hot or cold. They are flavored with dill and sour cream – flavors that seem made for each other.

¾ lb. ground beef	*½ cup sour cream*
⅓ cup onion, finely chopped	*2 tablespoons parsley, minced*
1 teaspoon butter	*2 teaspoons dill*
2 cups mushrooms, chopped	*2 teaspoons Worcestershire sauce*
1 tablespoon flour	*Pie crust for 2-9" pies*
1 teaspoon salt	

Sauté beef and onion in butter in a heavy pan until onions are transparent and beef is crumbly. Add mushrooms and cook, stirring, until mushrooms are tender and moisture has evaporated. Add flour and salt. Stir in remaining ingredients and cook until thick, stirring constantly. Cool. May be made ahead to this point and refrigerated. Remove any grease which has accumulated on top before proceeding. Roll pie crust ⅛" thick on a floured surface and cut into 4" circles. Put 1 teaspoon of filling in center of each circle, fold pastry in half, and press edges together to form a half circle. Bake in a preheated 425° oven 8 to 10 minutes, or until crust is brown. Makes 5 dozen pastries.

» Sausage Pinwheels «

2 cups flour	*¼ cup plus 1 tablespoon vegetable shortening*
1 tablespoon baking powder	*⅔ cup milk*
¾ teaspoon salt	*1 lb. bulk pork sausage, at room temperature*

Combine flour, baking powder, and salt. Cut in shortening until mixture resembles coarse meal. Add milk and blend. Turn out dough on a lightly floured surface. Knead about 4 to 5 times. Roll dough into an 18"x12" rectangle. Spread uncooked sausage over dough. Leave a ½" margin on all sides. Roll lengthwise in jelly roll fashion. Pinch seams and ends to seal. Cover and refrigerate 2 hours or longer. Slice in ¼" slices. Place 1" apart on baking sheet, and bake in preheated 350° oven for 10 minutes. Remove and turn over pinwheels; return to oven and bake 10 more minutes, or until browned. Serve warm. Makes 20 to 24 servings. These appetizers can be prepared in advance, frozen, and warmed when ready to use.

– Jane Jacobs (Mrs. Brent A.)

Louis-Marin Bonnet, 1736-1793, French,
"The Woman Taking Coffee," 1774, color engraving, 1943.417.
Bequest of Herbert Greer French

» Barbecued Spare Ribs «

The combination of orange juice, honey, sherry, and ginger gives an Oriental flavor to these ribs.

6 lbs. pork spare ribs,
  halved
2 cups orange juice
1 cup honey
½ cup dry sherry

4 cloves garlic, mashed
½ teaspoon pepper,
  coarsely ground
2 teaspoons ground ginger
Mustard Sauce

Have butcher saw ribs in half so they are about 3″ long. Mix orange juice, honey, sherry, garlic, pepper, and ginger together in a large bowl or heavy plastic bag. Add ribs and marinate at least 4 hours, turning often. Bake in preheated 350° oven for about 1½ hours on a rack set in a roasting pan. Baste often with marinade. Makes 15 to 20 appetizer servings. Serve with Mustard Sauce.

Mustard Sauce

½ cup butter
1 tablespoon flour
½ tablespoon dry mustard
1 cup dry white wine
½ teaspoon salt

¼ teaspoon pepper
3 tablespoons Dijon
  mustard
2 to 3 tablespoons
  whipping cream

Cook all but cream together in the top of a double boiler until thick; add cream just before serving. Makes 2 cups.

» Schwadenmagen «

There are no precise measurements for this old German dish, but it makes an excellent cocktail appetizer. Don't be scared off by the headcheese – it was a favorite snack of my brother's children. While it is best if consumed in a day or two, it will keep in the refrigerator for a week or two. It's particularly nice to serve when your other snacks are on the bland side, and it's a natural with beer. Buy good, meaty headcheese, sliced about 1″ thick. Cut into bite-size cubes and place in covered jar. Mix equal parts of water and vinegar; add a generous portion of sliced onion and mixed pickling spices. Cover headcheese cubes with vinegar mix. Marinate in refrigerator for 24 to 48 hours. Serve as snack or hors d'oeuvre.

– Audrey McCafferty

» Sauerkraut Balls «

1 lb. potatoes
Milk
Butter
1½ lbs. sauerkraut,
  squeezed dry
½ lb. ham, finely diced
¼ cup parsley, finely
  chopped
2 scallions, finely chopped

1 tablespoon mustard
Salt and pepper
1 egg, well beaten
2 tablespoons cold water
Flour
¾ cup fine dry bread
  crumbs
Oil

Peel and cook potatoes; mash with enough milk and butter to make a stiff mixture. Combine with sauerkraut, ham, parsley, scallions, and mustard; season with salt and pepper to taste. Shape into 32 walnut-sized balls. Combine beaten egg with water; blend thoroughly. Roll sauerkraut balls in flour, dip in egg, and coat with bread crumbs. Deep-fry in 350° oil, or pan-fry until brown and finish off in oven. Makes 32 meatballs.

– Grammer's Restaurant

» Sauerbraten Meat Balls with Gingersnap Gravy «

These meat balls have an excellent flavor. The spices may seem overwhelming in the mixing but they blend delightfully in the cooking. If serving from a chafing dish, the gravy might be thinned or the gravy recipe doubled. This dish can be made ahead and refrigerated until time to reheat for the party.

1½ lbs. ground beef
½ medium onion,
  chopped
1 egg, beaten
1 teaspoon salt
¼ teaspoon thyme
¼ teaspoon garlic powder
⅛ teaspoon pepper
½ cup vinegar
⅓ cup water

2 tablespoons catsup
1 tablespoon oil
3 tablespoons brown
  sugar
12 cloves
8 peppercorns
1 bay leaf
8 gingersnaps, crumbled
Water, if needed for
  thinning gravy

Mix ground beef, onion, egg, salt, thyme, garlic powder, and pepper in large mixing bowl. Roll into balls about 1″ in diameter. Refrigerate while you make gravy. Combine all remaining ingredients in a large, heavy skillet; stir until gingersnaps are soft and well blended. Drop meat balls into gravy; cover and simmer over medium heat for 1 hour, stirring occasionally; thin gravy with water if too thick. Serve from chafing dish with cocktail picks. Makes 3 dozen appetizer meatballs.

– Audrey McCafferty

» Taramosalata «

This is a feature of the Athens Hilton. It is excellent served with cocktails on party rye, Syrian bread, or crackers. Mullet roe is available in Greek food stores and specialty shops.

4 oz. mullet roe	*water and squeezed dry*
1 medium potato, boiled	*¾ cup olive oil*
and peeled	*Juice of 1 lemon*
1" thick piece of dry white	*Lemon wedges*
bread, soaked in cold	*Whole Greek black olives*

Force roe, potato, and bread through a fine sieve, or purée in a food processor. Beat in olive oil and lemon juice, a drop at a time, with a wire whisk. Garnish with lemon wedges and olives. Makes 1 lb.

– Sally Brown (Mrs. Fred I., Jr.)

» Seafood Tartlets «

This dough can be refrigerated for up to 1 week before rolling out and baking.

2 cups self-rising flour	*3 oz. pkg. cream cheese,*
½ cup butter, frozen or	*softened*
chilled thoroughly	*¼ cup mayonnaise*
½ cup Parmesan cheese,	*2 tablespoons lemon juice*
freshly grated	*4 drops Tabasco sauce*
½ teaspoon salt	*1 green onion, cut into*
⅓ teaspoon pepper,	*1" pieces*
freshly ground	*¼ teaspoon dry mustard*
½ cup or less of ice water	*¼ teaspoon curry*
7¾ oz. can red salmon, or	*Salt and freshly ground*
1 cup crab meat	*pepper*

Place flour, butter, Parmesan cheese, salt, and pepper in a food processor; blend quickly until mixture resembles coarse meal. Add only enough ice water to make mixture form a stiff ball while processing. Wrap pastry dough

securely and refrigerate at least 1 hour. Drain salmon and remove bones and skin; set aside. Place the remaining ingredients in a food processor and blend until smooth; blend in salmon for a few seconds. Chill overnight. Roll pastry until thin on a floured surface. Cut 24-2½" circles out of pastry and fit the circles into miniature muffin tins. Prick the tartlets with a fork; bake in a preheated 400° oven for 15 minutes, or until browned. Remove from pans and cool. Fill tartlets with 1 tablespoon of filling just before serving. Makes 24 tartlets.

– Rosemarie Culver

» Tostadas de Carne «

Party appetizers such as these meat-topped fried tortillas are called "antojitos" or "little whims" in Mexico.

4 lbs. beef chuck,	*8 Ancho chiles*
trimmed and cut into	*4 cloves garlic, minced*
2" cubes	*1 large onion, chopped*
6 tablespoons olive oil	*12 flour tortillas, cut into*
2 tablespoons chili	*quarters*
powder	*Oil for frying*
2 teaspoons salt	*2 cups Colby cheese,*
1 onion, chopped	*grated*

Brown beef in 4 tablespoons olive oil. Place in a large saucepan; cover with water and add chili powder, salt, and onion. Cook, partially covered, for 2 to 2½ hours, or until meat is tender enough to slice. Let cool in broth. Shred and set aside. While meat is cooking, put the Ancho chiles in boiling water to cover; let sit 30 minutes. Remove stem and seeds; purée in food processor, adding enough of the soaking water to make a smooth paste. Sauté garlic and onion in remaining 2 tablespoons olive oil. Add shredded meat and chile purée. Taste and correct the seasonings, if necessary. Deep-fry the flour tortilla triangles in 375° oil until golden and crisp. Drain on paper towels. Put a spoonful of the meat mixture on each triangle and top with grated cheese. Put in a 400° oven just until cheese melts. Serve immediately. Makes 48 appetizers.

– Marilyn Harris
L.S. Ayres 4th Street Market

» Terrine de Canard aux Raisins «

This classic French terrine of duck with raisins is superb served with a glass of chilled Chablis or Macon wine. Cornichons, the tart, crisp imported gherkins, are a wonderful contrast to the texture and flavor of this terrine.

1 duck breast, skinned	8 duck livers or chicken
2 cups chicken broth	livers
8 teaspoons Cognac	Salt and pepper
brandy	1 pinch allspice
8 teaspoons Port wine	1 cup cream
1½ teaspoons white	5 egg yolks
raisins	Cornichons
6 oz. fresh pork fat,	Dijon mustard
unsalted	

Cook duck breast in broth for 15 minutes. Cool; cut meat from bone, and dice small. Warm Cognac, Port, and raisins. Allow to cool and chill. Add duck and marinate 1 hour. Place pork fat, duck liver, salt, pepper, and allspice in food processor; blend until creamy. Add cream and egg yolks; continue blending 30 seconds. Fold in duck and raisin mixture. Pour into an earthenware terrine. Place terrine in a high-sided roasting pan and add enough boiling water to come halfway up the side of the mold. Cover with foil and bake 30 to 40 minutes in preheated 400° oven, until firm in center. Serve cold with garnish of cornichons and Dijon mustard. Makes 12 servings.

– Chef de Cuisine Otis Sherrer
Pigall's French Restaurant

» Tiropita «

These three-cornered cheese-filled Greek appetizers are made of crisp phyllo dough and filled with fragrant Feta cheese.

½ lb. Feta cheese,	2 eggs
crumbled	1 egg yolk
8 oz. package cream	1 lb. frozen phyllo sheets
cheese, at room	1 lb. butter, melted
temperature	

Blend Feta and cream cheeses thoroughly. Add two eggs, one at a time, blending thoroughly. Add egg yolk and mix well. Cut phyllo into strips 2″ wide and stack on top of each other. Cover with a dampened towel to prevent phyllo from drying out while assembling the tiropita. Take one strip of phyllo and brush with melted butter. Place 1 teaspoon of the filling at one corner of the end of a phyllo strip. Fold corner over to form a triangle. Continue folding from side to side in the form of a triangle until phyllo strip is used. This is the way you used to fold an American flag at Scout camp. Proceed until all phyllo and filling is used. Place on a greased baking sheet and brush with additional butter. Bake in a preheated 350° oven for 15 to 20 minutes, until golden brown. Makes 80 pastries.

– Cleo Seremetis (Mrs. William G.)

» Raspberry Champagne Cocktails «

We enjoyed this refresher in Munich after a strenuous day of sightseeing.

1 pint fresh raspberries	¾ cup raspberry liqueur
Sugar	Champagne

Sprinkle fresh berries with sugar and allow to sit for a few minutes. Crush berries slightly and add liqueur. Put a tablespoon in each glass and pour cold champagne over. Makes 8 glasses.

– Joanne Lynagh (Mrs. James)

» Sangria «

This icy summer drink brings a respite from the bright hot heat of a Spanish summer.

1 quart red wine	Sugar
1 quart soda water	1 cup chopped fruit,
½ cup cognac	optional
1 lemon, sliced	

Mix wine, soda water, cognac, lemon, and sugar as desired. Stir well, chill, and add fruit before serving. Makes 2 quarts.

– Carlos Casariego

» Tzatziki «

This fresh and crunchy spread is wonderful served with cocktails on a summer evening.

1 cup cucumber, peeled, seeded, and finely diced
2 cups sour cream
1 clove garlic, crushed
1 tablespoon olive oil

Salt and white pepper
4 tablespoons fresh mint or dill, chopped
French bread, thinly sliced

Place chopped cucumber in a paper or linen towel and squeeze out excess liquid. Mix with the remaining ingredients and chill well. Serve with French bread. Makes 3 cups.

– Stanley Demos
Coach House Restaurant, Lexington, Ky.
From his book, "Stanley Suggests"

» Jamaica Flower Water «

The rich ruby color and tangy flavor of this refreshing Mexican summer drink can be strengthened or weakened by adding more dried flowers or increasing the amount of water used. Dried jamaica hibiscus flowers are available in health food stores.

¾ cup dried hibiscus flowers
8 cups water

Sugar
Orange slices

Place dried hibiscus flowers in a pitcher and add water. Let steep overnight in refrigerator. Pour through a strainer and discard flowers. Stir well and add sugar to taste. Serve in tall glasses with ice cubes, garnished with orange slices. Makes 8 servings.

– Lupe A. Gonzales-Hoyt

» Irish Coffee «

Although Irish coffee dates back only about to 1950, when it was invented by bartender Joe Sheridan, few travelers can pass through Shannon Airport without sampling this warming concoction.

1 cup strong black coffee
1 heaped teaspoon sugar

2 ozs. Irish whiskey
1 tablespoon whipping cream

Warm a heavy stemmed or clear glass. Add the coffee and sugar; mix to dissolve the sugar. Add the whiskey. Hold a teaspoon, curved side up, across the glass; pour the cream slowly over the spoon, so cream floats on top. Do not stir into the coffee. Serve at once. The hot coffee is drunk through the cold cream. The cream may also be whipped before it is spooned on top of the hot coffee. Makes 1 serving.

» Turkish Coffee «

Turkish coffee should be made in small amounts, no more than 3 or 4 servings at a time. Turkish coffee pots are cone-shaped brass containers with long handles. A small saucepan or butter warmer may be substituted.

1 cup cold water
2 tablespoons sugar
⅛ teaspoon ground cardamom

2 tablespoons pulverized dark roast coffee

Combine water and sugar in a Turkish coffee pot. Heat to boiling over high heat, stirring just until sugar is dissolved. Add cardamom and coffee; stir constantly until mixture is thick and smooth, about 1 minute. Continue heating until a thick foam rises, about 30 seconds. Remove pot from heat and spoon foam into each of 3 demitasse cups. Reduce heat and bring coffee to boiling twice more. Remove pot each time foam rises and divide foam evenly among the 3 cups; add coffee. Makes 3 servings.

– Vesta Kitchens Dajani (Mrs. Adnan)

Iznik Ware, earthenware with underglaze polychrome painting,
Turkey, Ottoman Period, late 16th century, jug, 1948.145,
tallest tankard, 1948.140, tankard, 1948.143.
Given in honor of Mr. and Mrs. Charles F. Williams by their children.
This colored reproduction donated
by Mrs. J. Richard Andre and Mrs. J. Gordon Dixon

Tin-glazed earthenware, called majolica in Italy, faience in France and Delft in Holland, is Iznik ware when its geographical point of origin is the Iznik area of Turkey. Admirably suited to ceramics, the local clay was used to produce some of the most decorative and colorful of all Islamic wares, particularly during the period of Ottoman rule.

These late 16th century pieces are from that era and are fine examples of the prevailing style of decoration, expressed in strong colors against a white ground. Red bodies, less effective than white, characterized earlier work. On the two generously sized tankards stylized floral motifs retain a natural feeling, while the graceful shapes of small sailboats form a pattern on the jug.

Soups, Salads, and Sauces

» Ajiaco «

This Columbian dish may be classified as either a soup or a one-pot meal.

1 large frying chicken,
  cut up
1 stalk celery, chopped
1 large onion, chopped
2 bay leaves
1 tablespoon parsley,
  chopped
1 tablespoon cumin
1 tablespoon coriander
1 tablespoon vinegar
1 cayenne pepper, or

½ teaspoon crushed
  hot pepper
Salt and pepper
6 medium red potatoes,
  cut into bite-sized
  pieces
6 ears corn, cut into
  2″ lengths
2 avocados, peeled and
  chopped
Garlic bread

Place the chicken in a soup pot. Add the celery, onion, bay leaves, and parsley. Place the cumin and coriander in the blender with enough cold water to grind the spices; add to the soup pot with enough additional water to cover the chicken. Add the vinegar, cayenne, and salt and pepper to taste. Bring to a boil; cover; simmer for 1 hour. Add the potatoes and the corn; cook until tender, about 10 to 15 minutes. Add the avocado pieces just before serving. Serve with garlic bread.
Makes 4 servings.

— *Mary Anna DuSablon (Mrs. Sean T. Bailey)*

» Cream of Almond Soup «

This Scottish recipe uses mace, which is actually the outer hull of the nutmeg seed. You may substitute nutmeg if you have no mace. Both spices complement and strengthen the flavor of almonds.

1 cup blanched almonds,
  grated
1 cup milk
¼ cup fine bread crumbs
2 tablespoons butter

2 tablespoons flour
4 cups rich chicken stock
Pinch of mace
Salt and pepper
1 cup whipping cream

Simmer almonds and milk slowly until nuts are very soft. Add bread crumbs and purée in a blender or food processor or press through a sieve. Melt butter and flour together and cook over low heat for a few minutes; add chicken stock and cook, stirring until mixture is thickened and smooth. Add almond purée, mace, salt, and pepper and simmer for 5 minutes, stirring constantly. Add cream and heat to boiling, but do not allow to boil; serve immediately. Makes 8 servings.

» Cream of Asparagus Soup «

3 lbs. fresh asparagus,
  prepared for cooking
1 medium onion, chopped
⅓ cup butter
3 cups chicken broth

1 tablespoon lemon juice
1½ cups whipping cream
2 tablespoons fresh
  tarragon, chopped
Salt and white pepper

Cook asparagus until tender in a small amount of boiling water. Cut into 1″ pieces, reserving tips. Sauté onion in butter until soft. Place asparagus bottoms, onions, chicken broth, and lemon juice in a food processor or blender; process until smooth. Add cream and tarragon; season with salt and pepper to taste; process again. To serve, heat soup gently or chill thoroughly. Garnish with reserved asparagus tips. Makes 6 servings.

— *The Heritage Restaurant*

» Chilled Essence of Apricot Soup «

2 cups chicken stock
2 cups apricot nectar
1½ cups dry white wine
1 cup water
½ cup dried apricots
¼ teaspoon cinnamon
¼ teaspoon cloves
Pinch of salt
2 tablespoons cornstarch
Water
2 tablespoons apricot
   liqueur
2 tablespoons apricot
   brandy
1 cup whipping cream
Fresh apricots, diced

In a large saucepan, combine chicken stock, apricot nectar, wine, water, dried apricots, cinnamon, cloves, and salt. Simmer the mixture, covered, for 1 hour. Mix cornstarch with a little water and add to soup. Cook over medium heat, stirring, until soup thickens. Strain the soup, chill, and stir in apricot liqueur, apricot brandy, and cream. Serve soup garnished with fresh apricots. Makes 8 servings.

» Burgoo «

No one seems to know the origin of the name, but burgoo is a hearty soup that is a staple at political rallies in Kentucky, as well as other festive occasions such as racing meets, court days, and elections. Traditionally, it is made in a huge iron pot and cooked slowly over smoldering wood, imparting a rich, smoky flavor. For best results using a new-fangled range, cook the day before and let it rest overnight to mingle the flavors.

5 to 6 lb. hen
2 lbs. beef shanks
2 lbs. lamb shanks
2 lbs. pork shanks
2 lbs. veal shanks
Cold water
6 large potatoes, peeled
   and diced
5 large onions, coarsely
   chopped
6 carrots, peeled and
   diced
2 cups celery, diced
2 cups corn
2 cups lima beans
4 cups fresh tomatoes,
   chopped, or 4 cups
   canned tomatoes,
   undrained
2 green peppers, chopped
2 dried red peppers, or
   Tabasco sauce to taste
Salt
2 tablespoons
   Worcestershire sauce
1 bunch parsley, minced

Place the chicken and other meats in a heavy 20-quart stock pot. Cover the meat with cold water and bring to a boil over high heat. Cover, reduce heat, and simmer for 3 to 4 hours, until the meat is tender and begins to fall off the bone. Remove the chicken and meats from the stock, cool, and remove bones and skin. Dice the meat and return it to the stock. Add vegetables; slowly simmer until vegetables are cooked and the mixture is thick. Stir frequently to prevent the mixture from sticking. Add salt to taste, Worcestershire sauce, and parsley. Makes 10 quarts or 25 servings.

— Karen Rafuse (Mrs. Peter B.)

» Alouette's Cold Avocado Soup «

Alouette was a young girl from New Zealand who stayed with me for several months. She was an excellent cook and this is one of the recipes she introduced to us.

3 ripe avocados, peeled
   and cut into 1" cubes
1 cup milk
1 cup whipping cream
½ cup chicken stock
Salt and pepper
Fresh chives for garnish,
   chopped

Purée avocado in blender or food processor until smooth. Remove and place in a large bowl. Stir in milk, whipping cream, and chicken stock. Add salt and pepper. Whip mixture by hand. Serve in chilled bowls and garnish with chives. Makes 4 servings.

— Henrietta Kauffman (Mrs. Ted)

» Curried Avocado Soup «

1 medium avocado, peeled
   and seeded
2 cups chicken broth
1 cup half and half cream
¼ cup light rum
1 teaspoon curry powder
Salt and pepper
1 lemon, cut in quarters
Sprigs of fresh basil

Put all ingredients except lemon and basil in blender. Pureé. Chill in refrigerator. Serve in bowls with a lemon quarter on the side. Garnish with fresh basil, if available. Makes 4 servings.

— Anne Ziebarth (Mrs. John)

» Kentucky Bean Bash Soup «

This recipe generously serves 8, but may be multiplied ad infinitum to serve large groups. In Kentucky, it's often accompanied by crisp and buttery corn bread and hours of politicians' speeches.

3 to 4 cups dried navy
   beans
1 ham hock
1 onion, coarsely chopped

½ stalk celery
1 tablespoon brown sugar
Salt and pepper

Soak navy beans in water to cover in large saucepan overnight. In the morning, combine beans, ham hock, onion, celery, and brown sugar. Add water to cover. Bring to boil, lower heat, and simmer until beans are tender. Cooking time will be about two hours or more, depending on the beans. Add water as necessary to maintain a thick soup consistency. Season with salt and pepper to taste. Makes 8 servings.

» Creole Calico Bean Soup «

This soup is best when you use a variety of beans. Choose at least four of navy, great northern, pinto, red kidney, black, or lima beans, or lentils or dried peas.

1 to 1¼ lbs. dried beans,
   washed and drained
3 quarts boiling water
1 ham hock
2 teaspoons bouquet garni
1 bay leaf
6 to 10 cloves
1 large onion, quartered
2 tablespoons parsley,
   chopped
2 tablespoons celery tops,
   chopped

8 oz. can tomatoes,
   undrained
1 large onion, chopped
3 to 4 carrots, chopped
6 to 7 stalks celery,
   chopped
2 to 3 cloves garlic, finely
   chopped
About six quick shakes
   Tabasco sauce
Salt and pepper
½ cup parsley, chopped
¼ cup red wine

Soak beans in cold water overnight, or at least 4 hours; drain. Have a large pot of boiling water ready; add beans, ham hock, bouquet garni, bay leaf, cloves, onion, parsley, and celery tops. Bring to a boil and simmer until beans are tender, about 1½ to 2 hours. Remove ham hock and set aside. Drain beans and reserve liquid. Discard remainder of vegetables, herbs, and spices. Return beans and liquid to pot; add tomatoes, onion, carrots, celery, garlic, Tabasco sauce, and salt and pepper to taste. Simmer about 1 hour until ingredients are soft. Add chopped parsley and red wine. More water may be added to bean liquid, if needed. Simmer about 10 to 15 minutes more. Cut ham from hock into small pieces and add to soup. Additional ham may be added, if desired. Makes 10 to 12 servings.

– Dottie Jacobs (Mrs. Donald)

» Pennsylvania Dutch Chicken Rivel Soup «

For 200 years, Pennsylvania Dutch cooks have been rubbing a mixture of flour, salt, and egg through their fingers so that it flakes into boiling soup. They call it rivel, and it has a tasty texture similar to boiled rice or German spaetzle.

3 lb. chicken, cut up; or
   backs, necks, and 6
   chicken wings
3 quarts water
½ cup celery leaves,
   chopped
¼ cup fresh parsley,
   chopped
1 large onion, peeled and
   quartered

Salt and pepper
4 medium carrots, cut into
   small pieces
2 eggs, beaten
2 cups flour
¼ teaspoon sage
¼ cup parsley, minced
Few shakes of Tabasco
   sauce

Bring first six ingredients to a boil, lower heat, and simmer until chicken is tender. Remove chicken, celery, parsley, and onion from broth; discard vegetables. Remove bones and skin from chicken; cut into bite-size pieces; set aside. Cook carrots in a little chicken broth until tender. Put carrots in blender and blend until smooth. Combine carrot purée with chicken. Bring the rest of the broth to an easy boil. Combine eggs, flour, and sage until egg mix is crumbly. Rub mixture through hands into boiling broth. Add parsley and Tabasco; cook about 10 minutes more. Add chicken and carrots; serve. Add more water if soup is too thick.
Makes 10 to 12 servings.

– Dottie Jacobs (Mrs. Donald)

» Soupe de Choux Fleur et Poireaux «

This unusual French-inspired leek and cauliflower soup is served at LeRuth's in New Orleans, which consistently appears on lists of the finest restaurants in the country.

1 head cauliflower, cut into florets
4 leeks, white part only, cut into 4 pieces
1 large onion, finely chopped
½ cup butter, clarified
4 cups chicken stock
1 cup whipping cream
Pinch nutmeg
2 tablespoons cold butter

Sauté cauliflower, leeks, and onion in butter over low heat for a few minutes. Add stock and cook 45 minutes or until vegetables are tender. Puree in blender or food processor until smooth. Return to saucepan and add cream and nutmeg. Bring to boil, reduce heat, and simmer 10 minutes. Add cold butter and whisk into soup. Makes 4 servings.

– Ann Trufant (Mrs. S. A., III)
New Orleans, Louisiana

» Cock-A-Leekie Soup «

This soup from the British Isles was appropriately served during the Cincinnati Art Museum's exclusive showing in the United States of "Arms and Armor from the Tower of London."

3 lb. chicken, cut up
4 cups water
½ cup carrots, finely chopped
½ cup celery, finely chopped
¼ cup onion, finely chopped
2 sprigs parsley
2 teaspoons salt
¼ teaspoon white pepper
1 bay leaf
½ lb. leeks, thinly sliced
1 small potato, peeled and chopped
½ cup quick-cooking barley
2 cups half and half cream

In a large kettle or Dutch oven, combine chicken and water. Add carrots, celery, onion, parsley, salt, pepper, and bay leaf. Cover; simmer 25 minutes, or until chicken is tender. Remove chicken, bay leaf, and parsley from broth. Discard bay leaf and parsley. Cool chicken until it can be easily handled; remove meat from bones; discard bones and skin. Chop meat. Skim off excess fat from broth. Add leeks, potato, and barley to soup; bring to boiling. Reduce heat; simmer, covered, 15 to 20 minutes. Blend in cream and chicken. Heat through. Makes 8 servings.

– Davis Catering

» Family Style Onion Soup Metropole «

This recipe dates back to 1910, when my father used to stay at the old Metropole Hotel when he had to work too late for the 2-hour train ride to Hamilton. He loved their onion soup, and got the recipe from the chef – it became a part of every festive family dinner after that.

8 large or 16 medium onions, sliced
2 tablespoons butter
1 tablespoon flour
3 pints beef broth
Salt and pepper
½ lb. Swiss cheese, grated
4 thin slices bread, toasted

Sauté onions in butter in saucepan for about 30 minutes, until golden. Mix in flour and continue cooking for 5 minutes. Add broth, and salt and pepper to taste; simmer 10 minutes. Add ¼ lb. Swiss cheese. Put toasted bread in cocottes or individual baking dishes, pour the soup over it, and sprinkle top with remaining Swiss cheese. Bake in a preheated 400° oven for 30 minutes, until golden brown on top. Serve immediately. Makes 4 servings.

– Edna Holle

» Cheddar Soup «

3 tablespoons onion, grated
3 tablespoons carrot, grated
¼ cup butter
2-13 oz. cans chicken broth
½ teaspoon dry mustard
¼ cup cornstarch
¼ cup milk
1 cup sharp Cheddar cheese, grated
Garlic croutons

Sauté onion and carrot in butter for 3 minutes. Add broth and dry mustard; simmer for 5 minutes. Blend cornstarch and milk; add to the broth, stirring continuously with a wire whisk. Simmer until the soup is smooth and thick. Add the cheese; continue beating and stirring until the cheese melts. Serve in heated cups, topped with croutons. Makes 6 servings.

– Stanley Demos
Coach House Restaurant, Lexington, Kentucky
From his book, "Stanley Suggests"

» Cuban Black Beans «

4 lbs. dry black beans	¼ cup cumin powder
6 medium onions, chopped	¼ cup curry powder
4 large green peppers, sliced	2 tablespoons crushed red pepper
1 cup olive oil	¼ cup salt
8 cloves garlic, mashed	2 tablespoons sugar
11 bay leaves	Cooked rice

Soak black beans overnight in three times the amount of water needed to cover beans. Cook onions and green peppers in olive oil until soft; set aside. Add garlic, bay leaves, cumin powder, curry powder, red pepper, salt, and sugar to beans and cook in at least double the amount of water needed to cover the beans, using first the water in which the beans were soaked. Cook slowly together for three hours until beans are soft on the inside but still somewhat firm on the outside. Add the olive oil, green peppers, and onions. Cook slowly for another half hour. Serve over rice. Makes 50 servings.

– Fred Lazarus III

» Velvet Sweet Corn Soup «

This thick, nourishing soup is often served as a first course in Chinese restaurants in America.

1 whole chicken breast, skinned, boned, and minced	1¼ teaspoons salt
	3 tablespoons cornstarch
	3 tablespoons water
1 egg white	1 egg white, beaten
3 tablespoons cold water	½ teaspoon peanut oil
4 cups chicken broth	3 tablespoons ham, finely minced
1 cup canned cream style corn	

Mix minced chicken breast with egg white and water. Combine chicken broth, corn, and salt in a heavy saucepan; bring to a boil. Add chicken and egg mixture; blend well with a spoon. Bring to a boil once more. Combine cornstarch and water and add to pan, stirring until mixture is smooth and thick. Add egg white, stirring, and remove mixture from heat immediately. Quickly add oil and garnish with ham. Makes 8 servings.

– Kathleen J. Baker

» Russian Cabbage Borscht «

This should be made the day before so it can season properly. It freezes extremely well and tastes even better the second time it's warmed. It's marvelous with dark pumpernickel bread.

1 lb. beef short ribs	4 small yellow onions, quartered
1 lb. beef soup meat	½ cup light brown sugar
1 knuckle bone	¼ cup granulated sugar
3 marrow bones	Juice of 2 lemons
1 gallon water	14 oz. bottle catsup
1 medium head cabbage	1 teaspoon salt
15 oz. can skinned and seeded Italian tomatoes, plus juice	½ teaspoon white pepper
	1 teaspoon caraway seeds

Wash the meat and bones in cold water. Place in a 2-gallon pot with water. Cut cabbage into quarters and remove the thick core. Use steel blade of processor and chop cabbage with several on/off pulses; add to the pot. Place the tomatoes, onions, brown sugar, and white sugar in bowl of processor; process for 30 seconds. Add to the soup pot. Add lemon juice, catsup, salt, pepper, and caraway seeds. Cover and bring to a boil. Simmer for 3 to 4 hours, until meat is tender. Remove from heat and let cool. When cooled, refrigerate overnight. One hour before serving, skim off any congealed fat and remove bones from soup. Remove marrow from bones and add to soup. Remove meat from the bones, cut into small pieces, and add to soup. Reheat over low heat for 30 minutes. Makes 15 to 20 servings.

– Zell Schulman (Mrs. Melvin)
From her book, "Something Different for Passover"

» Cream Cucumber Soup «

3 large cucumbers, peeled
   and seeded
1 large clove garlic

2 cups sour cream
Salt and white pepper
Cucumber slices

Using a blender or food processor, purée cucumbers and garlic. Add sour cream; season with salt and pepper to taste; blend well and refrigerate for at least 4 hours. Serve in chilled cups, decorated with cucumber slices. Makes 6 servings.

– Stanley Demos
Coach House Restaurant, Lexington, Kentucky
From his book, "Stanley Suggests"

» Garlic Soup «

Garlic is very much a part of French cooking, and has been dubbed "the vanilla of Marseille." The amount of garlic in this French soup may be intimidating at first, but the result is surprisingly mild and savory.

1 head garlic
   (approximately 16
   cloves), separated but
   unpeeled
2 cups boiling water
6 cups water
3 teaspoons salt
3 grinds fresh pepper
   from mill
2 whole cloves
½ teaspoon sage

½ teaspoon thyme
4 sprigs parsley, minced
1 bay leaf, crushed
3 tablespoons olive oil
3 egg yolks
4 tablespoons olive oil
Croutons or croutes au
   fromage – rounds of
   French bread sprinkled
   with grated cheese and
   olive oil

Drop garlic cloves into boiling water. Boil 1 minute, refresh in cold water, drain, and peel. In a large saucepan, place garlic, water, salt, pepper, cloves, sage, thyme, parsley, bay leaf, and 3 tablespoons olive oil. Bring to a boil and simmer for 30 minutes. Strain broth, pressing juice from garlic cloves. Beat egg yolks until thick and lemon colored. Add 4 tablespoons olive oil, drop by drop, beating until thickened. Add hot soup gradually, being careful not to curdle egg mixture. Serve at once with croutons or croutes au fromage. Croutes au fromage are made with slices of French bread cut on the bias. Place in preheated 350° oven on a baking sheet and brown the bread lightly. Spread bread with grated cheese and drizzle with olive oil. Continue browning under a hot broiler and serve at once. Soup may be prepared ahead of time up to egg yolk addition, and final steps done just before serving. Makes 6 servings.

– Barbara Godard
Chatham, Massachusetts

» Cold Cucumber and Yogurt Soup «

In Turkey, this is served as a soup course, or as an accompaniment to the main course.

1 large cucumber
¼ teaspoon salt
2 cups yogurt
1½ tablespoons olive oil
2 teaspoons white vinegar

1 tablespoon mint leaves,
   finely chopped
1 tablespoon dill, finely
   chopped
6 cucumber slices
Mint sprigs

Cut peeled cucumber in half lengthwise; remove seeds and grate coarsely. Sprinkle with salt and let stand for 15 minutes. Whisk yogurt with olive oil, vinegar, mint leaves, and dill. Drain cucumbers well and stir into yogurt mixture. Cover and refrigerate until served. Garnish with cucumber and mint. Makes 6 servings.

– Anne Seasholes Cozlu (Mrs. Cem)

» Gazpacho El Bodegon Restaurante, Madrid «

Every visitor to Madrid tries the gazpacho, a sort of liquid salad that is a refreshing beginning to the meal. Each one is a little different.

2 medium size
   cucumbers, seeded and
   coarsely chopped
5 medium size tomatoes,
   coarsely chopped
1 large onion, coarsely
   chopped
2 teaspoons garlic cloves,
   finely chopped
4 cups croutons
4 cups cold water

¼ cup red wine vinegar
4 teaspoons salt
¼ cup olive oil
2 green onions, finely
   chopped
1 green pepper, finely
   chopped
1 cucumber, finely
   chopped
1 cup toasted croutons

If the cucumbers have thick skins, peel them before chopping. Mix cucumbers, tomatoes, onion, garlic, croutons, water, vinegar, salt, and olive oil in a large bowl. Process in blender 1 minute or until well puréed. Chill in a covered container in refrigerator. Stir well before serving and season to taste. Ladle into chilled soup bowls. Serve the green onions, green pepper, cucumber, and toasted croutons as garnishes in separate bowls, to be added to the gazpacho. Makes 4 servings.

– Elizabeth K. Fern (Mrs. Jules)

» Gazpacho Malaca «

The ingredients of this traditional cold vegetable soup from Spain may be changed in proportions to suit individual tastes. If too tart, add a little sugar. The more bread used, the whiter the soup. Malaca was the Phoenician name for the famous Spanish seaport and resort now known as Malaga.

1 or 2 slices bread, soaked in water	Salt and pepper
2 large tomatoes, peeled	1 green pepper, chopped
1 large onion	1 tomato, peeled and chopped
2 cloves garlic, peeled	1 cucumber, chopped
1 medium cucumber, peeled	1 onion, chopped, or 4 tablespoons scallions, chopped
¼ cup oil	
½ cup wine vinegar	Toasted croutons
Cold water	

Mash bread, tomatoes, onion, garlic, and cucumber in a mortar or mix in a blender or food processor until smooth. Strain; add oil and vinegar to the strained liquid, mixing well. Refrigerate 1 hour, preferably in a pottery bowl. Mix and add enough cold water to make 5 cups; season with salt and pepper to taste. Serve very cold. Pass chopped vegetables and croutons to be added to soup as desired. Makes 5 servings.

– Barbara Eveland (Mrs. Joseph)

» Egg Flower Soup «

Sesame seeds, when crushed and squeezed, yield the light oil that gives this soup its distinctive flavor. The oil may be found in Oriental groceries or specialty food shops.

3 cups chicken stock	2 tablespoons green onion, chopped
1 tablespoon soy sauce	1 egg, beaten
⅛ teaspoon pepper	½ teaspoon sesame oil
¼ teaspoon salt	
2 cups bok choy or nappa, shredded	

In a heavy saucepan, bring the chicken stock to a boil with the soy sauce, pepper, and salt. Add the bok choy or nappa and green onion; boil together for 1 minute. While stirring, add the beaten egg slowly; the cooled egg will float and form egg "flowers." Add sesame oil and serve immediately in individual bowls. Makes 6 to 8 servings.

– Dora Ang (Mrs. Francis)

» Hot and Sour Soup «

4 dried lily pods	2 tablespoons vinegar
2 large dried Chinese black mushrooms	1 tablespoon sugar
6 tree ear mushrooms	1 teaspoon bead molasses
¼ lb. pork, cut into matchsticks	14 oz. cake tofu, cut into matchsticks
2 tablespoons oil	1 teaspoon freshly ground pepper
½ cup bamboo shoots, cut into matchsticks	1 tablespoon cornstarch
1 teaspoon fresh ginger root, minced	2 tablespoons water
1 tablespoon soy sauce	2 large eggs, beaten
5 cups rich chicken broth	2 scallions, green and white part, chopped
½ teaspoon salt	Sesame oil

Put lily pods, black mushrooms, and tree ears in a shallow bowl and cover with boiling water; let stand 20 minutes and then drain. Trim stems and any tough, woody parts. Cut into matchsticks. In a wok or heavy skillet, stir-fry pork in oil. Add mushrooms, tree ears, lily pods, bamboo shoots, ginger, and soy sauce; stir-fry for 1 minute. Add chicken broth, salt, vinegar, and sugar. Bring to a boil rapidly and skim off any foam that appears. Add bead molasses, tofu, pepper, and cornstarch dissolved in water. Stir until mixture thickens slightly. Add beaten eggs while stirring; cook until egg is set. Put soup into bowls and serve immediately, garnished with chopped scallions and a drop of sesame oil. Makes 6 to 8 servings.

– Bing Moy, China Gourmet Restaurant

» Lentil Soup «

½ lb. lentils
5 cups cold water
4 slices bacon, cut into small pieces
1 cup leeks, chopped
½ cup onions, chopped
¼ cup carrots, chopped
¾ cup green pepper, chopped
¾ cup tomatoes, chopped

3 tablespoons butter
3 tablespoons flour
10½ oz. can condensed beef broth, undiluted
2 teaspoons salt
2 tablespoons vinegar
4 wieners or frankfurters, cut into ¼" slices, optional

Place lentils in 5 cups of cold water in a large pan; bring to a boil. Reduce heat; simmer covered 1 hour. Meanwhile, sauté bacon pieces in a large skillet until crisp. Add leeks, onions, carrots, peppers, and tomatoes; sauté over low heat about 5 minutes. Combine with cooked lentils and liquid. Melt butter in skillet; remove from heat. Stir in flour until smooth, then gradually stir in beef broth. Add salt and vinegar, return to heat, and bring to the boiling point, continuing to stir. Mix into cooked lentils and simmer over low heat, stirring occasionally, about 30 minutes. Add wieners or frankfurters during the last 10 minutes.
Makes 6 servings.

– Mary Wanek (Mrs. Robert)

» Cream of Lettuce Soup with Popcorn Croutons «

The crunchy popcorn croutons complement the delicate flavor of this unusual soup from The Netherlands.

1 ham hock
2 quarts water
2 heads lettuce, shredded
1 cup whipping cream
4 thin slices onion
1 bay leaf

3 whole cloves
3 sprigs parsley
2 tablespoons butter
1 tablespoon flour
Popcorn

Simmer ham hock in water for 1½ hours. Set aside to cool and skim fat from broth. Rinse lettuce, shake only lightly so it retains moisture, and place in kettle without water. Cover and cook slowly until tender, about 30 minutes. Purée lettuce in blender or food processor; add to ham stock. Scald cream with onion, bay leaf, cloves,

and parsley; strain. Blend butter and flour over low heat; stir in cream; add to soup mixture. Cook gently for 10 minutes; bring to a boil. Serve hot with popcorn as croutons. Makes 8 to 10 servings.

» Easy Mock Turtle Soup «

1 lb. ground beef
3 to 4 carrots, grated or thinly sliced
1 onion, finely chopped
2 quarts water
5 tablespoons Worcestershire sauce
14 oz. bottle catsup

2 to 3 tablespoons mixed pickling spices, placed in a small cheesecloth bag
1 lemon, thinly sliced
1 cup flour, browned
1 hard-cooked egg, chopped

Boil beef, carrots, and onion in water until tender. Add all but the flour and egg. Brown the flour by placing in a heavy pan over very low heat. Stir frequently until flour is evenly browned to a tan color. Do not overheat or flour will scorch. Add a little cold water to make a paste; stir into the soup. Simmer over low heat for 1 to 2 additional hours; remove bag of spices. This soup tastes better if cooled and refrigerated overnight. Before serving the next day, reheat and add chopped egg.
Makes 6 to 8 servings.

– Mrs. Marion Palmer

» Mock Turtle Soup «

This family recipe came from our father's older brother, who lived in Posen, Prussia. We still prepare it for our Texas neighbors.

1 calf head or 2 lbs. boiling beef or veal
1 fresh tongue
1 set of brains
3 quarts water
6 large potatoes
1 large onion
A pinch of cloves, cayenne, mace, basil, and lemon thyme, tied in a cheesecloth bag

Salt and pepper
1 lemon, sliced and seeded
2-12 oz. bottles catsup
½ cup white vinegar, or less to suit taste
3 tablespoons flour
3 hard-cooked eggs, chopped
2 tablespoons parsley, finely chopped

Place calf head or beef or veal in a large kettle; add tongue and brains; cover with water. Bring water to a boil, add potatoes, onion, and seasoning bag. Cover and cook until the meat is very tender. Remove meat, vegetables, and seasonings; strain broth and reserve. Remove bones and the skin from the tongue. Grind meats and vegetables in grinder or food processor. Return the mixture to the strained broth; add salt, pepper, sliced lemon, catsup, and vinegar. Bring soup to a boil, reduce heat, and simmer for at least 1 hour. Meanwhile, brown flour in a heavy iron skillet over low heat, stirring constantly to prevent scorching. Sprinkle over the soup and stir in well to thicken the broth. Add eggs and parsley; boil soup for a few minutes longer. Makes 12 to 14 cups.

– Submitted in honor of our mother,
Mrs. May Ida Thiel,
by Dr. John Thiel and Mrs. Angela T. Silcox

» Menudo Soup «

Mexicans like to eat tortillas with this soup as bread, dipped into the soup and used to scoop up the hominy and onions.

2-12 oz. cans whole hominy, yellow or white	12 corn tortillas
10 oz. can enchilada sauce, hot or mild	1 onion, chopped
	½ cup oregano, dried
5 tablespoons water	2 lemons, cut in wedges

In a large saucepan mix hominy, sauce, and water. Simmer for 10 minutes, stirring occasionally. One at a time, heat corn tortillas directly over stove burner, turning often to avoid burning. Remove from flame, stack, and wrap in a dish towel to keep warm. Tortillas may also be heated by placing under a broiler, 3″ or 4″ from the heat. Turn with a fork or tongs until the tortillas are heated through, softened, and lightly blistered. They may also be heated in a heavy ungreased iron skillet over medium heat. Place onion, oregano, and lemon wedges in small separate bowls. Serve soup in bowls and each guest may add as much chopped onion, oregano (crushed in the palm of the hand and sprinkled into soup), and lemon juice as desired. Makes 6 servings.

– Lupe A. Gonzales-Hoyt

» Cuban Seafood Soup «

This soup is both dramatic and delectable. Serve it as a sensational first course or as a meal in itself.

1½ cups onions, chopped	6 clams or mussels in the shell, scrubbed
1½ cups green peppers, chopped	6 large shrimp, heads and shells removed
2 cloves garlic, minced	2 crab legs, cut in 3 pieces each
3 tablespoons olive oil	
1 tablespoon parsley	3 to 4 lb. sea bass or other
1 teaspoon basil	strongly flavored fish
2 bay leaves	such as cod or haddock,
3 tomatoes, peeled and puréed, or about 1 cup	cleaned and cut in 6 pieces
1 quart water	
6 oysters in the shell, scrubbed	

In a large soup pot, sauté the vegetables and garlic in oil for a few minutes. Add parsley, basil, and bay leaves; sauté for a few minutes, stirring frequently. Add the tomatoes and water; bring to a boil. Reduce heat and simmer about 15 minutes. Add seafood to soup. Simmer another 15 to 20 minutes, covered. Serve in deep bowls, each serving containing one portion of each fish. A table knife and sturdy napkin are essential with this soup; the knife is for opening any stubborn shellfish. Makes 6 servings.

– Mary Anna DuSablon (Mrs. Sean T. Bailey)

» Cold Raspberry Soup «

This is a soup that can double as dessert. You may also use fresh or frozen strawberries in place of raspberries.

10 oz. pkg. frozen red raspberries, thawed	2 cups sour cream

Using a blender or food processor, purée raspberries; add sour cream and blend together. Refrigerate for at least 4 hours; serve in chilled glass bowls. Makes 6 servings.

– Stanley Demos
Coach House Restaurant, Lexington, Kentucky
From his book, "Stanley Suggests"

Tureen with Cover, English, Charles Kandler, 1728-29,
Silver, 1982-187. Bequest of Paul E. Geier

» Pretzel Suppe «

2 slices bacon, diced
½ lb. smoked sausage or
   frankfurters, sliced
1 cup celery, finely diced
½ cup onion, finely diced
1¼ cups water
1 bay leaf

1 cup frozen hash brown
   potatoes
Salt and pepper
10¾ oz. can cream of
   chicken soup
1¼ cups milk
4 soft pretzels, warmed

Partially cook bacon in a large saucepan. Add sausage
and continue to cook until bacon is brown; remove and
keep warm. Add celery and onion to the bacon and
sausage drippings; sauté until tender. Add water, bay
leaf, potatoes, and salt and pepper to taste. Cover and
simmer 10 to 15 minutes. Stir in soup, milk, and sausage,
reserving bacon for garnish. Remove bay leaf and serve.
Garnish soup with bacon and serve with warm pretzels
or float pretzels on top of soup. Makes 4 servings.

— *Peggy Andre (Mrs. J. Richard)*

» Potato-Onion Soup «

5 slices bacon, diced
3 cups onion, sliced
5 cups potatoes, peeled
   and diced

3 cups water, salted
2 to 3 cups milk
Salt and pepper

Sauté diced bacon slowly in heavy Dutch oven. When
bacon is browned, add the sliced onions and cook slowly,
covered, stirring occasionally, until onions are
transparent and yellow, but not mushy. Meanwhile, add
potatoes to water and cook slowly, until potatoes are
soft. Remove potatoes and add water to the bacon and
onion; mix well. Mash the cooked potatoes and add to
Dutch oven mixture. Add the milk and blend. Although
this is a heavy soup, it can be thinned by adding more
milk. Heat slowly, just to the boiling point, while stirring
frequently. Add salt and pepper to taste. Serve
immediately. Makes 4 to 6 servings.

— *Johanna Clark (Mrs. Roger W.)*

» Red Pottage «

½ cup dried Great
   Northern beans
2 tablespoons butter
2 stalks celery, chopped
1 red beet, cooked and
   quartered

1 onion, peeled and
   chopped
3 tomatoes, chopped
4 cups chicken stock
Salt and pepper
1 tablespoon fresh mint,
   chopped

Cover the beans with water and soak two hours. Drain the beans. Melt butter in a large pan and add beans and vegetables; sauté for five minutes. Pour in stock and season to taste. Bring to a boil; lower heat and simmer for three hours or until beans are very soft. Remove beet and then purée the soup in a blender. Reheat and serve garnished with chopped mint, if available. Makes 4 to 6 servings.

– Aurelia Klayf (Mrs. Bernard)

» Leith's Restaurant Stilton Soup «

We celebrated my husband's birthday at this remarkable restaurant in London. He enjoyed this superb soup and the chef was kind enough to share his recipe with us.

1 medium size onion, or 4
   shallots, finely chopped
2 stalks celery, finely
   chopped
2 tablespoons butter
1½ tablespoons flour
3½ cups chicken broth or
   veal stock

¼ cup dry white wine
2 cups milk
½ cup Stilton cheese,
   grated or crumbled
3 tablespoons whipping
   cream
Salt and pepper

Sauté onion or shallots and celery in butter until softened. Add flour and cook, stirring, for a minute or two. Remove from heat and add broth and wine. Return to heat and bring to a boil, stirring. Reduce heat and simmer for 45 minutes or until wine has lost its harsh alcoholic flavor. Add the milk, cheese, and cream; heat only until the cheese has melted. Do not allow the soup to boil. Add salt and pepper to taste and serve hot with croutons or cheese straws, or serve well chilled. For a smooth, velvety texture, place the soup in a blender or food processor or through a sieve. Makes 4 servings.

– Pat Matthews (Mrs. A. Pierce)

» Tomato Soup au Gratin «

Bacchus was originally an Elm Street row house in Cincinnati, and is now a beautifully restored restaurant, specializing in continental cuisine. It's a favorite stop for opera and symphony patrons from nearby Music Hall.

1 small onion, diced
1 clove garlic, minced
3 tablespoons butter
10 large ripe tomatoes,
   peeled, seeded, and
   puréed
1 tablespoon fresh basil,
   minced
1 teaspoon fresh oregano

1 tablespoon fresh thyme,
   minced
2 teaspoons fresh
   marjoram
½ cup whipping cream
Ricotta cheese
Parmesan cheese, grated
Romano cheese, grated
Celery leaves, diced

Sauté onion and garlic in butter in a heavy saucepan until they are lightly browned. Add the puréed tomatoes; bring to a boil. Reduce heat and simmer the mixture for 30 minutes. Carefully skim the residue from the tomato mixture. Add the herbs and whipping cream; simmer for an additional 15 minutes. Ladle soup into individual heatproof bowls; add a dollop of Ricotta cheese to each, sprinkle with Parmesan and Romano cheeses, and place under a broiler for 2 to 3 minutes to brown the cheese lightly. Sprinkle with diced celery leaves and serve immediately. Makes 1 quart.

– Chef Craig Paden
Bacchus Restaurant

» Spinach Borscht «

10 oz. pkg. frozen chopped
   spinach
1 quart water
Juice of ½ lemon
1 tablespoon granulated
   chicken bouillon
1 teaspoon salt

½ teaspoon pepper
1 egg, beaten
1 teaspoon onion flakes
1 cup sour cream
Additional sour cream
Parsley sprigs

Cook spinach in water until thawed. Add lemon juice, chicken flavoring, salt, and pepper. Add beaten egg and onion flakes. Beat together; chill overnight. Before serving, add sour cream; beat well. Pour into soup bowls; garnish with a dollop of sour cream and a sprig of parsley. Serve chilled. Makes 6 servings.

– Phyllis T. Karp (Mrs. Gilbert)

» Mim's Easy Vegetable Soup «

I have given this recipe to a number of my friends and they tell me they are forever grateful. It is easy and very nourishing – an ideal one-dish meal for couples or those who live alone. And leftovers freeze well.

10 oz. pkg. frozen peas
10 oz. pkg. frozen mixed vegetables
10½ oz. can vegetable soup
10½ oz. can beef barley soup

24 oz. can cocktail vegetable juice, or more if desired
½ teaspoon sugar
Salt and pepper
A mixture of herbs, such as thyme, basil, tarragon, or oregano, to taste

Defrost peas and frozen vegetables. Mix vegetable and beef barley soups together; add cocktail vegetable juice along with sugar. Put into a 3-quart pot and bring to a simmer. Add peas, mixed vegetables, salt, pepper, and herbs. Cook until vegetables are tender. Makes 6 to 8 servings.

– Miriam Stern (Mrs. Joseph, Sr.)

» Wild Rice Soup «

This is a tradition in Minnesota, where the Ojibwa Indians still harvest the rice by shaking it over canoes as their ancestors did. This hearty soup may be frozen. If a thinner soup is desired, add more chicken broth.

¼ cup butter
1 tablespoon onion, minced
¼ cup flour
2 cups chicken broth
1 cup half and half cream
2 cups wild rice, cooked

⅓ cup cooked ham, minced
¼ cup carrots, finely grated
¼ cup almonds, toasted and chopped or slivered
2 teaspoons Madeira wine
Minced chives, for garnish

Melt butter in saucepan and sauté onion until tender. Blend in flour; gradually add broth and cream. Cook, stirring constantly, until mixture thickens slightly. Stir in rice, ham, carrots, and almonds. Simmer about 10 minutes. Blend in wine. Serve immediately, garnished with chives. Makes 4 servings.

– Peggy Andre (Mrs. J. Richard)

» Black Walnut Soup Chantilly «

1 lb. ground beef
2 onions, chopped
5 stalks celery, chopped
3 stems parsley
1 teaspoon ground cinnamon
1 teaspoon ground pickling spices
½ teaspoon ground allspice

2 cups flour
1 gallon water
½ cup black walnuts, chopped
1 pint cream
½ cup sherry
1 oz. brandy
Salt and pepper
Whipped cream for topping

Sauté beef, onions, celery, parsley, and spices together. Stir in flour and gradually add water, stirring to keep from lumping. Simmer 1½ hours. Strain, removing the meats and vegetables. Add walnuts, cream, sherry, brandy, and salt and pepper to taste. Serve hot topped with whipped cream. If desired, glaze cream by putting it into a preheated 500° oven for 3 to 5 minutes. Makes 10 generous servings.

– Chef Andre Leriche
Queen City Club

» One-of-Each Soup «

You may not believe the ingredients, but the result is tantalizingly good. It's nice as a first course, served chilled in old-fashioned glasses, before you go to the dinner table or buffet.

1 onion
1 apple
1 potato
1 banana
1 celery heart
2 cups chicken broth

1 cup half and half cream
1 tablespoon butter, melted
1 rounded teaspoon curry powder
1 teaspoon salt

Peel and chop vegetables and fruits; cook until soft in chicken broth. Put through food mill or blend in blender or food processor until smooth. Mix in cream, butter, curry powder, and salt. Chill in refrigerator for at least two hours. Serve cold. Makes 4 servings.

– Audrey McCafferty

» Soup Accessories «

Mix in or float the following garnishes on your favorite soups – and they become party fare.

- Thin salami slices in tomato, pea, or celery soup
- Crumbled bacon in celery, bean, or tomato soup
- Grated cheese on all chowders and onion soup
- Olive rings on jellied consomme
- Lemon slices on clam chowder
- Toasted almonds on most cream soups
- Popcorn on tomato, pea, or corn soup
- Walnuts, pecans, or toasted almonds on cream of chicken or celery soup.

– Elaine Hocks (Mrs. Harry J.)

» Molded Avocado Salad «

6 oz. pkg. lemon gelatin
2 cups boiling water
1 cup avocado, mashed
½ cup sour cream
½ cup mayonnaise
1 tablespoon onion, finely chopped
¼ teaspoon salt
Dash of Tabasco

Dissolve gelatin in boiling water and cool. Add the rest of ingredients and stir. Coat a 4-cup mold with mayonnaise; add gelatin mixture; chill. Unmold when ready to serve. Makes 4 servings.

– Marie Clift (Mrs. Robert G.)

» Cinnamon Apple Salad «

This is an original recipe from Hood River, Oregon, the Apple Kingdom of the U.S. and the country's top apple-raising region.

1 cup sugar
1 cup water
¾ cup cinnamon "red hot" candies
6 apples, peeled and cored
½ cup celery, finely chopped
½ cup walnuts, finely chopped
½ cup mayonnaise
6 leaves of lettuce

Combine sugar, water, and red hots in a heavy saucepan. Simmer over medium heat until candy is melted. Place

apples in hot syrup and cook very slowly until apples are tender; you may use a toothpick for testing. Cool in syrup. Mix celery and walnuts with enough mayonnaise to moisten; stuff apples with mixture. Serve on lettuce leaves and top with additional mayonnaise, if desired. Makes 6 servings.

– Naomi Bergert (Mrs. Jack R.)

» Beet Salad Vinaigrette «

3 large beets, cooked and peeled
1 large onion, sliced in rings
1 tablespoon oil
1 tablespoon lemon juice
½ teaspoon sugar
Salt and pepper
¼ teaspoon dry mustard

Slice beets in rounds. In a glass dish, alternate a layer of beets and a layer of onions until all are used. Mix remaining ingredients together; pour over the beets. Chill for at least 3 hours before serving. Makes 4 servings.

– Jennifer-Ann Fernandes (Mrs. Allan)

» Indiana Cabbage and Lettuce Salad «

The original recipe for this salad came from my mother in Indiana. It gave instructions like "plenty of onion, preferably green," assuming that you did it by feel and by taste. This salad can be made ahead – it's a good dish to take to picnics or potluck suppers.

4 cups cabbage, shredded
4 cups lettuce, shredded
1 green pepper, chopped
4 green onions, sliced
6 hard-cooked eggs, sliced
1 cup mayonnaise, more if needed
Dash of lemon juice or tarragon vinegar
Salt and coarsely ground pepper
Tomatoes, optional
Ham slivers, optional

Mix cabbage, lettuce, green pepper, onions, and eggs with mayonnaise, adding more if needed to moisten. Add lemon juice or tarragon vinegar, and season with salt and pepper to taste. If desired, tomatoes may be added or ham slivers may be substituted for part of the eggs. Makes 8 to 10 servings.

– Jane Durrell (Mrs. John)

» Lookout House Caesar Salad «

During the halcyon days of the Lookout House in northern Kentucky in the 1940s, I was the nightclub columnist for The Cincinnati Post and covered the opening nights of all the top show business entertainers whom the late Jimmy Brink booked to headline his floor shows. A fond culinary memory of the Lookout House was its famous Caesar Salad, priced in those days at $1.50 for two!

1 clove garlic, peeled	1 teaspoon Worcestershire
2 heads Bibb or 1 small	sauce
head romaine lettuce,	Salt and freshly ground
leaves separated,	pepper
crisped, and dried	2 tablespoons Parmesan
3 tablespoons olive oil	cheese
Dash of Tabasco sauce	1 egg
Juice of 1 lemon	10 to 12 croutons
	5 anchovy fillets, quartered

Rub a chilled salad bowl with the garlic clove. Place lettuce in bowl. If using romaine, remove large outer leaves and break remainder into bite-size pieces. Mix together olive oil, Tabasco sauce, lemon juice, Worcestershire sauce, salt, pepper, and Parmesan cheese. Pour this over lettuce. Scald the egg in boiling water for 1 minute. Break it over salad; add croutons and anchovies; toss well. Makes 2 servings.

– Mary Wood

» Cervelat Salad «

Cervelat is marvelous combined with these aromatic herbs in this French sausage salad.

1 lb. cervelat, skinned,	1 tablespoon chives,
sliced ¼" thick	chopped
¼ cup olive oil	1 tablespoon parsley,
2 tablespoons white wine	chopped
vinegar	1 tablespoon shallots,
1 tablespoon chervil,	chopped
chopped	Lettuce leaves

Place sausage slices in a bowl. Whisk together oil and vinegar; add chopped chervil, chives, parsley, and shallots. Pour over sausage and marinate several hours.

Taste and correct seasonings, adding salt and pepper if necessary. Serve on lettuce leaves as salad or as hors d'oeuvres on toothpicks. Serves 6 as salad.

– Sarah Headley (Mrs. Grant)

» Maurice Salad «

There have been many variations of the original Maurice Salad, but many people say this is the best. This salad brings back memories of Saturday luncheons at the old Netherland Plaza Hotel prior to shopping trips or visits to the theater. Somehow, no other julienne salad has ever tasted the same.

1 cup mayonnaise	¾ cup cooked ham,
¼ cup tarragon vinegar	julienned
½ cup olive oil	¾ cup cooked turkey,
1 teaspoon chives	julienned
2 eggs, hard-cooked and	¾ cup Swiss cheese,
quartered	julienned
2 tablespoons sweet or	½ cup tomatoes, chopped
dill pickle relish	Chives, finely chopped
1½ teaspoons	3 tomatoes, medium size,
Worcestershire sauce	quartered
Salt and pepper	2 eggs, hard-cooked,
1 head iceberg lettuce,	quartered
shredded and crisped	

Blend mayonnaise, tarragon vinegar, olive oil, chives, eggs, relish, Worcestershire sauce, and salt and pepper to taste slowly in blender. It should pour like molasses. Toss lettuce, ham, turkey, cheese, and tomatoes with dressing. Divide into portions and mound on plate, sprinkling with chives. Place tomato and egg quarters at corners. Add additional ground pepper, if desired. Makes 4 to 6 servings.

» Vichy Carrot Salad «

4 carrots, peeled and	Juice of 1 lemon
shredded	Salt and pepper
1 apple, peeled, cored,	1 to 2 tablespoons honey,
and shredded	optional

Mix carrots and apple with lemon juice; season with salt and pepper. Add honey if salad is too tart. Chill until serving. Makes 4 servings.

– Barbara Lauterbach (Mrs. Peter)

» Oriental Chicken Sprout Salad «

2 cups chicken, cooked
   and diced
1½ cups fresh bean
   sprouts, or 8 oz. can
   bean sprouts, drained
1 cup cooked rice
1 cup celery, chopped
1 cup carrots, shredded
2 tablespoons green
   pepper, chopped
¼ cup French dressing
2 tablespoons soy sauce
¼ teaspoon salt
Juice of ½ lemon
3 green onions, chopped
½ cup almonds, slivered
   and toasted
½ cup mayonnaise
1 head lettuce
2 hard-cooked eggs,
   quartered
8 ripe olives

Combine first 11 ingredients in a large bowl; chill thoroughly. Just before serving, add almonds and mayonnaise; toss well. Serve on lettuce leaves and garnish with egg wedges and ripe olives. Makes 8 servings.

— Barbara Wagner (Mrs. James H.)

» Sesame Chicken Salad «

3 whole chicken
   breasts, boned
   and split
2 cups chicken broth
¼ cup soy sauce
1 head lettuce, cut into
   ⅛" strips
2 stalks celery, cut into
   julienne strips
4 to 6 scallions, cut into
   julienne strips
¼ cup sesame seeds,
   toasted
3 ozs. rice sticks
Oil
3 tablespoons wine
   vinegar
2 tablespoons sugar
1 teaspoon salt
½ teaspoon pepper
1 teaspoon sesame oil

Simmer chicken in broth and soy sauce until tender. Remove skin and shred the flesh into julienne strips. Toss with lettuce, celery, scallions, and sesame seeds. Fry unsoaked rice sticks, a few at a time, in deep 375° fat for about 5 seconds or just until they puff and rise to the top. Remove and drain well on paper towels. Toss with salad just before serving. Combine rest of ingredients to make dressing; pour over individual salads as served. Makes 6 to 8 servings.

— Cheryl Omori Brinker (Mrs. Barry)

» Cranberry Marble Mold «

6 oz. pkg. cherry gelatin
2 cups boiling water
8 oz. can crushed
   pineapple, undrained
16 oz. can whole
   cranberry sauce
1 cup sour cream

Dissolve gelatin in boiling water; add pineapple. Chill until partially set. Fold in cranberry sauce; pour into an 8"x8" pan. Spoon in sour cream; swirl it thoroughly through the mixture for a marbled effect. Chill. Makes 6 to 8 servings.

— Kay Groll (Mrs. Fred L.)

» Greek Summer Salad «

3 tomatoes, cut in wedges
1 cucumber, sliced
1 red onion, sliced
2 green peppers, seeded
   and cut in rings
6 tablespoons olive oil
2 tablespoons wine
   vinegar
Salt and pepper
½ lb. Feta cheese, cut into
   ½" cubes
2 dozen black olives,
   pitted
Fresh parsley, chopped
½ teaspoon oregano

Place first 4 ingredients in a large bowl. Shake olive oil, vinegar, salt, and pepper together; pour over the salad. Top with Feta cheese and black olives. Sprinkle with parsley and oregano; toss. Toss again just before serving. Makes 6 to 8 servings.

— Gloria Nutini (Mrs. Louis J.)

» Cucumbers with Yogurt «

A Near East version of an old Midwestern summer favorite, this is particularly refreshing on a hot day.

1½ cups plain yogurt
1 cup cucumbers, peeled
   and chopped
½ teaspoon salt
3 cloves garlic, mashed
1 teaspoon dried or fresh
   mint, chopped

Mix all together; serve well-chilled. Makes 5 servings.

— Vesta Kitchens Dajani (Mrs. Adnan)

» Longboat Key Salad «

16 oz. loaf sandwich bread
1 cup butter, softened
4 green onions, finely
    chopped
6 hard-cooked eggs,
    grated
3 cups mayonnaise
2 teaspoons lemon juice

6.5 oz. can crabmeat,
    drained
2-4.25 oz. cans small
    shrimp, rinsed in cold
    water and drained
2 teaspoons seasoned salt
Lettuce leaves
Tomatoes, optional

Trim crusts from bread, butter each side, and cut into cubes. Mix with green onions and eggs, cover, and refrigerate overnight. Next day, add mayonnaise, lemon juice, crabmeat, shrimp, and seasoned salt. Refrigerate until ready to serve. Toss again and serve on lettuce leaves, or as a filling for tomatoes. Fresh crabmeat and shrimp may be used if available. Makes 8 to 10 servings.

– Barbara McDonald (Mrs. John C.)

» Salade Elégante «

The addition of foie gras as well as the formal arrangement of the separate elements of the salad give this a French elegance.

2 heads Bibb lettuce, or 1
    head Boston lettuce
2 celery stalks, strings
    removed, cut into
    julienne strips
¼ lb. green beans
2 cups water

1 teaspoon vegetable oil
2 artichoke hearts
4 ozs. foie gras, cut into ½"
    cubes or diamonds
White pepper
Parsley, minced
Vinaigrette dressing

Wash and dry the lettuce and cut into long, fine shreds. Place in the bottom of an attractive salad bowl. Place celery in a mound to one side of the bowl. Cook green beans in boiling water and oil until al dente; rinse immediately in cold water, dry, then place them in a mound to another side of the lettuce in the bowl. If using fresh artichoke hearts, remove from the artichoke oval, cook in usual fashion, rinse when done, and cut into small ½" cubes. Coat them in lemon juice to preserve their color; place them in the salad bowl as the third round surrounding the lettuce. Place foie gras in the center of the salad. Grind a few twists of white pepper over top. Sprinkle parsley over the top and serve from

the table. Ladle the vinaigrette dressing over the individual servings as they are apportioned. Makes 4 servings.

Vinaigrette Dressing

2 tablespoons wine
    vinegar or lemon juice
⅛ teaspoon salt

¼ teaspoon dry mustard
6 tablespoons oil
Pinch pepper

Beat vinegar, salt, and mustard with a whisk until salt is dissolved. Continue beating while adding oil, drop by drop. Or, process or mix all in a blender. Makes ½ cup.

– Jeremy C. Gibson

» Brussels Endive Salad «

4 to 6 heads of Belgian
    endive, cut into 1"
    diagonal slices
1 tablespoon prepared
    horseradish
1 cup catsup

1 cup cottage cheese
1 tablespoon fresh lemon
    juice
1 teaspoon Cognac brandy
½ teaspoon sugar
Salt and pepper

Wash the endive slices and drain thoroughly. Mix all the other ingredients well and toss with the endive. Makes 4 servings.

» Endive with Bacon Sauce «

This Belgian recipe is akin to wilted lettuce or German hot slaw. The contrasting flavors and textures are fascinating.

4 to 6 Belgian endive, cut
    diagonally in 1" slices
6 slices bacon, finely diced
1 medium onion, chopped
2 tablespoons vinegar
2 tablespoons butter

4 slices white bread,
    crusts removed and cut
    into ½" cubes
Salt
Freshly ground pepper
2 tablespoons chives,
    chopped

Wash endive and drain well. Sauté bacon and onion over medium heat until bacon is brown and onion is transparent. Add the vinegar; mix together. Remove the sauce from the pan and keep warm. Melt the butter and add the bread cubes; toast over medium heat until the cubes are golden brown, stirring often to prevent burning. Add the endive and bacon sauce; season with salt and pepper to taste. Sprinkle with chives and serve immediately. Makes 4 servings.

» Salade des Lentilles «

This substantial French lentil salad is a welcome winter variation for the dinner table. The colorful garnishes create an attractive picture with the brown lentils.

2 cups dried lentils
1 onion stuck with 2 cloves
1 bay leaf
1 tablespoon salt
3 or 4 cloves of garlic, peeled and crushed
1 slice orange zest
½ cup crisp bacon, crumbled
15 scallions, white and green part, minced
Several sprigs parsley, chopped
½ cup olive oil
1 tablespoon red wine vinegar
1 tablespoon lemon juice
Salt and pepper
Chopped egg, parsley, or black olives, optional

Soak lentils overnight in cold water. Drain water and place lentils in saucepan; cover with water by 2 inches. Add onion, bay leaf, salt, garlic, and slice of orange zest. Bring to a boil, reduce heat, and simmer until lentils are firm but tender. Drain at once and refresh under cold water; drain completely. Toss lightly with remaining ingredients. Refrigerate at least 1 hour. Garnish with chopped egg, parsley, or black olives, if desired. Makes 4 to 6 servings.

– Winnie Love (Mrs. Wesley)

» Picnic Pasta Salad «

1 lb. spiral or curly pasta
¼ cup pine nuts
½ cup Parmesan cheese, grated
1 cup cooking oil
½ cup olive oil
⅓ cup vinegar
1 clove garlic
10 oz. pkg. frozen spinach, thawed, drained, and chopped
10 oz. pkg. frozen green peas, thawed, left uncooked
1 pint cherry tomatoes
1 red onion, thinly sliced
Salt and pepper

Cook pasta according to directions; drain. Combine pine nuts, Parmesan cheese, oils, vinegar, garlic, and spinach.

Purée in a blender or food processor. Add to pasta and toss well; chill. Add peas, tomatoes, and red onion just before serving. Season with salt and pepper to taste. Makes 8 to 10 servings.

– Gayle Trump (Mrs. Vincent A.)

» Endive, Orange, and Walnut Salad «

4 to 6 Belgian endive, cut diagonally into 1" slices
4 oranges, peeled and segmented or sliced
½ cup walnuts, chopped
1 cup yogurt
¼ cup olive oil
1 teaspoon Worcestershire sauce
1 teaspoon lemon juice
Pinch of cayenne pepper
Salt and pepper

Wash endive and drain well. Mix with the oranges and walnuts. Whisk together the yogurt, olive oil, Worcestershire sauce, lemon juice, cayenne; season with salt and pepper to taste. Toss with the endive, oranges, and walnuts. Chill and serve. Makes 6 servings.

» Pasta Salad with Sausage «

1 lb. ziti pasta
1 teaspoon Dijon mustard
1 clove garlic, minced
¼ cup oil
⅓ cup vinegar
1 teaspoon sugar
Salt and freshly ground pepper
2 tablespoons green pepper, minced
2 tablespoons onion, minced
2 tablespoons parsley, chopped
1 stalk celery, chopped
2 ozs. summer sausage, cubed
2 ozs. goat cheese, cubed
2 ozs. ripe olives, sliced
12 to 15 cherry tomatoes, halved

Cook ziti as directed on package. Drain and run under cold water; drain again. Combine mustard, garlic, oil, vinegar, sugar, and salt and pepper to taste; mix well. Toss pasta with this mixture. Add remaining ingredients; toss. Chill for several hours or overnight. Makes 8 servings.

– Patty Paquette, Kramer's Kitchen

» Rainbow Pasta Salad «

A can of tuna or salmon makes this a quick and easy anytime dish, but it's a favorite way at our house to use up a couple of leftover fish fillets smoked in a kettle grill. Fresh salmon, swordfish, or other meaty fish is excellent when lightly smoked with water-soaked wood chips in a covered grill.

Boiling, salted water
8 ozs. multi-colored pasta ribbons, or spinach and egg noodles, mixed
5 small stalks of celery heart, and some leaves, chopped
1 large green pepper, cut in slivers
4 green onions, sliced with tops

6.5 oz. can chunk tuna, 7¾ oz. can salmon, or 1 cup leftover smoked fish, coarsely chopped
1 tablespoon sesame seeds
Garlic salt, as desired
5 shakes of Tabasco sauce
1 teaspoon dried basil
2 tablespoons olive oil
2 tablespoons red wine vinegar

Have a large amount of salted water at a rapid boil. Add the pasta and cook according to package directions. Meanwhile, place celery, pepper, and green onions in large serving bowl. When pasta is cooked al dente, drain in large colander and shake a few times. Then dump while steaming hot on top of vegetables in bowl; do not mix. Drain the liquid from tuna or salmon if packed in water; if oil-packed, add some to salad for extra flavor. Flake fish and add to pasta. Sprinkle on sesame seeds, garlic salt, Tabasco sauce, basil, olive oil, and vinegar. Toss well; taste and adjust salt and vinegar seasonings. Serve immediately, while still warm. Makes 8 servings.

– Joyce Rosencrans
Food Editor, The Cincinnati Post

» Greek Potato Salad «

2 large potatoes
½ cup onions, thinly sliced
2 tablespoons parsley, minced

½ cup olive oil
¼ cup red wine vinegar
Salt and freshly ground pepper

Boil potatoes in their skins until tender, about 30 minutes. Drain and cool until warm enough to handle. Remove the skins, cut potatoes into quarters, and slice the quarters. Toss carefully with onions, parsley, and oil, being careful not to break slices if possible. Add vinegar; season with salt and pepper to taste; blend. Chill and serve. Makes 4 servings.

– Stanley Demos
Coach House Restaurant, Lexington, Ky.
From his book, "Stanley Suggests"

» Sweet and Sour Potato Salad «

Sauerkraut and potatoes seem so much a part of the German cuisine that it's surprising to find that they are relative latecomers to Germany. Sauerkraut was unknown until the 13th Century, and potatoes didn't reach Germany until the 17th Century when they were imported from South America. And at first, King Frederick of Prussia had to threaten to cut off their noses and ears to get the peasants to plant them.

3 cups potatoes
5 strips bacon, diced
1 heaping tablespoon flour
½ cup white vinegar
½ cup water

2 tablespoons sugar
1 tablespoon salt
1 medium onion, finely chopped
½ teaspoon celery seed

Cook the unpeeled potatoes the day before they are to be used. Peel and slice when cold. Sauté bacon slowly in a large, heavy pan until crisp; remove from pan. Add flour to pan and simmer a few minutes, stirring. Add vinegar and water and continue to cook, stirring, until sauce is thick and smooth. Salad should be built in layers: potatoes, onions, sugar, salt, celery seed, ½ of the bacon, and sauce. Repeat the layers and blend while the sauce is hot. Serve at room temperature. Makes 6 servings.

– Mrs. Marion Palmer

» Sillsalad «

The Swedish are among the best fish cooks in the world. But the wonderful combination of flavors in this herring salad makes it special even in Sweden. You'll almost always find some variation of this on a smorgasbord table, or it might be served individually on lettuce as an appetizer. It's also a refreshing touch for an hors d'oeuvres table, particularly when your other snacks are creamy or rich.

1 cup pickled herring, diced	2 tablespoons sugar
1½ cups potatoes, boiled and diced	2 tablespoons water
1½ cups pickled beets, diced	¼ cup vinegar or liquid from pickled beets
⅓ cup dill pickles, diced	Dash of pepper
½ cup apple, diced	2 hard-cooked eggs
¼ cup onion, finely chopped	2 tablespoons parsley, chopped
	Sour cream

In a large bowl suitable for serving, gently mix the herring, potatoes, beets, pickles, apple, and onion, being careful not to mash the ingredients. Combine sugar, water, vinegar, and pepper; blend well. Gently stir liquid mixture into the herring mixture. Chill in refrigerator for 3 to 4 hours. Slice egg whites and arrange as garnish on salad. Put yolks through sieve and sprinkle over salad, along with chopped parsley. Serve with sour cream. Makes 8 servings.

» Spring into Summer Salad «

1 clove garlic, mashed	1 teaspoon Dijon mustard
¼ teaspoon salt	½ to ⅔ cup virgin olive oil
2 tablespoons white wine vinegar	Lettuces, vegetables, herbs, and/or flowers

Mash garlic and salt together until they form a smooth paste. Add vinegar and mustard; mix well. Gradually add the oil and whisk together. Add more or less oil according to your individual taste. This makes enough dressing for 6 to 8 servings. Serve vinaigrette dressing over your choice of salad ingredients. Use any edible salad ingredient that grows in your garden. Combine several lettuces, vegetables, herbs, and/or flowers, with attention to variety of color and texture. Some choices: romaine, leaf lettuce, Bibb lettuce, spinach, Swiss chard, carrots, radishes, broccoli, cauliflower, peas, tomatoes, lovage, marjoram, thyme, tarragon, chives, salad burnet, basil, nasturtium leaves and flowers, calendula petals, wild violets, primroses, borage, and johnny jump-ups.

— Marge Haller (Mrs. Hugh)

» Zucchini and Cucumber Salad «

This is a flexible salad from Africa. Extra onion, zucchini, cucumber, or cooked or canned wax or green beans may be added if a larger number of servings is desired. The marinade ingredients remain the same.

2 large zucchini, peeled and thinly sliced	¼ cup sugar
2 tablespoons oil	1 tablespoon salt
2 large cucumbers, scored with a fork and thinly sliced	1 cup hot water
	1 cup white vinegar
2 large onions, thinly sliced and divided into rings	¾ teaspoon black pepper, coarsely ground
	½ teaspoon crushed red pepper
	¼ teaspoon garlic powder

Sauté zucchini for a few minutes in oil, until slightly cooked but still crisp. Alternate layers of zucchini, cucumbers, and onions in a large bowl. Dissolve sugar and salt in hot water; add remaining ingredients and blend well. Pour over vegetables, cover, and refrigerate until ready to serve. Makes 10 to 12 servings.

— Anne Glass Anthony

» Tabbouleh Salad «

Tabbouleh has been called the star of Lebanese salads. The chopped onions, parsley, and mint blend delightfully with the nutty-flavored bulgur wheat.

2 cups fine cracked wheat or bulgur	Juice of 2 lemons
4 large bunches fresh parsley, stemmed and very finely chopped	⅓ to ½ cup olive oil, as desired
	10 green onions, finely chopped
24 sprigs of fresh mint, very finely chopped	4 tomatoes, finely chopped
	Salt

Wash cracked wheat in cold water; cover with fresh cold water and soak 10 minutes; drain well. Mix with rest of ingredients and let stand at least 30 minutes before serving. Makes 10 servings.

— Vesta Kitchens Dajani (Mrs. Adnan)

» Sunomono «

Sunomono translates as "things made of vinegar," and this Japanese salad is served as a refreshing complement to main dishes, or as a second course after soup.

1 daikon radish, about the size of a medium cucumber, peeled and grated
2 tablespoons sugar
¼ cup rice vinegar or white distilled vinegar
Pinch of salt

4 medium cooked shrimp, chopped
½ medium cucumber, peeled and diced
1 teaspoon horseradish, grated
1 teaspoon fresh ginger root, grated

Squeeze grated daikon in paper towels to remove some of liquid. Mix with sugar, vinegar, and salt; add shrimp, cucumber, horseradish, and ginger. Shape into mounds and serve on lettuce or spinach leaves. Makes 4 servings.

» Fruit Salad Dressing «

This is an excellent dressing for fresh fruit or tangy fruit gelatin salads, such as cranberry.

Juice of 1 large lemon
Juice of 1½ tangy oranges
½ cup sugar

1 egg
1 cup whipping cream, stiffly beaten

Mix the first four ingredients well; cook, stirring constantly, for about 10 minutes, or until thickened. Cool; fold into the whipped cream. Makes 2 cups.

– Mrs. Marion Palmer

» Pineapple Salad Dressing «

¾ cup pineapple syrup
1 cup salad or olive oil
½ cup vinegar
1 tablespoon brown sugar
1 teaspoon garlic salt
1 teaspoon onion salt

1 teaspoon paprika
½ teaspoon oregano
½ teaspoon ground pepper
½ teaspoon dry mustard
¼ teaspoon thyme

Mix all ingredients well. Serve over green salad. Makes 2½ cups.

– Jo Price (Mrs. Stanley)

» Hot Mustard «

½ cup dry English mustard
1 cup vinegar
3 eggs, beaten

½ cup brown sugar, packed
½ cup sugar
¼ teaspoon salt

Combine mustard and vinegar; let sit overnight. Mix with rest of ingredients. Cook, stirring, over low heat for about 5 minutes or until mixture thickens. Hot mustard is very good with hot dogs, brats, or Chinese egg rolls. This mustard may also be mixed with 1 part honey to 2 parts mustard and served as a tangy sauce with ham. Makes 2 cups.

– Dorothy Kornmann (Mrs. Milton)

Bottle, 386-589 A.D., Chinese, Hopei Province, glazed stoneware, 1950.46. Museum purchase

» Amanda's French Dressing «

This dressing is the best I have ever tasted. It is excellent for marinating vegetables which have been cooked crisp-tender – such as cauliflower, green beans, peas, baby beets, or tiny new potatoes. A combination of vegetables makes a beautiful platter for a buffet supper.

2 tablespoons
    Worcestershire sauce
1 tablespoon salt
2 tablespoons dry
    mustard
2 tablespoons paprika

1 teaspoon white pepper
1 cup sugar
1 cup vinegar
2 cups oil
1 clove garlic, mashed,
    optional

Beat above ingredients with a hand beater, wire whisk, or blender until well blended. The dressing can be stored in the refrigerator for a month. Makes 1 quart.

– Miriam Stern (Mrs. Joseph, Sr.)
From her book, "Mim in the Kitchen"

» Sour Cream Sauce «

This is a super topping that brings vegetables to life. It is good over crisply cooked fresh asparagus, green beans, artichoke hearts, broccoli, cauliflower, Brussels sprouts, or whatever seasonal vegetable comes to your mind.

2 eggs
1 cup sour cream
½ teaspoon salt

Juice of 1 lemon
¼ cup butter

Beat eggs and blend well with sour cream, salt, and lemon juice. Melt butter over boiling water in top of double boiler. Add sour cream mixture and stir constantly until mixture thickens. Sauce may be kept warm over hot water. Stir briskly just before serving. Makes 1½ cups.

– Ann Hinckley (Mrs. Charles C.)

» Aunt Dannie's Sour Cream Hollandaise «

1 cup sour cream
1 cup mayonnaise
¼ cup lemon juice

½ teaspoon salt
¼ teaspoon Tabasco sauce
⅛ teaspoon white pepper

Combine ingredients in a saucepan; warm slowly over low heat, stirring. When warm, serve over asparagus, eggs Benedict, or anything else that requires Hollandaise sauce. Makes 2 cups.

– Jessie Mae Helms (Mrs. J. A.)

» Rhubarb Chutney «

1 lb. fresh rhubarb, cut
    into 1" pieces, or 1 lb.
    package frozen rhubarb
1 cup light brown sugar,
    packed
¾ cup onion, chopped
½ cup malt or cider
    vinegar

1 large apple, cored and
    chopped
½ cup walnuts, coarsely
    chopped
⅓ cup raisins
1 teaspoon curry powder
½ teaspoon ground ginger
½ teaspoon salt

Mix all ingredients together in a heavy enameled saucepan. Heat to boiling, stirring. Reduce heat and cook for 30 minutes, stirring often. May be kept in refrigerator for up to 3 months. Makes 2½ cups.

– Fern Storer (Mrs. Sheldon)

» Claridge's Sauce Balmoral «

This recipe for a piquant brown sauce that is excellent with roast beef or Beef Wellington is named for the Scottish castle of the British royal family.

3 cups beef bouillon
3 sprigs parsley
1 stalk celery, cut in
    1" pieces
5 to 6 medium
    mushrooms, diced
1 tomato, peeled, seeded,
    and chopped
½ bay leaf

1 pinch dried thyme
½ clove garlic
2 tablespoons onion,
    finely chopped
3 tablespoons butter
3 tablespoons flour
½ cup Madeira wine
3 tablespoons sweet
    butter

Heat bouillon, parsley, celery, mushrooms, tomato, bay leaf, thyme, and garlic in a heavy saucepan; bring to a boil. Lower heat and simmer, covered, for 1 hour. Cool and strain. In a skillet, sauté onions in butter until limp and golden. Over low heat, whisk in flour until well blended. When butter and flour mixture is smooth, gradually add strained stock, stirring constantly, until blended and smooth. Bring sauce to a boil, lower heat, and simmer for ½ hour, stirring occasionally to keep sauce smooth. Cool. Just before serving, heat; add Madeira and swirl in the butter to give richness and glaze to the sauce. Makes 3 cups.

» Unheated Relish «

This relish keeps for several months and I enjoy giving it for gifts. If red bell peppers are available, use some of them for color.

18 green peppers	2 tablespoons mustard
1 large solid head cabbage	seed
6 to 8 medium yellow	2 tablespoons celery seed
onions	4 cups sugar
¼ cup salt	4 cups vinegar

Trim and cut peppers, cabbage, and onions into wedges. Grind medium fine in food processor or grinder. Mix well and cover with salt. Let stand three hours. Mix with remaining ingredients. Put into sterilized jars and seal. Makes 10 to 12 pints.

— Jane C. Sweeder (Mrs. Willard)

» Individual Luncheon Sandwich «

½ English muffin, or 1 slice of bread, toasted	1 tablespoon French dressing
2 slices bacon, crisply cooked	2 tablespoons white sauce, or cream of celery soup
1 slice tomato	1 tablespoon Cheddar
1 poached egg	cheese, grated

Arrange sandwich in the above order. Put under broiler to brown cheese. Makes 1 serving. Duplicate for as many people as you are serving.

— Edith Magrish (Mrs. James)

» Cranberry Nut Relish «

This is a nice accompaniment to a Thanksgiving or Christmas turkey.

1 lb. fresh cranberries, rinsed	1 cup walnuts or pecans, coarsely broken and
1 cup sugar	toasted in 250° oven
1 cup orange marmalade	10 minutes
	Juice of 1 small lemon

Spread cranberries over the bottom of a 9″x13″ baking dish. Sprinkle sugar evenly over berries. Cover tightly with aluminum foil. Bake in preheated 325° oven, without stirring, until berries look candied and most have popped, about 20 to 25 minutes. Remove from oven and gently stir in the marmalade, nuts, and lemon juice. Refrigerate in covered container. Makes 8 servings.

— Laura Young (Mrs. Eugene)

» Cincinnati Herb Society's Saltless Salt «

This recipe is a lifesaver for people who are on salt-restricted diets, as well as those who just enjoy the fresh flavor it gives to foods. It will keep indefinitely.

1 tablespoon cumin seed, ground	2 tablespoons instant minced onion
4″ stick cinnamon	1 tablespoon fenugreek
5 whole cloves	seed
1 teaspoon cardamom seeds, hulled	2 tablespoons ground turmeric
1 teaspoon black peppercorns	4 teaspoons ground coriander
2 bay leaves	1 teaspoon ground ginger
¼ cup dried parsley flakes	3 cups instant non-fat dry milk

Crush whole seeds in mortar and pestle, food processor, or blender. Combine all and use in place of salt. Makes 3 to 4 cups.

— Betty Barnett (Mrs. Joseph)

Dining Room, Cary House, American, College Hill, Ohio,
1816, 1939.297. Gift of Mrs. Samuel Joseph.
This color reproduction donated by Mrs. Elsie H. Warrington

If the first requirement for a house is to provide shelter, surely the second is to lend itself to hospitality. William Cary must have had that generous thought in mind when he built his large new house in a farming settlement a few miles north of the young city of Cincinnati, in 1816. Elegance was then uncommon in this corner of Ohio and invitations to the Cary home must have been eagerly accepted. The furnishings reflect the taste of well-to-do households of this area from early to mid-19th century. An English Staffordshire tea set is in readiness on the tiger maple table of American manufacture. The slat back chairs with their rush seats are also American. Imported hollow ware of Sheffield silver plate and Cincinnati-made pewter beverage pots are nearby.

Among those who would have enjoyed the warmth of this well-proportioned fireplace were the owner's nieces, Alice and Phoebe, who lived not far away before they moved to New York City and gained modest fame as poetesses. A son of the house eventually ran for vice president of the United States on the Greenback ticket. Cary himself was a farmer and the owner of a mill.

Meats

» Ayrshire Hot Pot «

Ayr is on the coast of in Scotland where the River Clyde joins the Firth of Clyde. This warming casserole helps to ward off the icy blasts from the sea.

1 lb. lean beef chuck, cut into 1½" cubes	4 large potatoes, peeled and sliced
½ lb. pork sausage links, halved	1 apple, peeled, cored, and sliced
Flour	1 onion, sliced
2 cups tomato juice	Salt and pepper
2 bouillon cubes	

Toss beef cubes and sausage with flour until meat is thoroughly coated. Heat tomato juice to boiling and add bouillon cubes; set aside. Layer meats, potatoes, apple, and onion in a greased 2-quart casserole, sprinkling layers with salt and pepper to taste. Pour hot tomato juice over, cover tightly, and bake in a preheated 350° oven for 90 minutes. Makes 4 servings.

» Beef and Borscht Skillet «

½ lb. lean ground beef	1 envelope brown gravy mix
1 cup water	1 tablespoon brown sugar
6 large carrots, peeled and cut into julienne strips	2 tablespoons cider vinegar
6 large fresh beets	½ teaspoon salt
	Sour cream

Sauté ground beef in a heavy pan, stirring to crumble. Pour off excess fat; add water and carrots. Cover and simmer about 20 minutes, or until carrots are just tender. Meanwhile, cook beets in boiling water until tender, peel, and slice thinly. Add these to beef mixture along with gravy mix, brown sugar, vinegar, and salt. Stir and cook until heated through. Serve topped with sour cream. Makes 4 servings.

– Audrey Raabe (Mrs. Victor)

» Eggplant and Beef with Yogurt «

Turkish dishes often combine meat with yogurt and this recipe is an especially successful combination.

1 lb. eggplant	1 cup plain yogurt
½ teaspoon salt	⅛ teaspoon freshly ground pepper
1 lb. lean ground beef, or ½ lb. ground beef and ½ lb. ground lamb	1 tablespoon parsley, chopped
1 clove garlic, minced	Paprika

Broil eggplant in shallow baking dish 4" from heat, rotating eggplant a quarter turn every 5 minutes, until skin blisters, or about 25 minutes. Cool slightly, about 30 minutes; remove skin from eggplant. Chop eggplant into ½" pieces. Sprinkle with salt and drain in colander or strainer for 15 minutes. Sauté beef and garlic in small skillet over medium heat, stirring frequently, until brown. Drain off excess fat; add ¼ cup yogurt and pepper. Arrange drained eggplant in a greased shallow casserole. Spoon meat mixture over eggplant. Preheat oven to broil or 550°. Spread remaining yogurt over meat mixture; sprinkle with parsley and paprika. Broil 4" from heat until hot and bubbly, about 4 minutes. Makes 4 servings.

– Anne Seasholes Cozlu (Mrs. Cem)

» Beef Olives «

A masala is a mixture of ground spices and herbs used for flavoring of a dish. The name "olive" refers to the fact that a small piece of beef is filled with seasonings and stuffing and rolled up like an olive.

1 lb. beef, preferably steak	2 slices bacon
1" piece of ginger root	1 slice bread, soaked in
10 peppercorns	water and drained
1 bunch mint leaves	2 large onions, minced
½ teaspoon ground	¼ cup ghee or clarified
cinnamon	butter
1 tablespoon raisins,	2 teaspoons flour
optional	1 cup water
1 green chili	Salt

Flatten the meat with a cleaver or cut 2" cubes and flatten each piece with cleaver; set aside. Grind together the ginger, peppercorns, mint, cinnamon, raisins, and the green chili. Cut the bacon fine and mix in with this masala. Add the drained bread and one minced onion. Place a teaspoon of this stuffing on meat if making individual olives, or all of the stuffing if making just one roll. Roll up tightly and secure with string. Sauté the beef olives in a little ghee until brown. Remove and set aside. In the same pan, add the remaining minced onion, flour, water, and salt. Cook for 5 minutes over low heat; add the beef olives, and stew gently until tender. If making one large roll, remove the string, slice, and serve warm with the gravy over it. Makes 6 servings.

– Jennifer-Ann Fernandes (Mrs. Allan)

» Bobotie «

Both British and East Indian influences are evident in this dish from Africa.

2 medium onions, sliced	1 thick slice white bread,
2 tablespoons butter	soaked in 1 cup milk
2 tablespoons curry	3 eggs
powder, or more to taste	Salt and pepper
1 teaspoon salt	2 bay leaves, broken in
Pepper	pieces
1 tablespoon sugar	Butter
2 tablespoons vinegar	Cooked rice
2 lbs. lean beef, finely	Peach Chutney
ground	

In a skillet, sauté onions in butter until transparent. Add curry powder, salt, pepper, sugar, vinegar, and meat. Cook thoroughly over low heat, crumbling ground meat. Drain the milk from the bread, and mash the bread with a fork and add to the meat mixture. Set remaining milk aside. Be sure to scoop off any extra fat from the meat mixture. Add one beaten egg to the meat mixture and mix well. Put in a shallow buttered ovenproof casserole; bake, uncovered, in preheated 375° oven for about 30 minutes. Beat remaining 2 eggs, add to reserved milk, adding additional milk, if necessary, to make a total of 1 cup. Season with salt and pepper to taste, and pour over top of the meat mixture. Stick in a few pieces of bay leaf, and dot with small pieces of butter. Stand the casserole in a pan of cold water and bake gently for 30 to 40 minutes in preheated 350° oven until the custard is set and lightly browned. Serve with rice and Peach Chutney. Makes 6 servings.

– Margaret Macpherson (Mrs. Colin R.)

» Châteaubriand Farci «

This method of preparing beef was invented by the chef of a 19th century French statesman, Vicomte François de Chateaubriand.

8 to 9 lb. fillet of beef	1 teaspoon
1 lb. boneless lean pork,	Worcestershire sauce
cut in 1" cubes	1 tablespoon fresh
1 lb. boneless veal, cut in	tarragon, chopped, or
1" cubes	1 teaspoon dried
½ cup onion, minced	tarragon
2 teaspoons garlic,	1 teaspoon freshly ground
crushed	pepper
⅓ cup whipping cream	Salt
4 egg yolks	Bordelaise or truffled
1½ teaspoons salt	Madeira sauce, optional

Trim the fat, gristle, and membrane from the beef. Cut off the pointed ends and save for another meal. Blend remaining ingredients in a food processor. Cover and chill at least 2 hours. Roll out the blended forcemeat between two sheets of oiled waxed paper until it is large enough to completely enclose the fillet. Remove the top sheet of paper and carefully wrap the mixture around the fillet. Tuck in the ends and smooth out the seams.

Roll the covered fillet into the pan. Gently pull away the remaining piece of waxed paper, taking care not to tear the forcemeat. Roast in preheated 375° oven for 35 to 40 minutes for a rare fillet. If using a meat thermometer, the internal temperature should be 120°. Serve as is, or with a Bordelaise or truffled Madeira sauce. Makes 8 to 10 servings.

– Anne Ziebarth (Mrs. John)
New York City

» Peach Chutney «

Serve this chutney with the Bobotie. The chutney improves with time, and will keep for years.

4 lbs. ripe peaches, pitted
2 medium onions, sliced
2 cloves garlic, peeled
½ lb. candied ginger
16 oz. pkg. seedless raisins

1 quart cider vinegar
2.625 oz. pkg. mustard
*   seed*
1½ lbs. brown sugar

Chop the peaches rather coarsely, leaving the skins on. Process onions, garlic, ginger, and raisins through food processor or grinder. This should be a rough texture, not smooth. Combine with all the rest of the ingredients in a heavy pot and simmer until thickened. Simmering time is about 1½ hours, depending on the weather. While hot, put into sterilized jars and seal with paraffin. Makes about 12 medium-sized jelly jars.

– Margaret Macpherson (Mrs. Colin R.)

» Brown Sugar Brisket «

This is so good you may not have any left over. But if you do, it freezes very well.

4 to 5 lbs. beef brisket
1 clove garlic, peeled and
*   chopped*
2 onions, medium size,
*   sliced*
½ cup cold water

Salt and pepper
½ lb. brown sugar
½ cup orange juice
1 tablespoon cornstarch
1 tablespoon brandy

Place brisket in a 10"x15" roasting pan. Add garlic, onions, and water; season with salt and pepper to taste. Pack brown sugar over the entire top and sides of the brisket. Cover brisket and bake for 3 hours in a preheated 275° oven. Add orange juice and bake 1 hour or more, until brisket is tender. Remove from oven. Place brisket in foil, cool, and refrigerate. Pour liquid from roasting pan into food processor or blender; add cornstarch and brandy. Blend until onion is puréed. Cool and remove any fat that has congealed. Before serving, slice brisket against the grain and place in an ovenproof casserole. Pour puréed liquid over meat. Cover with aluminum foil and heat in a pre-heated 300° oven for 30 minutes, or until bubbling. Makes 8 to 10 servings.

– Jan Shulman (Mrs. Sy)

» Daube de Campagne «

The title for this recipe for country braised beef comes from the French word for a covered casserole, daubiere. Almost every region of France has its own variation of daube.

2 to 3 lbs. top sirloin, cut
*   into 1" cubes*
2 tablespoons bacon
*   drippings*
½ lb. ham, cut into 1"
*   cubes*
2 large onions, chopped
25 stuffed green olives
5 cloves garlic, peeled and
*   wrapped in a small*
*   square*
*   of cheesecloth*
¾ teaspoon thyme

½ cup golden raisins,
*   soaked in hot water and*
*   drained*
3 cups dry red Burgundy
*   wine*
2 tablespoons whole black
*   peppercorns*
1 teaspoon salt
¼ cup brandy
¾ cup whipping cream
Flour and water or
*   arrowroot*

Sauté sirloin cubes in bacon drippings until browned; add ham and onions and continue cooking for 3 to 4 minutes or until onions are golden. Place in a heavy, heatproof casserole and add olives, garlic, thyme, raisins, and wine. Cover and place in a preheated 350° oven for 40 minutes. Add peppercorns, salt, brandy, and cream; continue cooking in oven for 30 additional minutes. Arrange meats on a serving platter and keep warm. Strain juices into a heavy saucepan; heat and add enough flour and water or arrowroot to thicken the sauce to desired consistency. Pour the sauce over the ham and beef and serve at once. Makes 6 to 8 servings

– Winnie Love (Mrs. Wesley)

» Spiced Beef «

This is traditional Christmas fare and may be purchased in Irish butcher shops, often decorated with red ribbon and a sprig of holly.

6 lb. beef roast
3 bay leaves, crumbled
1 teaspoon cloves
6 blades mace
1 teaspoon whole black
    peppercorns
1 clove garlic, mashed
1 teaspoon allspice
2 heaping tablespoons
    brown sugar
1 lb. coarse or rock salt

2 heaping teaspoons
    saltpetre or curing salt
1 celery rib, chopped
1 medium onion, chopped
3 carrots, sliced
3 cloves
1 teaspoon ground cloves
1 teaspoon allspice
Water
1 cup Guinness stout

Rub roast with a mixture of the next 9 ingredients. Place in a large dish with excess mixture. Store in a cool place or in the refrigerator for 1 week. Turn the joint daily and baste with the spices from the bottom of the dish. Wash the roast and tie for cooking. Place in a large saucepan on a bed of the celery, onion, and carrots sprinkled with the cloves and allspice. Cover with water and bring slowly to a boil; skim. Simmer gently for 4 hours, adding the stout during the last hour. Makes 12 servings.

– Pud Preston (Mrs. Robert H.)

» Non-Irish Baked Corned Beef «

Growing up in Cincinnati, I never questioned the fact that corned beef had to be boiled. "Corned beef and cabbage" were almost inseparable words, and trained as I was in the clean-plate philosophy of my formative years, I duly ate, without question, the soggy vegetable and the stringy, tasteless meat. I've learned differently. Baked corned beef is a delightful and different dish. Corned beef usually comes from the brisket, and brisket is virtually all tough muscle. It takes long, slow, moist cooking to come up with tender results. But it's worth it.

3 to 4 lbs. lean corned
    beef
½ cup dry red wine

1 packet dried onion soup
2 tablespoons dark
    brown sugar

Put the corned beef into a roasting pan with a tight-fitting lid. Pour the wine over it and then spread the dried onion soup over the top. Pat it down with your hand so it covers the meat well. Roast the meat, covered, in a preheated 275° to 300° oven until it is fork-tender. This usually takes 2 to 3 hours or more, depending on the size of the beef. When the meat is tender, spread the brown sugar evenly over the meat, return it to the oven, and cook it, uncovered, until the sugar melts. If you remove the meat from the oven about 30 minutes before you're ready to serve, it's easier to carve. Make certain your knife is very sharp, so you can carve very thin slices. Corned beef frequently has a lot of fat, which it loses in cooking, so you can figure that it takes about 3 lbs. of meat to serve 6 people. You may have some left over. When you start making sandwiches from cold, baked corned beef, you'll wish you had more.
Makes 6 to 8 servings.

– Jerry Ransohoff

» Curried Beef «

Serve this for luncheon with a frozen fruit salad.

2 medium onions,
    chopped
½ green pepper, chopped
2 tablespoons butter
1 lb. ground beef
1 teaspoon salt
½ to 1 tablespoon curry
    powder
1 cup seedless raisins

1 bay leaf
1 cup water
1 tablespoon cornstarch
2 tablespoons water
½ cup salted peanuts,
    chopped
4 oz. can or jar of
    pimientos, chopped
10 oz. pkg. frozen peas

Sauté onions and green pepper in butter until transparent. Add beef; brown and drain off excess fat. Add salt, curry powder, raisins, bay leaf, and 1 cup water. You may want to add only part of curry powder now and correct the seasonings after completion of the next step. Cover and simmer 10 minutes, add cornstarch mixed with water, and cook until slightly thickened. Add peanuts and pimientos and place in a 2-quart ovenproof dish. Bake in a preheated 350° oven for 25 minutes. Remove from oven and stir in peas, bake an additional 5 minutes. Makes 4 servings.

– Dorothy Sells (Mrs. Bert E.)

» Genoese Beef «

Genoa, on the Italian Riviera, lends its name to this delicious braised beef.

3 onions, sliced
2 stalks celery, sliced
3 to 4 slices bacon, diced
½ cup butter
1 cup oil, part olive oil,
    if preferred

3 lb. beef eye of
    round roast
Salt and pepper
8 oz. can Italian tomatoes
½ cup dry red wine
Linguine or fettuccine
    noodles

Sauté onions, celery, and bacon in butter and oil until onion becomes translucent. Drain and place in an ovenproof casserole; arrange roast on top of vegetables; season with salt and pepper to taste. Cover and bake in preheated 325° oven for 1½ hours. Add canned tomatoes and wine; bake another ½ hour or until meat is tender. Remove meat and slice. Vegetables and juices may be used for sauce, as is; reduce over heat on top of stove if necessary, or purée in blender or food processor and reheat. This is good served with pasta such as linguine or fettuccine. Makes 6 to 8 servings.

— Mrs. Donna Schott

» Keftedes «

These Greek meat balls are delicious in pita bread, with salad, or as an appetizer.

10 thin slices firm white
    bread
2 cups warm water
1½ lbs. ground chuck
1 egg
2 medium onions, finely
    chopped
3 tablespoons oregano

16 oz. can tomatoes,
    chopped
1 teaspoon dried mint
Salt and freshly ground
    pepper
Flour
1 cup oil

Soak bread in water and squeeze dry. Crumble and combine with chuck, egg, onions, oregano, tomatoes and juice, mint, and salt and pepper to taste. Form in 1" balls and roll in flour, shaking off excess. Brown meat balls in oil in a heavy pan. Serve hot or cold. Makes 6 servings.

— Eldora Masterson (Mrs. William V.)

*Adriaen Van Ostade, 1610-1685, Dutch, "The Hog Butcher,"
ca. 1642, etching, 1943.338.
Bequest of Herbert Greer French*

» Mackinac Broil «

This version of London Broil is a Michigan favorite. The marinade is also excellent for shish kabob.

½ cup catsup	1 teaspoon salt
½ cup water	1 teaspoon lemon juice
2 tablespoons sugar	¼ cup dry red or white
2 tablespoons olive oil or	wine
salad oil	Freshly ground pepper
2 tablespoons red wine	1 clove garlic, minced
vinegar	3 lbs. flank steak,
2 tablespoons	unscored
Worcestershire sauce	

Mix well all ingredients except meat. Place meat in glass dish; pour the marinade over the meat. Cover with foil or plastic wrap; let stand 2 to 3 hours at room temperature, turning occasionally. Remove meat from marinade; grill over hot coals about 5 minutes on each side, or until it reaches desired doneness. Slice diagonally across the grain in thin slices and serve. Makes 8 servings.

– Nancy Angus (Mrs. John W.)

» Pastitsio «

This pastitsio meat sauce may be prepared days or weeks in advance and frozen until needed. It may also be used with spaghetti or moussaka.

1 lb. box cut macaroni	6 oz. can tomato paste
½ cup butter	1 garlic clove, chopped
½ cup flour	1 bay leaf
4 cups milk	1 teaspoon oregano
1 egg, beaten	1 teaspoon basil
Salt and pepper	Pinch of ground cloves
Dash of nutmeg	1 dried red pepper
2 large onions, finely	Salt
chopped	1 tablespoon sugar
¼ cup olive oil	Bread crumbs
1 lb. ground beef	Freshly grated
1 cup dry white wine	Parmesan cheese
8 oz. can tomato sauce	Butter

Cook macaroni in salted boiling water until al dente. Drain and reserve. Melt butter and flour together in a heavy pan and cook, stirring, for 4 to 5 minutes over medium heat. Add milk; stir and cook until mixture is thick and smooth. Add a small amount of hot mixture to beaten egg and mix together. Return mixture to hot sauce and stir well. Add salt, pepper, and nutmeg to taste. Set white sauce aside and prepare meat sauce. Brown onions in olive oil in a heavy pan; add meat and brown, separating with 2 forks, if necessary. Drain off excess fat. Add wine, tomato sauce, tomato paste, garlic, herbs, salt, and sugar. Cook over low heat about 1 hour, stirring occasionally. To assemble the casserole, butter generously a 3-quart ovenproof dish. Coat it with dry bread crumbs and arrange a layer of macaroni over the bottom. Sprinkle with grated cheese and some of the white sauce. Add the meat sauce and another layer of macaroni. Cover with remaining white sauce; sprinkle with additional grated Parmesan and bread crumbs. Dot generously with butter. Bake in a preheated 350° oven until golden brown, about 30 minutes. Makes 6 to 8 servings.

– Andreas Nomikos
Greensboro, N.C.

» Sauerbraten «

This traditional German dish may be prepared ahead and refrigerated or frozen until serving. Each section of Germany, and sometimes each cook, has a different marinade for the beef.

4 lbs. chuck or rump roast	12 whole cloves
1 cup cider vinegar	3 bay leaves
1 cup dry red wine	½ cup parsley, chopped
2 medium onions, sliced	3 allspice berries
2 carrots, sliced	3 tablespoons butter
1 stalk celery, chopped	3 tablespoons bacon
2 tablespoons sugar	drippings
2 teaspoons salt	12 gingersnaps, crushed
10 whole peppercorns	

Marinate meat with next 12 ingredients in an earthenware or glass dish or heavy plastic bag for 5 days in refrigerator, turning once or twice a day. Remove meat from marinade and pat dry with a paper towel. Put butter and bacon grease in a heavy deep pot or Dutch oven; add beef and brown well on all sides over medium heat. Meanwhile, bring marinade to a boil and simmer five minutes. Strain and add to pot with beef. Simmer slowly, covered, for 2 to 3 hours or until beef is very tender. Remove meat and cool. Let gravy cool completely and skim off fat. Add crushed gingersnaps and heat slowly to thicken and season gravy. Slice beef in thin slices, across grain of meat, if possible. Pour gravy over beef slices, cover with foil, and heat through and until bubbling in a preheated 350° oven. Makes 8 servings.

– Mary Wood

» Corned Beef Salad «

6 oz. pkg. lemon gelatin
1½ cups boiling water
Pinch of salt
1 cup mayonnaise
2 cups celery, diced
1 medium onion, finely chopped
½ green pepper, finely chopped
1 cup corned beef, shredded
Lettuce leaves
¼ cup mayonnaise
1 tablespoon Dijon mustard

Mix gelatin with water and salt. Cool; fold in mayonnaise, celery, onion, pepper, and corned beef. Mix thoroughly and spread in a 9″x13″ dish. Refrigerate overnight. Cut into squares and serve on lettuce leaves as a luncheon dish. Garnish with mayonnaise and Dijon mustard mixed together. Makes 8 to 12 servings.

– Anne Nethercott (Mrs. J. W.)

» Cuban Picadillo «

This meat and vegetable hash-type dish is found in endless variations throughout Latin America. The addition of capers and raisins adds a special Latin dash.

2 large onions, chopped
1 clove garlic, minced
1 large green pepper, chopped
2 tablespoons oil
1 lb. lean ground beef
1 lb. can Italian tomatoes
¼ teaspoon oregano
¼ teaspoon thyme
¼ teaspoon basil
Salt and freshly ground black pepper
1 tablespoon capers
1 tablespoon red wine vinegar
¼ cup olives with pimientos, sliced
½ cup raisins, finely chopped
Cooked rice

Sauté onions, garlic, and green pepper in oil in a heavy pan until vegetables are transparent. Add ground beef and cook until beef is lightly browned, crumbling it with a fork as it cools. Drain excess fat. Add tomatoes and liquid from can, oregano, thyme, basil, salt and pepper to taste, capers, vinegar, olives, and raisins. Cover and simmer over low heat for 1 hour, stirring occasionally to prevent sticking and to break up tomatoes. Serve over rice. Makes 4 servings.

– Suzanne Cahill

» Beef Rouladen «

The waiters and waitresses at Forest View Gardens are music students at the University of Cincinnati's College Conservatory of Music. They'll serve your meal, then entertain you with everything from opera to Broadway musicals to Roll Out the Barrel.

4 thin slices beef top round steak, 6 ozs. each
½ cup mushrooms, chopped
½ cup onions, diced
¼ cup parsley, chopped
1 cup celery, diced
1 cup ham, diced, or ½ cup bacon, cooked and crumbled
2 cloves garlic, pressed
½ cup dill pickles, chopped
Salt, pepper, and bouquet garni herbs
¼ cup butter
2 tablespoons flour
1 cup bouillon
1 small onion, chopped
1 carrot, chopped
Salt and pepper
1 cup Burgundy wine
1 cup mushrooms, chopped
Parsley, chopped
Spaetzle

Trim fat from beef, sprinkle with meat tenderizer, and pound. Set aside. Sauté mushrooms, onions, parsley, celery, ham, garlic, dill pickles, and salt, pepper, and bouquet garni to taste in butter until heated through and onions are limp. Place ¼ of mixture in the center of each steak, roll, and fold together, fastening with toothpicks. Roll each in flour, sauté in heavy iron skillet in melted butter until lightly browned. Remove rolls from skillet and add flour; stir in. Add bouillon, onion, carrot, and season to taste with salt and pepper. Place rolls in a baking dish; pour gravy over, cover, and bake in preheated 350° oven for 1 hour. Add Burgundy wine and mushrooms; bake ½ hour longer, or until tender. Sprinkle with parsley, and serve with spaetzle. Makes 4 servings.

– Forest View Gardens

» Brandy Steak «

1 teaspoon cooking oil
6-6 oz. beef steaks, filet
   mignon preferred
2 tablespoons butter
½ lb. mushrooms, sliced

1 pint half and half cream
1 splash brandy
Salt and cracked black
   pepper

Wipe heavy frying pan with oil and heat until it is hot, but not smoking. Place steaks in pan and cook until done, according to taste – rare, medium, or well done. Remove to hot serving dish. Lower the heat under frying pan, melt butter, and sauté mushroom slices briefly. Pour the cream and brandy over mushrooms; season with salt and pepper to taste. Pour sauce over steaks and serve immediately. Makes 6 servings

– Margy Gale (Mrs. William M.)

» Spiced Beef with Fresh Asparagus «

The fresh ginger and soy sauce lend a tang to this beef that is especially Chinese.

1 lb. lean beef, cut into
   1"x½" pieces
2 tablespoons soy sauce
2 tablespoons dry sherry
½ teaspoon cornstarch
1 teaspoon sugar
6 tablespoons oil, divided
1 clove garlic, crushed
1 teaspoon fresh ginger,
   minced
⅛ teaspoon cayenne pepper

5 green onions, cut into 1"
   lengths
½ lb. fresh asparagus, cut
   into 1" lengths
1 medium tomato, cut into
   wedges
½ tablespoon cornstarch
2 tablespoons soy sauce
½ tablespoon sesame oil
Cooked rice

Marinate beef in soy sauce, sherry, cornstarch, and sugar for 30 minutes. In a wok or heavy skillet, stir-fry beef in 4 tablespoons oil for 2 minutes; remove and set aside. Add 2 tablespoons of oil to wok and stir-fry garlic and ginger for 2 minutes. Add cayenne pepper, green onions, asparagus, tomato, and reserved beef pieces; cook until vegetables are tender but still very crisp. Add cornstarch and soy sauce which have been mixed together into a paste; stir-fry for 1 minute. Add sesame oil, blend well, and serve immediately with rice. Makes 6 servings.

– Dora Ang (Mrs. Francis)

» Picadillo «

This version of Picadillo is a Mexican-inspired recipe that is popular in Texas and also familiar in Florida, due to that state's Spanish heritage. It's as easy as making Sloppy Joes. Tomato sauce may be added to make a dip for tortilla chips.

1 lb. ground beef
1 lb. ground pork
2 medium onions, finely
   chopped
1 large green pepper,
   finely chopped
1 lb. can stewed tomatoes
   with juice
1 teaspoon salt, scant
1 garlic clove, minced or
   crushed
Several grindings black
   pepper

Dash of cayenne or hot
   pepper sauce
1 tablespoon brown sugar
¼ cup red wine vinegar
⅓ cup stuffed green olives,
   chopped
½ cup raisins
1 tablespoon capers,
   optional
½ cup red wine
Cooked brown rice;
   shredded, steamed
   cabbage; or spaghetti
   squash

Break up ground beef and pork in a Dutch oven and place over medium heat. Stir frequently to break up chunks of meat while it browns. When some drippings have accumulated, add the onions and green pepper. Sauté the vegetables while the meat finishes browning, stirring frequently. Turn mixture into a large colander set over a pan to catch the drippings. Meanwhile, return Dutch oven to heat and add the tomatoes and juice, salt, garlic, pepper, cayenne, brown sugar, vinegar, olives, raisins, capers, and red wine. Return the drained meat-vegetable mixture to the Dutch oven and blend with all other ingredients. Bring to a boil and then reduce heat to simmer. Simmer, uncovered, for nearly 1 hour. Serve over brown rice or over a bed of shredded, steamed cabbage, or spaghetti squash. Makes 6 to 8 servings.

– Joyce Rosencrans
Food Editor, The Cincinnati Post

» Hot Chinese Beef Shreds «

Chinese cooking styles are divided into Shanghai, Peking, Manchurian, Szechuan, Fukien, and Cantonese – each very distinctive. This dish is spicy hot and typical of the cuisine from the Szechuan province.

1 lb. flank steak, sliced into very thin strips
3 tablespoons soy sauce
1 teaspoon dry sherry
¾ cup oil
1 tablespoon powdered ginger
1 tablespoon hot pepper flakes
½ cup carrots, shredded
1 cup celery, finely chopped
8 oz. can water chestnuts, drained and sliced
8 oz. can bamboo shoots, drained
2½ oz. can or jar of sliced mushrooms, drained
10 oz. pkg. frozen pea pods, optional
1 teaspoon salt
¼ teaspoon monosodium glutamate, optional
Cooked rice or Chinese noodles

Combine flank steak strips, soy sauce, and sherry in a bowl; marinate for at least 30 minutes. Pour ½ cup oil into a hot wok or skillet. Add beef mixture and stir-fry constantly over high heat for 8 to 10 minutes, or until brown. Remove beef and oil to a colander or strainer over a large bowl, reserving the liquid. Add remaining ¼ cup oil to wok. Stir powdered ginger, hot pepper flakes, and shredded carrots into oil. Stir-fry for 1 minute. Add celery and stir-fry for 1 minute. Add water chestnuts, bamboo shoots, mushrooms, pea pods, beef, salt, and monosodium glutamate. Stir constantly and let cook until all ingredients are tender and hot. Serve immediately with reserved beef liquid over rice or Chinese noodles. Makes 4 to 6 servings.

– Gretchen Mehring

» Kümmel Steak «

The German word for caraway is kümmel. Caraway also flavors aquavit, which is used here to make a spectacular flaming entree.

4 boneless beef strip steaks, about 10 oz. each
Freshly ground pepper
3 tablespoons oil
Salt
1 teaspoon cracked caraway seeds
3 medium onions, diced
¼ cup sour cream
1 teaspoon parsley, chopped
3 drops Tabasco sauce
Salt and pepper
3 ozs. aquavit
Spaetzle dumplings

Rub generous amount of pepper on all sides of steaks; fry in skillet in hot oil for 3 to 4 minutes, turn, and fry for

an additional 3 to 4 minutes. Remove to serving dish, season with salt to taste, and sprinkle caraway seeds over the steaks. Set aside and keep warm. Saute onions in oil remaining in skillet until golden brown. Mix in sour cream, parsley, Tabasco sauce, and season with salt and pepper to taste. Pour over steaks. Heat aquavit, flame, and pour over steaks. Serve with spaetzle.
Makes 4 servings.

– Black Forest Restaurant

» Korean Beef «

2 to 3 lbs. flank steak, thinly sliced
½ cup soy sauce
2 tablespoons sugar
1 teaspoon sesame oil
1 tablespoon sake or dry vermouth
½ cup green onions, chopped
Flour
2 eggs, beaten
2 cups vegetable oil

To make slicing beef easier, partially freeze steak before slicing in very thin strips. Combine soy sauce, sugar, sesame oil, wine, and onions; marinate steak strips in the mixture for 4 hours. Drain well and dip into flour to cover surface. Dip floured steak into beaten egg and fry at once in 1″ hot oil until crispy. Drain and serve with vegetables and fluffy rice. Makes 6 to 8 servings.

– Cheryl Omori Brinker (Mrs. Barry)

» Queen Stroganoff «

3 lbs. beef sirloin tip, cut in strips
3 large onions, sliced
3 teaspoons salt
½ teaspoon pepper, coarsely ground
2 tablespoons Worcestershire sauce
2 tablespoons Kitchen Bouquet
2 tablespoons parsley, chopped
¼ cup catsup
1 lb. mushrooms, sliced
2 tablespoons cornstarch
¼ cup water
2 cups sour cream

Combine beef, onions, salt, pepper, Worcestershire sauce, Kitchen Bouquet, parsley, catsup, and mushrooms in a heat-proof casserole; bake in a preheated 275° oven for 2 hours. Check after 1¾ hours; if juices need to be thickened, stir in cornstarch and water mixed together; continue cooking until juices are smooth and thickened. Stir in sour cream and heat, but do not allow the mixture to boil as the sour cream will separate. Serve at once, or cover, cool, and refrigerate or freeze. To reheat, place in preheated 350° oven until just bubbling. Defrost frozen casserole before baking. Makes 8 servings.

— Meg Sexton (Mrs. Owen)

» Croatian Stuffed Cabbage «

This is very good cooked a day ahead and reheated. An extra Croatian touch: serve brown gravy as an accompaniment, with mashed potatoes, of course.

1 solid head cabbage, core removed	Salt and pepper
1 large onion, chopped	¾ cup rice, simmered in water long enough to remove starch
½ green pepper, chopped	
1 clove garlic, chopped	1 egg, beaten
2½ tablespoons butter	16 oz. can tomatoes
2 lbs. ground chuck, or 1 lb. chuck, ½ lb. pork, and ½ lb. veal, ground	16 oz. can sauerkraut, drained
	10½ oz. can beef bouillon

Scald cabbage head in very hot, salted water. As leaves soften enough to roll meat in them, remove from head, leaf by leaf, and dry on paper towel. Sauté onion, green pepper, and garlic for a few minutes in skillet with butter. Add ground meat; season with salt and pepper to taste; cook until meat is lightly browned. Remove from skillet, put in large bowl, and add drained cooked rice, beaten egg, 2 tomatoes squeezed from can (reserve tomato juice). Mix all ingredients well. Fill individual cabbage leaves with mixture. Fold in side of leaf, roll, and place seam side down on wax paper or aluminum wrap. Put ½ of sauerkraut on bottom of roasting pan or casserole. Chop up any leftover cabbage and add to sauerkraut. Squeeze a tomato over this. Place cabbage rolls side by side. Then sprinkle remaining sauerkraut, tomatoes, and juice over all. Add ½ of beef boullion and more later, if needed to keep moist. Bake approximately 2 hours, covered, in preheated 300° oven. Keep warm in oven until serving time. Makes 12 servings.

— Babs Deming (Mrs. Dorman)

» Stuffed Cabbage Roll with Sauerkraut «

1 large head cabbage	1 tablespoon parsley, minced
Boiling water	
1½ lbs. ground beef	⅛ teaspoon oregano
2 cups milk	2 cups rice, cooked
2 eggs	2 to 3 cups sauerkraut
1 onion, finely chopped	1 bay leaf
1½ teaspoons salt	½ teaspoon caraway seeds, optional
¼ teaspoon pepper	
	1-14 oz. can tomato sauce

Core cabbage and separate the leaves. Put into boiling water until the leaves are limp enough to roll; drain and let cool. Meanwhile, combine ground beef, milk, eggs, onion, salt, pepper, parsley, and oregano. Fold in cooked rice. Place 2 tablespoons of meat mixture on each cabbage leaf; fold the leaf around the mixture, making a neat roll. Place seam side down around the edges of a large covered ovenproof casserole or roaster. Continue until all of the meat mixture has been used. Drain and rinse sauerkraut; place in the center of the cabbage rolls; add bay leaf and caraway seeds. Pour tomato sauce over cabbage rolls and sauerkraut. Bake in a preheated 350° oven for 1½ to 2 hours, or until cabbage is tender and easily cut. Remove bay leaf before serving. Makes 8 servings.

— Zenia U. Kobylski

» Teriyaki Roast Tenderloin «

Teriyaki means "glaze-broiled." Traditional Japanese teriyaki dishes could be made from beef, pork, chicken, or fish. Recipes usually call for soy sauce, some kind of sweetening, wine such as dry sherry or sake, and often ginger and garlic. They are broiled or grilled over coals.

½ cup dry sherry	2 tablespoons brown sugar
¼ cup soy sauce	
2 tablespoons dry onion soup mix	2 tablespoons water
	2 lbs. beef tenderloin

Combine sherry, soy sauce, onion soup mix, brown sugar, and water. Place tenderloin in plastic bag; add marinade and close bag tightly. Let stand 2 hours at room temperature, or overnight in the refrigerator, turning bag several times to distribute marinade evenly over the meat. Remove meat from bag, reserving marinade. Place in shallow roasting pan and bake in preheated 425° oven for 45 to 50 minutes, basting with ½ marinade during cooking. Heat remaining marinade. To serve, slice meat ¼″ thick and baste with heated marinade. Makes 6 to 8 servings.

– Jean McCafferty (Mrs. Edward)

» Sukiyaki «

This is a country Japanese meal of meat and vegetables simmered together. Sukiyaki means "broiled on the blade of a hoe," from the early practice of Japanese farmers cooking meals in the field.

1 lb. beef tenderloin, cut into thin strips	following vegetables, thinly sliced –
3 cups beef stock	carrots, onion, broccoli,
¼ cup sake wine	mushrooms, bamboo
¼ cup sugar	shoots, spinach, or
½ cup soy sauce	bean sprouts
1 cup each of any 4 of	Cooked rice

Simmer the beef in a broth made of stock, sake, sugar, and soy sauce for 3 minutes. Add vegetables and simmer for an additional 5 minutes. Serve in bowls with separate bowls of rice as an accompaniment. Makes 4 to 6 servings.

– Kiyo Ya Restaurant
Atlanta, Georgia

» Stuffed Cabbage «

20 leaves of cabbage, approximately 2 small heads	2 onions, sliced
	2 cloves garlic, chopped
Boiling water	2 tablespoons butter
2 lbs. lean ground beef	10 oz. can tomatoes with purée, chopped
Salt and pepper	2 tablespoons lemon juice
1 onion, chopped	½ cup brown sugar
⅓ cup rice, uncooked	6 to 8 ginger snaps, crushed

Separate cabbage leaves and cover with boiling water while preparing stuffing and sauce. Combine beef with salt, pepper, chopped onion, and rice. Use a little tomato juice from can, if needed, to moisten. Sauté sliced onions and garlic in butter until softened. Add tomatoes and purée; simmer 15 minutes. Add lemon juice and brown sugar; cook 5 minutes. Adjust seasonings and set aside. Place 3 tablespoons of meat mixture in each leaf and roll up, tucking in sides. With the seam side down, place rolls 1-layer deep in a heatproof pan. Pour tomato sauce over. Cover and simmer over low heat 3 hours. After 2½ hours, remove a small portion of the sauce and mix with the crushed ginger snaps. Return to pan and cook until sauce is thickened. Makes 20 rolls, about 8 servings.

– Barbara Wagner (Mrs. James H.)

» Ma Po Hot Tofu «

Five-spice powder – the "Spices of Five Fragrances" – is a mixture of ground anise seed, cinnamon, cloves, ginger, and nutmeg or other spices. It is used in Chinese recipes requiring a strong spice flavor.

1 lb. tofu, cut into 1″x¼″ cubes	⅛ teaspoon five-spice powder
1½ cups oil	1 cup beef or chicken stock
½ lb. ground beef or pork	1 tablespoon soy sauce
3 tablespoons oil	½ tablespoon cornstarch
2 cloves garlic, minced	1 teaspoon water
½ tablespoon soya bean paste	1 teaspoon sesame oil
½ teaspoon cayenne or chili powder	3 green onions, chopped

Deep-fry tofu in hot oil for 1 minute; drain and set aside. In another pan, brown meat in oil; add garlic and cook until golden, stirring. Add bean paste, cayenne, five-spice powder, and stock; bring to a boil. Mix soy sauce, cornstarch, and water to make a paste; add to broth mixture; heat and stir until the broth thickens. Add fried tofu and simmer for 4 minutes; add sesame oil and mix lightly. Serve on a warm platter garnished with chopped onions. Makes 8 servings.

– Dora Ang (Mrs. Francis)

» Red Hot Spicy Tofu «

Tofu is bean curd, made from milk produced by cooking soybeans, and it has been a dietary staple in the Orient for more than 2,000 years. Now that it is regularly available in food stores, Americans are learning to appreciate tofu – low fat, low calorie, and a good source of protein.

¼ lb. ground pork or beef
1 teaspoon soy sauce
1 teaspoon dry sherry
½ teaspoon sugar
½ teaspoon salt
1 tablespoon oil
1 garlic clove, minced
1 teaspoon ginger root, grated
1 tablespoon green onion, chopped

½ teaspoon chili oil or hot sauce, or 1 small dry hot
  chili pepper, seeded and crumbled
14 oz. cake tofu, cut in ½"x½" squares, drained
¾ cup water
2 tablespoons soy sauce
2 tablespoons water blended with 2 tablespoons cornstarch

Marinate meat in soy sauce, sherry, sugar, and salt for 15 minutes. Heat skillet or wok and add oil. Stir-fry garlic, ginger, and onion in skillet briefly. Add marinated meat, stirring until it loses its pinkness. Add chili oil, tofu, water, and soy sauce; simmer 3 minutes. Reblend cornstarch and water, add to mixture and stir gently until sauce thickens. Makes 4 servings.

» Baked Lamb with Feta «

This rich casserole is perfect served with a crisp Greek salad and baklava. Feta is a common Greek cheese made in almost every small village. It is salty, white, and moist, and crumbles easily with a fork.

2½ lbs. boneless leg of lamb, cut into ¼" slices
1 lb. can plum tomatoes, drained and chopped
1 onion, thinly sliced

4 garlic cloves, minced
¼ teaspoon oregano
¼ teaspoon lemon pepper
½ lb. Feta cheese, crumbled

Cover bottom of 1½-quart casserole with ⅓ of lamb. Cover with ½ of the tomatoes and ½ of the onions. Sprinkle with some of the garlic, oregano, and lemon pepper. Continue layering, ending with lamb. Top with Feta cheese; bake in a preheated 300° oven for 3 to 3½ hours, or until tender. Spoon off juices and brown 6" from broiler before serving. Makes 8 servings.

– Mary Wydman (Mrs. Robert)

» Serundeng «

Lemon thyme or lemongrass is a favorite addition to Indonesian cookery, as it is in this beef recipe. It is available in some specialty food stores.

½ lb. beef tenderloin, sliced ⅛" thick
1 teaspoon salt
2 tablespoons oil, peanut or sesame
¼ lb. coconut, grated
2 cloves garlic, chopped
1 small onion

2½ teaspoons sugar
2 teaspoons ground coriander
½ teaspoon ground cumin
Dash of turmeric powder
1 sprig lemon thyme, optional, or leaf from lemon tree

Season beef slices with ½ teaspoon salt. Sauté for 5 minutes in hot oil in wok. Remove from oil; keep warm. Add all other ingredients to wok; stir-fry over low heat about 8 minutes. Add beef; stir until coconut is crisp and golden brown. Let cool and serve. Makes 4 to 6 servings.

– Dora Ang (Mrs. Francis)

» Kumback Barbecue Sauce «

This is my brother David Helms' recipe for barbecue sauce, and it makes enough for several sessions. He took great pride in his barbecuing, particularly steaks grilled outdoors. I have a feeling he came by this sauce from stag parties at Moon Lake, which were great fish-fry, barbecue, beer, and bourbon times when we lived in the Mississippi Delta. However he came by it, his barbecuing was as good as he thought it was... which was considerable. I add a pinch of brown sugar to mine, for like a lot of Southern cooks, I think a little pinch of sugar improves almost anything.

2 cloves garlic, minced
1 cup mayonnaise
¼ cup chili sauce
¼ cup catsup
1 teaspoon prepared mustard
½ cup vegetable oil

1 tablespoon Worcestershire sauce
1 teaspoon black pepper
Dash of Tabasco sauce
Dash of paprika
Juice of grated onion
2 tablespoons water

Combine all ingredients in a quart jar and shake well. Keep it in the refrigerator and use as needed. Marvelous for basting steaks, chops, spareribs, or chicken. Makes 1 pint.

– Jamie Sue Spurgeon (Mrs. C. E.)

Horace Pippin, 1888-1946, American,
"Christmas Morning, Breakfast." 1945, oil on canvas, 1959.47.
The Edwin and Virginia Irwin Memorial.
This color reproduction donated by Joan and George Rieveschl

The comfortable bulk of the wood stove at left and the decorated tree at right provide domestic sentinels guarding either side of this perfectly ordered painting. The artist's remembered child-self is shown obediently at table before opening his presents in "Christmas Morning, Breakfast." Greens brighten the frugal room and the boy's filled stocking hangs tantalizingly from a shelf just behind him.

Horace Pippin's considerable talent was shaped only by himself and the circumstances of his life that made physical labor impossible, allowing him to foster the interest in art that had been his since childhood. A sniper's bullet in World War I left his right hand almost paralyzed. To paint, he used his left hand to hold the right wrist, starting at one side of the canvas and working to the other with small brushes and neat strokes, painting over anything that dissatisfied him. "Pictures just come to my mind, and I tell my heart to go ahead," he said.

Pippin was 42 years old when he completed his first oil, and nearly 50 when he was discovered by the art world in 1937. His style became increasingly assured but was not altered by the sophistication of his new contacts. "Christmas Morning, Breakfast" was a late work, painted in 1945, the year before the artist died.

» Agneau sans Egal «

This curried lamb dish incorporates some of the traditional condiments within the recipe, making it a less complicated version of the Indian staple.

1 medium onion, finely chopped	1 teaspoon thyme
1 tablespoon butter	1 bay leaf
1 tablespoon oil	1 clove garlic, crushed
⅔ cup rice, uncooked	1⅓ cups water
1½ teaspoons curry powder	¼ cup raisins
	¼ cup almonds, slivered
2 lamb shoulder chops, boned and cubed	Salt and pepper
	Minced parsley

Sauté onion in butter and oil over medium heat until it begins to turn brown. Add rice and cook for about 1 minute, or until rice becomes translucent. Add curry powder and heat until aroma fills the air, 10 to 15 seconds. Add lamb, thyme, bay leaf, garlic, and water. Bring to a boil; lower heat and simmer, covered, about 18 minutes, or until most of water has been absorbed. Add raisins and almonds; season with salt and pepper. Set aside for a few minutes. Sprinkle with parsley before serving. This may be prepared in advance and reheated, adding a little water, if necessary. Makes 2 servings.

– Jeremy C. Gibson

» Lamb and Apricot Pilaf «

Pilaf or pilau is a steamed rice dish made of meat, chicken, fish, fruit, or vegetables in a broth. It came from the Middle East, where the word means "rice porridge," but long ago became so popular in the United States that Marjorie Kinnan Rawlings, in "Cross Creek Cookery," called it "almost a sacred Florida dish."

1 cup onion, chopped	½ teaspoon cinnamon
½ cup butter, divided	¼ teaspoon pepper
1 lb. lamb, cut into 1" cubes	1¾ cups water
½ cup dried apricot halves	1½ cups long grain rice
3 tablespoons raisins	3 cups boiling, salted water
1 teaspoon salt	

Sauté onion in 2 tablespoons butter until golden. Add lamb and cook, stirring, until well-browned on all sides.

Stir in apricots, raisins, salt, cinnamon, pepper, and water. Simmer, covered, for 90 minutes or until lamb is tender. Meanwhile, rinse rice thoroughly and drain. Add to boiling, salted water; reduce heat, cover, and simmer for 15 minutes. Stir in remaining butter; layer rice and lamb mixture in a heavy saucepan, beginning and ending with rice. Cover and simmer 25 minutes, or until rice is tender and fluffy. Makes 4 to 6 servings.

– Helen Voelkerding

» Persian Leg of Lamb «

This versatile marinade from Iran is as good with chicken as it is with lamb.

1 tablespoon sesame seeds	black pepper
1 tablespoon rosemary, crushed	Drop of Tabasco sauce
	Juice of 2 or 3 fresh lemons
1 teaspoon ground cumin	¼ cup vegetable oil
1 teaspoon cinnamon	5 to 6 lb. leg of lamb, boned and trimmed
1 teaspoon dried dill	
1 teaspoon fennel seeds	8 oz. pkg. pitted prunes
1 teaspoon garlic salt	8 oz. pkg. dried apricots
1 teaspoon Maggi	Juice and zest of 1 lemon
1 teaspoon monosodium glutamate	½ cup honey
	¼ cup dark brown sugar
Pinch of freshly ground	Cooked rice

Combine sesame seeds, rosemary, cumin, cinnamon, dill, fennel, garlic salt, Maggi, monosodium glutamate, pepper, Tabasco sauce, lemon juice, and oil. Rub meat inside and out with the marinade; place in a covered casserole or heavy ziplock plastic bag. Refrigerate and continue marinating for 1 to 2 days, turning occasionally. Roast in a preheated 350° oven for 1 hour for medium-rare lamb; use a meat thermometer to obtain the precise doneness desired (170°). While lamb is roasting, combine prunes, apricots, lemon juice, and lemon zest in a heavy pan; simmer until fruit is tender, adding water if necessary. Remove lamb from oven and place on ovenproof serving platter. Raise oven temperature to 425°. Arrange the fruit around the lamb and sprinkle both with honey and brown sugar mixed together. Return to oven for 10 to 15 minutes. Serve with rice. Makes 8 to 10 servings.

– Virginia L. Cope (Mrs. Paul E.)

» Agneau aux Petits Fruits «

This combination of fruits and vegetables with lamb creates a marvelous stew with a sophisticated French flavor.

¼ teaspoon freshly ground
   pepper
¾ teaspoon salt
½ teaspoon thyme
1 teaspoon seasoned salt
3 ozs. tomato paste
1½ cups dry Burgundy
   wine
1 bay leaf
1 cinnamon stick
1 clove garlic
2 lbs. lean boneless lamb

3 cups carrots, sliced
   crosswise
10 oz. pkg. mixed dried
   fruits
¾ cup frozen whole baby
   onions
½ cup white raisins
1 lb. mushroom caps
¾ cup frozen pie cherries
Superfine flour for
   thickening

Mix pepper, salt, thyme, and seasoned salt. Stir in tomato paste and add wine slowly. Tie bay leaf, cinnamon stick, and garlic in a small square of cheesecloth and add to marinade. Cube lamb; add to marinade and stir to coat meat well. Marinate lamb for 4 to 6 hours, stirring occasionally. Place marinated mixture in a heavy pan and simmer over low heat for 30 minutes; use an asbestos pad over burner to help in preventing sticking. Add carrots and dried fruits; simmer for an additional 30 minutes. Add onions and raisins; simmer until carrots and lamb are tender. Remove cheesecloth bag of herbs and add mushrooms and cherries. Simmer for an additional 15 minutes. Correct seasonings and add flour for thickening, if necessary. Makes 6 servings.

– Barbara Rosenberg (Mrs. Berton)

» Carre d'Agneau «

This rack of lamb roasted quickly in the French manner remains moist and succulent, and is excellent served with a fine red Bordeaux or Medoc wine.

1-3 lb. rack of lamb
½ cup Dijon mustard

¼ cup olive oil

Coat rack of lamb with a paste made from mustard and olive oil. Roast on a rack in a roasting pan in a preheated 425° oven for 25 minutes. Lamb will be pink on the inside and crusty on the outside. Makes 4 servings.

– Winnie Love (Mrs. Wesley)

» Lube a fe Lahem «

The touch of cinnamon imparts a Lebanese dash to this fragrant lamb and green bean dish.

2 lbs. fresh green beans,
   washed and trimmed
1 lb. lean lamb, cubed
1 medium onion, minced
1 clove garlic, minced
2 tablespoons butter
1 cup hot water

2 cups fresh or canned
   tomatoes, diced
1 teaspoon salt
½ teaspoon pepper
¼ teaspoon cinnamon
Cooked rice
Pita bread

Cook beans in boiling water to cover until just tender; do not overcook. Drain and set aside. Brown lamb, onion, and garlic in butter. Add hot water and simmer for 10 minutes. Add beans, tomatoes, salt, pepper, and cinnamon; simmer for an additional 20 to 25 minutes. Lamb should be tender and most of the moisture evaporated. Serve immediately with rice and pita bread. Makes 6 servings.

– Marcia Joseph (Mrs. Ronald G.)

» Lebanese Lamb-Stuffed Cabbage «

1 cup long grain rice,
   cooked and rinsed in
   water
1 lb. lamb or beef, finely
   chopped
½ cup canned tomatoes,
   drained
½ teaspoon allspice
Salt and pepper

2 medium heads cabbage
1 cup canned tomatoes
1 teaspoon salt
Dash dried mint
1 clove garlic, minced
Water or tomato juice
   sufficient to cover
   cabbage rolls
Juice of 3 lemons

Mix rice with meat, tomatoes, allspice, salt, and pepper. Remove thick core from center of cabbages. Drop into salted boiling water, cored end down. Boil a few minutes until leaves are softened. While boiling, loosen leaves with a fork. Remove and cool. Remove heavy center stems from leaves, halving leaves if large. Fill each leaf with 1 tablespoon of stuffing and roll into cigar shape. Place cabbage stems on the bottom of a large heavy pan. Arrange cabbage rolls on top of stems. Add tomatoes, salt, mint, and garlic. Press down with a flat dish that fits inside pan. Add water or tomato juice to cover rolls. Cover pan and simmer 25 minutes; add lemon juice and cook 10 minutes more. Makes about 50 rolls.

» Roast Leg of Lamb «

Lamb is the staple meat of Greece. Roasted with garlic and lemon, it is truly a feast for the gods.

5 lb. leg of lamb	¼ cup olive oil
Salt and freshly ground pepper	Juice of 2 lemons
	1 cup water
6 to 8 cloves of garlic, peeled, more if desired	Small potatoes, peeled
	Small onions, peeled

Wash the lamb well and place in a roasting pan. Mix salt and pepper with garlic in a small bowl. Using a small, sharp knife, make several deep incisions in the leg of lamb; insert a garlic clove in each incision. Rub the remaining salt and pepper over the leg of lamb, along with the olive oil. Pour the lemon juice over all. Cover the pan with aluminum foil or a lid; roast in a preheated 350° oven. After about 1 hour, remove the lid and pour 1 cup water into the roasting pan. Use the pan liquids to baste the lamb during the final 30 to 60 minutes. At this time, the potatoes and onions may also be added. For rarer lamb, cook 20 minutes to the pound, or until the internal temperature reaches 160° to 165°; for more well-done lamb, roast 30 minutes to the pound, to an internal temperature of 175° to 180°. Makes 8 servings.

– Cleo Seremetis (Mrs. Wm. G.)

» Baten Gen Mihshee «

The eggplant is related to the tomato or love apple, and was once called the mad apple. This stuffed baked eggplant dish from Lebanon is both sane and savory.

3 small eggplants	½ teaspoon cinnamon
1 lb. ground lamb	2 tablespoons pine nuts
1 medium onion, finely chopped	1 tablespoon butter
	6 oz. can tomato paste
2 tablespoons butter	1 cup water
1 tablespoon salt	Rice
½ teaspoon pepper	Pita bread
½ teaspoon allspice	

Remove stem of eggplant. Score the eggplant skin lightly several times and place in a broiler pan. Broil 4″ from flame, turning so eggplants brown evenly but do not become charred. The flesh should be soft but the skin intact; set aside. Sauté lamb and onion in butter until lamb is browned; pour off excess butter and add spices. Meanwhile, brown pine nuts in additional butter in a heavy skillet. Add to meat mixture. Slice each eggplant in half and place in a casserole just large enough to hold eggplant halves snugly. Push the center flesh of the eggplant aside, or scoop it out, until eggplant resembles a boat. Stuff with the meat mixture. Mix tomato paste with water and pour over the eggplant. Bake in a preheated 350° oven for 45 minutes. Serve with rice and pita bread. Makes 6 servings.

– Marcia Joseph (Mrs. Ronald G.)

» Turkish Lamb Kabobs «

1½ lbs. lean lamb, cut into 1″ cubes	2 tablespoons olive oil
	½ teaspoon salt
2 green peppers, cut into 1″ cubes	½ teaspoon thyme
	½ teaspoon oregano
2 sweet red peppers, cut into 1″ cubes	Freshly ground pepper
	1 tablespoon fresh mint leaves, minced
1 onion, cut into wedges	
3 tablespoons lemon juice	

Place lamb and peppers in a shallow bowl. Blanch onion wedges in boiling water for 3 minutes; drain. Mix remaining ingredients together and add to lamb, peppers, and onions. Mix gently so all is coated well. Cover and marinate at least 1 hour at room temperature, stirring occasionally. Thread lamb, peppers, and onions on 4 skewers, alternating. Broil in oven 4″ from heat or over charcoal for 10 to 15 minutes, or until lamb is done. Makes 4 servings.

– Anne Seasholes Cozlu (Mrs. Cem)

» Eight-Boy Curry «

This curry may be made ahead and refrigerated overnight – in that case, add a cup of chicken broth or bouillon before reheating. Curry or "rijstafel" – rice table – is one of the traditional Dutch dishes that were originally brought back to the Netherlands from Dutch colonies in the East Indies. The "boys" refer to the side dishes or garnishes because each dish was carried in separately in a ceremonial procession ... eight side dishes equals 8-boy curry, and 20 dishes would be a 20-boy curry.

3 lbs. stewing lamb or
    veal, cut into bite-size
    pieces
¼ cup butter or oil
4 large onions, chopped
6 cloves garlic, crushed
2 tablespoons curry
    powder

2 lemons, sliced and
    seeded
4 apples, cored, peeled,
    and chopped
1½ cups chicken broth
½ teaspoon salt
¼ teaspoon black pepper
Cooked rice
"Boys"

Brown meat in butter or oil; remove from pan. Sauté onions and garlic in remaining fat, stirring constantly, until onions are soft but not brown. Add curry powder and cook, stirring, for 5 minutes. Return meat to pan; stir in lemons, apples, chicken broth, salt, and pepper. Bring to a boil, reduce heat, cover, and simmer 1½ to 2 hours, or until meat is tender and apples and onions have cooked down into sauce. Stir curry from time to time. Serve with fluffy rice and "boys" or garnishes. Combine each bite of curry with rice and a "boy" so the blend of flavors comes through. "Boys" can be salty, sweet, hot, sour, creamy, crispy, crunchy, chewy – the more variety the better. Makes 6 servings. Some suggestions for "boys" are:

Crisp bacon bits
Grated egg yolks or
    chopped hard-cooked
    eggs
Chopped pecans or
    peanuts
Watermelon pickle
Raisins
Mandarin oranges

Relish
Coconut
Chutney
Chopped green pepper
Chives
Sour cream
Olives
Capers
Chopped banana

– Marjory Van Lieu

» Lamb Bhuna «

This complicated Indian combination of lamb and spices is perfectly complemented by fluffy rice.

3 medium onions, thinly
    sliced
¼ cup oil
1 lb. lean lamb, cubed
3" piece of ginger root
12 cloves garlic
1 cup fresh coriander
    leaves
1 cup fresh mint
3 small hot green peppers
1 tablespoon vinegar
1 teaspoon salt

1 heaping tablespoon
    yogurt
2 tomatoes, quartered
1 tablespoon cumin
1 tablespoon powdered
    coriander
½ tablespoon garam
    masala
1 tablespoon paprika
1½ cups water
Cooked rice

Sauté onions in oil until they are transparent. Add the meat, stir-fry for 1 minute, cover, and cook for 1 minute. Remove the cover and continue cooking until most of the moisture has evaporated. Meanwhile, combine all the rest of the ingredients except water in a blender or food processor. Process until they form a smooth paste. Add to the meat mixture, stirring for 1 minute until well combined; add water; simmer over low heat for 30 minutes. Increase heat and cook, stirring, until moisture evaporates. Serve at once with rice. Makes 4 servings.

– Annapurna Restaurant
New York City

» Moussaka «

1 large eggplant, peeled
    and cut into ¼" slices
1 cup butter, divided
1 medium onion, finely
    chopped
2 lbs. lean ground lamb
8 oz. can tomato sauce
½ cup dry red wine
½ cup parsley, chopped
¼ teaspoon cinnamon

Salt and freshly ground
    pepper
¼ cup flour
1½ cups milk
¾ cup chicken broth
4 eggs, beaten until frothy
Dash of nutmeg
1 cup cottage cheese
1 cup Parmesan cheese,
    freshly grated

Brown eggplant slices quickly, a few at a time, in ¼ cup butter in a heavy pan; remove and set aside. Add ¼ cup butter to pan and sauté onion until translucent. Add ground meat and continue cooking until lamb is browned, about 10 minutes. Drain excess fat and add tomato sauce, wine, parsley, cinnamon, and salt and pepper to taste. Simmer over low heat, stirring frequently, until all liquid is absorbed; remove from heat. In another heavy pan, melt ½ cup butter with flour; cook together a few minutes, stirring constantly. Remove pan from heat and add milk and broth. Return pan to heat and cook, stirring, until mixture thickens. Cool slightly and stir in eggs, nutmeg, and cottage cheese. Grease an 11"x16" casserole, and sprinkle the bottom with some of the Parmesan cheese. Arrange alternate layers of eggplant and meat sauce in pan, sprinkling each layer with Parmesan cheese. Pour the white sauce over the top and bake in a preheated 375° oven for 1 hour, or until top is puffed and golden. Remove from oven and let stand for 20 to 30 minutes before serving. The flavor is improved if the dish is served the next day. Cool and refrigerate; reheat before serving. Makes 8 to 10 servings.

— Jill Ford (Mrs. Starr, Jr.)

mixture to a boil; simmer 2 minutes. Cover the pan and cook over the lowest heat for 15 minutes. Remove the pan from heat, place a piece of waxed paper under the cover, and let stand 10 minutes. Place lamb in a large mixing bowl. Remove crust from bread, soak it in a small amount of cold water, and squeeze it dry. Crumble and mix with lamb, adding salt and pepper. Knead and shape into walnut-sized balls. Roll in flour and then brown in butter in a heavy pan. Drain and set aside. Add tomato to the pan and cook until the moisture is almost evaporated. Meanwhile, sprinkle the eggplant with salt and drain in a colander for 10 minutes. Coat the cubes with flour and brown in the remaining butter. Add the eggplant, tomato, and meatballs to the cooked rice; let stand for 15 minutes. Place in a greased heatproof casserole; sprinkle with cinnamon and cloves; garnish with mint leaves. Bake in a preheated 325° oven for 20 to 25 minutes. This dish may be made ahead and reheated at 325° for 20 to 25 minutes. Makes 6 servings.

— Hermine Wirthlin (Mrs. C. Ray)

» Sultan Reshat Pilavi «

This rice, lamb, and vegetable dish was served to us as a main course at a restaurant in Istanbul. It was appetizingly accompanied by a cucumber and zucchini salad with an olive oil, lemon, and yogurt dressing.

½ cup pine nuts
1 small onion, finely chopped
1 tablespoon butter
4½ cups chicken broth
½ cup dried currants or raisins
1 teaspoon salt
½ teaspoon pepper
2 cups rice
3 tablespoons butter
½ lb. ground lamb
1 slice white bread

½ teaspoon salt
Pinch of pepper
½ cup flour
2 tablespoons butter
1 large tomato, diced
1 medium eggplant, peeled and diced
2 tablespoons salt
2 tablespoons flour
2 tablespoons butter
Pinch of cinnamon
Pinch of cloves
Mint leaves

Brown pine nuts and onion in butter in a heavy saucepan. Add broth, currants, salt, and pepper. In another heavy saucepan, sauté rice in butter for 10 minutes over medium heat, stirring constantly. Pour the onion and broth mixture over the rice and bring the

» Jambon Veronique «

The French call a dish which uses grapes in combination with meat or poultry Veronique. This one is an unusual marriage of flavors.

1 tablespoon butter
1 tablespoon shallots, finely chopped
1½ lbs. ham steaks, ⅜" thick
2½ tablespoons Madeira wine

2 cups seedless white grapes
1 cup whipping cream
1 teaspoon arrowroot or cornstarch

Melt part of the butter in the bottom of a large heavy sauté pan. Add shallots and ham steaks dotted with remaining butter; pour 2 tablespoons of Madeira around ham. Cover loosely and cook 5 minutes over medium heat. Remove cooking liquid from steaks to another sauté pan; keep steaks covered and warm. Bring liquid to boil, add grapes and cook for 3 minutes. Add cream and cook 5 minutes over high heat. Blend arrowroot with remaining teaspoon of Madeira and stir into sauce. When smooth and thick, pour over ham, and serve at once. Makes 4 servings.

— Barbara Lauterbach (Mrs. Peter)

» Jambon au Saupiquet «

This wonderful way of cooking ham with a piquant sauce is from Madame Connel's Chateau Cooking School. The wine and juniper berries combine to create a unique aromatic flavor.

8 slices cooked ham,
    ½" thick
5 tablespoons butter
3 shallots, minced
1 tablespoon flour
¼ cup wine vinegar
¾ cup chicken stock
¼ cup white wine

8 juniper berries
Few green peppercorns,
    optional
Salt and freshly ground
    black pepper
1 cup whipping cream
¼ cup parsley, chopped

Sauté ham slices in 4 tablespoons butter for a few minutes on each side. Remove to a serving dish and keep warm. In the same pan, melt additional 1 tablespoon butter and sauté shallots until golden. Add flour and cook together a few minutes; add wine vinegar, chicken stock, and white wine. Add juniper berries and peppercorns; season with salt and pepper; bring sauce to a boil, reduce heat and simmer while stirring for about 10 minutes, or until thickened. Strain the sauce and add cream and parsley. Heat again, pour over reserved ham slices, and serve at once.
Makes 8 servings.

– Ruth Swigart (Mrs. Eugene)

» Ham and Asparagus Casserole «

2 cups soft bread crumbs
¾ cup Cheddar or
    American cheese,
    grated
¼ cup butter, melted
1 lb. fresh asparagus

2 tablespoons butter
¼ cup flour
Salt and white pepper
1½ cups milk
1 cup cooked ham, diced

Mix crumbs, cheese, and butter together. Put half of this mixture in bottom of casserole. Peel and steam asparagus and arrange spears on top. Melt butter over low heat; stir in flour until well-blended; add salt and pepper to taste. Stir in milk slowly; simmer and stir with a wire whisk until sauce has thickened and is smooth. Add ham to sauce and pour over asparagus in casserole.

Top with remaining crumb mixture. Bake in preheated 350° oven for about 25 minutes, or until bubbling. Makes 4 servings.

– Charlotte Kruse (Mrs. Henry O.)

» Filet Mignon de Porc en Croute «

Anchovies are often used by the French in unlikely combinations. Here they lend a delightful piquancy to a rather bland cut of meat.

Pastry or puff pastry
1 lb. pork tenderloin
12 anchovy fillets
Freshly ground pepper

2 tablespoons fresh
    thyme, minced, or 1
    tablespoon dried thyme
1 egg yolk
1 tablespoon water

Roll pastry or puff pastry into a ½" thick rectangle large enough to encase the pork. Place anchovy fillets on top, bottom, and sides of pork tenderloin; sprinkle with pepper and thyme. Roll up like a parcel, tucking in the ends. Place seam-side-down on an oiled baking sheet. Mix egg yolk and water and brush onto pastry. Roll may be decorated with leftover pastry cut into leaves or strips. Bake in a preheated 350° oven for 30 minutes. Remove from oven and let rest for 10 minutes before slicing. Makes 4 servings.

– Mme. M. Preston Jones
Roquefort-les-Pins, France

» Chuletas de Cerdo a la Madrileña «

These Madrid-style pork chops may be prepared easily and are a favorite recipe from my bachelor days, even before my first trip to Spain in 1962. My love of things Spanish, particularly that country's paintings from her golden age in the Seventeenth Century, is reinforced by her cooking. The starkness of the Spanish landscape is sometimes reflected in her cuisine, but Spanish cookery is usually exciting, tasty, and colorful – like the works of Zurburan, Murillo, and Velasquez, all of whom are represented in the Cincinnati Art Museum's collection.

¼ cup olive oil
1 small clove garlic,
 minced
4 large sprigs parsley,
 minced
½ bay leaf
Pinch paprika
Pinch thyme

Pinch salt
Pinch pepper
½ to 1 teaspoon Tabasco
 sauce, as desired
4 large pork chops,
 1½" thick
4 cups cooked rice

Combine olive oil, garlic, parsley, bay leaf, paprika, thyme, salt, pepper, and Tabasco sauce in a shallow ovenproof dish. Marinate the pork chops in this mixture for 1 hour, turning once in order for both sides of the pork chops to absorb the marinade. Cover the dish with foil and bake the chops in a preheated 350° oven for 30 to 40 minutes, or until well-cooked, but not dry; baste the meat occasionally. Serve with rice. Makes 4 servings.

– Millard F. Rogers, Jr.
Director, Cincinnati Art Museum

» Stuffed Pork Loin «

In 1872, Anton Grammer founded the restaurant that still bears his name. A magnificent turn-of-the-century bar and beautiful leaded glass windows dominate the main dining room.

3 oz. bacon, chopped
½ onion, diced
1 cup dried raisins,
 apricots, and dates,
 soaked in white wine
¼ lb. cornbread, cut in
 1" cubes
1 teaspoon sage
1 teaspoon thyme
½ teaspoon cinnamon

¼ teaspoon allspice
¼ cup molasses or
 maple syrup
3 lb. boneless center-cut
 pork loin
Salt and pepper
1 quart beef stock or
 bouillon
½ cup flour
1 tablespoon molasses

Sauté bacon and onion together until onions are clear and bacon is crisp. Drain; toss lightly with fruit, cornbread, sage, thyme, cinnamon, and allspice; mix in molasses. With a sharp slicing knife, make two intersecting cross cuts from end to end through the center of the pork loin. Push out a passage through the loin; force stuffing mixture through with fingers. Sprinkle outside of loin with salt and pepper to taste; place on rack in a roasting pan and bake in a preheated

400° oven for 40 minutes, or until a thermometer inserted into the center of the meat registers 180°. To make the sauce, skim fat from the roasting pan, add beef stock, flour, and molasses; simmer over medium heat until thick, stirring frequently. Season to taste; pour over slices of loin before serving. Makes 8 servings.

– Grammer's Restaurant

» Pork and Watercress «

Stew served with rice is typical of African cuisine, particularly in West Africa, where rice paddies abound.

2 lbs. lean pork, cut into
 2" cubes
1 tablespoon oil
4 cups water
2 teaspoons salt

6 peppercorns, or 1 dried
 red pepper
4 cups watercress,
 chopped coarsely
Cooked rice

Sauté pork in oil until lightly browned. Add water, salt, and pepper and simmer slowly, covered, until pork is nearly soft. Uncover and reduce liquid; add watercress and cook until reduced to sauce consistency. Correct seasonings, if necessary, and serve with hot rice. Makes 6 servings.

» Japanese Sweet and Sour Pork «

1 lb. boneless lean pork,
 cut into ½" cubes
1 tablespoon sherry wine
2 tablespoons soy sauce
2 eggs
1 tablespoon water
½ cup cornstarch
Peanut oil for frying
2 carrots, cut into
 1" pieces
1 green pepper, cut into
 1" cubes

1 green onion, cut into
 1" pieces
4 slices pineapple, cut into
 1" pieces
3 tablespoons oil
6 tablespoons sugar
1 tablespoon sherry wine
¼ cup soy sauce
3 tablespoons vinegar
¼ cup tomato sauce
1 tablespoon cornstarch
½ cup water

Mix pork cubes with sherry and soy sauce. Dip cubes into eggs and water which have been beaten together; dip into cornstarch. Fry in deep oil until golden brown;

drain. Meanwhile, blanch the carrot slices in boiling water for 6 to 8 minutes. Drain; sauté them with green pepper, green onion, and pineapple in oil for a few minutes. Combine sugar, sherry, soy sauce, vinegar, tomato sauce, cornstarch, and water. Add to vegetables and cook, stirring constantly, until mixture boils. Add reserved fried pork; serve immediately. Makes 4 servings.

– Mieko Johnston

» Pork, Shrimp, and Mushroom Loo Mein «

Dried noodles and Chinese black mushrooms may be purchased in specialty stores and supermarkets. The mushrooms have a much more pungent flavor than those that are domestically available, and the black color is attractive.

5 ozs. dried Oriental noodles	4 dried black Chinese mushrooms
4 cups boiling water	Boiling water
1 tablespoon soy sauce	3 tablespoons oil
1 tablespoon peanut oil	1/4 lb. nappa or green cabbage, cut in strips
1 teaspoon sesame oil	
1/2 lb. shrimp, peeled and deveined	6 green onions, cut into 1/2" lengths
1/2 teaspoon salt	3/4 cup snow peas
1/2 teaspoon cornstarch	1 to 2 tablespoons soy sauce
1/2 lb. lean pork, cut into 3/4" cubes	
1 tablespoon soy sauce	1/2 teaspoon salt
1/2 teaspoon cornstarch	1/8 teaspoon pepper
	1/2 teaspoon sesame oil

Boil noodles in water for 3 to 4 minutes. Remove and immediately rinse in cold water. Drain well, place in a shallow bowl, and add soy sauce and oils; mix well. Mix shrimp with salt and cornstarch; set aside. Mix pork, soy sauce, and cornstarch; set aside. Place mushrooms in a shallow bowl and pour boiling water over. Let stand 10 minutes, remove stems and discard, and slice mushrooms into strips. Heat 3 tablespoons of oil in a wok or heavy skillet; stir-fry pork for 2 minutes, remove and set aside. Add shrimp to wok and stir-fry for 2 minutes. Remove and set aside. Add nappa, green onions, snow peas, sliced mushrooms, soy sauce, salt, and pepper. Add noodles, reserved pork and shrimp; mix well and stir-fry until vegetables are done but still crisp. Add sesame oil and serve immediately. Makes 6 to 8 servings.

– Dora Ang (Mrs. Francis)

» Pork Vindalho «

This spicy hot Indian dish is sparked with chilies and tamarind juice.

16 Kashmiri chilies	Warm water
1 teaspoon cumin	6 whole green chilies, cut with slits
1/2 teaspoon peppercorns	
1 teaspoon turmeric	1 teaspoon sugar
10 cloves garlic, minced	1 teaspoon salt
2" piece of ginger, minced	Walnut-sized ball of tamarind, soaked in 3/4 cup water
6 onions, sliced thinly	
2 tablespoons oil	
1 lb. boneless pork, cut into 1" cubes	2 tablespoons vinegar

Grind together chilies, cumin, peppercorns, turmeric, and 1/2 of the garlic and ginger to make the masala. Sauté onion and remaining garlic and ginger in oil until lightly browned. Add the pork and the masala; sauté for 10 minutes. Add water to barely cover pork; cook until water has been reduced by 1/2. Add green chilies, sugar, salt, tamarind juice, and vinegar. Simmer over low heat until liquid is thickened. Makes 6 to 8 servings.

– Jennifer-Ann Fernandes (Mrs. Allan)

» Barbecued Spareribs «

The addition of pineapple juice to this marinade gives it an Oriental sweet/sour flavor.

1/2 cup pineapple juice	1 teaspoon dry ginger
2 tablespoons lemon juice	1/4 teaspoon dry mustard
1/2 cup dark corn syrup	1/8 teaspoon garlic powder
1/4 cup soy sauce	4 lbs. baby ribs, cut into serving pieces

Mix together pineapple juice, lemon juice, corn syrup, soy sauce, ginger, dry mustard, and garlic powder. Pour into a large baking dish; add ribs, cover, and marinate in refrigerator overnight, turning occasionally. Drain ribs and save marinade. Place ribs in shallow baking dish. Cover and bake in a preheated 350° oven for 1 hour. Remove ribs and transfer to a rack; drain fat. Replace rack and ribs in baking pan; return to oven. Bake 30 minutes more, or until ribs are well done, basting with marinade and turning frequently. Makes 4 to 6 servings.

» Dublin Coddle «

This dish originated in the Eighteenth Century and is a traditional Sunday night supper in Ireland.

8 thick slices bacon	8 large potatoes, peeled
1 lb. pork sausage links	and sliced
4 cups water	½ cup parsley, chopped
4 large onions, sliced	Salt and pepper

Boil bacon and sausages in water for 5 minutes. Drain, reserving water. Place meats and remaining ingredients in an ovenproof casserole and add enough reserved liquid to cover. Cover and bake in a preheated 250° oven for about 1 hour, or simmer slowly on top of the stove for 1 hour. Makes 8 servings.

– Pud Preston (Mrs. Robert H.)

» Pancit Cuisado «

In the Philippines, many dishes combine two or more basic ingredients, such as pork, chicken, and ham, as in this hearty meat and cabbage casserole. Filipino cooking reflects the many culinary styles that have influenced the country – Tagalog, Spanish, Chinese, and American.

4 cloves garlic, peeled and crushed	½ cup cooked ham, sliced in matchstick strips
1 medium onion, sliced thinly	¼ cup oil
½ cup shrimp, sliced in half lengthwise and boiled, reserve 1 cup liquid	3 tablespoons soy sauce
	Salt and pepper
	1 cup cabbage, shredded
	1 lb. rice sticks
½ cup pork, sliced in matchstick strips and boiled	Boiling water
	Peanut oil
	Lemon wedges
½ cup chicken, boiled and shredded	2 eggs, hard-cooked and sliced

Sauté garlic, onion, shrimp, pork, chicken, and ham in oil until onion is transparent. Remove 4 tablespoons of mixture for garnish. To the rest, add soy sauce, 1 cup liquid reserved from shrimp, and salt and pepper to taste. Cook together for 5 minutes; add cabbage, mix well, and simmer until most of the liquid evaporates. Meanwhile, blanch rice sticks for 2 minutes in boiling water to cover, drain well, and then sauté in peanut oil until lightly browned. Mix all together and arrange on a serving dish. Garnish with reserved mixture, lemon wedges, and eggs. Makes 8 servings.

– Nellie Obial (Mrs. Guadencio)

» New Year's Day Sauerkraut «

In a tradition handed down from our German ancestors, our family eats sauerkraut on New Year's Day to insure good luck throughout the year. Chicken is "verboten," for as a chicken scratches in the ground, so will chicken eaten on New Year's Day scratch back bad luck. This is our favorite way to serve sauerkraut, with dark rye bread, and white wine or steins of ice cold beer.

2 lbs. sauerkraut	4 Idaho potatoes
½ cup butter	1 teaspoon Maggi
1 large onion, diced	½ cup parsley, chopped
2 tart apples, peeled and diced	1 lb. fresh mett sausage
	1 lb. bratwurst
2 cloves garlic, minced	1 lb. smoked breakfast
1 cup dry white wine	sausage
6 juniper berries, crushed	1 lb. garlic franks
1 bunch carrots	½ cup parsley, chopped

Using a stainless steel or enamel pan, cover sauerkraut with cold water. Bring to a boil and then drain well in a colander. Melt butter, sauté onion for a few minutes; then add apples, garlic, wine, juniper berries, Maggi, parsley, and the blanched, drained sauerkraut. Simmer 30 minutes. Place cooked sauerkraut in a large ovenproof casserole. Place sausages on sauerkraut; peel carrots and cut into ½″ rounds; peel potatoes and cut into ½″ rounds. Blanch both for 10 minutes in boiling water and place on top of sausages. Sprinkle with additional parsley. Cover and bake in a preheated 350° oven for 40 minutes. Makes 12 servings.

– Virginia Cope (Mrs. Paul E.)

» Sausage and Cheese Casserole «

6 slices bread, crusts
    removed
1 lb. bulk sausage
1 teaspoon prepared
    mustard
½ lb. Swiss cheese,
    shredded
¼ cup milk

¾ cup light cream
3 eggs, lightly beaten
1 teaspoon
    Worcestershire sauce
1 teaspoon salt
Freshly ground pepper
1 teaspoon nutmeg

Arrange bread slices on bottom of 9″x13″ ovenproof casserole. Brown sausage in a heavy pan, stirring to crumble. Pour off excess fat and add mustard. Sprinkle sausage over bread and cover with cheese. Combine remaining ingredients and pour over cheese. Bake 35 minutes in a preheated 350° oven, or until topping has set and is lightly browned on top. Makes 6 servings.

    – Audrey Raabe (Mrs. Victor)

» Tamale Pie «

Your crowd will enjoy this hearty recipe given to us by the author of the best-selling book, "Our Crowd."

½ lb. ground pork sausage
1 lb. lean ground beef
1 clove garlic, minced
1 cup onion, chopped
2 cups celery, sliced
1 lb. can tomatoes
2 cups canned or
    fresh corn

Salt
2 teaspoons chili powder
½ cup yellow corn meal
1½ cups pitted ripe olives
1½ cups American,
    Cheddar, or Monterey
    Jack cheese, shredded
Paprika

Cook sausage until lightly browned, stirring to keep crumbly. Pour off excess fat, add beef, and continue cooking and stirring until browned. Stir in garlic, onion, and celery; cook until vegetables are tender, but not browned. Stir in tomatoes, corn, salt to taste, and chili powder, adding more chili powder for a spicier dish; simmer 15 minutes. Slowly stir in corn meal; cook until thickened. Remove from heat; stir in olives. Turn into a buttered 2-quart casserole; top with cheese and dust with paprika. Bake, uncovered, in a preheated 350° oven for 45 minutes. Serve immediately. Makes 8 servings.

    – Stephen Birmingham

Affronted Ibexes, relief, ceramic (stucco), Iran, Sasanian period, 5th or 6th century, 1972.541. Museum purchase

» Swiss Sausage Casserole «

6 slices bread, crusts
 trimmed
1 lb. bulk sausage
1 teaspoon prepared
 mustard
½ cup Swiss cheese,
 shredded
1¼ cups milk

¾ cup half and half cream
3 eggs, lightly beaten
1 teaspoon
 Worcestershire sauce
1 teaspoon salt
Pepper
1 teaspoon nutmeg

Place bread on bottom of 9"x13" pan. Brown sausage, drain fat, and stir in mustard. Sprinkle sausage over bread and top with cheese. Combine the rest of the ingredients and pour over bread, sausage, and cheese. Bake 35 minutes in preheated 350° oven. Makes 6 servings.

– Audrey Raabe (Mrs. Victor)

» Spinach and Sausage Casserole «

Italian sausage, with its aroma and taste of fennel, gives this casserole a special flavor.

12 crepes, about 7" size, at
 room temperature
10 oz. pkg. frozen chopped
 spinach
1 lb. mild or hot Italian
 sausage
1 large onion, chopped
¾ teaspoon oregano
 leaves

¾ teaspoon dry basil
2 cups prepared spaghetti
 sauce or seasoned
 tomato sauce
2 eggs
2 cups small curd cottage
 cheese
6 tablespoons Parmesan
 cheese, grated

Prepare crepes, using your favorite recipe. Thaw spinach and squeeze out as much moisture as possible. Remove casing and crumble sausage into frying pan. Cook until lightly brown; drain off fat. Add onion and cook until transparent. Stir in oregano, basil, and spaghetti sauce. Simmer 10 minutes. Lightly beat together eggs; stir in cottage cheese, drained spinach, and 4 tablespoons Parmesan cheese. Arrange 6 crepes, overlapping, in a greased 9"x13" baking dish, so they completely cover the bottom and come up the sides of dish. Spread half of the spinach and cheese over the crepes, then top with half of the meat sauce. Top with remaining crepes, cheese, and

meat sauce. Sprinkle with remaining Parmesan cheese. Cover with foil and chill if made ahead. Bake, covered, in a preheated 375° oven for 45 minutes, or 55 minutes if casserole has been refrigerated. Let stand 15 minutes before cutting into squares. Makes 6 to 8 servings.

– Toni Eyrich (Mrs. David J.)

» Toad-in-the-Hole «

This is one of those traditional English recipes with marvelous, irresistible names like Bubble and Squeak, Spotted Dog, and Roly Poly. Vegetable extract is a concentrated yeast spread that is thick and black like molasses. It is made in England and Canada and available at supermarkets.

1 tablespoon vegetable
 extract
1 cup water
1 cup flour
½ teaspoon salt
2 eggs

4 tablespoons drippings
 from bacon or other
 fat meat
¾ lb. sausage, rolled in
 1" balls
Thick brown gravy or
 tomato sauce

Mix vegetable extract with water. Put flour in a large shallow bowl; add salt. Make a well in the center and break the eggs into it. Gradually mix together the flour, eggs, and half the water. Beat until quite smooth, and then add remaining water. Let stand at room temperature for at least 1 hour before proceeding. Heat the drippings in a flat 2-quart ovenproof casserole in a preheated 425° oven until smoking hot. Remove from oven, pour in the batter, and drop in the sausage balls. Return to oven and bake for 50 minutes, reducing the oven temperature to 350° after the first 15 minutes. Serve with thick brown gravy or tomato sauce. Makes 4 to 6 servings.

– Jeanna Horwitz (Mrs. Harry)

» Medaillon de Veau au Beurre d'Avocat «

Medallions of Veal with Avocado Butter

Pigall's is one of Cincinnati's four-star French restaurants, featuring superb French cuisine served in an elegant and intimate setting.

2 ripe avocados, peeled and seeded	6-4 oz. veal medallions
½ cup unsalted butter, softened	½ cup olive oil
	1 lb. mushrooms, sliced
Juice of 2 lemons	¼ cup dry white wine
Salt and pepper	Julienne of fresh vegetables, for garnish

Purée avocado, butter, lemon juice, salt, and pepper together until very smooth. Lightly flour the veal and sauté in the oil about 10 to 12 minutes. Remove from pan and keep warm. Discard oil. Add avocado purée, mushrooms, and wine. Sauté for 5 minutes, or until butter is completely melted. Pour over veal, and garnish with julienne of fresh vegetables. Makes 6 servings.

– Chef de Cuisine Otis Sherrer
Pigall's French Restaurant

» Vitello alla Fiorentina «

This exquisite veal in the style of Florence, Italy, could be preceded by a first course of fettuccine tossed with heavy cream and butter, or tortelloni topped with a fresh tomato cream sauce.

3 tablespoons flour	1 lemon slice
1 teaspoon salt	¾ cup onions, chopped
⅛ teaspoon pepper	2 tablespoons parsley, minced
1½ lbs. veal scallops, pounded until ¼" thick	1 cup mushrooms, sliced
¼ cup olive oil	¾ cup dry white wine
1 clove garlic, minced	¾ cup chicken broth

Combine flour, salt, and pepper; dip veal into mixture until covered on all sides. Sauté veal in oil in a heavy sauté pan; when veal is almost browned, add garlic and sauté until veal and garlic are lightly browned. Reduce heat and add lemon slice, onions, parsley, and mushrooms. Combine wine and broth; add ⅓ of the mixture to the pan. Cover and simmer gently for 25 to 30 minutes, adding wine and broth as needed to keep sauce from becoming too thick. Correct seasonings and serve at once. Makes 6 servings.

– Sue Cahill

» Veal Florentine with Sauce Choron «

Boiled new potatoes are a pleasant accompaniment to this veal dish. Choron Sauce is a variation on the French standard, hollandaise, which calls for the addition of tomato.

3 tablespoons sweet butter	2 tablespoons dry white wine
2 cloves garlic	2 tablespoons tarragon vinegar
2 tablespoons leeks, minced	2 teaspoons shallots or onions, minced
⅓ cup sweet red peppers, diced	3 egg yolks
½ lb. mushrooms, sliced	½ cup sweet butter
4 veal scallops, ¼" thick	3 tablespoons tomato paste at room temperature
¾ cup dry white wine	
½ tablespoon superfine flour	Salt and pepper
2 cups fresh spinach	Parsley, optional

Melt 3 tablespoons butter with garlic cloves. Sauté leeks in 1 tablespoon of this butter until very lightly browned. Add red peppers and continue cooking until tender. Set aside. Sauté mushrooms in 1 tablespoon butter; set aside with above. Sauté veal in 1 tablespoon butter 1 minute on each side; remove from pan. Add juices from leeks, peppers, and mushrooms, meat juice, and ¾ cup wine to skillet. Deglaze pan and simmer until reduced one half. Thicken with flour. Return meat to pan and coat with sauce. Top with reserved leeks, peppers, and mushrooms; simmer 3 minutes. Meanwhile, steam spinach lightly with salt and pepper to taste. You may do this by cooking it in a heavy, covered pan over medium heat, using just the water that clings to it from washing. Serve the veal with seasoned spinach topped with Sauce Choron. To make sauce, simmer wine, vinegar, and shallots or onions until 1 tablespoon liquid remains. Place in food processor with steel blade and process with egg yolks, switching on and off quickly. Heat butter to boiling. With processor running, add butter in a steady stream. This should take less than a minute. Add tomato paste; turn on and off immediately. Correct seasoning and add parsley, if desired. Keep warm over hot, not boiling, water until ready to serve. Makes 4 servings.

– Barbara Rosenberg (Mrs. Berton)

» Roast Veal Dijon «

Be sure to use the finest white milk-fed veal for the best results. The French use veal between 5 and 12 weeks old, before the animal begins to eat grain or grass.

2 to 3 lb. leg of veal, boned and rolled	*10½ oz. can chicken consommé*
½ cup butter, melted	*¼ cup sherry*
8 oz. jar Dijon-type mustard	*Chopped parsley, for garnish*

Place veal in a shallow roasting pan. Blend butter and mustard well and pour over veal, covering all sides. Roast in a preheated 300° oven for 4 hours. During the final hour, baste every 20 minutes with a mixture of the consommé and sherry. Remove meat from oven and cover loosely with foil. Let meat rest in a warm place for 20 minutes before carving. Meanwhile, deglaze roasting pan and reduce liquid to make a gravy for the roast, adding flour or arrowroot to thicken, if necessary. Garnish with chopped parsley before serving. Makes 4 to 6 servings.

– Dottie Kreeger (Mrs. John)

» Veal Morels «

8-6 oz. veal steaks from top round or loin	*3 ozs. Cognac brandy*
1/4 lb. butter	*5 ozs. Madeira wine*
1 lb. fresh morels, or 1/4 lb. dry morels	*1 cup whipping cream*
	Salt and pepper
1 oz. shallots	*2 tablespoons fresh parsley, chopped*

In a heavy skillet, sauté the veal steak in half the butter. Brown on both sides. Remove and keep hot. Add the remaining butter to the skillet and sauté the morels. Add the shallots. Cook for two minutes. Deglaze with Cognac

and Madeira; reduce for 2 minutes. Add the cream, salt, and pepper; reduce until the sauce is slightly thickened. Add chopped parsley and pour over veal. Makes 8 servings.

*– Chef de Cuisine George Haidon
Maisonette Restaurant*

» Medallions of Veal Celestial «

When Cincinnatians sit in the glass-enclosed Celestial Restaurant atop Mt. Adams and watch the sunset overr downtown Cincinnati as they dine, they're continuing a tradition that dates back to 1875, when a huge restaurant and beer garden called the Highland House was opened on the site. It is said that evening crowds numbering as many as 8,000 people rode the incline railway up the steep hill to dine elegantly to classical music or to quaff a beer with friends. The Highland Towers, a modern, high-rise apartment building in which the Celestial is located, was named after the famous restaurant.

3 lbs. boneless leg of veal, cut into 24 medallions, slightly pounded	*½ cup white wine*
	Salt and pepper
	½ lb. cooked crabmeat
2 tablespoons butter	*2 large ripe avocados, peeled*
1 pint whipping cream	
1 pinch thyme	*1 lb. Swiss cheese, sliced*
1 pinch cayenne pepper	*Watercress for garnish*
1 bay leaf	

Sauté medallions of veal in butter until lightly browned. Remove veal from the pan. Add to the pan the cream, thyme, cayenne pepper, bay leaf, and white wine; allow to reduce over medium heat. Season with salt and pepper to taste; remove bay leaf. On ovenproof dinner plate, arrange 3 medallions of veal per person. Top with 1 oz. of chunked crabmeat, 3 thin slices of avocado, and the white wine sauce. Place 2 thin slices of Swiss cheese diagonally over the entree and brown under broiler, or in the oven. Garnish each dish with a sprig of watercress. Complement the veal with such vegetables as baby Belgian carrots and wild rice. Makes 8 servings.

– Celestial Restaurant, Highland Towers

» Ossobuco «

This famous Italian braised veal dish came from Milan, where it is often served with the equally famous risotto – rice flavored with saffron and Parmesan cheese. It's good with spaghetti, too.

4 ossibuchi – 1½" long crosswise cuts of meaty veal shanks with bone and marrow	1 cup water
	¼ cup tomato paste
	2 carrots, sliced
	2 medium onions, sliced
Salt and freshly ground pepper	3 tablespoons parsley, chopped
Flour	2 cloves garlic, minced
½ cup butter	Juice of ½ lemon
1½ cups broth	Risotto or spaghetti
1 cup red wine	

Tie each ossobuco with string to hold the meat in place around the bone during cooking. Salt and pepper the meat and roll in flour. Melt the butter in a large saucepan and brown the shanks. Add the liquids and tomato paste. Cover and cook over medium heat for 45 minutes. Add the rest of the ingredients except risotto or spaghetti; cook 45 minutes longer, uncovering the pot the last 10 minutes to thicken the sauce. Serve with risotto or spaghetti. Makes 4 servings.

– *Eunice Gronauer (Mrs. Raymond)*

» Piccata di Vitello «

The piquant lemon juice gives this veal in lemon and wine sauce a freshly light touch.

1½ lb. veal scallops, cut ⅜" thick	½ cup white wine
	1 lb. mushrooms, sautéed, reserve juices
Salt	
Pepper	1 tablespoon lemon juice
Flour	3 tablespoons capers
2 tablespoons butter	¼ cup parsley, chopped
2 tablespoons olive oil	1 lemon, thinly sliced

Pound veal to ¼" thickness between two pieces of waxed paper. Sprinkle with salt, pepper, and flour. Melt butter and olive oil in skillet. Sauté veal in a single layer for 1 minute. Turn and cook on second side. Remove to platter and continue until all veal is cooked. Pour off excess fat. Pour wine, mushroom juice, and lemon juice into skillet; deglaze pan, cooking and scraping the bottom of the pan to loosen any caramelized juices from the veal. Simmer to reduce to 1 cup. Add capers and reserved mushrooms. Return meat to skillet and simmer 3 minutes, or until tender. If desired, thicken pan juices with a little flour sprinkled over. Sprinkle with parsley and garnish with lemon slices. Makes 4 servings.

– *Barbara Rosenberg (Mrs. Berton)*

» Veal Patties with Mushroom Cream Gravy «

1½ lbs. ground veal	2 tablespoons flour
2 tablespoons onion, chopped	¼ cup butter
	1 cup mushrooms, sliced
Salt and pepper	½ cup half and half cream
1 teaspoon thyme	2 tablespoons parsley, chopped
Dash of nutmeg	

Mix veal, onion, salt, pepper, thyme, and nutmeg. Make into patties and flour lightly. Melt 2 tablespoons butter in skillet until bubbling. Add patties and cook briefly, about 5 minutes on each side. Remove patties from skillet and keep warm in oven. Wipe skillet clean; add remaining butter; sauté mushrooms for about 6 minutes. Add cream, stir well, and add parsley. Remove veal patties from oven. Place on serving plate and pour mushroom cream gravy over patties. Makes 6 servings.

– *Anne Ziebarth (Mrs. John)*

» Scallopini of Veal with Lemon Zest «

Lemon lends a snappy twist to the Parmesan crumbs coating this Italian delicacy.

1 lb. veal scallops	1½ teaspoons salt
1 cup flour	½ teaspoon pepper
2 cups fresh bread crumbs	3 eggs
1 cup Parmesan or Romano cheese, freshly grated	3 tablespoons water
	¼ cup butter
3 tablespoons lemon zest, grated	¼ cup olive oil
	Watercress
	Parsley

Pound veal scallops very thin. Cut into 2"x2" pieces. Dry between paper towels and powder with flour, shaking off excess. Set aside. Combine crumbs, cheese, lemon zest, salt, and pepper in a flat plate. Lightly beat eggs and water together in a shallow bowl. Heat butter and olive oil together in a heavy sauté pan until bubbling. Dip veal scallops first in egg wash and then bread crumb mixture. Sauté about 2 minutes on each side or until lightly browned. May be kept warm in a low oven for up to 30 minutes. Serve on a platter garnished with watercress and parsley. Makes 12 servings.

– Lu Dixon (Mrs. J. Gordon)

» Veal Scallopini with Mushrooms «

The Italians have an infinite number of ways to prepare boneless, thin slices of veal. This marriage with mushrooms is an especially appealing one.

2 lbs. veal scallops, cut in	*or white wine*
thin rounds	*1 lb. fresh mushrooms,*
Flour	*sliced*
Salt and freshly ground	*2/3 cup whipping cream*
pepper	*Fresh parsley, chopped*
2 tablespoons olive oil	*Parmesan cheese, freshly*
1/2 cup butter	*grated*
4 to 6 tablespoons cognac	*Saffron rice*

Pound veal with wooden mallet until paper thin. Lightly flour and sprinkle with salt and pepper to taste. Heat olive oil and half the butter. When pan is hot, sauté veal on both sides until meat begins to turn white around the edges. Remove and keep warm. If using cognac, add to sauté pan and when warm, ignite carefully with match and let burn until flame dies. If using wine, heat until boiling. Add remaining butter. Sauté mushrooms briefly; add cream. Heat until almost boiling. Place veal on a serving platter. Top with mushrooms, sauce, parsley, and Parmesan cheese. Serve with saffron rice. Makes 8 servings.

– Marilyn Reichert (Mrs. David)

» Veal Scallopini with Roquefort Sauce «

French cuisine, so it is said, was uninspiring until Catherine de Medici married the Dauphin and brought her Florentine cooks to the court. The buttery texture of the veal and the rich bite of Roquefort cheese combine to make this modern combination of French and Italian a superb offering.

8 to 10 veal scallops	*1 to 1 1/2 cups whipping*
6 tablespoons butter	*cream*
1 cup dry white wine or	*1/4 lb. Roquefort or bleu*
dry vermouth	*cheese*
	1/2 cup butter, softened

Pound the veal until it is paper thin. Sauté veal in butter, 1 minute on each side. Set aside and keep warm. Simmer the white wine or vermouth until reduced to approximately 2 tablespoons. Add cream and reduce the mixture again to 1/2. In the meantime, blend the Roquefort and butter until smooth. Add it, little by little, to the simmering wine and cream mixture until well combined. Put through a sieve or blend in a blender or food processor; pour over the scallopini and serve. Sauce may be prepared ahead of time and reheated in a double boiler. Makes 6 servings.

– Andreas Nomikos
Greensboro, North Carolina

» Weisswurst «

Weisswurst is a small, white, spicy but unsmoked veal sausage that is a specialty of Munich. Bratwurst may be substituted.

8 weisswurst	*1 teaspoon herbs: thyme,*
2 tablespoons unsalted	*basil, rosemary*
butter	*1/2 cup apple juice or*
2 slices bacon, diced	*apple cider*
4 cups onions, sliced	*2 tart apples, thinly sliced*
2 cloves garlic, minced	*Salt and pepper*
1/2 cup dry white wine	*2 tablespoons parsley,*
	minced

Prick sausage with fork. Sauté in butter in skillet until brown, about 8 minutes. Drain on paper towel. Add bacon and onions to skillet; sauté until bacon is brown and onions are transparent. Add garlic and herbs; sauté 2 more minutes. Add wine, bring to boil, cook 3 minutes, and stir in cider. Replace the sausage, cover, and simmer 10 minutes; add apple slices and cook 10 more minutes. Add salt and pepper to taste. Sprinkle with parsley. Makes 6 to 8 servings.

» Wiener Schnitzel «

This specialty from Vienna, or Wien, may also be garnished with hard-cooked egg, anchovies, and olives. A schnitzel is a little slice or cutlet.

4 veal cutlets, no more than ¼" thick	1 egg, beaten with 2 tablespoons milk
1 teaspoon salt	1 cup fine bread crumbs
¼ cup flour	2 tablespoons oil
	1 lemon, sliced

Place veal between two pieces of waxed paper and use wooden meat mallet to pound cutlets thin. Salt both sides lightly and powder with flour. Dip into egg/milk mixture, then into bread crumbs. Place on waxed paper and refrigerate 5 minutes. Melt oil in large skillet. Add veal and saute both sides over medium heat until golden brown, about 10 to 15 minutes. Serve hot with lemon slices. Makes 4 servings.

» Beef with Beer «

This is an interesting variation of the traditional Belgian Carbonnade Flamande or beer stew. The piquant mustard adds a distinctive flair.

3½ lbs. beef chuck, cut into ½" cubes	2 tablespoons parsley, minced
2 cloves garlic, minced	½ teaspoon thyme
1 medium onion, chopped	½ teaspoon rosemary
2 tablespoons oil	1 bay leaf, crumbled
½ lb. mushrooms, sliced	4 to 6 slices soft French bread
1 teaspoon salt	
½ teaspoon freshly ground black pepper	Dijon mustard
	12 ozs. beer

Brown chuck, garlic, and onion in oil in a heavy pan over medium heat. Mix with mushrooms, salt, pepper, parsley, thyme, rosemary, and bay leaf. Place in a

heatproof casserole. Spread mustard on bread and place on top of beef mixture, mustard side up. Use enough bread to completely cover the meat mixture. Pour beer over and allow it to soak into bread. Bake in a preheated 300° oven for 1½ hours, basting several times while cooking. Makes 6 to 8 servings.

– Suzanne Cahill

» New Year's Stew «

A New Year's night buffet has become a tradition at my house. It's a laid-back evening, meant for recuperation from excesses of New Year's Eve, and by request, the menu has been the same for the past several years. Preparation should, ideally, begin 2 to 3 days ahead. The stew is better reheated, and it involves a good many steps.

4 lbs. boneless pork loin roast	Salt and pepper
½ cup olive oil or unsalted butter, divided	4 teaspoons bouquet garni
	1 cup beef stock
2 tablespoons garlic, crushed	Water to cover beef
	4 large onions, puréed
2 tablespoons dried rosemary leaves, crushed	1 bunch celery, very thinly sliced
6 lbs. boneless beef chuck, cut in 1" cubes	2 lbs. carrots, very thinly sliced
½ cup flour, or more if needed, for dredging beef	2 lbs. Kielbasa or other good quality cased sausage, cut into ½" slices
	Additional butter or oil

Rub pork loin with a paste of 1 tablespoon olive oil, garlic, and rosemary. Wrap tightly in aluminum foil and refrigerate overnight. Remove from refrigerator. Roast at 325° for 2 hours. Cool. Cut in 2" cubes. Refrigerate until ready to use. Divide beef into 4 equal parts. Dredge beef in flour and brown in remaining oil or butter, in 4 batches. When each batch is well-browned, season with salt, pepper, and 1 teaspoon of bouquet garni. Remove last batch of beef from skillet. Add beef stock to skillet and deglaze the pan. Transfer beef and deglazing liquid to a large Dutch oven. Add water just to cover the beef. Cover and cook beef in a 325° oven for 1 hour. Add the puréed onions and cook for ½ hour. Add celery and carrots; cook beef until fork-tender. Remove from oven.

Stir in cubes of roast pork. Stew can now be refrigerated until a few hours before serving. I generally make it 2 days ahead. Several hours before serving, allow stew to come to room temperature. Meantime, sauté the Kielbasa slices in butter or oil, drain, and add to stew. Cook until bubbling. All you need now is dry red wine, a green salad, and crusty bread. Makes 24 servings.

– Charles E. Bolton

» Estofado «
Philippines Beef Stew

1 lb. boneless beef, cubed or left whole	1 bay leaf
¼ cup flour	Water
Salt and pepper to taste	6 small whole onions, peeled
½ cup vegetable oil	
2 cloves garlic, mashed	2 cups green beans
2 onions, finely chopped	2 carrots, quartered
1 cup tomatoes, peeled, seeded, and chopped	2 tablespoons cornstarch, dissolved in ¼ cup water

Rub beef with flour, salt, and pepper. Sauté in oil until brown on all sides. Remove beef from oil and sauté garlic until golden. Add onions and tomatoes; cover and simmer 5 minutes. Add reserved beef, bay leaf, and water to cover. Correct seasonings, bring to a boil, and simmer, covered, until meat is tender. Add whole onions, green beans, and carrots; cook until vegetables are tender. Remove beef to serving platter and surround with vegetables; keep warm. Stir cornstarch and water mixture into sauce and cook, stirring, until thickened. Spoon sauce over beef and vegetables and serve at once. Makes 6 servings.

– Nellie Obial (Mrs. Gaudencio)

» Hungarian Goulash «

Hungarian paprika is fiery red, but sweet and mildly pungent. It is made from the ground capsicum pepper, often blended with other varieties which grow especially well in Hungarian soil.

1½ cups onions, chopped	1 teaspoon marjoram
4 tablespoons oil	1 teaspoon cloves
4 lbs. chuck, cut into 1" pieces	¼ cup lemon juice
	Salt
1 clove garlic, minced	1 cup tomato juice
2 teaspoons paprika, preferably Hungarian	8 oz. pkg. noodles, cooked
1 teaspoon ginger	4 tablespoons butter
½ teaspoon pepper	1 tablespoon caraway seeds

Sauté onions in oil until transparent. Remove onion and brown meat cubes in remaining oil. Add onions, garlic, paprika, ginger, pepper, marjoram, cloves, lemon juice, salt to taste, and tomato juice. Simmer over low heat for 1½ hours. Cook noodles in salted water according to directions on package. Drain and toss with butter and caraway seeds. Serve goulash over noodles. Makes 8 servings.

– Barbara Wagner (Mrs. James H.)

» St. Nicholas French Stew «

The old St. Nicholas Hotel was built in 1865 at the corner of 4th and Race Streets in Cincinnnati. In 1911, it was sold and became the Sinton Hotel, since razed. The St. Nicholas was an elegant hotel and one of the most popular dishes served was their French Stew. This is the recipe as it appeared in the Cincinnati Enquirer in 1932.

1½ lbs. stewing lamb, breast, neck or sides boned and cut into 1" cubes	4 onions, thinly sliced or diced
	1 leek
2 tablespoons fat	1 bay leaf
10 oz. can tomato purée	Pinch allspice
4 carrots, diced	6 small new potatoes or potato balls
1 stalk celery, chopped	

Brown the lamb very slowly in the heated fat, allowing about 15 minutes for cooking. Season well with salt and pepper; add the tomato purée. Cover tightly and cook slowly for half an hour. No water is added, as the meat will furnish liquid if covered closely. Add carrots, celery, onions, leek, bay leaf, and allspice. Cover and cook for 1½ hours. Add the potatoes 25 minutes before serving time; cook until tender. Makes 6 servings.

» Sauté de Lapin au Vin «

The French call a rabbit stew a sauté, and this rabbit in wine sauce is a delicious example of a classic.

1 rabbit, about 3 lbs., cut
   into 6 pieces
Salt and pepper
¼ cup olive oil
½ teaspoon thyme
½ teaspoon tarragon
1 bay leaf
2 teaspoons parsley
2 chopped shallots

1 tablespoon wine vinegar
   or lemon juice
½ cup dry red
   or white wine
Flour
1 tablespoon butter
½ cup additional wine
1 cup beef bouillon or
   more wine to provide
   more sauce

Marinate rabbit overnight or longer with salt, pepper, olive oil, thyme, tarragon, bay leaf, parsley, shallots, vinegar, and wine. Remove rabbit pieces from marinade. Dip in flour and brown on all sides in butter in an iron skillet, adding more butter if necessary. Add marinade and additional wine. Cover and cook about 45 minutes, adding beef bouillon or more wine gradually. Check seasonings, and serve at once. Makes 6 servings.

– Mrs. George Whitman

*A. de Loarte, ca. 1622-1626, Spanish, "Still Life," oil on canvas,
1956.10. Bequest of Mrs. Frieda Hauch, by exchange*

» Philippine Pork Stew «

3 cloves garlic, mashed
1 medium onion, sliced
3 tomatoes, peeled, seeded, and diced
¼ cup peanut oil
2½ cups lean pork, diced
1 cup pork liver, diced
½ cup water
1 teaspoon salt
½ teaspoon pimientos, optional
3 potatoes, peeled and diced
⅓ cup dried garbanzo beans

Sauté garlic, onion, and tomatoes in peanut oil until onions are transparent. Do not allow garlic to brown. Add pork and pork liver; continue sautéing for 5 minutes. Add water, salt, pimientos, potatoes, and garbanzos. Cook until potatoes and garbanzos are tender. Makes 8 servings.

– Nellie Obial (Mrs. Guadencio)

» Veal Stew «

½ cup butter
2 lbs. boneless veal, cut in 1" cubes
1 medium onion, finely chopped
1 clove garlic, crushed, or ¼ teaspoon garlic powder
1 teaspoon salt
1 teaspoon pepper
1 lb. fresh mushrooms
1 cup beef bouillon
2-8 oz. cans water chestnuts, drained and sliced
¼ teaspoon nutmeg
1 bay leaf
2 cups whipping cream
¼ cup cognac, optional
¼ cup parsley, chopped

In a heavy skillet, melt ¼ cup butter. When bubbling, stir in veal; brown. Remove veal and place in an ovenproof casserole. Sauté onions and garlic in skillet until golden brown. Add to veal and season with salt and pepper. Melt remaining ¼ cup of butter in skillet and sauté mushrooms briefly. Add mushrooms to veal. Gently stir in beef bouillon, water chestnuts, nutmeg, and bay leaf. Cover casserole and bake at 375° for 1 to 1½ hours, or until veal is fork tender. Remove from oven, discard bay leaf. Slowly stir in whipping cream. Return to oven, uncovered, and reheat for 15 minutes. Before serving, add cognac, if desired, and stir in chopped parsley. Makes 6 servings.

– Stephen Birmingham

» Stifado «

The aromatic spices give this beef stew an unusual and distinctively Greek flavor. It is delicious when served with crisp bread and a fresh green salad.

3 lbs. lean stew beef, cut into 1½" cubes
Salt and freshly ground pepper
½ cup butter
2½ lbs. small onions, peeled
6 oz. can tomato paste
⅓ cup dry red wine
2 tablespoons red wine vinegar
1 tablespoon brown sugar
1 clove garlic, minced
1 bay leaf
1 small cinnamon stick
½ teaspoon whole cloves
½ teaspoon ground cumin

Season meat with salt and pepper to taste. Melt butter in Dutch oven or heavy kettle with cover. Add meat and coat with butter, but do not brown. Arrange onions over meat. Mix tomato paste, wine, vinegar, sugar, and garlic; pour over meat and onions. Add bay leaf, cinnamon, cloves, and cumin. Cover onions with an ovenproof plate in order to keep them intact. Cover kettle and simmer 3 hours, or until meat is very tender. Do not stir. As you serve, stir sauce gently to blend. Makes 4 to 6 servings.

– Mrs. Pat Rutledge
Cincinnati Art Museum

» Zucchini Stew «

1 lb. lean ground beef
1 lb. hot Italian sausage, bulk or with casings removed
2 cups Italian whole tomatoes
2 cups celery, chopped
1 cup onion, chopped
1 teaspoon pepper
2 lbs. zucchini, chopped
Salt
1 teaspoon Italian seasoning
1 tablespoon oregano
Cooked noodles or rice
½ cup fresh Parmesan cheese, grated

Brown beef and sausage in a heavy sauté pan; drain excess fat. Add next eight ingredients; simmer until zucchini is tender but not mushy. Serve over noodles or rice, and sprinkle with Parmesan. Makes 10 servings.

– Mary Ann Shaffer

» Sweetbreads and Ham «

3 pairs sweetbreads
Cold water
1 quart water mixed with
   1 tablespoon vinegar
Ice water
4 tablespoons butter
2 cups ham, cubed
1 green pepper, seeded
   and thinly sliced
½ lb. fresh mushrooms,
   sliced
Salt and pepper
1 cup whipping cream,
   unwhipped
½ cup dry sherry
1 tablespoon flour
Pastry shells or toast

Sweetbreads should be cooked as soon as you bring them home. Soak them for 1 hour in cold water to release any blood, changing water several times; drain. Put sweetbreads in saucepan in water/vinegar mixture; bring slowly to a boil, lower heat, and simmer about 10 minutes. Drain sweetbreads in a colander and pour ice-cold water over them. When they are cool and drained, remove all connective tissue and covering. Refrigerate at once until ready to cook. Cut cooked sweetbreads into 1″ pieces. Melt butter in a large saucepan. Add sweetbreads, ham, and green pepper. Cook over medium heat, about 10 minutes, stirring frequently. Add mushrooms and cook a few minutes longer. Season with salt and pepper. In a skillet, combine cream and sherry, heat slightly, and add flour. Stir well and blend into the sweetbread mixture. Cook over low heat for about 10 minutes. Do not boil. Serve in pastry shells or over toast. Makes 6 to 8 servings.

– Karen Rafuse (Mrs. Peter B.)

» Kidney and Mushroom Toast «

Kidneys and mushrooms are a favorite combination in the British Isles. The toast soaks up the delicious juices in this breakfast or luncheon dish.

4 lamb kidneys
Salt and pepper
½ cup flour
¼ cup butter
2 cups mushrooms, sliced
1 cup chicken stock
½ teaspoon
   Worcestershire sauce
4 slices toast
Chopped parsley

Remove skin and core from kidneys and slice them. Season with salt and pepper to taste and dredge with ½ of flour. Melt butter in a heavy pan; sauté kidneys and mushrooms for a few minutes, sprinkling with remaining flour. Add stock and Worcestershire sauce and cook, stirring, for about 5 minutes, or until sauce is thickened and kidneys are tender. Divide and place on toast. Sprinkle with parsley before serving. Makes 4 servings.

» Ris de Veau, Madeira «
Sweetbreads with Madeira Wine

4 large veal sweetbreads
3 bay leaves
Flour
6 tablespoons butter
1 lb. fresh mushrooms,
   sliced
2 large shallots, minced
1 cup Madeira wine
½ cup brown stock or
   consommé
Salt and pepper
Whipping cream, optional

Trim sweetbreads of tissue and membranes. Cover with cold water, add bay leaves and simmer 10 minutes. Refresh in cold water and dry. Slice and dust with flour. Melt butter in a heavy sauté pan and cook sweetbreads, turning them until they are light in color, being careful not to burn butter. Add mushrooms, shallots, Madeira, and stock. Simmer slowly until done, about 20 minutes; correct seasonings. Add cream if desired; bring to a boil and serve immediately. Makes 4 servings.

– Chef Bruno Fatino
The Met Club, Tequesta, Florida

*Black-figured Amphora attributed to the
Swing Painter, painted and incised terra-cotta, Greek, Attic,
ca. 540 B.C., 1959.1. Museum Purchase.
This color reproduction donated by Dr. and Mrs. George M. Callard*

Among the practical purposes for Greek vases was their use for storage of food and drink. Wine was kept in slip-painted vases of this shape, called amphorae, with two handles close to the mouth. The human inclination to decorate the things we use means that such works give as much pleasure to moderns as they presumably did to the Greeks. This is a fine, late example of the black-figured style, attributed to the Swing Painter, whose deftly handled details were first identified in a portrayal of a girl in a swing. Humor is an unusual element, for Greek vase painters, which also marks the work of the Swing Painter. Here he shows a scene requiring the suspension of disbelief asked by cartoonists. Herakles, on the verge of being sacrificed by the Egyptian ruler, Busiris, rises up in his lion skin, smartly dispatches the unfriendly king and turns on his captors, grasping one priest by the neck and another by the ankle. Apparently they will serve as weapons in the absence of Herakles' usual club and bow. White and a deep red as well as black form the picture, with tiny incised markings to suggest fabric patterns and the hair and beards of those involved in this animated moment.

Poultry and Seafood

» Chicken Breast for One «

You may increase this recipe to as many people as you want to serve. Oven time for a larger quantity will be slightly longer. This chicken, served with salad and fruit, makes a nutritious and easy meal.

1 boned chicken breast half	½-10 oz. can chicken broth
¼ teaspoon dried tarragon	¼ cup sherry or dry white wine
Salt and pepper	
1 tablespoon butter	½ cup medium thin noodles

Wash and dry chicken breast. Season with tarragon and salt and pepper to taste. Put in small casserole. Dot with butter and add chicken broth and wine. Place, covered, in a preheated 350° oven for 10 minutes. Turn chicken breast over; add noodles, and cook for about 10 more minutes, or until chicken and noodles are tender. Makes 1 serving.

— Margaret Minster (Mrs. Leonard)

» Chilaquiles «

This layered Mexican tortilla dish may be made ahead and heated at the last minute for a hearty buffet.

18 corn tortillas	3 Jalapeno chiles
1 cup lard or peanut oil	Salt and pepper
1 medium onion, peeled and quartered	4 chicken breasts
	Chicken broth
4 sprigs of cilantro	1 cup whipping cream
10 oz. can Mexican tomatillos, undrained	⅔ cup Parmesan cheese, grated

Slice tortillas into ½″ strips and fry in lard or oil in a heavy iron skillet for a few minutes; do not brown. Drain on paper towels and reserve. Place onion, cilantro, tomatillos and juice, and chiles in the port of a food processor; chop finely. Season with salt and pepper; sauté in a heavy skillet for 5 to 10 minutes, until sauce becomes reduced and thickened. Meanwhile, poach chicken breasts until tender in boiling broth to cover. Skin, bone, and cut or pull into shreds. Oil a shallow 2-quart casserole; place a layer of the tomatilla sauce in the bottom. Top with a layer of the tortilla strips, and top with ½ of the cream. Add the chicken, the rest of the sauce, the remaining cream, and sprinkle with cheese. Bake in a preheated 350° oven for 20 to 30 minutes, or until hot and bubbling and the cheese is lightly browned. Makes 8 to 10 servings.

— Mary Courter (Mrs. Sanford)

» Chicken with Bing Cherries «

4 large half chicken breasts, skinned and boned	¼ cup flour
	¼ cup butter
	16 oz. can Bing cherries
Salt and pepper	2 tablespoons cornstarch

Sprinkle each breast with salt and pepper to taste; roll in flour, coating evenly. Melt butter in a heavy pan and saute breasts over medium heat until they are golden and done. This should take 10 to 15 minutes; juices inside breasts will be clear when they are pricked with a fork. Remove them from pan and keep warm until serving time. Meanwhile, place cherries and juice in a pan, reserving ¼ cup of the juice. Bring the cherries and juice to a boil and add the reserved juice which has been mixed with the cornstarch. Simmer for a few minutes, until the sauce thickens and is transparent. Spoon cherries and sauce over chicken breasts and serve at once. Makes 4 servings.

– Stanley Demos
Coach House Restaurant, Lexington, Kentucky
From his book, "Stanley Suggests"

» Chicken Cacciatore «

This Italian-American Hunter's Stew has many variations, but this version is my family's favorite.

4 chicken breast halves	1 medium green pepper,
2 or 3 green onions,	cut into strips
chopped	½ lb. fresh mushrooms,
3 cups water	sliced
Pinch salt	¼ cup olive oil
1 clove garlic, minced	8 oz. can tomato sauce
1 tablespoon basil	¼ cup dry white wine
1 tablespoon oregano	1 teaspoon salt
1 tablespoon parsley,	½ teaspoon pepper
minced	1 cup pitted black olives
1 medium onion, cut into	
strips	

Place chicken breasts, green onions, water, and salt in a heavy skillet. Bring the water to a boil, cover loosely, and cook for 7 minutes. Remove the pan from heat and let the chicken cool in the broth for 5 minutes. Meanwhile, sauté garlic, basil, oregano, parsley, onion, green pepper, and mushrooms in olive oil in a heavy pan until the vegetables are soft, about 10 minutes. Add tomato sauce, wine, salt, and pepper; simmer over low heat for an additional 15 minutes. Meanwhile, remove the chicken from the broth; remove the meat from the bones, discarding skin. Add chicken and olives to the tomato mixture; continue simmering for another 10 minutes. Serve with buttered pasta or rice, a green salad, and hot garlic bread. Makes 4 servings.

– Nina Rogers (Mrs. Millard F., Jr.)

» Curried Chicken Breasts «

8 split chicken breasts	cubed, with seeds
1 large onion, diced	removed
2 or 3 carrots, peeled and	1 large apple, peeled,
sliced	cored and cubed
2 stalks celery with	½ cup golden raisins
leaves, sliced	1 cup cream of chicken
Small bunch of parsley	soup
½ teaspoon salt	2 tablespoons raisins
1 medium sweet potato,	2 tablespoons whole
peeled and cubed	almonds, toasted
1 cucumber, peeled and	1 teaspoon curry powder
	Steamed rice

Place chicken breasts in pan with enough water to barely cover. Add onion, carrots, celery, parsley, and salt. Simmer, covered, until tender. Cool chicken in broth. Remove chicken; using 1½ cups of the broth, simmer sweet potato, cucumber, apple, and ½ cup raisins until tender; blend or whirl in food processor until smooth. Skin and bone chicken breasts and separate into large shredded pieces. Mix cream of chicken soup with 1 soup-can of the sweet potato/cucumber/applesauce mixture; add shredded chicken, 2 tablespoons raisins, almonds, and curry. Simmer over low fire for a few minutes, stirring constantly. Cool and layer in an ovenproof casserole with the remaining sweet potato/cucumber/ applesauce mixture. This should be done ahead and refrigerated a few hours or overnight to marinate properly. Bake 30 to 40 minutes in a preheated 400° oven. Serve over rice with bowls of desired condiments which may include (chopped peanuts, coconut, chives, chutney, kumquats, chopped hard-cooked egg, sliced bananas, grapes, or orange segments. Makes 8 servings.

– Launcey Roder (Mrs. Frank)

» Chicken with Sherry Sauce «

2 whole chicken breasts,	1 teaspoon salt
split, skin removed	1 teaspoon white pepper
2 cups herb-seasoned	¼ cup parsley, coarsely
stuffing mix	chopped
1 cup grated Parmesan	½ cup butter, melted
cheese	Sherry Sauce
1 teaspoon garlic powder	

Rinse and wipe dry chicken breasts. Process herb mix in a blender or food processor until the crumbs are fine and uniform. Mix with Parmesan cheese, garlic powder, salt, pepper, and parsley. Dip chicken breasts in butter and roll in the crumb mixture, pressing crumbs into chicken on both sides. Place chicken in a shallow, foil-lined pan, taking care not to let pieces overlap. Bake in preheated 350° oven for approximately 1 hour. Check after 50 minutes to see that chicken is not too brown. Serve with Sherry Sauce. Makes 4 servings.

Sherry Sauce

1 teaspoon cornstarch	1½ cups chicken broth
½ cup cooking sherry	Parsley

Mix cornstarch with sherry. Combine with broth and cook for 1 minute, stirring constantly. Chop parsley and add for garnish.

– Fanny Smith (Mrs. George R.)

» Chicken Breasts with Herb Stuffing «

The sauce is delightful to serve with chicken, and it's great over other dishes as well.

4 whole chicken breasts, split just enough to fold	2 tablespoons parsley, chopped
¼ cup flour	¼ teaspoon poultry seasoning
½ teaspoon salt	½ cup butter, melted
Dash of pepper	¼ cup chicken stock or bouillon
¼ teaspoon paprika	Mushroom Sauce
2 cups dry bread crumbs	
1 tablespoon onion, chopped	

Wash and pat dry chicken breasts. Combine flour, salt, pepper and paprika in a paper or plastic bag. Add chicken breasts and shake to cover. Mix dry bread crumbs, onion, parsley, poultry seasoning, 2 tablespoons melted butter, and chicken stock. Season with salt and pepper to taste. Fill breasts with this stuffing. Then pour remainder of melted butter over the breasts. Bake in preheated 325° oven for 45 minutes; turn and bake an additional 45 minutes. Serve with Mushroom Sauce. Makes 4 servings.

Mushroom Sauce

½ lb. fresh mushrooms, sliced	½ cup whipping cream
¼ cup onion, minced	½ cup sour cream
2 tablespoons butter	½ teaspoon salt
2 tablespoons flour	¼ teaspoon pepper

Sauté mushrooms and onion in butter, Cover and cook over low heat 10 minutes. Add flour, mix well, and then add heavy cream, sour cream, salt, and pepper. Heat, but do not allow to boil.

– Dorothy Sells (Mrs. Bert E.)

» Pollo alla Margherita «

The combination of smoky Italian Prosciutto and creamy mild Fontina cheese makes these chicken breasts with ham and cheese a memorable dish.

3 whole chicken breasts	2 oz. Prosciutto, thinly sliced
¼ cup flour	¼ lb. Fontina cheese, thinly sliced
1 teaspoon salt	½ cup dry white wine
⅛ teaspoon freshly ground pepper	½ cup chicken broth
4 tablespoons butter	

Remove skin from chicken breasts and slice 2 to 3 fillets from each side of a breast. Combine the flour, salt, and pepper and lightly dredge the fillets. Heat the butter in a heavy pan and cook the fillets slowly over medium low heat for 2 to 3 minutes; do not overcook. Remove to a shallow 2-quart ovenproof casserole. On each piece of chicken, arrange a thin slice of Prosciutto and top with Fontina cheese. Deglaze the pan with wine and chicken broth, scraping to mix in brown bits clinging to pan. Simmer until liquid is reduced and slightly thickened. Pour over chicken breasts. At this point, the casserole may be covered and refrigerated until cooking time. Uncover and bake in a preheated 350° oven for 15 minutes or until hot and bubbly. Makes 6 servings.

– Dottie Kreeger (Mrs. John)

» Pecan Chicken «

This Chinese dish incorporates pecans, which add a distinctive Western touch.

½ lb. chicken breasts, skinned, boned, and cubed	blanched 1 minute
2 tablespoons light soy sauce	3 tablespoons peanut oil, divided
½ teaspoon sugar	1 green onion, cut into 1" slices
1 tablespoon dry sherry	3 slices fresh ginger root
1 teaspoon cornstarch	Salt
¼ lb. snow peas,	½ cup pecans, warmed in peanut oil and drained

Marinate chicken for at least 1 hour in mixture of soy sauce, sugar, sherry, and cornstarch. Stir-fry peas in 1 tablespoon peanut oil until jade green; remove. In remaining 2 tablespoons of oil, stir-fry onion and ginger until ginger is golden. Add chicken and cook until browned; return peas and add salt to taste. Toss in pecans and remove from heat. Serve at once. Makes 2 servings.

– Kathleen J. Baker

» Pastel de Choclo «

This popular Chilean dish is a chicken and beef pie topped with a corn crust instead of pastry. Other meats or fish are sometimes used.

3 lbs. chicken breasts, boned and skinned	Dash of Tabasco sauce
2 tablespoons oil	6 cups fresh corn, grated
1 large onion, sliced	1 tablespoon sugar
1 teaspoon salt	1 teaspoon salt
1 teaspoon oregano	¼ cup butter
3 lbs. lean beef round, ground	6 cups onions, chopped
2 tablespoons oil	6 hard-cooked eggs, quartered
2 tablespoons butter	1 cup pitted ripe olives
1 teaspoon salt	1 egg
1 teaspoon oregano	1 teaspoon water
½ teaspoon paprika	½ teaspoon sugar

Cut chicken into bite-sized pieces and brown in oil in a heavy pan. Add onion, salt, and oregano; cook until onion is transparent. Remove and set aside. Brown beef in oil and butter; add salt, oregano, paprika, and Tabasco. Cook over medium heat until beef is tender. Remove and set aside. Cook corn with sugar, salt, and butter until tender and thickened. Remove and set aside. Cook onion in butter remaining in beef pan until transparent. Add more butter and oil, if necessary. Using a 6-quart casserole, place the beef and onion as a first layer. Cover with quartered eggs and olives. Add the chicken mixture and top with corn. Beat egg and water together and pour over corn mixture; sprinkle with sugar. Bake in a preheated 400° oven until the top is golden brown. Makes 16 servings.

– Maryetta Courter (Mrs. Sanford R.)

» Princess Chicken «

¾ lb. chicken breast, boned, skinned, and cut into ½" cubes	1 teaspoon dry sherry or rice wine
1 teaspoon soy sauce	1 tablespoon soy sauce
1 teaspoon dry sherry or rice wine	¼ teaspoon monosodium glutamate, optional
3 tablespoons water	1 tablespoon sugar
2 teaspoons cornstarch	½ teaspoon sesame oil
½ cup oil	1 teaspoon vinegar
½ cup dried hot peppers	1 teaspoon cornstarch
	1½ tablespoons water
	Cooked rice

Mix chicken cubes, soy sauce, sherry, water, and cornstarch; marinate for 20 minutes. Heat oil in a wok or heavy skillet. Stir-fry hot peppers for 10 seconds; add chicken and stir-fry until meat turns white. Add sherry, soy sauce, MSG, sugar, sesame oil, vinegar, and cornstarch dissolved in water. Cook 10 seconds until thickened. Serve immediately with rice.
Makes 3 servings.

– House of Hunan Restaurant

» Chicken Parmesan «

The city of Parma in northern Italy gives us the pungent cheese which complements the mild, sweet flavor of the chicken breasts in this recipe. The people of Parma have been making this wonderful cheese for two thousand years.

2 whole chicken breasts
½ cup flour
Salt and freshly ground
  pepper
¾ teaspoon nutmeg
2 eggs

1 cup fresh bread crumbs
¼ cup Parmesan cheese,
  grated
6 tablespoons butter
2 tablespoons oil
4 lemon slices or wedges

Skin and bone the chicken breasts; cut into halves. Place chicken breasts between two sheets of paper and flatten to ¼" thick with a mallet. Mix flour, salt, pepper, and nutmeg together in a shallow bowl. Beat the eggs lightly in another shallow bowl. Mix the crumbs and Parmesan cheese in a third bowl. Dip chicken breasts lightly in flour mixture, then into beaten eggs, and finally into crumb mixture. Heat butter and oil together in a large skillet; cook the chicken breasts until golden brown on both sides, about 20 to 25 minutes. You may need additional butter. Serve garnished with lemon. Makes 4 servings.

– Candy Clark-Baron

» Chicken Saltimbocca «

Saltimbocca means "leap into the mouth" – a subtle Italian way of telling us that this dish is at its best when served promptly.

5 chicken breasts, split,
  skinned, and boned
Flour
¼ cup unsalted butter,
  clarified
Flour
10 very thin slices of
  prosciutto
10-⅛" to ¼" thick slices of
  provolone, mozzarella, or
  Monterey Jack cheese
3 tablespoons shallots,
  chopped

3 large garlic cloves, finely
  minced
½ lb. mushrooms, sliced
½ cup Chablis or other
  dry white wine
1 cup chicken broth
½ teaspoon oregano
½ teaspoon thyme
1 tablespoon flour
½ cup dry sherry
½ cup half and half cream
Salt and pepper

Dredge the chicken in flour; brown in the clarified butter. To clarify butter, melt it and let it stand a few minutes until solids settle to the bottom of the pan. Pour off the clear liquid butter and use for cooking. Arrange chicken in a buttered 9"x13" baking dish. Top each piece with 1 slice proscuitto and 1 slice cheese. Cook shallots and garlic in butter remaining in pan until tender; add mushrooms, white wine, broth, and herbs. Bring to a boil and simmer for 10 minutes. Mix flour and a small amount of sherry; add to the sauce. Stir in remaining sherry and the cream; season with salt and pepper to taste. Pour sauce over chicken. Bake in preheated 375° oven for 20 minutes. Makes 10 servings.

– Jane Link and Mary Hager
College of Mount St. Joseph
Consumer Science and Nutrition Department

» Chicken Tikka Masala «

Yogurt acts as a tenderizer in this dish, as well as adding a creamy richness.

2-16 oz. cartons yogurt
3" piece of ginger root,
  finely chopped
12 cloves garlic
1 tablespoon cumin
1 tablespoon coriander

1 tablespoon garam masala
1 tablespoon paprika
1 teaspoon salt
2 tablespoons oil
6 chicken breast halves,
  skinned, boned, and cut
  into 1" cubes

Combine all of the ingredients except the chicken; blend well. Add the chicken, cover, and marinate in the refrigerator for 24 hours. Remove from the refrigerator 1 hour before serving. Thread the chicken on skewers and place on a wire rack above a baking pan. Place in a preheated 350° oven and cook for 7 to 10 minutes, or until chicken is tender. Makes 4 servings.

– Annapurna Restaurant
New York City

» Salade Mignonne «

The astringent, slightly bitter flavor of Belgian endive combines wonderfully with the richness of the chicken breasts.

6 whole chicken breasts
Boiling, salted water
1 lb. Belgian endive
1¼ cups mayonnaise
1 cup whipping cream,
  whipped

Salt and pepper
1 medium-size truffle,
  finely chopped
2 hard-cooked eggs, cut
  into quarters
French bread

Poach the chicken breasts in a shallow, covered pan, with just enough salted water to cover. Cook 15 to 20 minutes, remove from heat, and allow the chicken to cool in the broth. Remove skin and bones; cut chicken and ¾ of endive into thin, match-like strips. Blend mayonnaise lightly with whipped cream; season with salt and pepper to taste; toss with strips of chicken and endive. Place the remaining endive leaves in a star design in the bottom of a salad bowl or on individual plates. Spoon chicken mixture into the center of the endive. Sprinkle with chopped truffle and garnish with egg quarters. Serve with crusty French bread. Makes 6 to 8 servings.

» Lasagne Verdi «

Rolling the lasagne noodles with the filling inside gives a new twist to the Italian classic.

1 lb. package spinach
   lasagne noodles
1 quart boiling salted
   water
¼ cup button mushrooms
2 tablespoons butter
1 tablespoon flour
1 cup milk
1 egg, beaten

Salt and pepper
2 cups cooked chicken,
   chopped
½ cup Parmesan cheese,
   grated
2 medium tomatoes, cut in
   wedges
2 tablespoons parsley,
   chopped

Cook lasagne for 5 minutes in water. Drain well and lay each piece flat on a tea towel. Sauté mushrooms in butter for 2 to 3 minutes or until lightly browned. Remove mushrooms and add flour to remaining butter. Cook for 3 minutes, stirring well. Remove from heat and gradually add milk. Return to heat and bring to a boil, stirring constantly, until mixture becomes thick and smooth. Quickly add beaten egg and stir until smooth; add salt and pepper to taste. Combine half of the sauce with the chicken and spread the mixture over the lasagne. Roll lasagne and place rolls, seam side down in a buttered, oven-proof dish. Pour the remaining sauce over the lasagne rolls, sprinkle with Parmesan cheese, and garnish with tomato wedges, sautéed mushrooms, and parsley. Bake in a preheated 350° oven for 15 minutes or until bubbling. Makes 6 servings.

    – Guilia Kinneary (Mrs. William)

» Skewered Chicken «

Shish kabob, the name commonly given to broiled combinations of meat, poultry, seafood, or vegetables on skewers is Turkish, and that country claims credit for the dish. But it's enjoyed throughout the Middle East, as well as in Cincinnati kitchens and backyards.

4 split chicken breasts,
   skinned and boned and
   cut into 1½" pieces
2 green peppers, cut into
   1" pieces
2 tomatoes, cut in wedges

¼ cup lemon juice
3 tablespoons olive oil
1 teaspoon paprika
½ teaspoon salt
Dash cayenne pepper

Combine chicken, green peppers, and tomatoes in a large bowl. Mix remaining ingredients and toss gently with chicken and vegetables. Cover and marinate at room temperature for at least 1 hour, stirring occasionally. Thread chicken and vegetables alternately on 4 skewers. Broil 4" from heat or over charcoal. Turn and baste with remaining marinade for about 20 minutes or until chicken is tender. Makes 4 servings.

    – Anne Seasholes Cozlu (Mrs. Cem)

» Lamb-Stuffed Chicken «

The flavor of lamb combined with the texture of pine nuts gives this Lebanese dish a special flair.

¼ cup butter
1 lb. ground lamb
Salt and pepper
1 cup rice

½ cup pine nuts, browned
   in butter
Chicken broth
4 to 5 lb. roasting chicken
1 cup water

Melt butter; add lamb; season with salt, and pepper to taste; sauté until lamb is browned. Add rice and pine nuts; simmer for 10 minutes. Add enough chicken broth to cover; bring to a boil, cover pan, lower heat, and cook until all liquid is absorbed and rice is tender, about 20 minutes. Set aside until cooled. Put lamb and rice mixture inside chicken and secure opening with string or skewers. Place in a roasting pan with water; cover and roast in a preheated 325° oven for 2½ hours. Remove cover; let the chicken brown for an additional 20 minutes. Carve and serve immediately. Makes 6 servings.

    – Marcia Joseph (Mrs. Ronald G.)

Habit de Rôtisseur

» Chicken Cutlets with Swiss Cheese Crust «

2 whole chicken breasts,
   boned, skinned, and
   split in half
¼ cup flour
½ teaspoon salt
⅛ teaspoon pepper
⅛ teaspoon nutmeg
1 egg
½ teaspoon oil
½ teaspoon water
½ cup fine bread crumbs
⅔ cup Swiss cheese,
   grated
¼ cup butter
Lemon wedges

Pound chicken breasts between sheets of waxed paper until ¼" thick. Combine flour with salt, pepper, and nutmeg; spread on a sheet of waxed paper. In a pie dish or other deep plate, beat egg with oil and water. On another sheet of waxed paper, mix the bread crumbs with the cheese. Coat chicken with seasoned flour, shaking off excess; dip in egg; then coat well with the crumbs/cheese mixture. Melt butter in a large skillet; add chicken, being careful not to crowd; sauté until golden brown and cooked through, about 5 minutes on each side. Garnish with lemon wedge to serve. Makes 4 servings.

– Karen Berkemeyer (Mrs. James)

» Hawaiian Chicken Ono-Ono «

4 green onions, chopped,
   include tops
1 clove of garlic, mashed
¼ cup butter, melted
2 tablespoons flour
1 cup dry white wine
1 teaspoon salt
7¾ oz. can water
   chestnuts, sliced
1 cup mushrooms, fresh
   or canned, sliced
5 oz. can bamboo shoots,
   drained
4 oz. can pineapple
   chunks, drained,
   reserve syrup
3 cups chicken breast,
   cooked and sliced
1 pimiento, cut into strips
½ cup macadamia nuts
½ cup chicken stock, if
   needed

Sauté onions and garlic in butter. Blend in flour and cook for a few minutes; add wine; cook until mixture thickens, stirring constantly. Add salt, water chestnuts, mushrooms, and bamboo shoots. Simmer 5 minutes. Add pineapple chunks and chicken. Stir until heated through. Transfer to a warm 2-quart casserole. Place strips of pimiento like spokes out to border of macadamia nuts surrounding edge of casserole, and serve. Makes 4 to 6 servings. This can be made a day ahead, and reheated until bubbling. Add chicken broth and pineapple syrup if needed for moisture.

– Jo Price (Mrs. Stanley)

» Peasant's Chicken in a Pot «

This is an adaptation from an old French recipe. Served with a simple salad or jellied cranberries, it is a satisfying and easy dinner. You may use more vegetables, or fewer, as you like.

4 to 5 lb. roasting chicken
Salt and pepper
1 teaspoon poultry
   seasoning
⅓ cup celery leaves,
   chopped
¼ teaspoon dried
   rosemary, or 4 fresh
   sprigs
¼ teaspoon dried
   tarragon, or 4 fresh
   sprigs
⅓ cup butter
½ cup dry white wine
½ cup chicken broth,
   preferably homemade
12 small new red potatoes,
   unpeeled
10 small carrots, or larger
   ones cut in half
10 small white or yellow
   onions, peeled
10 fresh mushrooms, cut
   in half
Fresh parsley and
   tarragon

Wash chicken, dry, and season inside and out with salt, pepper, and poultry seasoning. Place ½ of celery leaves, rosemary, and tarragon in cavity. Truss chicken as you would for roasting, tying legs together, tucking wings under, and closing open ends by sewing, or with skewers. Melt butter in an ovenproof casserole large enough to hold the chicken and vegetables. Brown the chicken on all sides in the butter. This will take about 30 minutes. When chicken is nicely browned, add wine, chicken broth, and remaining celery leaves and herbs to casserole. Cover and bake in a preheated 350° oven for 30 minutes. Remove from oven and place vegetables around chicken in this order: potatoes on the bottom, then carrots, onions, and mushrooms. Baste chicken and vegetables. Return to oven and bake until both chicken and vegetables are tender, about 45 minutes, basting once again about 15 minutes before serving. Serve chicken on a large platter, surrounded by vegetables and garnished with fresh parsley and tarragon if available. The sauce from the casserole may be served in a sauce boat, or if you wish, chicken may be carved and served with vegetables and sauce in a shallow soup bowl. Makes 4 to 6 servings.

– *Margaret Minster (Mrs. Leonard)*

» Nona Sauce for Pasta «

Arnold's is the oldest tavern in continuous operation in Cincinnati, dating back to 1861. It once gained fame for its upstairs dining room that contains a bathtub from the old days, but now Cincinnatians visit this restaurant for the offbeat menu offering everything from American to French country cooking, along with summertime jazz in the courtyard.

3 lb. whole chicken	*10 cloves garlic, peeled*
2 heads garlic	*and chopped*
Water	*Salt and pepper*
Oil	*¼ teaspoon crushed red*
2 medium green peppers,	*pepper*
cut in thin strips	*¼ cup fresh basil,*
2 medium red bell	*chopped*
peppers, cut in thin	*30 oz. can whole*
strips	*tomatoes, chopped*
½ lb. hot Italian sausage	*30 oz. can tomato purée*
Oil	*1 cup chicken stock*
2 medium onions,	*6 oz. can tomato paste*
chopped	

Stuff chicken with 2 heads of garlic; bake 2 hours in preheated 350° oven. Allow to cool; pull meat off bones and set aside. Boil the bones and skin in water to make stock. In a large skillet, sauté the red and green peppers in a small amount of oil in small batches until soft; set aside. Brown the Italian sausage over low heat in the same skillet. In a large pan, sauté in oil the onions, garlic, salt and pepper to taste, crushed red pepper, and basil, being careful not to brown the garlic. Add the whole tomatoes, tomato purée, and chicken stock. Stir in the tomato paste; add chicken meat, peppers, and sausage. Serve over mostaciolli or other pasta. Makes 16 servings.

– *Arnold's Restaurant*

» Yakitori «

In Japanese, yakitori means "grilled chicken," and the soy marinade is traditional.

3 to 4 lb. chicken, boned	*¾ cup soy sauce*
and cut into 1½" cubes,	*¼ cup sugar*
or 2 lbs. boned chicken	*¾ cup sake or rice wine*
breast, cut into 1½"	*1½ teaspoons fresh ginger*
cubes	*root, grated*
10 scallions or green onions,	*1½ teaspoons cornstarch*
cut into 1½" lengths	*Cooked rice*

Thread chicken pieces alternately with scallion pieces on wooden or metal skewers. Mix soy sauce, sugar, wine, ginger, and cornstarch; baste the chicken with the mixture. Broil in broiler or 4" above charcoal for about 5 minutes, basting with sauce 3 or 4 times while cooking and turning. Do not overcook or chicken will dry out. Serve at once with rice. Makes 4 servings.

» Chicken and Cheese Enchiladas «

Las Mananitas, a delightful restaurant in Cuernevaca, Mexico, cured many tourists of the stereotyped opinion that all Mexican food is hot and spicy. This recipe is reminiscent of their specialty, Chicken Enchiladas covered with a delicate cream sauce. The marvelous food is enhanced by dining on a terrace overlooking a rolling lawn where colorful peacocks stroll.

¼ cup vegetable oil	*6 ozs. Monterey Jack*
1 large onion, halved and	*cheese, shredded*
thinly sliced	*2 tablespoons butter*
1 dozen 6" to 8"	*2 tablespoons flour*
refrigerated-type	*2 cups rich chicken broth*
corn tortillas	*1 cup sour cream*
1½ cups chicken, cooked	*4 oz. can mild green*
and chopped	*chilies, diced*
1 cup black olives, sliced	*Chili powder, optional*

In a large skillet, heat the oil. Add onions and sauté briefly, just enough to wilt and to tone down the flavor. Lift out with slotted spoon, allowing onions to drain back into skillet. Next, soften corn tortillas by placing one at a time in hot, onion-flavored oil. Keep in skillet only a few seconds, picking up each tortilla with a fork or tongs, and allowing it to drain back into the skillet. Stack the tortillas to keep them warm. Add the chicken and olives to the bowl with the onions. Toss with cheese. To assemble, place a clump of the chicken-cheese mixture to one side of each tortilla; roll. Arrange filled tortillas side-by-side in 9"x13" baking dish. Distribute any leftover mixture over the top. In a saucepan, melt the butter and add flour. Let heat a minute or two, then whisk in chicken broth and cook until bubbly. Remove from heat and whisk in sour cream. Stir in undrained chilies; do not use Jalapenos. Pour evenly over rolled tortillas. Chili powder may be sprinkled on top before baking, if desired. Bake, uncovered, in preheated 425° oven for about 25 minutes. Makes 6 servings.

– Joyce Rosencrans
Food Editor, The Cincinnati Post

» Cold Curried Chicken «

This chicken dish can be made up to 48 hours ahead and the recipe can be easily doubled or quadrupled.

2 frying chickens, cut into serving pieces	1½ tablespoons curry powder
6 tablespoons butter	1¼ cups whipping cream
½ cup water	Pinch of tarragon
2 onions, sliced	Lemon slices
Salt and pepper	Parsley

Wash and dry chicken. Melt butter in a heavy sauté pan; add chicken and brown well on all sides. Remove chicken; add water and deglaze pan, scraping well to remove all the brown bits from bottom of pan. Add chicken, onions, salt, and pepper. Sprinkle the chicken with the curry powder, turning several times to cover. Cook, covered, over low heat until chicken is very tender, 1¼ to 1½ hours. The onions will be wilted and there will be broth. Remove chicken and cool. Debone chicken and discard skin, bones, and gristle. Put chicken pieces in a shallow dish with sides. To chicken broth and onions, add cream and tarragon. Heat gently but do not boil. Remove onions and pour sauce over chicken. Refrigerate at least 6 hours. Unmold by dipping dish in warm water. Place on serving dish and garnish with lemon slices and parsley. Makes 6 servings.

– Carolyn Fovel (Mrs. Donald R.)

» Chicken Adobo «

Adobo is a Philippine stew which is made by first simmering, and then sautéing, the meat ingredient. This results in a tender, yet crisp and browned, meat.

1 chicken, cut into pieces	½ cup vinegar
1 teaspoon salt	2 cups water
1 clove garlic, minced	4 tablespoons lard or
½ teaspoon pepper	peanut oil
½ bay leaf	

Place chicken, salt, garlic, pepper, bay leaf, vinegar, and water in a saucepan. Bring to a boil, cover, and simmer until chicken is almost tender. Remove cover and boil rapidly until liquid has almost completely evaporated. Add lard or oil and sauté chicken until brown on all sides. Serve hot or cold. Makes 4 servings.

– Nellie Obial (Mrs. Guadencio)

» East Indian Casserole «

This richly spiced dish utilizes many of the pungent seasonings that are available in India.

½ cup oil	2 cups rice, uncooked
1 medium onion, diced	1½ teaspoons salt
1 lb. boneless chicken, lamb, or beef, cubed	⅛ teaspoon saffron
	Additional water
2 cups chicken or beef broth	2 medium carrots, finely slivered
1 teaspoon salt	1 teaspoon sugar
½ teaspoon cinnamon	¼ cup oil
½ teaspoon cloves	1 cup golden raisins
½ teaspoon cumin	¼ cup slivered almonds
½ teaspoon cardamom	

Heat oil in a heavy pan and sauté onion and meat until lightly browned. Add broth, salt, and spices; cover and simmer until meat is tender. Remove meat and set aside. Add rice, salt, and saffron to broth; add enough water to cover rice with 2" of liquid. Cover and cook for 15 minutes. Meanwhile, combine carrots and sugar; sauté in oil until browned and tender; remove and drain. Cook raisins in the oil over low heat until they are plump; remove and drain. Sauté almonds in the oil until lightly browned; remove and drain. Mix meat and rice; place in a greased 2-quart casserole. Cover and bake in a preheated 350° oven for 25 minutes. Serve at once, sprinkled with carrots, raisins, and almonds. Makes 4 to 6 servings.

– Susan Pfau (Mrs. Daniel)

» Poulet Dijonnais «
Dijon Chicken

The French Burgundian capital of Dijon is the home of perhaps the most renowned mustard in the world, a perfect complement to roasted chicken. In Dijon, there are shops that sell nothing but mustard, offering an amazing variety of flavors and styles.

6 tablespoons butter	1½ to 2 cups seasoned
2 tablespoons Dijon	croutons
mustard	4 chicken legs and thighs,
	or two breasts, split

Melt butter over medium heat in small frying pan. Stir in mustard, blending well. Set aside. In blender or food processor, chop croutons to fine crumbs. Roll chicken pieces in butter mixture, then coat with crumbs. Place skin side down on a rack in roasting pan. Bake, uncovered, in preheated 400° oven for 20 minutes. Turn skin side up. Drizzle with any remaining butter mixture. Bake an additional 25 to 30 minutes. Makes 4 servings.

– Mrs. Molly Fox

» Chicken Stuffed with Pork, Spinach and Pine Nuts «

This chicken may be served hot or at room temperature. Since it is boneless, it may be sliced through. Thin slices are best if you are serving it at room temperature.

3 to 4 lb. roasting chicken	1 tablespoon fresh thyme,
½ lb. lean pork, ground	or 1 teaspoon dried thyme
2 10 oz. pkgs. frozen	2 tablespoons pine nuts
spinach, or 1½ lbs. fresh	1 teaspoon salt
spinach, slightly cooked	½ teaspoon freshly ground
3 cloves garlic, minced	pepper
1 tablespoon fresh sage,	1 egg, beaten
or 1 teaspoon dried sage	Salt and pepper
	2 tablespoons olive oil

Bone chicken, leaving in the wing bones. To prepare the stuffing, grind the pork in a food processor or have the butcher do it for you. Thaw, drain, and squeeze-dry the frozen spinach. If using fresh, do the same and then chop it. Add spinach, 1 clove minced garlic, sage, thyme, nuts, salt, pepper, and egg to pork. Mix well. Push some of the stuffing into the boned legs and thighs and the rest into the cavity of the chicken. Sew or skewer the chicken, as for normal roasting. Mix remaining 2 garlic cloves and salt and pepper to taste with olive oil. Rub the entire chicken with this mixture. Roast on a rack in a shallow pan in a preheated 350° oven for approximately 1½ hours, basting frequently. Makes 4 to 6 servings.

– Marge Haller (Mrs. Hugh)

» Chicken with Mole Sauce «

First-time visitors to Mexico are always shocked when they learn that mole sauce contains chocolate. But mole is not sweet, just rich and dark, and very, very good.

6 tablespoons cooking oil	1½ teaspoons ground
3 cups onion, sliced	cumin
3 cloves garlic, crushed	1½ teaspoons ground
3 tablespoons raisins	oregano
½ cup sesame seeds,	¼ teaspoon ground cloves
toasted	¼ teaspoon ground anise
¾ cup slivered almonds,	1½ oz. unsweetened
toasted	baking chocolate
3 tablespoons flour	3 cups Mexican tomatoes
1 tablespoon salt	and mild chiles,
3 tablespoons sugar	undrained
1½ to 3 tablespoons	3 small tortillas, broken
imported chili powder	into pieces
1½ teaspoons ground	3 cups turkey or chicken
cinnamon	broth
1½ teaspoons ground	Chicken pieces for 12 to
coriander	15 servings

In hot oil, sauté onion, garlic, raisins, sesame seeds, and almonds about 5 minutes. Add a bit more oil if needed. In a large bowl, combine remaining ingredients. Stir into sautéed mixture. Simmer about 15 minutes. Puree briefly in blender or food processor, but take care that raisins and nuts retain their identity. In a preheated 350°

oven, bake enough chicken pieces to serve 12 to 15 for about half the time needed to complete the cooking process, about 30 minutes. Remove any accumulated fat. Cover with mole sauce and bake for an additional 30 minutes. Serve chicken covered with the remaining mole sauce. Makes 12 to 15 servings.

– Jan Denton (Mrs. M. Drue)

» Puerto Rican Paella «

1 onion, chopped
2 cloves garlic, minced
2 tablespoons oil
1 frying chicken, cut into serving pieces
4 pork chops, boned and cubed, or 1½ lbs. pork tenderloin, cubed
1 teaspoon paprika
1 teaspoon saffron

Salt and freshly ground pepper
1 lb. can Italian tomatoes
2 to 3 cups chicken broth
2 cups uncooked rice
10 oz. pkg. frozen baby lima beans
1 cup crab meat
½ lb. shrimp, peeled and deveined
2 pimientos, sliced

Brown onion and garlic slightly in oil in a large, heavy pan. Add chicken and pork; brown meats on all sides. Add paprika, saffron, salt and pepper to taste, and tomatoes and liquid from can; simmer for 10 minutes. Add enough chicken broth to cover the ingredients, cover the pan, and simmer until the chicken and pork are tender. Add rice and cook for 15 minutes. Add lima beans and cook for another 5 minutes. Add crab and shrimp; stir to distribute the seafood. Remove from heat, cover, and let stand 15 minutes. Serve on a platter decorated with pimiento slices. Makes 8 servings.

– Suzanne Cahill

» West Indies Chicken Pilau «

3 lb. chicken, cut into pieces
3 cloves garlic, minced
Salt and pepper
Cayenne
3 large onions, sliced

½ lb. bacon, diced
1 green pepper, seeded and sliced
3 teaspoons curry powder
Boiling water
1 lb. uncooked rice

Rub chicken with mixture of garlic, salt, pepper, and cayenne; add onions. Sauté bacon in a heavy pan until brown and crisp; remove and drain. Add chicken, onion slices, and green pepper slices to bacon fat; stir and sauté for a few minutes until chicken is golden. Add curry powder and enough boiling water to cover chicken by ½". Cover and simmer until chicken is tender, about 45 minutes. Add rice, stir well, cover and simmer another 20 minutes. Remove from heat and let stand 5 minutes, covered, before serving. Makes 4 to 6 servings.

» Paprika Huhn «

This rich and creamy German stewed chicken dish is sparked with paprika and accented with the tangy addition of fresh dill.

5 lbs. chicken pieces
½ tablespoon salt
½ cup butter
1 large onion, diced
2 tablespoons paprika
½ tablespoon flour

2 cups chicken stock or bouillon
1 tablespoon whipping cream
1 cup sour cream
2 tablespoons fresh dill, chopped

Rinse chicken, pat dry, season with salt, place in a bowl, and refrigerate, covered, for 30 minutes. Heat butter in a deep pot or Dutch oven until light brown. Add onion and sauté until transparent. Stir in paprika, add chicken, and cook slowly until chicken is golden. Cover and cook 30 minutes longer, or until chicken is tender. Sprinkle flour over chicken, add stock or bouillon and heavy cream. Stir, cover, and simmer for 15 minutes. Remove chicken and keep warm on serving platter. Stir sour cream into sauce and simmer 5 minutes. Pour sauce over chicken, sprinkle with dill, and serve at once.
Makes 4 to 6 servings.

» Chicken Teriyaki «

The Japanese marinade serves to tenderize the chicken as well as impart a delicious flavor and moistness.

3 to 4 lb. chicken, cut into pieces
⅔ cup soy sauce
3 tablespoons sherry wine
3 tablespoons sugar

1 clove garlic, chopped
2 green onions, chopped
2 slices fresh ginger root, chopped

Wash chicken and pat dry. Mix soy sauce, sherry, sugar, garlic, green onion, and ginger root; place in a plastic bag with the chicken pieces. Close bag tightly and marinate for 5 to 6 hours in refrigerator. Remove chicken from marinade and place in a shallow baking pan. Bake in a preheated 325° oven for 1 hour, basting 1 or 2 times with marinade. Serve hot or room temperature. Makes 4 servings.

— Mieko Johnston

» Smoored Pullets «

From the days of Bonnie Prince Charlie, many Scots emigrated to the New World, particularly to the Carolinas, where an annual Highland Games celebration is held. This fried chicken from the Isle of Skye was probably a forefather of Southern fried chicken.

2-3 lb. chickens,	*2 tablespoons oil*
quartered	*1 cup sour cream*
Salt, pepper, and flour	*Chopped parsley*
½ cup butter	

Toss chicken with salt, pepper, and flour to cover completely. Melt butter and oil in a heavy pan and sauté chicken pieces until browned on all sides. Cover tightly, reduce heat, and simmer very gently for 40 minutes. If necessary, add a small amount of water or stock to chicken to prevent burning. Remove chicken and keep warm; add sour cream to pan and stir and scrape to deglaze the roasting pan. Heat gently but do not allow to boil. Correct seasonings and pour over chicken. Serve immediately, sprinkled with parsley. Makes 4 servings.

» Circassian Chicken with Walnuts «

4 lb. stewing chicken, cut	*Freshly ground black*
into 8 pieces	*pepper*
3 cups water	*1½ cups walnuts,*
2 onions, cut into wedges	*chopped and toasted*
2 tablespoons parsley,	*2 tablespoons onion,*
chopped	*chopped finely*
1 tablespoon tomato paste	*2 cups fresh bread crumbs*
1 teaspoon salt	*1 teaspoon paprika*
	Parsley sprigs

Place chicken, water, onions, parsley, tomato paste, salt, and pepper in a large covered pan. Bring to a boil and simmer until chicken is tender, about 45 minutes. Remove chicken and strain broth through fine sieve or cheesecloth. Boil broth, uncovered, until reduced to approximately 1½ cups liquid. Cool slightly and place in a blender or food processor with walnuts, onion, bread crumbs, and paprika. Purée until smooth. Meanwhile, remove skin and bones from chicken. Cut meat into bite-sized strips or chunks. Place in a serving bowl and toss gently with the walnut purée. Sprinkle with additional paprika and garnish with parsley. Makes 6 servings.

— Anne Seasholes Cozlu (Mrs. Cem)

» Coq au Vin «

In France, this chicken with wine dish is made with either red or white wine, but the Burgundy used in this recipe is most usual. The classic accompaniment is potatoes cooked with butter and parsley.

⅓ lb. salt pork, cubed	*1 clove garlic*
2 small onions, sliced	*Pinch of thyme*
2 tablespoons butter	*2 to 3 sprigs of parsley*
3 lb. chicken, cut into	*1 bay leaf*
serving pieces	*½ lb. mushrooms, sliced*
Flour	*3 tablespoons butter*
¼ cup brandy, warmed	*3 tablespoons flour*
1 quart dry red Burgundy	
wine	

Brown salt pork and onions in butter; remove from pan. Coat the chicken pieces with flour and brown in the remaining fat. Add the warmed brandy and carefully ignite with a match; burn until flame dies. Add Burgundy and bouquet garni of garlic, thyme, parsley, and bay leaf which have been tied in a small square of cheesecloth. Add salt pork and onions. Simmer slowly until chicken is tender. Meanwhile, sauté mushrooms in butter until moisture is evaporated; add flour and cook a few minutes. Add the mushroom mixture to the chicken; cook until mixture is thickened slightly. Remove bouquet garni and serve. Makes 4 servings.

— Sarah Headley (Mrs. Grant)

» Country Cornish Hens «

4 Cornish hens, rinsed
   and dried
Salt and pepper
Flour for dredging
2 to 3 tablespoons oil
2 tablespoons unsalted
   butter
4 strips bacon, diced
1 medium onion, chopped
1 clove garlic, minced
1 cup chicken stock
Few sprigs of thyme
Few sprigs of parsley
1 bay leaf
Splash of Madeira or a
   dry white wine

Cut backbone out of hens. Salt and pepper hens inside
and out. Flatten slightly with heel of hand by pressing
down on breast bones. Tie legs together, place wings
underneath bird. Dredge lightly with flour. Heat oil and
butter in a large skillet, add hens, and brown on all sides.
Remove hens from skillet and pour off grease. Add
bacon to skillet and sauté until almost crisp. Add onion
and garlic; sauté for about 2 minutes. Remove bacon,
onion and garlic; reserve. Deglaze the pan with a small
amount of chicken stock, 1 or 2 tablespoons. Return hens
to pan along with thyme, parsley, and bay leaf. Add
remainder of chicken stock and wine; add reserved
bacon, onion, and garlic. Liquid should come halfway up
on hens. Bring hens to boiling point, reduce heat, cover
and simmer until tender, basting occasionally. When
ready to serve, cut strings off legs and place on a serving
platter. Keep warm while straining sauce through a
sieve. Reheat sauce and pour over hens.
Makes 4 servings.

– Marge Haller (Mrs. Hugh)

» Peking Duck «

1 duck, not too fat
Boiling water
1 tablespoon soy sauce
1 tablespoon chives,
   minced
Pinch of powdered
   aniseed
1 rounded tablespoon
   brown sugar
1 teaspoon cinnamon
Pinch of powdered cloves
1 rounded teaspoon salt
1/8 teaspoon freshly
   ground pepper
2 teaspoons dry sherry
3 garlic cloves, crushed
2 tablespoons soy sauce
2 tablespoons honey
1 tablespoon white wine

Scald the duck 3 or 4 times in the boiling water and then
dry thoroughly. Combine soy sauce, chives, aniseed,
brown sugar, cinnamon, cloves, salt, pepper, sherry, and
garlic. Cook over low heat for 2 to 3 minutes, then stuff
the duck with this mixture. Sew the neck and abdominal
openings securely. Mix soy sauce, honey, and white wine.
Rub this mixture all over duck. Roast the duck in a
preheated 500° oven for 2 to 3 minutes, uncovered. Then
baste the duck with the soy sauce-honey mixture, reduce
the heat to 425°, cover the roasting pan, and roast the
duck for about 45 minutes. Uncover, baste, and continue
to roast for about 15 minutes longer, basting the duck
frequently so that it becomes evenly browned and crisp.
To serve, cut the duck into bite-size pieces.
Makes 4 to 6 servings.

– The Wah Mee Restaurant

» Canard en Civet aux Olives Noires «

This recipe is from LeRuth's Restaurant in New Orleans.
A civet is a stew made from furred or feathered game.
This recipe uses duck with black olives, with the addition
of a red wine marinade.

2-5 to 6 lb. ducklings, or
   4 duck breasts and
   4 legs
Zest of 1 orange, minced
1 carrot, finely chopped
1 onion, finely chopped
1 stalk celery, finely
   chopped
1/4 cup parsley, finely
   chopped
1 bay leaf
1/2 teaspoon thyme
1 quart red Burgundy wine
1/2 cup olive oil
1 tablespoon cornstarch
   or arrowroot
1/2 cup Port wine
Black Greek or Nicoise
   olives, seeded

De-bone ducks, reserving bones. Place in large bowl
with orange zest, carrot, onion, celery, parsley, bay leaf,
thyme, and Burgundy. Marinate 6 to 10 hours. Remove
duck pieces and pat dry with paper towels. Heat oil in a
large Dutch oven; add duckling and sauté until lightly
browned on all sides. Remove from pot and remove
excess fat. Add bones and vegetables from marinade;
brown for 10 minutes over medium heat, stirring. Return
duck meat and Burgundy marinade to pot and cook,
covered, for 45 minutes, until meat is tender. Remove

meat and bones from pot, strain sauce, and reduce liquid for approximately 15 minutes, skimming constantly. Mix cornstarch and Port wine and add to sauce mixture. Cook, stirring, until smooth and thickened. Meanwhile, poach olives in boiling water for 5 minutes, drain, and rinse well. Add to thickened sauce. Serve duck meat covered with sauce, garnished with additional olives. Makes 4 servings.

— Ann Trufant (Mrs. S. A. III)
New Orleans, Louisiana

» Pescado al Horno «

I learned to make this oven-baked fish dish while living in Spain. I've only used fresh fish, but frozen could be substituted if necessary.

½ cup onions, finely
   chopped
1½ tablespoons olive oil
3 medium tomatoes,
   peeled, seeded, and
   chopped, or 1 lb. can
   tomatoes, drained and
   chopped
1 tablespoon olive oil
1 large firm potato, peeled
   and cut crosswise into
   ⅛" thick rounds

Salt
2 lbs. cod or haddock
   fillets
1½ tablespoons lemon
   juice
1½ tablespoons olive oil
6 tablespoons water
¼ cup fine, soft bread
   crumbs
2 teaspoons parsley,
   minced
1 tablespoon olive oil

In a heavy frying pan, sauté onions in oil for 8 to 10 minutes, stirring frequently, until they are soft and lightly browned. Add tomatoes and continue cooking for 10 to 15 minutes, stirring and mashing the tomatoes with a wooden spoon, until mixture is thick enough to hold its shape almost solidly in the spoon. Grease bottom and sides of an 8"x10"x2" baking dish with oil. Arrange the potato slices in a single layer in the bottom of the dish, overlapping slightly. Sprinkle with salt and arrange the fish fillets on top of the potatoes. Sprinkle with additional salt, lemon juice, and oil. Spread tomato mixture over fillets and pour water in at the side of the dish. Mix breadcrumbs with parsley and sprinkle over top of dish. Drizzle with olive oil. Bring casserole to a simmer on top of stove. Cover loosely with foil; bake in the center of preheated 350° oven 20 to 25 minutes, or until fish flakes easily. Makes 4 servings.

— Beverly Mourning (Mrs. M.P.)

» Stuffed Quail «

12 quail
Salt and pepper
7 oz. pkg. long grain and
   wild rice
3 tablespoons parsley,
   chopped
3 tablespoons lemon zest
   and/or dried orange
   peel, grated
½ cup pine nuts, chopped,

or small green seedless
   grapes
3 tablespoons butter,
   melted
1 cup dry white wine
3 tablespoons lemon juice
3 tablespoons orange
   juice
½ cup chicken bouillon
Watercress for garnish
Orange slices for garnish

Rinse and dry quail. Season inside and out with a minimum of salt and pepper. Prepare rice according to directions on package. Add parsley, lemon zest and/or orange peel, and pine nuts or grapes. Brown quail in butter in broiler, or in skillet on top of stove. While still warm, stuff quail with seasoned rice and tie together with twine. Place quail in a shallow baking dish. Add wine, juices, and bouillon. Bake, uncovered, in a preheated 350° oven for 30 minutes. Serve garnished with watercress and orange slices. Makes 12 servings.

— Mrs. George Whitman

» Hake a la Cazuela «

Hake a la Cazuela is one of the best foods you can eat in Spain. This recipe leaves room for endless variations, depending on availability of ingredients and the whim of the cook. A cazuela is an earthenware cooking pot traditionally used to prepare this meal.

2 lbs. hake or other
   close-textured white
   fish, sliced
Salt
Flour
Olive or other vegetable
   oil
Onion, chopped
Garlic, mashed
Parsley, chopped

1 tablespoon flour
Pinch of paprika
Pinch of pepper
Water
Lettuce
Clams
Lemon
Cooked peas
Pimientos, cut into strips
Cooked asparagus

Season slices of hake with salt, dip in flour, and fry quickly in hot oil until lightly browned. Remove fish and set aside. Add onion, garlic, parsley, flour, paprika, pepper, and a small amount of water to oil left in frying pan. Cook for a few minutes, stirring, until thickened. Remove from heat and press the mixture through a sieve. Spread vegetable purée on the bottom of an ovenproof casserole and arrange hake slices on top. Put in a preheated 350° oven for a few minutes. Remove from oven and simmer on top of stove for 5 minutes. While still hot, garnish with seasoned lettuce, clams with a squirt of lemon, peas, strips of pimiento, and asparagus. Return to oven for a few minutes, until clams have opened. Serve immediately. Makes 6 to 8 servings.

– Carlos Casariego

» Creamed Finnan Haddie «

The Scottish town of Findon gives the name to the prime ingredient of this recipe – haddock smoked Findon style.

1 to 1½ lbs. smoked haddock or Finnan Haddie	¼ teaspoon salt Chopped parsley for garnish
1 to 1½ cups milk	Chopped chives for garnish
2 tablespoons butter	
2 tablespoons flour	1 hard-cooked egg, sliced
½ cup fish stock	1 teaspoon lemon juice

Soak the haddock in enough milk to cover for 1 hour. Place in a skillet and bring milk slowly to a boil, reduce heat, and simmer for 15 minutes. Remove from stove, drain, and reserve the milk for sauce. Cool the haddock, remove skin and bones, and flake the fish. Keep warm in low oven. Melt butter in a heavy saucepan over medium heat; remove from heat and blend in flour. Add ½ cup reserved milk and fish stock. Mix well and season with salt. Return to heat and cook for 1 minute. Remove from heat and pour sauce over flaked fish. Garnish with parsley, chives, and egg slices; sprinkle with lemon juice. Makes 4 servings.

– Margaret Minster (Mrs. Leonard)

» Potted Herrings «

Ireland is surrounded by water and dotted with lakes, so the Irish have developed many recipes for the abundant fresh fish. These are particularly good served with a green or Waldorf salad.

1 cup vinegar	¼ teaspoon thyme
¼ cup brown sugar	¼ teaspoon pepper
1 bay leaf	1 tablespoon salt
1 onion, chopped	6 herrings
¼ teaspoon pickling spices	1 onion, sliced
	6 bay leaves, halved

Combine vinegar, brown sugar, bay leaf, onion, spices, pepper, and salt in a small saucepan; boil for 3 minutes; set aside. Fillet the herrings and place a slice of onion and half of a bay leaf at the tail end of each fillet; roll up. Place rolled fillets in a shallow, ovenproof casserole just large enough to hold the fillets. Pour the marinade over the fillets, cover with lid or aluminum foil, and bake in a preheated 350° oven for 15 minutes. Cool; refrigerate until serving. Makes 6 servings.

» Baked Fish Mousse with Lobster Sauce «

The abundance of fresh fish from the cold waters of the North Atlantic makes this Swedish dish a popular one in that country.

Melted butter	½ lb. butter, melted
¼ cup dried bread crumbs	4 eggs, separated
½ cup flour	1 tablespoon salt
1 tablespoon potato flour	½ teaspoon white pepper
2 lbs. haddock, cod, or pike	½ teaspoon allspice
	2 cups milk

Butter a 9" tube pan generously; coat with the crumbs, turning to cover all surfaces. Sift the flours together. Purée fish in a food processor or use a mortar and pestle. Add the melted butter and egg yolks; beat vigorously with a wooden spoon. Sprinkle with flour mixture, salt, pepper, and allspice; stir in well. Gradually add milk; mix well. Beat egg whites until stiff; gently fold into fish mixture. Pour into a greased tube pan and place in a larger pan of boiling water. Place both pans in a preheated 350° oven for about 70 minutes, until a toothpick inserted in the center of the mixture comes out clean. If the top of the mousse begins to get too brown before it is done, cover with aluminum foil and continue baking. Remove pan from the oven and let the mousse cool for 5 minutes. Loosen edges with a spatula, and unmold carefully onto a warmed platter. Serve immediately with Lobster Sauce. Makes 6 to 8 servings.

Lobster Sauce

3 tablespoons butter
2 tablespoons flour
¾ tablespoon sugar
1 teaspoon salt
1½ teaspoons white pepper

2 cups half and half cream
2 egg yolks, slightly beaten
1½ cups cooked lobster, minced
2 tablespoons lemon juice

Melt butter, add flour, and cook over medium heat for a few minutes. Add sugar, salt, pepper, and cream. Cook over low heat, stirring constantly, until thick and smooth. Mix a little of this hot mixture into egg yolks; return all to the saucepan; cook for 1 minute longer. Add lobster; heat gently until lobster is hot; add lemon juice. Serve at once. Makes 4 cups.

— Karen Rafuse (Mrs. Peter B.)

» Indian Fried Fish «

The spices in the marinade give this dish its unusual Indian flavor.

1 lb. firm-fleshed fish fillets, or 1 lb. prawns or shrimp, shelled and deveined
¼ teaspoon chili powder

½ teaspoon turmeric
Juice of 1 lemon
Salt
Oil

Marinate fish fillets or prawns in a mixture of chili powder, turmeric, lemon juice, and salt for 30 minutes. Remove from marinade. Heat ½" of oil in a heavy pan; fry fish until tender and lightly browned. Makes 4 servings.

— Jennifer-Ann Fernandes (Mrs. Allan)

Pablo Picasso, Spanish, 1881-1973, "Lobsters and Fish," 1949, lithograph, 1955.715. Gift of Cincinnati Print and Drawing Circle in memory of Chalmers Hadley

» Saumon Grillé, Flambé au Fenouil «

On the French Riviera, the fish in this recipe is loup de mer, or sea bass, but salmon is equally delicious flamed with fennel. A fish-flaming basket on legs is used to cook the fish over glowing coals and to flame it over the smoking fennel and brandy. If you do not own a basket like this, you may improvise with two wire racks, tied together so they hold the length of the fish.

4 to 6 lb. whole salmon or sea bass, head removed
1 teaspoon salt
Freshly ground pepper
2 tablespoons fresh fennel, minced, or

1 teaspoon dried fennel
¼ cup butter, softened
2 tablespoons oil
6 dried fennel stalks, or 1 teaspoon fennel
⅓ cup brandy

Clean, and if you prefer, debone fish. Wash and dry inside and out with paper towels. Sprinkle with salt and pepper to taste. Combine fennel and butter; place inside the fish cavity. Brush the outside of the fish with oil. Place the fish in a fish basket or between two wire racks fastened together to hold the fish inside. Cook over coals of moderate heat for 10 minutes per inch of thickness of fish, or until the flesh feels springy to the touch rather than soft. Place dried fennel stalks or seeds on the bottom of a flameproof platter. Heat brandy in a chafing dish or over low heat; when it is warm, pour brandy over the fennel and ignite it. Turn the fish over the smoke for several minutes, slide it onto a heated platter, and serve at once. Makes 8 to 10 servings.

– Carl and Eleanor Strauss

» Cucumber and Chive Dressing «

1 cucumber, peeled and seeded
1 tablespoon lemon juice
1 teaspoon chives, minced

Dash of cayenne pepper
Salt
1 cup sour cream

Grate or blend the cucumber so that it retains a slight texture. Mix well with lemon juice, chives, cayenne pepper, and salt to taste. Fold mixture into sour cream. Chill thoroughly before serving with poached salmon.

» Dill Mayonnaise «

1 cup mayonnaise
3 teaspoons lemon juice
¼ teaspoon Worcestershire sauce

2 drops Tabasco sauce
3 tablespoons fresh dill, chopped, or 3 teaspoons dried dill weed

Mix all ingredients well. Serve with poached salmon. Makes 1 cup dressing.

» Salmon Poached in Foil «

In early America, the traditional meal served on Independence Day was poached salmon with new potatoes and peas. Salmon usually is poached in milk, wine, or a court bouillon. This version simplifies the job and provides a lovely blending of flavors from the vegetables and seasonings. Serve hot as an entree, or cold as a dramatic party dish.

6 to 8 lb. salmon, cleaned
2 carrots
1 medium onion
1 shallot
2 stalks celery
8 sprigs parsley
½ teaspoon thyme

Salt
Freshly ground pepper
1 bay leaf
1 clove garlic, minced
2 cups dry white wine
Cucumber slices

Wash salmon and pat dry with paper towels. Using a food processor or blender, finely mince carrots, onion, shallot, celery, and parsley. Put a large piece of heavy duty aluminum foil in a shallow roasting pan that is large enough to hold the fish. Place the fish in the center of the foil; sprinkle with the minced vegetables, placing half of the mixture inside the cavity of the fish. Sprinkle with thyme, and salt and pepper to taste. Add bay leaf, garlic, and wine. Bring up the edges of the foil and seal tightly. Bake in a preheated 400° oven for 50 minutes. Fish is done when the back fin pulls out easily with the fingers. Open the foil and serve at once, or let fish cool for 15 minutes and remove skin. Chill thoroughly and decorate with cucumber slices; serve with dill-flavored mayonnaise, horseradish sauce, or cucumber/chive sauce. Makes 8 to 12 servings.

– Karen Rafuse (Mrs. Peter B.)

» Horseradish Sauce «

1 cup whipping cream,
 whipped
1 tablespoon lemon juice
 or vinegar

2 teaspoons horseradish
1 teaspoon
 Worcestershire sauce

Mix all ingredients well. Chill thoroughly before serving with hot or cold poached salmon.

» Baked Red Snapper «

This is sort of a short-cut Cincinnati version of Mexico City's delightful Huachinango a la Veracruzana. This formula suits any size red snapper or other mild fish. Increase amounts for a larger fish.

Grease a piece of aluminum foil large enough to seal over fish and other ingredients. Place fish on foil in baking pan and smother fish with a mixture of sliced onion, sliced tomatoes, pimiento-stuffed green olives, chopped celery and leaves, and chopped parsley. Douse with a cup or two of water, or substitute white wine for part of water. Seal edges of foil; bake in a preheated 350° oven for 30 minutes, or until onions test fork tender.

» Grilled Shark with Ripe Red Peppers «

Thresher shark steaks from the ocean off Southern California are usually a bargain buy, since they taste like swordfish at about half the price. This is a beautiful presentation – on a bed of green fettuccine with red pepper sauce.

1½ lbs. thresher shark,
 halibut, or swordfish
 steaks
2 ripe red bell peppers
2 tablespoons olive oil
1 small onion, chopped
2 garlic cloves, minced
5 to 6 anchovy fillets
1 tablespoon parsley,
 chopped
3 shakes of Tabasco sauce

Lemon juice, if desired
2 tablespoons olive oil
2 tablespoons fresh lemon
 juice
½ teaspoon salt
Pepper
Green fettuccine, cooked
 al dente and drizzled
 with olive oil, red wine
 vinegar, and a few dashes
 of garlic salt and pepper

Rinse fish steaks with cold water and pat dry. Have charcoal ready for cooking, or heat broiler. Meanwhile, prepare red pepper sauce: place whole red peppers on grill or beneath broiler; char skin until nearly black all over, turning frequently with tongs. Enclose peppers in plastic bag to steam 5 minutes. Then strip off peel and quarter. Rinse off seeds and cut into small strips. Heat 2 tablespoons olive oil in small saucepan. Sauté onion and garlic until transparent. Add anchovies; stir to "dissolve." Add red pepper strips, parsley, Tabasco sauce, and squeeze of lemon, if desired. Heat through. When ready to cook shark, combine 2 tablespoons olive oil with lemon juice, salt, and pepper. Baste fish and broil or grill on each side until shark flakes when tested with a fork. This will be about 10 minutes total cooking time, depending on thickness of steaks and heat of coals. Place shark steaks on bed of green fettuccine. Top with red pepper sauce. Makes 4 servings.

*– Joyce Rosencrans
Food Editor, The Cincinnati Post*

» Trout and Bacon «

Trout abound in the sparkling streams of the Welsh mountains, and cooking them with bacon gives an added moistness and richness. In the U.S., fresh farm-raised trout are now regularly available in supermarkets and other stores specializing in seafood.

½ lb. bacon
4 fresh trout, cleaned
Salt and pepper
½ lb. mushrooms, sliced

½ cup butter
½ cup flour
2 cups milk
Salt and pepper

Put bacon slices on the bottom of a shallow, ovenproof casserole and cover with the trout. Sprinkle with salt and pepper, cover tightly, and bake in a preheated 375° oven for 40 minutes. Meanwhile, sauté mushrooms in butter for a few minutes, until moisture is evaporated. Add flour; stir and cook for a few minutes; add milk and cook, stirring, until mixture is smooth and thick. Add salt and pepper to taste and pour sauce over cooked trout. Serve at once. Makes 4 servings.

– Karen Rafuse (Mrs. Peter B.)

» Baked Stuffed Red Snapper «

6 tablespoons butter
¼ cup hot water
2 cups bread, cubed
1 medium onion, chopped
2 tablespoons parsley, chopped
½ cup celery and leaves, chopped
1 teaspoon salt
⅛ teaspoon pepper
3 to 4 lb. red snapper, cleaned and scaled
Bacon fat

Melt butter in hot water; pour over remaining ingredients except fish and bacon fat. Mix lightly and stuff fish. Grease a shallow baking dish. Cover bottom with waxed paper and grease well with bacon fat. Place fish on paper. Bake fish 10 minutes per pound in a preheated 400° oven, basting frequently with bacon fat. Makes 6 servings.

– Dottie Rockel (Mrs. John)

» Red Snapper with Raspberry Beurre Blanc «

The Village of Mariemont, Ohio, was planned by Mrs. Mary Emery in the 1920's to be a "national exemplar" for planned communities. Anchoring the center of the Old English-style village's commercial area is the Mariemont Inn. Mrs. Emery also was a patron of the Cincinnati Art Museum and bequeathed the Museum her extensive art collection.

⅔ cup raspberry vinegar
¼ cup shallots, minced
3 cups water
½ cup white wine
1 teaspoon salt
4 red snapper fillets
1 lb. butter, chilled
2 tablespoons whipping cream
Salt and pepper
1 lemon
Whole raspberries
Sprig of fresh mint

(If raspberry vinegar is not available, place 1 cup fresh raspberries and ¼ cup shallots in ⅔ cup champagne vinegar. Over heat, reduce mixture to 3 tablespoons and strain through cheesecloth. Set aside, and continue with instructions for poaching fish.) Bring mixture of raspberry vinegar and shallots to a boil and simmer until reduced to 3 tablespoons. Set aside. In a pan large enough to hold fillets, place water, white wine, and salt.

Bring to boil, add fish, reduce heat, and let simmer for 8 to 12 minutes, depending on the thickness of the fillets. Fish is done when a fork flakes the flesh easily. Make sure fish is covered with water; add more water if necessary. While fish is poaching, finish Beurre Blanc. Over very low heat, warm vinegar mixture. Whisk in butter, 1 tablespoon at a time, until all of butter has been incorporated. Mixture will mound and become glossy. Whisk in whipping cream; season with salt and pepper and a squeeze of fresh lemon. Cover warmed plate with sauce. Place poached fish on top. Spoon a bit more sauce over fish. Garnish with raspberries and mint. Makes 4 servings.

– The National Exemplar Restaurant Mariemont Inn

» Sole Florentine «

Murray Seasongood was one of Cincinnati's most admired citizens. He died in 1983 at age 104 after a lifetime devoted to improving his city. Mr. and Mrs. Seasongood were major contributors to the construction and maintenance of the Faculty Club at the University of Cincinnati.

10 oz. pkg. frozen leaf spinach
Salted water
1 lb. fresh or frozen sole, or other tender/flaky fish, such as orange roughy or flounder
1 medium onion, sliced and separated into rings
Dash of cayenne pepper
½ cup clam broth, chicken broth, or fish stock
2 tablespoons dry white wine
½ cup evaporated milk
1 tablespoon flour
½ teaspoon dried dill
¼ teaspoon dried oregano, crushed

Cook spinach in salted water until tender. Drain well and keep warm. Layer fish fillets and onions in skillet; sprinkle cayenne pepper over fish. Add broth and wine. Bring to a boil, cover, reduce heat, and simmer until fish flakes easily. Remove fish, reserving stock, and keep warm. Combine evaporated milk, flour, dill, and oregano; blend until smooth. Add milk mixture to reserved stock in skillet; continue to cook, stirring until mixture has become thickened and smooth. Serve fish and sauce over spinach. Makes 4 servings.

– The Agnes and Murray Seasongood Faculty Center University of Cincinnati

» Clams in Black Bean Sauce «

Turtle beans or small black beans are mixed with salt and spices by the Chinese and allowed to ferment for several months to bring out the distinctive flavor that adds much to the character of this dish.

1 dozen clams, soaked in fresh water for 3 hours
2 teaspoons cornstarch
1 tablespoon light soy sauce
¾ teaspoon salt
Dash of sugar
1 green pepper, cubed
1 tablespoon water

Dash of salt
1 cup peanut oil
2 cloves garlic, minced
Few slices fresh ginger root
2 tablespoons fermented black beans, mashed into a paste with ⅓ cup water

Scrub clams and remove from shells. Mix with cornstarch, soy sauce, salt, and sugar. Set aside. Stir-fry green pepper with water and salt for a few minutes. Remove and set aside. Heat oil until moderately hot; add clams and stir-fry. Remove clams and all but 1 tablespoon of oil. Add garlic and ginger; stir-fry until golden; add bean sauce, clams, and green pepper. Mix together well and serve immediately with rice. Makes 4 servings.

– Kathleen J. Baker

Plate, XII century, Iran of Syria, glazed earthenware. 1948.99, Purchase. Given in honor of Mr. and Mrs. Charles F. Williams by their children

» Linguine with Clam Sauce «

4 large shallots, peeled and finely chopped
3 carrots, peeled and finely chopped
½ cup olive oil
¼ bunch parsley, finely chopped
½ cup white wine

1 cup clam juice
7 oz. can clams and juice
Pinch of crushed red pepper
3 tablespoons unsalted butter
Linguine

In a large saucepan, sauté shallots and carrots in olive oil. When shallots are soft, add parsley, white wine, clam juice, clams and juice, and red pepper. Simmer over moderate heat until liquid is reduced by about half. Remove from the heat; stir in butter. Serve over linguine. Makes 6 servings.

– Arnold's Restaurant

» Spaghetti alle Vongole «

Spaghetti with Clam Sauce

Once you have become used to pasta cooked al dente, you won't want to go back to the overcooked American style pasta. Al dente means literally "to the tooth," and denotes pasta that is cooked but still offers some resistance to the bite. The best way to test it is to remove a strand and put it "to the tooth."

1 lb. spaghetti
3 tablespoons butter
⅔ cup whipping cream
¼ cup onion, chopped
2 tablespoons parsley, chopped
1 clove garlic, minced

3 tablespoons Parmesan cheese, freshly grated
½ cup Romano cheese, grated
8½ oz. can minced clams
½ teaspoon oregano

Cook spaghetti in large amount of boiling water until al dente. Drain and put into 2-quart ovenproof casserole. Add remaining ingredients, one at a time, mixing well after each addition. Bake in a preheated 350° oven for 35 minutes. Makes 6 servings.

— Mary Ann Shaffer

» Crabmeat au Gratin «

1 stalk celery, finely chopped
1 cup onion, finely chopped
¼ lb. butter
½ cup flour
13 oz. can evaporated milk

2 egg yolks, beaten slightly
1 teaspoon salt
½ teaspoon red pepper
¼ teaspoon black pepper
1 lb. white crabmeat
½ cup Cheddar cheese, grated

Sauté onions and celery in butter until onions are wilted. Blend flour into this mixture. Pour in milk gradually, stirring constantly. Add yolks, salt, red pepper, and black pepper; cook for 5 minutes. Put crabmeat in a bowl large enough for mixing and pour the cooked sauce over the crabmeat. Blend well and then transfer mixture into a lightly greased casserole; sprinkle with grated cheese. Bake in preheated 375° oven for 10 to 15 minutes, or until light brown. Makes 4 servings.

— Brenda Martin (Mrs. F. Gary)
Morgan City, Louisiana

» Maryland Crab Imperial «

French-fried potatoes and cole slaw make a good accompaniment for this dish.

1 green pepper, finely diced
2 large pieces canned pimiento, diced
1 tablespoon dry mustard
1 teaspoon salt
½ teaspoon white pepper
2 eggs, well beaten

1 cup mayonnaise (reserve 2 tablespoons for topping)
5 drops Tabasco sauce
3 cups lump crab meat, fresh or canned
Paprika for garnish

Blend all ingredients except paprika together very gently. Try not to break up lumps of crab meat. Divide mixture into 8 individual baking shells or ramekins. Coat each with reserved mayonnaise and a sprinkling of paprika. Bake in a 350° oven for 15 to 20 minutes, until bubbling. Serve hot or cold. Makes 8 servings.

— Lynn Jacobs (Mrs. Donald S.)

» Crawfish Etoufée «

This is a Cajun dish from the Louisiana bayou country. "Etoufee" means "smothered," and devotees of this dish claim it's smothered in goodness. This Louisiana specialty is a favorite in Breaux Bridge, Louisiana, the "Crawfish Capital of the World," which holds an annual festival where every possible kind of crawfish dish is served.

½ cup butter
1 onion, chopped
½ cup celery, chopped
1 clove garlic, minced
2 tablespoons green pepper, chopped
3 lbs. crawfish tails, peeled

Crawfish fat or tomalley, if available
½ cup green onions, chopped
Salt and red pepper
2 tablespoons flour
1 to 1½ cups water
¼ cup parsley, minced
Cooked rice

Melt butter in a heavy pan and sauté onion, celery, garlic, and green pepper for 10 to 15 minutes, or until tender. Add crawfish, and tomalley. Tomalley is actually the liver of shellfish and adds a rich, intense flavor to any dish. Add green onions, salt, and red pepper. Cook over medium heat for a few minutes; the crawfish will release juices. Sprinkle flour over mixture; stir until blended. Slowly add the water and stir in well. Reduce heat and cook for 20 minutes, adding parsley a few minutes before crawfish are finished cooking. Serve at once over steaming, fluffy rice. Makes 8 servings.

– Brenda Martin (Mrs. F. Gary)
Morgan City, Louisiana

» Crabmeat Key West «

1½ cups mayonnaise
1 teaspoon tarragon
   vinegar
1 teaspoon tarragon
½ cup chili sauce
Dash of Worcestershire
   sauce
Dash of Tabasco sauce
1 teaspoon dry mustard
½ teaspoon paprika
2 cups crab meat, canned
   or fresh, preferably
   back fin, drained
3 slices of bacon, fried
   crisp and crumbled
1 tablespoon parsley,
   finely chopped

Blend mayonnaise, tarragon vinegar, tarragon, chili sauce, Worcestershire sauce, Tabasco sauce, dry mustard, and paprika. Gently toss with crab meat. Divide evenly into 6 shells or ovenproof dishes. Sprinkle with bacon bits. Place in preheated 350° oven until just heated through; do not overcook. Remove from oven and sprinkle parsley on top of each dish before serving. Makes 6 servings.

– Margaret Minster (Mrs. Leonard)

» Oysters Mosca «

¼ cup virgin imported
   olive oil
¼ cup butter
¼ cup shallots, tops and
   bottoms, finely chopped
2 tablespoons parsley,
   finely chopped
1 tablespoon garlic, finely
   chopped
⅔ cup Italian seasoned
   bread crumbs
¼ cup Parmesan cheese,
   grated
½ teaspoon salt
¼ teaspoon black pepper
⅛ teaspoon cayenne
   pepper
½ teaspoon basil
½ teaspoon oregano
8 raw oysters, opened but
   in shell

Sauté the first 5 ingredients until the onions and garlic are soft and translucent. Blend in the rest of the ingredients except oysters. Place oysters in baking-serving dish. Divide mixture over oysters; bake 15 minutes in preheated 425° oven. Makes 1 serving.

– Brenda Martin (Mrs. F. Gary)
Morgan City, Louisiana

» Quenelles de Poisson avec Sauce Normande «

These delicate fish dumplings with shrimp and mushroom sauce were originally painstakingly made by French chefs using mortar and pestle, or a fine sieve. With the advent of the blender and food processor, the art of the quenelle became possible for all.

1 cup water
1 teaspoon salt
¼ cup butter
1 cup flour
2 eggs
2 egg whites
1¼ lbs. pike, halibut, or
   hake fillets
Pinch of nutmeg
½ teaspoon salt
¼ teaspoon pepper
2 to 6 tablespoons
   whipping cream
1 cup fish court bouillon
   or clam juice
1 cup dry white wine

Sauce Normande

1 cup butter
2 tablespoons clam juice
¼ cup whipping cream,
   heated
4 egg yolks
1 teaspoon lemon juice
¼ teaspoon salt
Pinch cayenne pepper
1 tablespoon brandy
7 oz. can tiny shrimp,
   drained
12 mushroom caps
Parsley for garnish

In a heavy saucepan, heat water, salt, and butter until water is boiling and butter is just melted. Remove pan from heat and add flour all at once, using a wooden spoon. Return pan to heat; beat mixture until some of the moisture evaporates and it pulls away from the sides of the pan to form a ball. Remove from heat, add eggs and egg whites, one at a time, beating after each addition. Process fish fillets in a food processor until the mixture is smooth and fine. Beat the purée into the flour and egg mixture along with nutmeg, salt, and pepper. Add enough cream, one teaspoon at a time, until mixture is just stiff enough to hold a shape when it is spooned up. Using two tablespoons dipped into cold water, form fish mixture into rounded ovals 1½″ long and drop carefully into shallow pan filled with 1″ of court bouillon/white wine mixture, gently simmering. Poach for 8 to 10 minutes, basting constantly. Remove quenelles with a slotted spoon and drain on paper towels; keep warm while preparing sauce. Heat butter, clam juice, and cream until bubbly. Place egg yolks, lemon juice, salt, cayenne pepper, and brandy in blender or processor fitted with steel blade. With motor running, add bubbling mixture from saucepan, and flick motor off and on twice. Return to saucepan and add shrimp and mushroom caps which have been sautéed in butter until light brown. Serve hot sauce over quenelles and garnish with parsley. Makes 4 servings.

– Mrs. Samuel Thompson

» Coquilles a la Nage «

Scallops in Cream

This French method of preparing seafood in a court-bouillon yields a delightful sauce with which to nap the scallops and vegetables. A court-bouillon is simply an aromatic liquid in which fish, meat, or vegetables are cooked or marinated.

¾ cup water	1 lb. scallops, sliced
1 tablespoon shallots or onion, chopped	4 to 5 mushrooms, sliced
1 carrot, peeled and thinly sliced	1 tablespoon butter
	1 tablespoon flour
½ teaspoon salt	½ cup whipping cream
¾ cup dry white wine	Salt and pepper
	Sherry

Combine water, shallots, carrot, and salt; cook, covered, for 10 minutes. Add wine and bring to simmer. Add scallops and poach about 4 minutes. Drain, reserving liquid. Sauté mushrooms in butter. Remove and add to drained scallops and vegetables. Reduce scallop liquid to half by boiling. Add flour to mushroom butter (add a little more if needed). Add reduced liquid and whipping cream; stir until sauce is smooth. Season with salt and pepper and a dash of sherry. Arrange scallops and vegetables in 6 ovenproof shells, pour sauce over each, and put into a preheated 400° oven for a few minutes. Makes 6 servings.

– Winnie Love (Mrs. Wesley)

» New England Clambake «

If you have access to fresh seaweed and lobster, this will result in the most succulent shellfish you've ever tasted.

Easy Method

On top of wood or charcoal fire built on base of rocks and stones, place old-fashioned copper boiler or large, covered pot. Fill with:

1st layer, seaweed and small amount of salt water	4th layer, corn in husks
	5th layer, seaweed
	6th layer, clams
2nd layer, lobsters	7th layer, seaweed
3rd layer, seaweed	

Cover with broiler lid or piece of heavy canvas. Cook at least 1 hour.

Hard Method

Line pit with stones or rocks. Heat the stones with a wood fire for 2 hours. Use same procedure as above, with 1st layer of seaweed directly on hot rocks and embers. Cover with heavy tarp. Cook for 2 hours.

– Tom and Leslie Bittenbender

» Scalloped Chicken and Oysters «

2 cups chicken broth	Salt and freshly ground pepper
6 chicken breasts, split	
6 chicken thighs	2 tablespoons fresh tarragon, minced, or 1 teaspoon dried tarragon
4 cups soda crackers, crumbled coarsely	
½ cup butter	1 cup half and half cream
2 lbs. mushrooms, sliced	½ cup herbed bread crumbs, optional
1 quart fresh oysters, drained, reserving liquid	Chopped parsley and tarragon

Heat chicken broth, chicken breasts, and thighs until simmering; cover and cook until tender. Cool chicken in stock; skin and bone chicken, reserving stock for later use. Grease a 2-quart casserole and sprinkle the bottom with a layer of cracker crumbs. Dot with butter; add a layer of chicken, a layer of mushrooms, and a layer of oysters. Season with salt, pepper, and tarragon. Sprinkle cracker crumbs over and dot with more butter. Repeat layers until all ingredients are used. Mix 1 cup of reserved chicken stock with cream and pour into casserole. Sprinkle crumbs over the top; bake in a preheated 350° oven for about 40 minutes. Oysters should be slightly wrinkled around the edges; do not overcook. Sprinkle with parsley and tarragon. Serve at once. Makes 10 to 12 servings.

– Karen Rafuse (Mrs. Peter B.)

» Salade Tiede de St. Jacques «

This is a typical French nouvelle cuisine recipe, with the surprising combination of cold, crisp greens with hot shellfish.

Salad greens (Bibb, romaine, red leaf lettuce, endive, or spinach)	2 tablespoons sherry or other flavor vinegar
16 large scallops	Fresh tarragon or other herbs
¼ cup olive oil	1 teaspoon soy sauce
	Salt, pepper, and sugar

Wash salad greens and dry thoroughly. A mixture of 3 or 4 greens is most attractive. Arrange on salad plates. Sauté scallops quickly on both sides in 2 tablespoons oil; do not overcook. In a separate pan, combine rest of ingredients with remaining oil; mix well over medium heat until quite hot. Arrange hot scallops over greens and pour hot vinaigrette over. Serve at once. Makes 4 servings.

– Ann Trufant (Mrs. S. A. III)

» Frikedel Jagung, Shrimp «

Frikadelle is the Danish meat ball. This Indonesian version changes the spelling and the concept somewhat.

½ lb. shrimp, finely chopped	¼ teaspoon pepper
5 to 6 large ears corn, scraped off cob	1 teaspoon salt
	1 tablespoon garlic, grated
1 to 2 eggs	1 tablespoon onion, grated
3 tablespoons flour	1 teaspoon coriander seeds, ground
3 tablespoons green onion, chopped	3 cups oil

Combine all ingredients except oil; mix together well. Heat oil in pan, preferably a wok, 325° to 350°. Pour about 1 tablespoon of the mixture into frying pan for each fritter, making 4 to 5 fritters at a time. Fry for about 3 minutes, or until golden brown. Makes 8 to 10 servings.

– Dora Ang (Mrs. Francis)

» Les Crevettes Gourmet «

1 slice white bread, toasted	½ teaspoon shallots, chopped
5 large shrimp, shelled and deveined	¼ cup sweet butter
½ cup mushrooms, sliced	1½ ozs. dry white wine
1 teaspoon garlic, chopped	Salt and pepper
	Chopped parsley

Cut bread into four triangles. Sauté shrimp, mushrooms, garlic, and shallots in a heavy skillet with butter and wine. Season with salt and pepper. Place toast triangles on a warm plate. Top with shrimp, mushrooms, and shallots. Garnish with parsley. Makes 2 to 3 servings.

*– Chef George Pulver
Gourmet Room, Terrace Hilton Hotel*

» Shrimp with Cashews «

¾ lb. shrimp, peeled and deveined	1 teaspoon ginger root, minced
¼ teaspoon salt	½ teaspoon dry sherry or rice wine
½ teaspoon dry sherry or rice wine	¼ teaspoon salt
½ egg white, beaten	¼ teaspoon monosodium glutamate, optional
2 teaspoons cornstarch	¼ teaspoon pepper
¼ lb. cashews	¼ teaspoon sesame oil
3 cups water	½ teaspoon cornstarch
½ teaspoon salt	1 tablespoon water
3 cups oil	Cooked rice
2 scallions, green and white, cut diagonally into 1" pieces	

Mix shrimp, salt, sherry, egg white, and cornstarch; marinate 20 minutes. Add cashews to boiling water along with salt. Boil for 6 minutes and drain well. Heat oil in a wok or heavy skillet. Add cashews and fry for 8 minutes, being careful not to burn. Remove and set aside. Add shrimp to oil and fry for 30 seconds; remove from oil. Remove all but 1 tablespoon of oil from wok. Stir-fry scallions and ginger for 3 to 4 seconds, add rest of ingredients; mix and stir-fry. Add shrimp and cashews; stir evenly. Serve immediately with rice. Makes 4 servings.

– House of Hunan Restaurant

» Shrimp Fu Yung «

4 dried Chinese black mushrooms
l cup hot water
6 eggs
½ teaspoon salt
Dash of pepper
½ lb. shrimp, shelled and deveined
6 tablespoons oil, divided
6 green onions, shredded

1 cup bamboo shoots, shredded
½ cup water chestnuts, shredded
1 cup bean sprouts
1 tablespoon soy sauce
¾ teaspoon salt
1 cup chicken broth
1 tablespoon soy sauce
1 tablespoon cornstarch
1 tablespoon water

Soak mushrooms in hot water for 10 minutes; drain and cut into strips and set aside. Beat eggs with salt and pepper until foamy; set aside. In a wok or heavy skillet, stir-fry shrimp with 3 tablespoons of oil until they just begin to turn pink. Combine with green onions, bamboo shoots, water chestnuts, reserved mushroom strips, bean sprouts, soy sauce, and salt; set aside. Heat 1 tablespoon of oil in wok and add ⅓ of shrimp mixture and then ⅓ of egg mixture; fry until brown on both sides. Remove and keep warm while repeating twice, making 3 Fu Yung. Meanwhile, bring chicken broth and soy sauce to a boil and thicken with a paste made from the cornstarch and water. Serve Fu Yung with sauce poured over. Makes 3 servings.

– Dora Ang (Mrs. Francis)

» Spicy Cajun Shrimp Remoulade «

The Heritage is a four-star Cincinnati restaurant that specializes in fresh American cuisine, most recently Cajun and Creole cooking. The restaurant also emphasizes game cookery, and during its annual November Wild Game Festival, such exotica as hippo, lion, and bear are offered in addition to the regular menu.

3 tablespoons vinegar
3 tablespoons Creole mustard
1½ teaspoons grated fresh horseradish
1 tablespoon paprika
Salt and pepper
6 tablespoons olive oil
1½ teaspoons hot pepper, minced

3 tablespoons celery, minced
½ cup green onion, finely chopped
1 tablespoon parsley, finely chopped
24 large shrimp, cooked, peeled, and deveined
Shredded lettuce

Combine vinegar, mustard, horseradish, paprika, salt, and pepper; blend 30 seconds in a food processor or blender. With machine running, gradually add olive oil and continue blending until well mixed. Place mixture in a bowl and add hot pepper, celery, onion, parsley, and shrimp; combine well, being sure shrimp are well coated with sauce. Cover and refrigerate 4 hours or overnight. Serve on a bed of shredded lettuce. Makes 6 appetizer servings.

– The Heritage Restaurant

» Paella «

Cook this saffron-flavored fish, meat, and rice stew in a special 2-handled iron paella pan or use a heavy shallow pan. It's a hearty, one-dish meal. Carlos Casariego lived for a year in Cincinnati as a foreign exchange high school student through the American Field Service, a program in which many Cincinnati families participate.

½ cup olive oil
5 cloves garlic, minced
2 green peppers, thinly sliced
12 shrimp, peeled and deveined
3 squid, cleaned and chopped
18 clams
1 chicken, cut into small pieces

1 tomato, peeled and chopped
2 cups rice
4 cups fish stock, bottled clam juice, or water
½ teaspoon salt
Pinch of saffron
¼ teaspoon paprika
6 mussels

Heat oil in heavy pan and add garlic, peppers, shrimp, squid, and clams. Sauté until clams have opened; remove shrimp, squid, and clams; keep warm. Add chicken and tomato; cook until chicken is browned. Add rice and sauté for 1 minute; add stock, clam juice, or water, salt, saffron, and paprika; cover and simmer for 10 minutes. Add mussels and continue to simmer another 10 minutes or until rice is tender. Return seafood to pan and remove from heat. Cover and let the paella rest for 5 minutes before serving to allow the rice to absorb the tasty broth. Makes 6 servings.

– Carlos Casariego

» Stir-Fried Shrimp and Ham Rice «

½ teaspoon salt
½ tablespoon dry sherry
½ tablespoon soy sauce
½ lb. shrimp, peeled, deveined, cut into pieces
2 tablespoons oil
3 eggs, beaten
¼ teaspoon salt
½ tablespoon dry sherry
Dash of pepper
3 tablespoons oil

½ lb. ham, cut into small cubes
3 tablespoons oil
1 yellow onion, sliced vertically
2 tablespoons green onion, chopped
½ teaspoon salt
1 tablespoon soy sauce
Dash cayenne pepper, optional
3 cups cooked rice

Mix salt, sherry, and soy sauce; marinate shrimp in mixture for a few minutes while preparing remaining ingredients. Heat 2 tablespoons oil in a heavy sauté pan or wok. Pour in eggs mixed with salt, sherry, and pepper; stir-fry quickly until eggs are in tiny pieces; remove and reserve. Heat 3 tablespoons of oil and stir-fry ham for 2 minutes, remove and reserve. Heat 3 tablespoons oil, add yellow onion, and stir-fry for 2 to 3 minutes; add green onion and cook until both are tender but not soft. Remove. Add salt, soy sauce, and cayenne to remaining oil; add rice and reduce heat. Cook, stirring, until rice is heated through. Add ham, shrimp, eggs, and onions; mix and heat well. Makes 4 to 6 servings.

– Dora Ang (Mrs. Francis)

» Seafood Dressing «

½ cup whipping cream, whipped
2 cups mayonnaise
½ cup chili sauce
¼ cup green pepper, finely chopped

¼ cup green onions, finely chopped
Salt and pepper
3 or 4 drops lemon juice
Shrimp or crabmeat

Fold whipped cream into mayonnaise. Mix with chili sauce, green pepper, and green onions. Season with salt, pepper and lemon juice. Serve over shrimp or crabmeat. Makes 3 cups.

Casserole with Lid, 1774-1814, German; Meissen, Porcelain, 1981.70. Centennial gift of the Cincinnati Institute of Fine Arts from the collection of Mr. and Mrs. Arthur Joseph

» Shrimp Toast «

This dish is also delicious served on hot buttered fresh pasta or wild rice.

16 large shrimp, peeled and deveined
¼ cup clarified butter
1½ cups tomatoes, peeled, seeded, and diced
1 cup leeks, cut into julienne slices
¾ cup whipping cream
3 cloves garlic, minced
1 large shallot, minced
1 teaspoon fresh thyme, minced
1 teaspoon fresh basil, minced
½ cup Parmesan cheese, freshly grated
4 pieces rye bread, toasted and quartered diagonally

Sauté shrimp in clarified butter for 2 to 3 minutes; set aside. To clarify butter, melt it in a heavy pan over medium heat, skim off the foam that rises to the top, and strain the clear liquid into another container, discarding the milky residue in the bottom of the pan. Add tomatoes, leeks, and cream to the pan in which the shrimp were sautéed. Reduce the mixture over medium heat for 3 to 5 minutes, until it is of a sauce-like consistency. Add garlic, shallot, thyme, basil, and Parmesan cheese. Remove from heat, arrange shrimp on toast points, and ladle the sauce over the shrimp. Makes 4 servings.

– Chef Craig Paden
Bacchus Restaurant

» Shrimp and Snow Pea Pods «

1 lb. shrimp, shelled and deveined
1½ teaspoons cornstarch
½ teaspoon salt
¼ teaspoon pepper
⅛ teaspoon ginger
1 tablespoon dry sherry or
lemon juice
2 tablespoons oil
½ lb. snow pea pods, trimmed, or 8 oz. pkg. frozen pea pods, thawed and drained
1 green onion, chopped
Cooked rice

Toss shrimp with cornstarch, salt, pepper, ginger, and sherry or lemon juice. Heat oil in a skillet or wok over medium heat. When hot, add shrimp and stir-fry for 2 to 3 minutes. Add pea pods and green onion; continue cooking and stirring for 3 minutes or until pea pods are cooked but still crisp. Serve immediately with rice. Makes 4 servings.

» Cucumber Aspic «

This delicate garnish is an unusual and pretty accompaniment for poached or grilled fish.

3 cucumbers, peeled
1 envelope unflavored gelatin
2 tablespoons cold water
½ cup boiling water
1 tablespoon herb-flavored vinegar
3 drops onion juice
1 tablespoon lemon juice
Salt
Green food coloring

Grate cucumbers into a bowl, saving both juice and pulp; put through strainer, pressing out all the juice, ending up with 1½ cups cucumber juice. Soften gelatin in cold water, then dissolve in boiling water. Mix with the cucumber juice, then stir in vinegar, onion juice, lemon juice, and salt to taste. Add a little food coloring to make the aspic a delicate green. Pour into a shallow dish or pan; refrigerate for several hours or overnight. When set, cut in cubes and serve with fish. Makes 1 pint.

– Eunice Luskey

» Grilled Shrimp «

1½ lbs. raw unshelled shrimp
½ cup olive oil
2 cloves garlic, minced or pressed
2 teaspoons salt
3 tablespoons fresh basil, chopped, or 1 teaspoon dried basil
1 tablespoon red pepper, crushed
2 teaspoons dried Italian herbs
3 tablespoons fresh parsley, chopped, or 1 tablespoon dried parsley

Remove shells from shrimp, leaving tail intact. Combine with remaining ingredients and stir until well coated. Cover tightly with plastic wrap and refrigerate for 6 hours or overnight. Remove from marinade and grill over charcoal, or broil for 2 minutes on each side, until just done. Makes 4 main course servings or 6 appetizer servings.

– The Heritage Restaurant

Thomas Gainsborough, 1727-1788, English, "Returning from Market," ca. 1770s, oil on canvas, 1946.110. Gift of Mary Hanna. This color reproduction donated by Mrs. Richard Thayer

In "Returning From Market" England's greatest portrait artist paints his favorite subject, a landscape. Suffolk-born Thomas Gainsborough learned early that portraits were in demand but landscapes, in the latter 18th century, had little popular appeal. Commissions became satisfyingly numerous but he continued to turn for his own pleasure to the lovely British countryside, as yet uncut by railway lines and accented only by church spires, not industrial smokestacks.

These weary marketgoers, sitting their mounts in the most casual fashion and accompanied by a dog who seems the most energetic member of the party, make their way home through the delicate and uncertain English sunlight, the painting itself an arrangement of diagonals so artful as to appear unplanned. The artist knew precisely what he was about, however. "One part of a picture ought to be like the first part of a tune...you can guess what follows, and that makes the second part of the tune," was Gainsborough's own comment on composition.

An engaging man, fond of the company of musicians and actors but less so of literary men, the artist fitted easily into the society of Bath, where he probably lived at the time of this work, as well as into London circles when the family later moved there.

Eggs, Cheese, Rice, and Pasta

» Chinese Prawn and Bean Sprout Omelette «

Imported oyster sauce may be purchased in Oriental groceries and some supermarkets. A thick brown sauce made of oysters, soy, and brine, it has a pungent aroma and nutty taste and is used in much the same way as soy sauce.

4 dried Chinese black
  mushrooms
2 tablespoons soy sauce
2 tablespoons oyster
  sauce
1 cup water
3 small onions, thinly
  sliced
2 tablespoons oil
¼ lb. medium prawns or
  shrimp, shelled and
  deveined

6 ozs. bean sprouts
6 eggs, lightly beaten
Salt to taste, if desired
Additional oil
1 cup warm water
1 tablespoon cornstarch
3 tablespoons catsup
1 tablespoon chili sauce
2 tablespoons sugar
2 tablespoons light soy
  sauce

Simmer mushrooms in soy sauce, oyster sauce, and water until soft; drain. Sauté onions in oil until soft. Add prawns, bean sprouts, and mushrooms; stir-fry for 2 minutes. Remove from pan and add to beaten eggs. Place a small amount of oil in bottom of a sauté pan. Put ¼ of egg mixture in pan and cook over low heat until egg is set; turn over, fold in half, and remove from heat. Keep warm while repeating 3 more times with remaining egg mixture. Meanwhile, mix all the rest of ingredients together and simmer slowly over low heat until thick. Serve omelettes on warm plates with sauce poured over. Makes 4 servings.

– Betty Pritz (Mrs. Walter)

» Sausage 'n' Egg Casserole «

This is a nice dish for Sunday brunch, a light luncheon, or dinner accompanied by a fresh green salad.

6 hard-cooked eggs, sliced
Salt and pepper
1 lb. hot bulk sausage
1½ cups sour cream

½ cup dry bread crumbs
1½ cups Cheddar cheese,
  grated

Place eggs in buttered casserole and season with salt and pepper to taste. Cook sausage, drain, and sprinkle over eggs. Spread sour cream over sausage. Combine crumbs and cheese; sprinkle over top of casserole. Place in preheated 350° oven until bubbling; brown under broiler. Makes 6 servings.

– Mary Whitehurst (Mrs. Junius)

» Tortilla de Patata «

Omelets of every kind are as popular in Spain as they are in France. This potato omelet is hearty enough for a winter brunch.

¼ cup olive oil
1 oz. slice of ham, cut
  into small cubes
1 small onion, sliced

1 medium potato, sliced
  thinly
2 eggs
Salt

Heat olive oil in a small heavy pan until very hot, almost smoking. Add ham and cook until slightly browned; add onions and cook until soft and golden. Add potatoes and cook until tender. Remove from heat, beat eggs with salt, and add to pan. Return to heat; shake pan and slide a spatula or knife around the edges of the omelet while it cooks to keep from sticking and to form a high, rounded edge. When the eggs are firm, hold a plate upside down over the frying pan. Invert and drop the omelet onto the plate; slide omelet back into pan, browned side up, and cook for 2 minutes more. Serve at once. Makes 1 serving.

– Carlos Casareigo

» Egg Curry «

This is a Malaysian-style curry, which is not prepared with the spicy powder with which we are most familiar. In Malaysia, each cook grinds and mixes spices to individual family tastes. Curry, by another definition, is a stew of meat, fish, or fowl with a spiced sauce.

1 large onion, thinly sliced
4 tablespoons oil
1 teaspoon fresh chili
   powder
1 teaspoon turmeric
   powder
1 teaspoon coriander
   seeds, ground
½ inch piece fresh ginger,
   crushed
2 fresh green chilies, split

lengthwise
2 cloves garlic, minced
15 oz. can tomatoes
12 oz. can coconut santan,
   or 1 cup water plus ¼
   cup yogurt
Salt
4 hard-cooked eggs, or 12
   hard-cooked quail eggs,
   halved
Cooked Malay or white rice

Sauté onion in oil in a heavy pan until brown. Add chili powder, turmeric, coriander seeds, ginger, chilies, and garlic; sauté 3 minutes. Add tomatoes and santan; bring slowly to a boil. If santan is unavailable, use water and add yogurt later to thicken. Simmer gently for 30 minutes to 1 hour or until curry thickens. Add salt and hard-cooked eggs; simmer for a few more minutes. Serve over Malay or white rice. Makes 6 servings.

– Betty Pritz (Mrs. Walter)

» Cardigan Savories «

Serve these with crisp bacon and tomatoes for a hearty Welsh breakfast.

¼ cup rolled oats
¼ cup flour
4 teaspoons baking
   powder

⅛ teaspoon salt
½ cup milk
Bacon fat

Mix dry ingredients together; add milk, mixing well. Let stand a few minutes, and then shape into small cakes. Fry in bacon fat until crisp and browned. Makes 4 servings.

» Crusty Luncheon Dish «

1 lb. loaf white bread,
   thinly sliced
Melted butter
½ lb. Cheddar cheese,
   grated
3 eggs, slightly beaten
1 cup half and half cream
1½ cups milk
1 teaspoon salt

¼ teaspoon paprika
Few grains cayenne
   pepper
½ teaspoon mustard
1 teaspoon
   Worcestershire sauce
½ lb. bacon, fried crisp,
   drained, and crumbled

Brush bread with melted butter on both sides. Fit slices together around sides and bottom of low, buttered baking dish. Bread should extend about 1" above dish. Cover bread with grated cheese. Combine all other ingredients except bacon; mix well and pour over cheese. Bake 30 to 40 minutes in a preheated 350° oven. Sprinkle with bacon and serve. Makes 6 servings.

» Spanakopita «

Phyllo is a Greek dough made from flour and stretched by hand or machine into paper-thin sheets. It is available frozen in supermarkets and specialty food shops.

1 lb. phyllo dough
½ lb. butter
2-10 oz. pkgs. frozen
   chopped spinach
1 lb. ricotta or cottage
   cheese
4 eggs, beaten

¾ lb. Feta cheese,
   crumbled
2 teaspoons onion,
   chopped
2 teaspoons butter
Salt and pepper

In an 11"x14" ovenproof casserole, spread 10 sheets of phyllo pastry, brushing each with melted butter. Cook spinach until moisture evaporates. Add ricotta, eggs, Feta cheese, onion which has been browned in butter, and salt and pepper to taste. Spread filling evenly over phyllo sheets. Cover with 10 more sheets of phyllo, again brushing each with melted butter. Bake in a preheated 375° oven for 40 minutes or until golden brown. Cut into squares to serve. Makes 16 squares.

» Goetta «

This Cincinnati German version of Philadelphia Scrapple is a treat when browned until very crisp in a little bacon fat and served with eggs and bacon, ham, or sausage. Pinhead oatmeal may be purchased in supermarkets and specialty food shops. Do not use regular oatmeal or the texture will not be right.

8 cups water
3 teaspoons salt
Pinch of pepper
2½ cups pinhead oatmeal
1 lb. ground beef
1 lb. ground pork
1 large onion, sliced
3 or 4 bay leaves
Bacon fat
Butter and confectioners'
    sugar, optional
Syrup, optional

Bring the water to a boil and add the salt, pepper, and oatmeal. Cover the pan, lower heat, and simmer for 2 hours, stirring often. Add ground meats, onion, and bay leaves; cook for an additional hour, stirring often. Pour the mixture into 2-3"x9"x5" loaf pans, let cool, cover, and refrigerate overnight. Cut into ⅓" thick slices; fry in bacon fat until crisp. Serve plain, with butter and confectioners' sugar, or with syrup. Makes 54 slices.

» Sausage Scrapple «

1 lb. bulk pork sausage
4 cups cold water
1 cup enriched yellow
    cornmeal
1½ teaspoons salt
¼ teaspoon grated nutmeg
¼ teaspoon dried sage
Syrup, optional

Brown sausage in large saucepan. Stir to break up lumps of meat. Drain the meat in a large sieve or colander and pour out the excess fat. Return saucepan to heat; stir together the cold water, cornmeal, salt, nutmeg, and sage in pan. Heat until boiling, then continue cooking and stirring slowly for 10 minutes, or until the cornmeal thickens. Remove from heat and stir in the drained, crumbled sausage. Pour into a greased 9"x5" loaf pan, cover and refrigerate overnight until scrapple is firm. When ready to serve, loosen edges of scrapple from loaf pan by running a thin-bladed knife along sides; invert onto a sheet of foil and then slice off pieces as needed, no thicker than ½". Fry as for plain cornmeal mush, until crisp on both sides, on a griddle with oil or a little butter plus oil. A skillet or griddle with a nonstick coating is best for frying mush or scrapple; otherwise it will tend to stick and so more oil will be needed. Serve with syrup, if desired. Makes 15 slices.

– Mrs. Sally Scott

» Chiles Rellenos con Queso «

You can also make traditional meat-filled Chiles Rellenos from this recipe by substituting Picadillo for the cheese stuffing. Mild California Anaheim chiles or green bell peppers may be used if Poblano chiles are not available.

12 fresh Poblano chiles
12½"x4" strips Monterey
    Jack cheese
½ cup flour
8 eggs, separated
Oil for frying
1½ lbs. tomatoes, peeled
    and finely chopped
1 medium onion, chopped
2 tablespoons olive oil
2 cups chicken stock
1 cinnamon stick
Salt and Tabasco sauce

Impale the chiles on a long-handled fork; hold them over an open flame, turning until the skin is charred and blistered, or put them under a preheated broiler, about 1" below the heat unit, turning on all sides until blistered and lightly browned. Put in a plastic bag, close tightly, and allow them to "sweat" for 20 minutes. Remove and peel off skins under running water. Cut out stem and carefully slit peppers on one side. Remove seeds and veins. Drain on paper towels. Put a piece of cheese inside each pepper, pressing cut seam together. Dredge in flour. Beat egg whites until stiff. Remove from mixer bowl and beat egg yolks until thick and lemon-colored. Fold the whites and yolks together. Coat the chiles with the batter, using two forks to remove and place into 375° oil. Fry until golden. Drain on paper towels. For the sauce, sauté the tomatoes and onion in oil, until the onion is tender. Add chicken stock, cinnamon stick, and salt and Tabasco sauce to taste; simmer for 15 minutes. To serve, top each chile with a spoonful of the tomato sauce. Makes 6 servings.

– Marilyn Harris
L.S. Ayres 4th Street Market

» Enchilada Breakfast «

This recipe came from Guatemala via a friend in
Chicago. Although neither of us could speak the other's
language with any fluency, we had no trouble
communicating over good food.

1 tablespoon oil
1 tablespoon flour
1 teaspoon chili powder
2 dashes salt
½ cup water
4 eggs

4 corn tortillas
½ cup Cheddar cheese,
  shredded
1 small onion, finely
  chopped

Blend the oil, flour, chili powder, and salt in a small pan,
heating over low heat until it bubbles for about 2
minutes. Stir in the water, bring to a boil, then lower
heat and simmer. The longer you heat it, the hotter the
sauce. Scramble the eggs soft. Put the tortillas into a
well-greased iron skillet, spoon on the eggs, dividing
equally. Sprinkle the cheese on the eggs, reserving a
little to sprinkle on top. Add the onion. Fold the tortillas
and turn them seam side down. Pour the sauce over the
enchiladas, add the reserved cheese, and bake in a
preheated 400° oven for 10 minutes. Makes 2 servings.

– Mary Anna DuSablon (Mrs. Sean T. Bailey)

» Quiche Lorraine «

If you are a purist, the classic Quiche Lorraine contains
no cheese. The French serve it often with a leafy green
salad, hot crusty bread, and a dry, cold white wine.

3 eggs
2 cups whipping cream
Dash of salt, pepper, and
  nutmeg
8″ pie shell, partially baked

6 to 8 slices bacon, fried
  until crisp
2 tablespoons butter,
  cubed

Beat eggs, cream, and seasonings until frothy and light.
Put bacon pieces in pie shell and pour custard over it.
Dot with butter. Bake in a preheated 375° oven for 25 to
30 minutes, or until puffed and brown.
Makes 4 to 6 servings.

– Sarah Headley (Mrs. Grant)

*Pilgrim Bottle, ca. 1700. Japan, Shodai (Kyushu). Glazed
stoneware, 1982.121. Bequest of Mary M. Emery, by exchange*

» Crêpes aux Roquefort «

This is a recipe from the chef of the French Paquebot "Antilles." The boat sank on the next trip out, but the recipe still thrives in our kitchen.

1 cup cold milk
1 cup cold water
5 eggs
Pinch of salt
2 cups flour, sifted
¼ cup butter or oil, melted

3 ozs. Roquefort cheese, crumbled
½ cup bread crumbs
½ cup half and half cream
½ cup whipping cream
3 ozs. Gruyère cheese

Mix milk, water, eggs, salt, flour, and butter in a blender or mix well with a wire whisk. Make crepes, stack, and refrigerate overnight. Mix Roquefort, crumbs, and half and half cream. Fill crepes with 1 tablespoon of mixture, roll up, and place in a shallow ovenproof dish. Pour whipping cream over crepes, sprinkle with Gruyère, and broil until hot and lightly browned. Do not dry out. Makes 16 crepes.

– Mme. M. Preston Jones
Roquefort-les-Pins, France

» Mushroom Pie «

1 bunch green onions, chopped
¼ cup butter
2 lbs. fresh mushrooms, cleaned
2 tablespoons lemon juice
Salt
1 teaspoon garlic salt
1 teaspoon Maggi
1 drop Tabasco sauce

½ cup half and half cream
Puff pastry for a 10″ quiche pan
2 tablespoons parsley, chopped
½ cup Parmesan cheese, grated
6 eggs, beaten
1 cup Swiss cheese, grated

Sauté onions in butter until transparent. Chop mushrooms coarsely and sprinkle lemon juice over them. Add mushrooms to onions and butter. Season with salt, garlic salt, Maggi, and Tabasco. Simmer for a few minutes and add cream. Continue to simmer over low heat for 20 minutes. Remove from heat and let cool. Roll puff pastry very thin; line a 10″ quiche pan with it. Sprinkle bottom of pastry with ½ of chopped parsley and 1 tablespoon of Parmesan cheese. Stir beaten eggs and remaining Parmesan cheese into cooled mushroom mixture. Pour into pastry-lined quiche pan. Top with grated Swiss cheese and remaining parsley. Bake in preheated 350° oven for 30 to 40 minutes, until quiche is set. Makes 6 to 8 servings.

– Virginia Jones (Mrs. Robert)

» Onion Custard Pie «

1 cup saltine cracker crumbs
½ cup butter, melted
2½ cups onion, thinly sliced
2 tablespoons butter

3 eggs, beaten
1½ cups milk, scalded
1 teaspoon salt
⅛ teaspoon lemon pepper
½ lb. sharp Cheddar cheese, shredded

Combine crumbs and butter; press into unbuttered 9″ pie pan. Sauté onions in butter until golden; put into crust. Slowly add the eggs to scalded milk, stirring constantly. Add the rest of the ingredients and pour over onions. Bake in preheated 350° oven for 40 to 45 minutes, or until a knife comes out clean. Makes 4 to 6 servings.

– Mary Wydman (Mrs. Robert)

» Chawanmushi «

This delicate steamed custard from Japan may be served as a first course or as a light luncheon dish.

3 eggs, beaten
3 cups chicken broth
5 teaspoons soy sauce
½ teaspoon monosodium glutamate
1 chicken breast, boned, skinned, and cut into

bite-sized pieces
4 shrimp, peeled and deveined
4 mushrooms, sliced
4 slices of bamboo shoots
4 sprigs parsley, or 4 scallions, chopped

Mix eggs, broth, and 4 teaspoons of soy sauce in a blender or food processor until whites and yolks are well blended; add MSG. Place 2 pieces of chicken, 1 shrimp, 1 sliced mushroom, and 1 bamboo shoot in each of 4 heatproof bowls or large custard cups. Divide remaining teaspoon of soy sauce among bowls. Pour egg custard over the mixture in bowls. Using a heavy pan with a close-fitting lid, bring about 2″ of water to a boil. Cover bowls loosely with aluminum foil and place in water. Cover and steam for 13 to 15 minutes. Pierce the surface of the chawanmushi with a toothpick. If juices do not emerge, it is ready to serve. Do not overcook or custard will separate. Makes 4 servings.

» Baked Cheese Grits «

This may be refrigerated overnight, or frozen, before baking. If frozen, defrost and stir well before baking.

1 cup grits	1 teaspoon salt
4 cups boiling water	¾ lb. sharp Cheddar or
¼ cup butter	Swiss cheese, grated
3 eggs, well beaten	

Cook grits in boiling water according to directions on package. Add butter, eggs, salt, and grated cheese. Stir well and put in a greased, shallow 2-quart casserole. Bake for 1 hour in preheated 350° oven, or until top is golden brown. Makes 6 servings.

– Bee Herschede (Mrs. John)

» Red Beans and Rice «

Red beans and rice are a Monday tradition in New Orleans. It's handy to simmer the spicy, smoky beans on Sunday, then serve them Monday night when there's only time to cook the rice.

1 large smoked pork hock, approximately 1 lb.	1 generous teaspoon mixed pickling spices, tied in cheesecloth
About 7 cups water	½ to 1 lb. smoked sausage, such as kielbasa, thinly sliced
1 lb. dried kidney beans, rinsed and sorted	
1 teaspoon Worcestershire sauce	Hot cooked brown or enriched white rice
¼ teaspoon Tabasco sauce	Fresh parsley or red onion, minced, optional
3 stalks celery, chopped	
1 large onion, chopped	Red wine vinegar
1 green pepper, chopped	Tabasco sauce
2 large garlic cloves, minced	

No prior soaking of the dried beans is necessary for this dish. Bringing them to a boil, then allowing a lively simmer to finish cooking the beans works fine, because the goal is to produce a creamy bean mixture. So stirring and bubbly cooking liquid is all right; no need for the beans to retain their shape, as for baked beans. Place the smoked hock, water, and kidney beans in a Dutch oven or heavy pot. While bringing the water to a boil, add the Worcestershire sauce, Tabasco, celery, onion, green pepper, garlic, and pickling spices. When boiling, stir well, then cover pot and reduce heat to maintain a lively simmer. Cook until the beans are very well done, at least 2 hours, probably no more than 3 hours. Uncover; stir the beans occasionally, adding a little more water as necessary. Do not add salt. Near end of cooking time, remove smoked pork hock and cool a bit. Continue simmering the beans, mashing a cupful or so to get the desired creamy texture. Strip off the meat from the pork hock; return to pot, along with sausage. Continue to cook at least another 15 minutes. Remove spice bag. Now taste for seasoning – the pork hock and sausage have probably added enough salt. Add more Tabasco, if you can stand it; the beans should be a little hot to team with the bland rice. Ladle generously over cooked rice. Sprinkle with parsley, if desired, or minced red onion. Serve with a cruet of red wine vinegar and a bottle of Tabasco sauce. Makes 8 or more servings.

– Joyce Rosencrans
Food Editor, The Cincinnati Post

» Basmati Rice «

Basmati rice is long, thin-grained rice that many consider the best in the world. The best variety is Dehradun and it is worth the extra price.

2 cups Basmati rice	¼ teaspoon whole black peppercorns
2 tablespoons ghee or clarified butter	½ teaspoon turmeric
4 whole cloves	Salt
1″ piece stick cinnamon	4 cups cold water

To prepare Basmati rice in the authentic Indian way, three steps are necessary: 1) Cleaning – spread rice on flat surface and remove any foreign objects. 2) Washing – put rice in large bowl and fill with cold water. Let rice settle, pour off water, repeat process until water runs clean and clear. 3) Soaking – add twice the amount of cold water as raw rice; soak ½ hour; drain, reserving

· 112 ·

liquid, because in Indian cooking, the rice is always cooked in the water in which it was soaked. Heat ghee in a heavy pan and sauté cloves, cinnamon, peppercorns, and rice for a few minutes, stirring so rice does not stick to bottom of pan. Add turmeric, salt, and water. Bring to a boil, cover pan, reduce heat, and cook 12 minutes. Makes 6 to 8 servings.

– Jennifer-Ann Fernandes (Mrs. Allan)
New Delhi, India

» Broccoli-Rice Casserole «

This can be made ahead and baked just before serving.

1 small onion, chopped
¼ cup butter
10¾ oz. can cream of mushroom soup
¼ lb. sharp Cheddar cheese, cubed

10 oz. pkg. frozen broccoli, defrosted and chopped
3 cups cooked rice
Salt and pepper

Sauté onion in butter; mix with undiluted mushroom soup. Add the cheese and cook over medium heat, stirring until cheese is melted. Add broccoli, rice, salt, and pepper. Stir well and place in a buttered 2-quart baking dish. Bake in preheated 350° oven 20 to 30 minutes, or until bubbling. Makes 6 to 8 servings.

– Ruth Noll (Mrs. Harry)

» Coconut Rice «

Mrs. Fernandes is a noted cook and author of "100 Easy-to-Make Goan Dishes." Several of her authentic Indian recipes are included in this cookbook.

1 large fresh coconut, grated
5 cups boiling water, separated
3 cups Basmati rice
1 large onion, sliced

3 tablespoons ghee or clarified butter
½ teaspoon whole black peppercorns
2 teaspoons turmeric
Salt
Fried onions

Grate coconut in food processor or by hand. Add 3 cups boiling water. When cooled to lukewarm, strain liquid from coconut and reserve. Add remaining 2 cups of

boiling water to coconut and repeat process. Keep extracts separate; one will be thick and the other thin. Discard coconut, which you have squeezed dry. Soak rice in water to cover for 30 minutes. See index for recipe for the authentic Indian way to prepare Basmati rice. Sauté onion in ghee until it begins to brown; add peppercorns, turmeric, and drained rice. Sauté 5 minutes; add thick coconut milk, thin coconut milk, and enough water to cover rice with 1" of liquid, if necessary. Bring to a boil, reduce heat, cover, and cook 12 minutes. Correct seasoning for salt and garnish with fried onions, if desired. Makes 9 to 12 servings.

– Jennifer-Ann Fernandes (Mrs. Allan)
New Delhi, India

» Lentils and Rice «

The lentil is a native of southwestern Asia and the Middle East.

1¼ cups lentils
2 tablespoons olive oil
4 cups boiling water
1 teaspoon salt
Dash pepper

1½ cups rice, uncooked
3 oz. can French-fried onions
3 cups plain yogurt or Tomato sauce

Clean lentils and soak in cold water to cover for 30 minutes. Drain and sauté in oil in a heavy pan for 5 minutes. Add 3 cups water, salt, and pepper; cook, uncovered, over medium heat for 10 minutes. Stir in rice and remaining boiling water. Bring to boil, reduce heat to low, cover, and simmer 25 minutes without stirring. To serve, place lentils and rice on a platter and cover with French-fried onions. Serve yogurt or Tomato sauce on the side. Makes 6 to 8 servings.

Tomato Sauce

¾ cup tomato paste
3 cups canned tomatoes, chopped
1 green pepper, chopped
¼ cup celery leaves, chopped

1 tablespoon sugar
½ teaspoon salt
1 teaspoon cumin
Pepper

Combine all ingredients in a heavy pan; simmer slowly 20 to 30 minutes, until sauce is thick.

– Vesta Kitchens Dajani (Mrs. Adnan)

» Arroz Mexicana «

In Mexico, rice is called "sopa seca" or dry soup, and it is served as a separate course following the "wet" soup, in much the same way that Italians serve pasta or risotto.

2 cloves garlic, minced
1 medium onion, chopped
2 Anaheim green chiles, chopped
1 to 2 Jalapeno chiles, chopped
¼ cup lard
2 cups long grain rice

3 medium fresh tomatoes, peeled and finely chopped
4 cups chicken stock
10 oz. pkg. frozen green peas
1 tablespoon cilantro, chopped

Sauté garlic, onion, and chiles in lard. Use mild Anaheim chiles and only 1 Jalapeno for a less hot flavor. Add rice and stir to coat. Stir in tomatoes and chicken stock. Cook, covered, over low heat for 20 to 25 minutes, or until all liquid is absorbed. Let rest 20 minutes. Cook peas according to the directions on the package and add to rice along with cilantro; serve immediately. Makes 8 servings.

– Marilyn Harris
L.S. Ayres 4th Street Market

» Nasi Minyak «
Malay Rice

In the Far East, butter may be made from either buffalo or cow's milk. It is clarified by heating it until the milk solids are separated from the clear fat. The clarified butter, or ghee, keeps longer in a hot climate and cooks without burning.

1 small clove garlic, sliced
1 tablespoon ghee or clarified butter
1 medium onion, sliced
½" piece of fresh ginger, minced

2 cloves
½" piece stick cinnamon
Salt
2 cups boiling water
1 cup Thai or Chinese rice

Sauté garlic in ghee until light brown; add onion, ginger, cloves, cinnamon, and salt; cook for 3 minutes. Add boiling water and rice, stir, cover pan tightly, reduce heat, and cook for 20 minutes or until liquid is absorbed. Turn heat off and let rice stand in covered pan for a few minutes. Stir before serving. Makes 4 servings.

– Betty Pritz (Mrs. Walter)

» Feathered Rice «

My mother-in-law sent this family recipe to me from Texas a few months after we were married. This rice can be browned several days in advance, stored, and baked when wanted. In this case, you may need to bake it a few minutes longer.

1 cup rice, dry
1½ teaspoons salt

2½ cups boiling water

Brown to golden-brown the dry rice in shallow pan in a preheated 375° to 425° oven. Place in casserole; add salt and boiling water and cover with a tight-fitting lid. Bake 30 minutes in preheated 400° oven, or 45 minutes at 350°. Makes 4 to 6 servings.

– Shirley Chewning (Mrs. John B.)

» Sartu di Riso alla Napoletana «

This rice timbale is a favorite from my birthplace, Naples. This dish may be cooked partially, refrigerated, and then reheated just before serving.

1 medium onion, chopped and divided
1¼ cups butter, divided
¼ lb. prosciutto or baked ham, diced
½ lb. mushrooms
10 oz. pkg. frozen peas
¾ cup chicken broth
5 mild Italian pork sausages, cooked and diced
Salt and pepper

3 cups long grain rice
4 cups chicken broth
Freshly grated Parmesan cheese
Chopped parsley
3 eggs, beaten
¾ lb. Mozzarella cheese, sliced and divided
2 eggs, hard-cooked and sliced
Bread crumbs

Sauté ½ of the onion in ¼ cup butter until transparent, add ¼ of the prosciutto and the mushrooms; cook for another 5 minutes, or until lightly browned. Add peas and broth; cook, covered, for a few minutes or until peas are done. Mix in the sausage, salt, and pepper; set aside. Meanwhile, sauté remaining onion in ¼ cup butter; add rice and cook, stirring, until rice begins to brown lightly. Add chicken broth, cover, reduce heat, and simmer for 15 minutes. Remove from heat and immediately add ¾

· 114 ·

cup of butter, and Parmesan cheese and chopped parsley to taste. Let mixture cool; add beaten eggs and ½ of the reserved mushroom and pea mixture. Spoon ½ of the rice mixture into a 2-quart ovenproof casserole which has been greased well on bottom and sides and sprinkled with bread crumbs. Pat the mixture down with wet hands. Top with ½ of the sliced Mozzarella, sliced hard-cooked eggs, and the rest of the prosciutto. Lightly cover with rice, and the rest of the mushroom and pea mixture. Cover with the remaining sliced Mozzarella and dot with butter. Cover with remaining rice, sprinkle with bread crumbs, and dot with butter. Bake in a preheated 375° oven for 1 hour, or until top has formed a golden crust. Remove from oven and cool for 10 minutes before slicing to serve. Makes 6 to 8 servings.

– Kay Foglia Bishop (Mrs. Dolloff F.)

» Risotto alla Milanese «

Rice, Milan Style

In Milan, you're more likely to be served rice than pasta. This is the typical northern Italian style, cooked with butter and chicken broth and flavored with golden saffron and Parmesan cheese. We particularly like it with Chicken Breasts alla Margherita and Braised Peas with Lettuce.

5 tablespoons butter	*½ teaspoon saffron*
1 onion, chopped finely	*threads*
1 cup dry white wine	*4 to 5 cups chicken broth*
2 cups long grain rice	*3 tablespoons butter*
1 teaspoon salt	*1 cup Parmesan cheese,*
¼ teaspoon white pepper	*freshly grated*

Melt the butter in a 4-quart saucepan. Add onion and cook, stirring, until transparent. Add wine and cook over a brisk flame until wine is evaporated. Add rice, salt, and pepper; stir until all rice grains are coated. Add saffron and approximately 2 cups of broth. Cook until broth is almost completely evaporated; add remaining broth, a little at a time. Reduce heat and continue to cook, uncovered, stirring frequently, for about 20-25 minutes until rice is al dente, or done but still firm, an almost nut-like texture. Remove from heat and add remaining butter and grated cheese. Makes 6 to 8 servings.

– Dottie Kreeger (Mrs. John)

» Riz au Four «

Oven Baked Rice

The French often sauté rice in hot fat before adding the cooking liquid. This cooks the flour coating of the rice and prevents it from becoming sticky.

2½ tablespoons butter	*3 sprigs parsley*
2 tablespoons onion,	*1 sprig thyme, or ¼*
minced	*teaspoon dried thyme*
½ teaspoon garlic, minced	*Salt*
1 cup rice	*Pepper*
1½ cups chicken broth	*½ bay leaf*

Melt ½ of butter in an ovenproof casserole. Add onion and garlic, stirring and sautéing until onion is translucent. Add rice and cook briefly, stirring to coat rice with butter. Stir in broth, making sure there are no lumps in rice. Add the parsley, thyme, salt and pepper to taste, and bay leaf. Cover tightly, place in preheated 400° oven for exactly 17 minutes. Uncover and remove parsley, thyme sprigs, and bay leaf. Stir in remaining butter. Serve immediately or keep warm.
Makes 4 servings.

– Barbara Lauterbach (Mrs. Peter)

» Rice Pilaf «

Orzo is the Italian word for barley. In this recipe, it is a barley or rice-shaped pasta that gives this Middle Eastern pilaf a nutty, rich taste.

2 cups uncooked brown	*3 tablespoons olive oil*
rice	*¾ cup orzo*
4 cups boiling water	*6 cups chicken broth*
1 tablespoon salt	*½ cup pine nuts, toasted*
1 cup onion, chopped	*⅓ cup currants*
6 tablespoons butter	*Fresh dill sprigs*

Cover rice with boiling water in a large bowl. Add salt and let stand 10 minutes; drain and rinse. Sauté onion in butter and oil in a heavy pan. When onion is golden, add orzo and continue sautéing until orzo is brown. Add drained rice and cook, stirring constantly, until rice sizzles. Pour in chicken broth and simmer, covered, over medium heat until broth is absorbed and rice is tender,

25 to 30 minutes. Stir in pine nuts and currants and simmer, uncovered, over medium heat for 2 minutes. Serve garnished with dill. Makes 10 servings.

– Anne Seasholes Cozlu (Mrs. Cem)

» Cracked Wheat Pilaf «

This is a good substitute for rice, but wonderful on its own. If you really want to eat in the Near Eastern style, serve the pilaf with crisp romaine lettuce leaves, which are used to scoop up the pilaf.

*1 cup coarse cracked
　wheat or bulgur
2½ tablespoons butter*

*1 medium onion, chopped
2 cups chicken stock
Salt*

Sauté cracked wheat in butter; add onion and cook until soft. Bring stock to a boil in a heavy saucepan; add wheat and onion; season with salt to taste. Return to boil, cover, and simmer 20 to 30 minutes, or until all liquid is absorbed. Makes 6 servings.

– Vesta Kitchens Dajani (Mrs. Adnan)

» Cheese Fondue «

When we lived in Zurich, our Swiss neighbors taught us a few rules for eating fondue. He who loses a piece of bread in the mixture has to pay for a bottle of wine or the next fondue. If the lady loses her bread, she must kiss the gentlemen on either side of her.

*1 clove garlic
½ cup dry white wine
5 oz. imported Gruyere
　and Emmental cheese,
　grated
1 tablespoon Kirsch
½ teaspoon potato flour,
　cornstarch, or
　arrowroot*

*Dash of freshly ground
　nutmeg
Dash of freshly ground
　pepper
Crusty French or Italian
　bread, cut or broken
　into cubes
Kirsch or black tea*

Rub the inside of a fondue pot with the garlic clove. Add wine and heat until bubbles begin to rise to the surface; add cheese gradually, stirring constantly with a wooden spoon in a figure 8 motion. Stir until cheese is melted. Mix Kirsch with potato flour and stir into cheese. Add

nutmeg and pepper. As soon as fondue has come to low boil, carry to the serving table and place over an alcohol burner or candle to keep hot. Dip bread cubes into the fondue, using a long-handled, 3-pronged fork, giving it a good stir each time. Serve Kirsch or black tea with the fondue. Makes 1 serving; multiply as needed.

– Barbara Eveland (Mrs. Joseph)

» Lukchen Kugel «

This is a sweet baked kugel which is served as an accompaniment to poultry or roast meat.

*1 lb. pkg. egg noodles
¾ cup butter
6 eggs
¼ cup sugar*

*Pinch of salt
¼ cup golden raisins
⅛ teaspoon cinnamon
1 teaspoon lemon juice*

Boil noodles according to directions on the package. Drain, refresh with cold water, and drain again. Meanwhile, melt some of the butter in a 9″x13″ baking pan and spread it over the bottom and sides of the pan. Combine drained noodles and other ingredients with the remaining butter, mixing well. Pour into the buttered pan; bake in a preheated 350° oven for 40 minutes. Serve hot. Makes 6 to 8 servings.

*– Sidney Glazer
Sidney's Just South Restaurant
Atlanta, Georgia*

» Crunchy Noodles «

These noodles have a surprising, pleasant texture. They're great with sauerbraten and gravy.

*3½ cups medium width
　noodles
5½ cups beef or chicken
　broth*

*6 tablespoons butter,
　melted
35 butter-style crackers,
　crumbled
Freshly ground pepper*

Cook noodles in boiling broth until just tender, about 15 minutes. Drain well and place in a large heavy pan with melted butter. Toss together with crackers and pepper to taste. Serve at once. Makes 4 to 6 servings.

– Dottie Jacobs (Mrs. Don)

Charles-Edouard Jenneret le Corbusier, 1881-1965, French,
"1920: Still Life," 1957, transfer lithograph,
1966.572. Gift of the Cincinnati Print and Drawing Circle
in memory of Mrs. Hugo L. Kupferschmid

» Gnocchi di Spinaci «

Maestro Coppola, one of Cincinnati's favorite guest conductors, has been charming Queen City opera goers for years. He has graciously consented to share one of his Italian culinary masterpieces with our readers. It arrived written on musical score paper.

2 lbs. fresh spinach
1 lb. ricotta cheese
1 egg
3 tablespoons flour
Salt and pepper

Additional flour
1 quart water
½ cup butter
1 cup Parmesan cheese,
freshly grated

Remove stems from spinach and cook a minute or two until just tender. Allow to cool and squeeze quite dry; chop. Combine spinach, ricotta, egg, flour, and salt and pepper to taste. Mix with hands and roll into 1½" balls. Roll balls in flour until coated. Bring water to a boil. Add gnocchi and cook until they pop to the top. Remove with a slotted spoon and place in a well-buttered ovenproof casserole. Cut butter into pieces and place around and between gnocchi. Sprinkle with Parmesan cheese. Place in a preheated 350° oven until hot through – 10 to 15 minutes. Makes 4 servings.

– Maestro Anton Coppola

» Pasta con Pesto «

With the availability of fresh herbs, pesto appears more frequently on American tables. Originally Italian cooks painstakingly prepared the pungent sauce using a mortar and pestle to crush the herbs and garlic.

1 cup fresh basil leaves	3 tablespoons imported
¼ cup fresh parsley	olive oil
¼ cup pine nuts, lightly toasted	2 tablespoons butter, softened
¼ cup English walnuts, chopped	¼ teaspoon salt
	Water
2 cloves garlic, crushed	8 oz. pasta
½ cup Parmesan cheese, freshly grated	2 quarts water

Place all ingredients except water and pasta in a blender or food processor. Process by turning the motor off and on for short periods, until the mixture is smooth and uniform but still retains some texture. Add enough water to make a paste the consistency of catsup. Meanwhile, boil the pasta in water for 6 to 8 minutes, or until it is al dente. Drain immediately in a colander or strainer. Toss the hot pasta in a large bowl with the pesto and serve immediately. Makes 4 servings.

– Jeanne Seddio

» Spaghetti alla Carbonara «

½ lb. bacon, diced	1 cup whipping cream
½ lb. Canadian bacon, cut into julienne slivers	1 lb. spaghetti
	4 quarts boiling water
4 egg yolks	1 tablespoon oil
2 whole eggs	½ cup butter, softened
Parmesan cheese, grated	

Cook bacon pieces for a few minutes; add Canadian bacon slivers and continue cooking slowly while preparing the pasta. Mix egg yolks and whole eggs; beat until light and frothy. Add enough Parmesan cheese to make a sauce as thick as gravy; set aside. When bacon is cooked, but not yet crisp, pour off excess fat and add whipping cream to the bacon in the pan. Bring just to a boil, lower heat, and simmer for 10 to 15 minutes. Meanwhile, place spaghetti in boiling water to which oil has been added. Cook al dente; drain quickly in a colander. Place spaghetti in serving dish, add butter, and toss quickly. Toss in egg and Parmesan cheese mixture. Toss in bacon and cream mixture. Serve at once. Makes 6 to 8 servings.

– Jo Lane (Mrs. Jerome J.)

» Spaghetti alla Bolognese «
Spaghetti with Meat Sauce

The essential Italian meat sauce is also called al ragu and al sugo. This is a variation on the classic meat sauce that derives its name from the northern Italian city of Bologna – where some of the best cooking in Italy is found.

Salt	Italian herb seasoning, or
1½ lbs. lean ground beef	a combination of basil,
1 large onion, chopped	oregano, thyme, bay
2 cups mushrooms, sliced	leaf, fennel
2-8 oz. cans tomato sauce	Garlic cloves, crushed
4 cups tomato juice	Spaghetti or other pasta, cooked al dente

Sprinkle a little salt on the bottom of a heavy skillet. Brown ground beef and onion over medium heat, stirring. Pour off excess fat. Add mushrooms, tomato sauce, and 2 cups of tomato juice. Add herb seasoning and garlic to taste. Stir and cover. Simmer for at least ½ hour, adding more tomato juice and stirring from time to time as it cooks. Longer cooking only makes it better. Serve over thin spaghetti or other pasta. Makes 8 servings.

– Fanny Smith (Mrs. George)

» Sun-Dried Tomatoes with Pasta «

You may buy imported sun-dried tomatoes in specialty stores where they are usually stored in olive oil flavored with rosemary. You also may dry your own small, firm, pear-shaped Italian tomatoes. Wash the tomatoes and slice lengthwise into halves. Sprinkle the cut side with salt and place, cut side up, on a wire rack in a shallow baking pan. Bake at 200° until the tomatoes are flat ovals which are dry to the touch but not brittle, about 7 to 9 hours. Remove and cover with oil to which you have added a sprinkling of rosemary; they will keep indefinitely as long as the oil remains fresh.

2 eggs
½ cup sun-dried tomatoes, finely chopped
½ cup oil from tomatoes
½ cup Parmesan cheese, freshly grated
½ cup parsley, chopped
2 cloves garlic, mashed
1 tablespoon lemon juice
8 ozs. linguine, fettuccine, or tagliarini
2 quarts water
Salt and pepper

Whisk the eggs, tomatoes, oil, cheese, parsley, garlic, and lemon juice together until well blended. Meanwhile, boil the pasta in water for 6 to 8 minutes, or until it is al dente. Drain in a colander or strainer; toss with two forks with the egg mixture. Add salt and pepper to taste; serve immediately. Makes 4 servings.

» Pasta Sauce with Beef and Mushrooms «

Dried Italian porcini mushrooms impart a special taste to this sauce, but fresh mushrooms may be used with great success.

½ cup butter
½ cup olive oil
2 large onions, chopped
3 large cloves garlic, minced
1 stalk celery, chopped
1 teaspoon ground cloves
4 large fresh metts, skinned
Salt
Freshly ground pepper
1½ lbs. ground chuck
28 oz. can Italian tomatoes
4-12 oz. cans tomato paste
1½ cups water
¼ cup dried funghi or imported Italian mushrooms, soaked in warm water and squeezed
Rotini or spaghetti

Sauté together butter, oil, onions, garlic, celery, cloves, 2 of the metts, salt, and pepper, until the onions are golden. Add ground chuck and cook until it begins to brown. Add tomatoes, tomato paste, water, and mushrooms; stir well and place remaining 2 sausages, cut into pieces, across the top of the sauce. Cook slowly for 2½ hours, stirring often to prevent sticking. Add more salt and pepper, if necessary, before serving. Serve with rotini or spaghetti. Makes 10 to 12 servings.

– Eunice Gronauer (Mrs. Raymond)

» Conchiglie e Luganega «
Pasta and Sausage

Conchiglie is the Italian name for seashells. The name describes the pretty shape of the pasta in this recipe, which is ideal for trapping tasty morsels of sausage with its delicate sauce. Luganega is a mild pork sausage. If not available, bratwurst is a good substitute. Do not use sweet Italian sausage or any flavored with fennel.

2 tablespoons shallots, chopped
2 tablespoons butter
2 tablespoons olive oil
½ lb. luganega sausage, skinned and crumbled
1½ cups whipping cream
Freshly ground pepper
Freshly grated nutmeg
1 lb. small conchiglie pasta
4 quarts water
Salt
Parsley, chopped
Parmesan cheese, freshly grated

Sauté shallots in butter and oil until soft. Add the sausage and sauté about 10 minutes, stirring frequently. Add cream and pepper to taste; cook, stirring frequently, until thickened. Add nutmeg to taste. Drop conchiglie into boiling salted water, stir to separate, and cook until al dente. Drain well, tossing gently to empty shells of water. Combine pasta with sauce and serve immediately on warmed plates. Sprinkle with parsley and pass a bowl of freshly grated Parmesan cheese.
Makes 4 to 6 servings.

– Dottie Kreeger (Mrs. John)

» Straw and Grass Pasta alla Edwards «

½ lb. bacon, chopped
½ cup onion, chopped
1½ teaspoons garlic, minced
½ teaspoon salt
Pinch of pepper
6 ozs. green peas
¼ teaspoon nutmeg
1 teaspoon ginger
1 tablespoon mint, fresh if available
3 cups whipping cream
½ lb. spinach fettuccine
½ lb. regular fettuccine
¼ cup Parmesan cheese, freshly grated
1 teaspoon salt
½ teaspoon pepper
Additional freshly grated Parmesan cheese
Additional freshly ground pepper

Edouard Vuillard, 1867-1940, French, "The Cook," 1899,
color lithograph, 1951.348. Gift of Albert P. Strietmann

Sauté bacon until crisp in a heavy pan. Pour off half the fat, add onion, garlic, salt, and pepper. Cook until onions are soft; add peas, nutmeg, ginger, mint, and cream. Bring to a boil and simmer for 1 minute. Meanwhile, cook green and white fettucine al dente and drain well. Add to above along with Parmesan cheese, salt, and pepper. Mix together well and put on warmed plates. Serve immediately with a bowl of grated Parmesan cheese and a pepper mill.

Makes 4 entree, or 8 appetizer, servings.

– Rob Fogel
Edwards Under 5th Cafe

» Fettuccine with Broccoli and Mozzarella «

Edwards is a delightful restaurant that is located in a building that formerly housed the Edwards Manufacturing Company. Diners enjoy northern Italian cuisine in the former Board Room and in the glass-enclosed turn-of-the-century offices.

2 pounds broccoli, cut into small flowerettes	*3 cups whipping cream*
Salt	*1 lb. egg fettuccine*
Pepper	*½ teaspoon salt*
Juice of 2 lemons	*1 teaspoon pepper*
½ cup unsalted butter	*¼ cup Parmesan cheese, freshly grated*
½ teaspoon salt ½ teaspoon pepper	*6 oz. Mozzarella cheese, grated*
½ teaspoon nutmeg	*Additional freshly grated Parmesan cheese*
½ teaspoon red pepper flakes	*Freshly ground pepper*

Poach or steam broccoli until just tender, using water flavored with salt and pepper to taste and the lemon juice. Drain and place in a heavy pan; add butter, salt, pepper, nutmeg, pepper flakes, and whipping cream. Bring to a boil, lower heat, and simmer for 1 minute. Meanwhile, cook fettuccine al dente; drain well. Add to the broccoli mixture; mix well along with salt, pepper, Parmesan, and Mozzarella. Serve immediately on warmed plates with additional Parmesan cheese and a pepper mill. Makes 4 entree or 8 appetizer servings.

Rob Fogel
Edwards Under 5th Cafe

» Creamy Cheese Noodle Casserole «

4 ozs. fine noodles, cooked and drained	*1 teaspoon Worcestershire sauce*
1 cup large curd cottage cheese, drained	*4 drops Tabasco sauce*
1 cup sour cream	*1 to 2 tablespoons flour*
⅓ cup onion, finely chopped	*¼ teaspoon salt*
1 clove garlic, minced	*⅛ teaspoon white pepper*
	¼ cup fine, dry bread crumbs, buttered

While noodles are cooking, mix next 6 ingredients together. Sprinkle with a mixture of the flour, salt, and pepper. Blend the cottage cheese mixture with the cooked noodles. Turn into a buttered 1½-quart casserole; sprinkle crumbs on top. Bake in a preheated 350° oven until crumbs are lightly browned, about 20 to 30 minutes. Makes 8 servings. This casserole freezes well.

– Charlotte Kruse (Mrs. Henry O.)

» German Spaetzle «

Spaetzle or "little sparrows" are tiny dumplings that make a wonderful accompaniment to roasted game or fowl. This dish has an intriguing combination of textures. In neighboring Austria and Hungary, spaetzle are often served with grated Parmesan cheese, poppy seeds, or sesame seeds.

2 cups flour	*2 eggs, well beaten*
⅔ cup water	*½ cup bread crumbs*
½ teaspoon salt	*¼ cup butter*

Put flour in a mixing bowl and make a well. Add water, salt, and eggs. Mix well. Drop by half teaspoonful into a large pot of salted, boiling water. Reduce heat to simmer and cook about 10 minutes until the spaetzle all rise to the top. Drain. Meanwhile, sauté bread crumbs in butter until lightly browned. Sprinkle crumbs over spaetzle. Makes 4 servings.

– Mrs. Donna Schott

» Tagliarini con Carne «

Tagliarini is a thinner version of the best-known egg noodle – tagliatelle, or as it is called in Rome, fettuccine. The golden strands of noodles are said to have been inspired by the long blonde hair of Lucretia Borgia.

2 lbs. ground beef
5 tablespoons olive oil
3 garlic cloves, minced
2 medium onions, minced
16 oz. can tomatoes
15 oz. can tomato paste
2 tablespoons Italian seasoning, or a mixture of basil, oregano, and thyme

2 tablespoons chili powder
1½ teaspoons celery salt
½ teaspoon cayenne pepper
12 oz. pkg. thin egg noodles, cooked al dente and drained
2 teaspoons Parmesan cheese, grated

In a heavy skillet, brown meat in olive oil. Remove meat from skillet and lightly sauté garlic and onions in remaining oil. Do not allow garlic to brown or it will have a bitter taste. Mix beef, garlic, onions, tomatoes, tomato paste, and seasonings together. Place noodles in a buttered heat-proof casserole and pour mixture over noodles. Stir gently and sprinkle cheese over the top. Bake in a preheated 350° oven for 15 to 20 minutes, or until bubbly. Makes 10 to 12 servings.

– Gloria Nutini (Mrs. Louis J.)

» Yorkshire Pudding «

This traditional English dish is marvelous served with a standing rib roast. All can be done ahead except the baking.

⅞ cup flour
½ teaspoon salt
½ cup milk
2 eggs, beaten well

½ cup water
¼ cup whipping cream
Drippings from roast beef, or melted butter

Sift flour and salt together; add milk and stir well. Add eggs; mix well. Add water; beat well until large bubbles rise to the surface. This mixing may also be done in a blender or food processor. Add whipping cream and blend. Prepare ahead to this point and let stand, covered and at room temperature, for at least 1 hour. While roast beef is resting prior to carving, raise the oven temperature to 400°. Place the beef drippings or butter into a well-greased 9″x13″ ovenproof dish. Stir the batter and pour over the drippings; bake for 20 minutes; reduce heat to 350° and bake for another 15 to 20 minutes. The pudding will be puffy, uneven, and browned on the top. Remove, cut in squares, and serve immediately with roast beef and pan juices. Makes 6 servings.

– Harold Poe

» Individual Yorkshire Puddings «

These small versions of the typical English roast accompaniment are also called popovers because they rise so high in the hot oven.

14 tablespoons flour, or 1 cup less 2 tablespoons
1 teaspoon salt
2 eggs

1 cup milk or skim milk
Pepper to taste, if desired
Beef fat from roast

Have all ingredients at room temperature. Mix all ingredients except beef fat together; beat by hand or with electric mixer until batter is very smooth. Do not underbeat batter; you can't beat it too much. About 50 minutes before serving, place a large teaspoonful of fat into each of 12 muffin tins. Iron tins are best, but aluminum will do. Place tins in oven until fat is hot and smoking – this will take 10 to 15 minutes. Beat batter one more time. Add batter to tins. Bake 10 minutes in preheated 475° oven; then reduce heat to 350° and continue baking for 30 minutes or more, until puffy and golden brown. Serve at once with gravy from roast beef. Makes 12 servings.

– Charlotte Stone Fullgraf (Mrs. Charles)

Isaak Soreau, 1604-after 1638, Flemish,
"Still Life with Dish of Strawberries," early 1630's?, tempera
on wood, 1960.496. Gift of Mrs. Robert McKay.
This color reproduction donated by
The Union Central Life Insurance Company, Cincinnati, Ohio

The natural world was of intense interest to painters in the Netherlands of the 17th century, as it was to their patrons. Still life, with meticulous concentration on detail, offered a satisfying means of presenting fruits, nuts, and flowers as well as the insects which in the real world accompanied them. Here the artist, Isaak Soreau, includes two house flies, one of them lighted on a raspberry, and a dragonfly pausing on the wine glass.

The domestic pleasures of attractive tableware frequently lent another element to these works. Soreau clearly liked this Chinese bowl, as he used it in several paintings. But despite the precision of his observation he allowed himself certain romantic departures from fact here, following conventions current at the time.

Tulips and grapes do not appear in the same season, nor do lily of the valley and roses, but such subjects were individually symbolic and their mingling carried added meaning to Soreau's contemporaries. Also, the deliberately unrealistic handling of shadow and proportion leaves the objects without firm anchoring to the table, which is in any case impractically tilted, and injects a lightheaded, dreamlike effect, counterbalancing the neatness of detail. Although some artists by this time were turning to oil paints, Soreau's choice of medium continued to be tempera.

Fruits and Vegetables

» Banana Fritters «

6 large bananas, peeled
   and mashed
2 eggs
Sugar
¼ cup flour

Pinch of salt
Milk
Clarified butter or oil
Confectioners' sugar

Combine bananas, eggs, sugar to taste, flour, salt, and enough milk to form a thick batter. Heat butter or oil in deep frying pan or heavy saucepan and drop spoonfuls of batter into oil. Cook on both sides until brown; drain on paper towels. Sprinkle with confectioners' sugar and serve while hot. Makes 2 to 3 dozen fritters.

– Jennifer-Ann Fernandes (Mrs. Allan)

» Artichoke, Mushroom, and Pine Nut Casserole «

This Lebanese casserole is great with roasts, fillets, or roasted chicken.

1 lb. mushrooms, sliced
¾ cup dry white wine
4 cups artichoke hearts,
   quartered

2-15 oz. cans whole
   tomatoes, drained
½ lb. pine nuts
1 cup Parmesan cheese,
   freshly grated

Mix together all ingredients except cheese; place in a greased 2-quart ovenproof casserole. Sprinkle Parmesan cheese on top. Bake in a preheated 350° oven for 30 minutes. Makes 8 servings.

– Mary Ann Shaffer

» Mama's Frijoles «

These beans can serve as a filling for tacos, burritos, or tostadas, or as a side dish topped with grated cheese, salsa, or guacamole.

½ lb. dried pinto beans
2 to 3 garlic cloves, peeled
   and crushed

¼ cup cooking oil
Salt
Chili powder

Wash beans well and remove pebbles and blemished beans. Place in a large heavy pan and add water, covering beans with 1″ of water. Boil for 1 hour, replacing water boiled away with warm water. Add garlic and simmer for another 90 minutes. Remove beans with a slotted spoon. Place beans in a heavy frying pan with cooking oil. Cook over medium heat, mashing with a potato masher, until beans are thick and pasty. Season with salt and chili powder to taste. Makes 6 servings.

– Lupe Gonzalez-Hoyt

» Western Style Baked Lima Beans «

This recipe originated in the western province of Alberta, Canada, in the area of the great wheat ranches.

1 lb. dried lima beans,
   soaked overnight in
   water to cover
2 to 3 teaspoons salt
½ teaspoon black pepper
½ teaspoon paprika
1 tablespoon butter

½ cup onions, finely
   chopped
½ cup green pepper, finely
   chopped
½ cup olive oil
2 tablespoons boiling
   water

Drain lima beans. Cook them in water to cover until tender; drain. Add salt, pepper, and paprika to beans and place in a buttered casserole. Sauté onion and green pepper in olive oil until tender and lightly browned. Pour this mixture over beans, add boiling water, and stir well. Cover and bake in preheated 400° oven for about 1 hour. If beans become dry, add a small amount of boiling water. Uncover toward end of cooking time to brown. Makes 4 to 6 servings.

– Naomi Bergert (Mrs. Jack)

» Mark's Lima Beans «

This is an old family recipe that our son Mark loved, so we always called them Mark's Lima Beans.

1 lb. dried large lima beans	*1 teaspoon dry mustard*
Water	*½ teaspoon salt*
½ teaspoon salt	*1 tablespoon molasses*
¾ cup brown sugar	*1 cup sour cream*
	¼ cup butter

Soak beans overnight in enough water to cover them. Drain beans and add fresh water to cover along with salt. Simmer over low heat until tender, about 1 hour. Drain and mix the beans with brown sugar, mustard, additional salt, molasses, and sour cream. Pour into a 2-quart ovenproof casserole and dot with butter. Bake in a preheated 350° oven 1 hour. Two large cans of butter beans may be substituted for the dried beans. Makes 8 servings.

– Jane Sweeder (Mrs. Willard C.)

» Kentucky Baked Beans «

This typical dish from the Kentucky Bluegrass was given to me by a jockey's wife. It's a great recipe for a crowd, and can be doubled or tripled, in which case it needs a longer cooking time. It is a recipe that almost cannot be overcooked – it improves with longer cooking time.

3-16 oz. cans baked beans, with or without pork	*½ cup chili sauce*
3 slices bacon, cut into 1" pieces	*1 teaspoon dry mustard*
2 medium onions, thinly sliced	*1 tablespoon brown sugar*
	¼ cup bourbon whiskey

Place ½ the beans in bottom of bean pot or casserole. Cover this layer with ½ the bacon and onions. Mix chili sauce, mustard, sugar, and bourbon together; pour over layer. Cover with rest of beans and top with the remainder of the bacon and onion. Bake at least 3 hours in preheated 250° oven, or until onion and bacon are thoroughly cooked. If using bean pot, keep covered until last ½ hour. If using casserole, keep covered until last ½ hour, then uncover for browning on top. Makes 6 servings.

– Margaret Minster (Mrs. Leonard)

» Sesame Green Beans «

These Oriental-inspired beans are equally good served hot or cold. They may be used as a salad or vegetable dish.

1 lb. fresh green beans	*1 tablespoon sugar*
1 quart boiling, salted water	*1 teaspoon salt*
¼ cup imported soy sauce	*1 teaspoon sesame seeds, toasted until light brown*

Plunge green beans into boiling water; cook for 8 to 10 minutes, or until cooked but still very firm. Drain in a colander and pat dry with paper towels. Combine soy sauce, sugar, and salt; pour over green beans. Add sesame seeds and toss together. Makes 4 servings.

– Cheryl Omori Brinker (Mrs. Barry)

» Schnitzel Beans «

These beans may be prepared several hours before serving time and reheated just before serving. Spinach or small, whole, cooked beets may also be prepared by this method.

1 lb. fresh green beans, trimmed and cut in half	*1 cup sugar*
4 slices bacon, chopped	*½ cup vinegar*
	1 small onion, chopped

Cook or steam beans until crisp-tender. Sauté bacon until browned. Add sugar and vinegar to bacon and fat; cook until dissolved. Add beans and onion; simmer for 20 minutes. Makes 4 servings.

» Green Beans in Olive Oil «

Middle Eastern cooks originated the happy combination of green beans with tomatoes. The result may be served cold as well as hot, and this dish improves with age.

½ cup onions, chopped
½ cup olive oil
1 lb. fresh green beans, strings removed if necessary and ends trimmed

2 medium tomatoes, chopped
1 cup water or tomato juice
1 teaspoon oregano
2 cloves garlic, mashed
Salt and pepper

Sauté onions in olive oil in a heavy pan until soft. Add beans and remaining ingredients; cook until tender. Makes 4 servings.

– Vesta Kitchens Dajani (Mrs. Adnan)

» Haricots Verts au Gratin «

These cheese-topped green beans may be prepared ahead and heated through just before serving. The French serve them with veal chops or scallops, or with roast lamb, veal, or chicken.

2 tablespoons butter
1 small onion, minced
2 tablespoons flour
½ cup chicken broth
½ cup half and half cream
Salt

Nutmeg
2 lbs. fresh green beans, trimmed
½ cup Swiss or Gruyere cheese, shredded

Melt butter; sauté onion until soft. Add flour; cook until golden. Remove from heat. Mix in broth and half and half. Return to high heat and bring to boil, stirring. Season to taste with salt and nutmeg. Set aside. Cook beans in boiling salt water until just crisp, not overdone; drain. Place in shallow 1½-quart casserole. Pour reserved sauce over beans. Sprinkle with cheese and broil until cheese melts. Makes 8 servings.

– Mrs. Molly Fox

» Indian Beans «

Coconut cream is made by mixing fresh grated coconut with boiling water and then squeezing the liquid from the shreds. More water and it's coconut milk. It is used in Indian curries, or as here, where it adds a distinctive flavor to these green beans.

1 lb. French-cut green beans
1 cup water
1 large onion, sliced
¼ teaspoon turmeric powder

1 tablespoon oil
½ teaspoon mustard seed
½ tablespoon curry
1 tablespoon coconut cream or grated coconut
Salt

Boil the beans in water with the onion and turmeric until all the liquid has evaporated. Combine oil, mustard seed, and curry; place over medium heat. When the mustard seeds stop spluttering, add to the boiled beans. Add coconut cream or grated coconut and season with salt to taste before serving. Makes 4 servings.

– Jennifer-Ann Fernandes (Mrs. Allan)

» Bean Sprouts with Ginger «

This recipe from Singapore makes a crisp vegetable accompaniment. Fresh bean sprouts are widely available year round in supermarkets and specialty stores.

1 large onion, thinly sliced
3 tablespoons oil
1½" piece of fresh ginger

Salt or soy sauce
3 cups fresh bean sprouts

Sauté onion in oil in a heavy pan until soft. Crush ginger; add and sauté another 3 minutes. Stir in remaining ingredients, increase heat, and stir-fry until bean sprouts are cooked, but still crisp. Makes 4 servings.

– Betty Pritz (Mrs. Walter)

» Green Beans with Buttered Breadcrumbs «

1 lb. fresh green beans, trimmed
Boiling, salted water
1 teaspoon salt
1 tablespoon butter

¼ cup herbed bread crumbs
Dash of pepper
Dash of garlic powder, or fresh garlic

Cook green beans, uncovered, in a large pot of boiling salted water, until crisp-tender, but not overdone. Drain and run cold water over them to prevent further cooking and to retain their color. Place in buttered casserole. Melt butter in a skillet and add bread crumbs. Brown crumbs slightly; add pepper and garlic. Mix well and sprinkle over beans. Bake in a preheated 350° oven until heated through. For a variation, sauté chopped onion in butter along with bread crumbs. Makes 4 servings.

– Barbara Deming (Mrs. Dorman)
Punta Gorda, Florida

» Rotkohl mit Äpfeln «

The Germans incorporate fruits in many dishes. They are particularly fond of apples, as in this pretty red cabbage dish from Bavaria. It makes a colorful accompaniment to beef or pork dishes.

2 tablespoons chicken fat or butter	Juice of ½ lemon
1 medium onion, sliced	2 cloves
2 tart apples, peeled and diced	1 bay leaf
3 cups water	1 medium head red cabbage, shredded as for slaw
½ cup red wine vinegar	2 tablespoons cornstarch
½ cup sugar	2 tablespoons water
1 teaspoon salt	Freshly grated nutmeg
¼ teaspoon pepper	

Heat chicken fat or butter in large saucepan. Sauté onion and apples for 3 to 4 minutes. Add water, vinegar, sugar, salt, pepper, lemon juice, cloves, and bay leaf; bring to a boil. Add cabbage, cover, and simmer for about 45 minutes, or until tender. Thicken juices with cornstarch dissolved in cold water. Sprinkle with nutmeg before serving. Makes 4 to 6 servings.

– Miriam Fischer (Mrs. Mel)

» Johanna's Red Cabbage «

It was rumored that Johanna once cooked for one of the czars of Russia. She subsequently emigrated to Cincinnati, where she became the cook for a well-known family. She retired at age 85. Among her many specialties was her red cabbage, which she often served with sauerbraten or duck. It can be made ahead and reheated when you are ready to serve.

2 small heads red cabbage, core and outer leaves removed	¼ cup brown sugar
	3 tablespoons white raisins
2 small onions, minced	1 tablespoon red wine vinegar
2 tablespoons butter	
2 tablespoons flour	1 tablespoon red wine
2 tart apples, peeled, cored, and thinly sliced	Salt and pepper

Shred cabbage and soak in cold water in refrigerator for several hours. In a large skillet, saute onions in butter, add flour, and stir. Remove from burner. Put cabbage in a colander, drain. Pour boiling water over it twice and drain. Return pan with onions to stove on medium heat. Add cabbage, apples, brown sugar, raisins, red wine vinegar, red wine, and salt and pepper to taste. Cover skillet and simmer about 1 to 1½ hours, stirring occasionally. Makes 6 servings.

– Margaret Minster (Mrs. Leonard)

» Hot and Sour Cabbage «

2 lbs. nappa, shredded in 1½" lengths	5 tablespoons sesame oil
1½ tablespoons salt	½ tablespoon peppercorns
⅓ cup hot red peppers, shredded	5 tablespoons sugar
1 tablespoon fresh ginger, minced	5 tablespoons vinegar

Put nappa in a large bowl and sprinkle with salt; mix well and let stand 4 hours. Drain and squeeze to remove as much moisture as possible. Add peppers and ginger. Heat sesame oil in a wok or heavy pan; fry peppercorns until dark and good smelling. Add sugar and vinegar, bring to a boil, and pour over nappa; mix well. Cover and let stand at least 4 hours. Serve immediately or store in refrigerator for up to a week. Makes 6 servings.

– House of Hunan

» Aberdeen Carrot Puff «

This fluffy casserole comes from the northern Scottish city that sits where the River Dee joins the North Sea. Upriver about 60 miles is the famed Balmoral Castle.

4 large potatoes, peeled
    and grated
6 carrots, peeled and
    grated
3 eggs, separated
1 teaspoon salt

¼ teaspoon pepper
Pinch of nutmeg
Bread crumbs or
    Parmesan cheese,
    freshly grated

Combine grated potatoes and carrots. Beat egg yolks until thick and light yellow. Mix into vegetables, along with salt, pepper, and nutmeg. Beat egg whites until stiff; fold gently into vegetables. Pour into a 2-quart casserole, buttered and sprinkled with bread crumbs or cheese. Bake in a preheated 350° oven for 35 minutes. Serve at once. Makes 8 servings.

» Carrot Soufflé «

This is a different and delicious variation of the French standard and it never fails. The carrots may be cooked and puréed hours ahead.

2 cups carrots, sliced
½ cup water or chicken
    broth
2 teaspoons lemon juice
2 tablespoons onion,
    minced
½ cup butter, softened

¼ cup sugar
1 tablespoon flour
1 teaspoon salt
¼ teaspoon cinnamon
1 cup milk
3 eggs

Place carrots and water or chicken broth in a covered pan; bring to boil and simmer until carrots are soft. Drain well and purée in blender or food processor. Add lemon juice and cover tightly until ready to use. Combine carrots with rest of ingredients, beat together until smooth. Pour into a lightly-buttered 2-quart casserole and bake in a preheated 350° oven for 45 minutes to 1 hour, until the center of the souffle is firm to the touch. Makes 8 servings.

– Dottie Kreeger (Mrs. John)

Lewis Wickes Hine, 1874-1940, American, "Radishes! Penny Bunch! Sixth Street Market, Cincinnati, Ohio, 10:00 p.m. August 22, 1908," toned gelatin silver print, 1975.359. The Albert P. Strietmann Collection

» Green Corn Cakes «

These are especially good served with fried chicken, as they come hot from the griddle.

8 ears fresh corn	Pinch of pepper
2 tablespoons flour	2 egg yolks, beaten well
½ teaspoon salt	2 egg whites, beaten stiff

Scrape, do not cut, the kernels from the ears of corn, reserving kernels and liquid. Add flour, salt, and pepper. Add egg yolks. Fold in beaten egg whites. Drop by teaspoons onto hot, greased griddle. When brown on the underside, turn and fry for about 1 minute more. Makes 6 servings.

» Japanese Eggplant Ratatouille «

This is a classic French recipe, despite its title. Japanese eggplants are the tender, small ones that we are now able to buy at some seasons of the year ... or grow in our own gardens.

4 Japanese eggplants, about ¼ lb. each, unpeeled and split lengthwise	1 tablespoon tomato paste
	2 cloves garlic, minced
	1 teaspoon fresh basil, minced
1 cup zucchini, diced	1 teaspoon fresh thyme, minced
1 teaspoon salt	
2 tablespoons olive oil	1 small bay leaf
1 cup onion, chopped	Salt and pepper
1 cup peppers, preferably a mixture of red, green, and yellow, chopped	2 tablespoons parsley, minced
2 tablespoons olive oil	Parmesan cheese, freshly grated
1 cup tomatoes, peeled, seeded, and chopped	Sweet butter, softened

Cut 3 slashes in the flesh of each eggplant. Sprinkle with salt and let drain, cut side down, on a rack 30 minutes. Pat dry. At the same time, toss zucchini with salt in a colander and let drain over a bowl for 30 minutes. Pat eggplants dry and place cut side down in a baking pan coated with 1 tablespoon olive oil; brush the skins with additional olive oil. Bake in a preheated 400° oven for 10 minutes, or until tender. Do not overbake. Transfer to rack and let cool. Scoop out pulp, leaving ¼" shell; chop the pulp. Meanwhile, sauté onions and peppers in 2 tablespoons olive oil for a few minutes, until the onion is wilted. Add zucchini and eggplant pulp; cook, stirring, for a few minutes. Add tomatoes, tomato paste, garlic, basil, thyme, and bay leaf; season with salt and pepper. Cover mixture with an oiled round of waxed paper and a lid; cook over low heat for 15 minutes. Remove lid and paper; cook over high heat, stirring, until almost all the liquid has evaporated. Watch carefully so that the mixture does not burn. Remove the bay leaf and add the parsley. Fill shells with mixture, sprinkle with Parmesan, and dot with butter. Broil in an oiled shallow casserole for a few minutes, or until the tops are lightly browned. If making ahead, reheat in oven before broiling. These may be frozen after filling. When ready to serve, thaw, bring to room temperature, and reheat in oven. Add Parmesan and butter after heating, and broil as directed. Makes 8 servings.

– Marge Haller (Mrs. Hugh)

» Spoonbread «

½ cup butter, melted	8 oz. can cream style corn
2 eggs, well beaten	8½ oz. pkg. corn muffin mix
1 cup sour cream	
8 oz. can corn, drained	

Mix butter and eggs together. Add sour cream, both cans of corn and corn muffin mix. Stir well. Place in a 1½-quart well-greased pan. Bake in preheated 350° oven for 45 to 50 minutes. The center of the spoonbread should be of a jelly-like consistency when done. Makes 8 servings. Serve at once.

» Braised Celery «

This is a tasty change from the usual vegetable recipe. It comes from the Bay Tree Hotel, Oxfordshire, England.

6 stalks celery	Salt and freshly ground pepper
1 medium onion, thinly sliced	2 tablespoons butter, softened
6 small carrots, thinly sliced	2 tablespoons flour
2 cups chicken stock	Chopped parsley

Cut celery in half lengthwise, remove the tops, and then cut into 3″ lengths. Blanch in boiling water 10 minutes. Drain well and place in a heavy pan with onion, carrots, and stock; season with salt and pepper. Cover and simmer until vegetables are tender, about 40 minutes. Meanwhile, combine butter and flour to make a smooth paste. Stir into vegetables 3 minutes before they are done and cook until broth is thickened and smooth. Sprinkle with parsley and serve. Makes 6 servings.

– Anne Gebbie (Mrs. Douglas)

» Endive en Casserole «

This is an easy but unusual Belgian vegetable accompaniment to roasted meat or poultry.

8 Belgian endive, washed and trimmed	1 cup dry white wine
2 tablespoons butter	1 tablespoon parsley, chopped
1 cup beef broth or bouillon	Pinch of nutmeg
	Salt and pepper

Wash the endive and cut off the bitter end. Melt the butter in a small saucepan. Add the beef broth, wine, and other ingredients. Mix with the endive and place in a covered 1-quart casserole. Bake in a preheated 400° oven for 20 minutes. Makes 4 to 6 servings.

» Ham-Wrapped Endive with Cheese Sauce «

Belgian endive is available all winter long in grocery stores and it makes an excellent cold weather fresh vegetable. This dish also could serve as a fresh light luncheon dish.

8 small Belgian endive	2 tablespoons butter
8 slices boiled ham	2 tablespoons flour
1 cup dry white wine	1 cup milk
Pinch of nutmeg	Nutmeg, salt, and pepper
¼ teaspoon salt	¼ lb. Emmental cheese, grated
¼ teaspoon pepper	

Wash the endive and cut off the bottom. Wrap each head with a slice of ham and place in a greased shallow ovenproof casserole. Heat the wine, nutmeg, salt, and

pepper together until boiling; pour over the endive and ham. Cover and bake in a preheated 400° oven for 20 minutes. Meanwhile, melt the butter and the flour together. Add milk, stirring constantly, until mixture comes to a boil. Season with nutmeg, salt, and pepper to taste; stir in the cheese. Pour the sauce over the endive and ham; return to the oven until cheese is melted, approximately 10 minutes. Serve immediately. Makes 4 to 6 servings.

» Hot Fruit Compote «

This is delicious served with beef, pork, or poultry.

½ cup prunes	1 teaspoon cinnamon
½ cup pears	½ teaspoon ginger
½ cup peaches	1 teaspoon nutmeg
½ cup pineapple	Juice of 1 lemon
1½ cups applesauce	Zest of 1 lemon, chopped

Mix all ingredients. Bake, covered, in a preheated 250° oven for at least 1 hour before serving. It may be baked up to 3 hours and the longer it bakes, the better it is. Other fruits may be substituted, and either fresh or canned fruits may be used. Makes 1 quart.

– Pat Rutledge

» Fruit Melange «

This is a marvelous winter dessert that is limited only by your imagination. Any combination of canned fruit may be used, including peach halves, pineapple spears or chunks, apricots, or pitted Bing cherries.

12 large macaroons, crumbled	½ cup slivered almonds, toasted
4 cups canned fruit, drained	¼ cup dark brown sugar
	¼ cup sherry
	Sour cream

Butter a 2-quart casserole and cover bottom with macaroon crumbs. Add a layer of fruit. Continue alternating crumbs and fruit until all are used. Sprinkle top with toasted almonds and brown sugar, and drizzle the sherry over it. Bake in preheated 350° oven for 35 minutes. Turn off oven, but leave the casserole in the oven for 20 more minutes. Serve warm with sour cream. Makes 8 servings.

– Edith Magrish (Mrs. James)

» Japanese Fruit Bowl «

Sweet desserts are not popular with Japanese meals. Instead, the light sweetness of chilled fruits is preferred to balance a meal.

¼ cup undiluted frozen
   orange juice
   concentrate
½ cup light corn syrup
3½ cups honeydew melon
   balls
3½ cups cantaloupe balls

2 cups pineapple cubes
1 cup Bing cherries,
   pitted, or 1 cup red
   apples, unpeeled,
   cored, and cubed
Mint sprigs for garnish

Combine orange juice concentrate and corn syrup. Fold into mixed fruit. Chill several hours and serve with mint garnish. Makes 8 servings.

– Mieko Johnston

» Flamiche aux Poireaux «

Leek Tart

A flamiche is a tart especially associated with the provinces of Burgundy and Picardy. Leeks are a nice change in the winter vegetable repertoire.

2 cups flour
1 tablespoon salt
¾ cup butter
1 tablespoon ice water
18 leeks, white part and
   tender part of green
1½ tablespoons butter
2 tablespoons flour

1½ cups milk, or half and
   half cream
Salt
Pepper
Pinch nutmeg
3½ tablespoons butter
½ cup Gruyère cheese,
   grated

Process flour, salt, and ¾ cup butter in food processor or mix with pastry cutter until mixture resembles coarse meal. Add water and continue mixing only until mixture gathers into a ball (more water may be needed, but use only enough to hold mixture together). Cover ball with waxed paper and refrigerate for at least 2 hours. Trim leeks, cut into four lengthwise parts to facilitate washing; wash thoroughly to remove sand. Blanch for 2 minutes in boiling water; refresh under cold water and dry. Melt 1½ tablespoons of butter and flour in heavy pan and cook together, stirring for a few minutes. Add milk, salt, pepper, and nutmeg; cook, stirring, until the sauce becomes smooth and thick. Remove from heat. Place

remaining butter and leeks in a heavy saucepan; cook, covered, for 20 minutes or until leeks are limp. Roll out dough to a ³⁄₁₆″ thick round; line shallow individual baking dishes or a shallow 9″ pie or quiche pan with dough. Line dough with leeks and cover with sauce. Sprinkle with Gruyère cheese. Bake in a preheated 400° oven 20 minutes, until cheese is melted and browned. Makes 8 servings.

– Ruth Swigart (Mrs. Eugene)

» Stuffed Mushrooms with Bechamel Sauce «

12 large mushrooms
1 tablespoon onion,
   chopped
2½ tablespoons butter
3 tablespoons cooked
   ham, finely chopped
Salt and pepper

Bechamel Sauce
3 tablespoons Parmesan
   cheese, grated
2 tablespoons dry
   bread crumbs
Butter

Wash mushrooms, dry thoroughly, and remove stems. Chop stems finely and set aside. Sauté onion in butter until pale gold; add ham and sauté for 1 minute. Add chopped mushroom stems, and season with salt and pepper to taste; cook for 2 or 3 minutes. Tip skillet and remove all fat. Mix mushroom-ham mixture into Bechamel sauce. Add Parmesan cheese and mix again. Meanwhile, place mushroom caps in a buttered baking dish. Fill each cap with mixture. Sprinkle with bread crumbs and dot with butter. Place in oven on rack placed at upper third of oven; bake in preheated 375° oven until crust forms, about 15 minutes. Cool 10 minutes before serving. Makes 6 servings.

Bechamel Sauce

1½ tablespoons butter
1½ tablespoons flour
1 cup milk, at room

temperature
¼ teaspoon salt
Pepper

Melt butter in a saucepan. Do not let it brown. Add flour and beat well with a wire whisk. Add milk, salt, and pepper to taste. When thickened, remove from heat.

– Rosemarie Culver

· 130 ·

Habit de Cuisinier

» Leek Pie «

Because of the cold climate and short growing season, root vegetables are popular in Scotland. This is a blend of two of the favorites — potatoes and leeks. It's a marvelous winter treat for any climate.

4 large potatoes, peeled and cut into ⅛″ slices	½ teaspoon pepper
6 leeks, thinly sliced	2 cups milk, heated to boiling
¼ cup butter	½ cup Cheddar cheese, grated
2 tablespoons flour	
½ teaspoon salt	Pinch of nutmeg

Arrange half of potatoes on the bottom of a well-greased, 2-quart casserole. Top with the leeks and then cover with the remaining potatoes. Melt butter and flour together in a heavy pan over medium heat. Add salt, pepper, and milk; stir well to blend all together until smooth. Add ⅔ of the cheese and nutmeg; combine well. Pour over potatoes. Cover casserole with a lid or foil; bake in a preheated 350° oven for 45 minutes. Uncover and sprinkle with remaining cheese; bake for an additional 15 minutes or until the cheese is lightly browned. Makes 8 servings.

» Mushrooms Supreme «

1 lb. mushrooms, sliced	and diced
¼ cup unsalted butter	3 eggs, well beaten
1 onion, chopped	2 cups milk
½ cup celery, chopped	10¾ oz. can cream of mushroom soup
½ cup green pepper, chopped	1 cup sharp Cheddar cheese, grated
½ cup mayonnaise	
Salt and pepper	¼ cup parsley, chopped
9 slices bread, untrimmed	12 whole mushrooms

Sauté sliced mushrooms in butter for about 7 minutes. Remove from skillet and set aside. Sauté onion, celery, and green pepper until slightly soft. Add sautéed mushrooms, mayonnaise, and salt and pepper to taste. Spread ½ of the diced bread on the bottom of a buttered 9″x13″ baking dish. Pour mushroom mixture evenly on top of bread cubes. Spread remaining bread cubes over the top. Mix beaten eggs and 1½ cups of milk; pour over bread cubes. Cover and refrigerate overnight. Before baking, spread mixture of mushroom soup and ½ cup of milk over prepared casserole. Bake in preheated 325° oven for 50 minutes. Top with grated cheese and parsley. Arrange the 12 whole mushrooms on top so that each is in center of 12 serving portions. Bake 10 or 12 minutes more. Serve immediately. Makes 12 servings.

– Kay Wanous (Mrs. E. E)

» Nappa in Cream Sauce «

2 small or 1 large head
   nappa, coarsely
   shredded
3 scallions, thinly sliced
1 tablespoon butter
Salt and pepper

1 tablespoon white wine
   vinegar
1 tablespoon sesame oil
½ cup half and half cream
2 teaspoons soy sauce
Cooked rice

Stir-fry nappa and scallions with butter for 3 minutes. Season with salt and pepper to taste; sprinkle with vinegar; continue stir-frying for 3 more minutes. Nappa should be cooked but still crisp. Stir in remaining ingredients; cook, stirring constantly, until sauce comes to a boil. Serve at once with rice. Makes 6 servings.

– Betty Pritz (Mrs. Walter)

» Plantation Onions «

This is a favorite holiday dish, good with Thanksgiving turkey or a Christmas ham.

2 tablespoons butter
2 tablespoons flour
½ teaspoon salt
Grinding of black pepper
2 cups milk, or half and
   half cream
2-16 oz. jars boiled small
   white onions, or 16 oz.
   bag frozen small white

onions plus 2 cups
   sliced celery
¾ cup toasted bread
   crumbs
⅔ cup roasted peanuts,
   coarsely ground in food
   processor or blender
3 tablespoons butter,
   melted, or bacon
   drippings

In medium saucepan, melt butter; stir in the flour, salt, and pepper. Let bubble a minute or two to eliminate the starchy taste from the sauce. Remove from heat; whisk in milk. Return to heat; stir until sauce is smooth and thickened. In another saucepan, heat the boiled onions in liquid from jars; drain. If using frozen onions plus

celery, cook briefly as directed on bag; drain. Arrange hot onions and celery in shallow 10"x6" baking dish; no greasing is necessary. Pour the thickened sauce over the vegetables. Stir bread crumbs and peanuts into melted butter or bacon drippings; toss to coat. Sprinkle crumb topping over onions; bake, uncovered, in preheated 350° oven for about 25 minutes. For a variation, crumbled bacon may be added along with the bread crumbs and crushed peanuts. Makes 8 servings.

– Joyce Rosencrans
Food Editor, The Cincinnati Post

» Oignons à la Monegasque «

This French dish that combines onions with raisins is great for picnics or as an accompaniment for roast meat or chicken.

1 lb. small white onions
1½ cups water
½ cup white wine vinegar
3 tablespoons tomato
   paste
3 tablespoons olive oil

½ cup seedless golden
   raisins
1 bay leaf
¼ teaspoon thyme
Salt and pepper
1 sprig parsley, chopped
2 tablespoons sugar

To remove skins from onions, pour boiling water over them to cover; let stand until water cools. Skins will then slip easily from the onions. Combine onions with rest of ingredients in a heavy saucepan; mix well. Cook over low heat until onions are just tender – do not overcook or onions will become mushy. Chill thoroughly before serving. Makes 4 servings.

– Winnie Love (Mrs. Wesley)

» Rösti nach Zürcherart «
Zurich Fried Potatoes

6 medium potatoes
6 tablespoons butter
1 medium onion, finely
   chopped

Salt and pepper
2 tablespoons hot water
Paprika

Boil the potatoes in their skins until tender; cool enough to handle and remove skins. Shred the potatoes or cut into julienne strips. Heat the butter in a heavy 10" pan and sauté onions until transparent. Add potatoes; season with salt and pepper to taste. Cook over low heat, turning frequently with a spatula, until potatoes are soft and yellow. Press potatoes down into a flat cake with the spatula and then sprinkle with hot water. Cover and cook over low heat for 10 to 15 minutes, or until potatoes are crusty on the bottom. Shake the pan frequently to prevent scorching; add more butter, if necessary, to prevent sticking. Turn onto a hot serving dish, crusty side up, sprinkle with paprika, and serve immediately. For a variation, add 3 slices of diced bacon or ½ cup diced Emmental cheese to the potatoes while sautéing. Makes 4 to 6 servings.

– Barbara Eveland (Mrs. Joseph)

» Piselli in Sugo Proprio con Prosciutto «

Green Peas with Italian Ham

1 tablespoon sweet butter	2 cups fresh peas, shelled
1 tablespoon olive oil	Salt and pepper
2 large sweet onions, thinly sliced	3 slices Prosciutto, minced

Heat butter and oil in a heavy skillet with a tight-fitting lid. Add onions and cook over very low heat until they are soft. Add washed and drained peas; stir and cover. Cook over low heat about 12 minutes, or until peas are just tender. Season with salt and pepper. Serve hot, garnished with Prosciutto. Makes 4 to 6 servings.

– Audrey McCafferty

» Colcannon «

This dish is also called champ or thump, and is eaten all year round, but particularly at Hallowe'en or All Hallows Day. A ring, a sixpence, a button, and a thimble are often added to the mixture. For the finder, the ring foretells marriage; the sixpence, wealth; the button, a bachelor; and the thimble, a spinster.

1 lb. Irish potatoes	2 tablespoons whipping
½ lb. cabbage or kale	cream
1 small onion, chopped	Salt and pepper
¼ cup butter	Additional butter

Boil potatoes in their skins until very tender. Boil or steam cabbage until tender; chop very finely. Meanwhile, sauté the onion in butter until transparent and soft. Peel the potatoes and put through a ricer or sieve; add the onions and butter, whipping cream, salt, and pepper to taste; beat until fluffy. Mix in the chopped cabbage or kale; heat in a heavy pan over a low flame until quite hot. Serve at once with additional butter melting over the top, or melted in a well in the center of the Colcannon. Makes 6 servings.

– Marianne O'Regan

» Clapshot «

This recipe is from the Orkney Islands, off northeastern Scotland, and illustrates the Scottish affinity for tuberous or root vegetables.

1 lb. potatoes	1 tablespoon chives, or
1 lb. turnips	4 shallots, minced
2 tablespoons butter	Salt and pepper

Peel and cook the vegetables separately. Drain well. Mash the vegetables separately, then combine. Add butter, chives, and salt and pepper to taste. Beat the clapshot over heat until well-mixed. Serve piping hot. Makes 8 servings.

– Aurelia Klayf (Mrs. Bernard)

» Potato Dumplings «

There is a "dumpling belt" in Europe which stretches from Poland to Alsace and includes parts of Germany, Switzerland, Austria, and Czechoslovakia. This is a typical example.

8 red potatoes, cooked and peeled	½ teaspoon nutmeg
	3 teaspoons salt
3 eggs, beaten	2 quarts boiling salted
1 cup flour, sifted	water
⅔ cup bread crumbs	

Force the potatoes through a ricer. Add eggs, flour, bread crumbs, nutmeg, and salt. Beat until fluffy. Shape into small balls. Drop in simmering salted water. Simmer until dumplings rise to surface. Cover and cook 3 minutes longer. Remove and drain. Makes 6 to 8 servings.

» Potato Cakes «

Grated raw potatoes are often added to this recipe in Ireland, resulting in boxty, which, taken with a steaming cup of "tay," makes a delightful and filling meal.

½ lb. cooked potatoes, sieved
½ cup flour
¼ teaspoon salt
¼ teaspoon baking powder
1 tablespoon butter, melted
Milk

Mix potatoes, flour, salt, baking powder, and butter to make a smooth dough, adding a little milk if necessary. Turn onto a floured board and knead until smooth. Divide into two pieces and roll each piece into a circle ¼" thick. Cut each circle into 6 to 8 triangles. Cook on a well-greased griddle until nicely browned on both sides. Makes 12 to 14 cakes.

– Pud Preston (Mrs. Robert H.)

» Pommes Anna «

The French have a special two-part pan for these marvelous potatoes, but a cast-iron skillet is perfect for creating a crisply browned crust.

4 large potatoes, peeled and very thinly sliced
Salt and pepper
½ cup or more butter, melted

Dry potatoes with a paper towel. Sprinkle with salt and pepper; dip into butter. Use a greased heavy au gratin pan or skillet. Arrange the slices in a decreasing circle around the pan, overlapping slices a bit; proceed until all potato slices are used. Bake in a preheated 350° oven until brown and crisp. Serve at once. Makes 4 servings.

– Ann Trufant (Mrs. S. A. III)
New Orleans, Louisiana

» Potato Kugel «

A kugel is a baked dish of German-Jewish origin which is often served as a separate course, or as an accompaniment to poultry or meat.

4 to 5 medium potatoes, peeled and grated
1 onion, finely grated
3 eggs
⅓ cup flour
1½ teaspoons salt
⅛ teaspoon pepper, or more to taste
¼ cup oil, or 2 tablespoons chicken fat

Combine potatoes and onions. Beat eggs until thick and add to potatoes and onions, along with the remaining ingredients. Mix well with fork. Place in a greased 2-quart casserole. Bake in a preheated 350° oven for 1 hour, or until kugel is light brown and crisp. It may be cut into sections and served hot or cold. Makes 4 servings.

– Bonnie Warton

» Double-Duty Potatoes «

This is known as using everything but the squeal! Start out with hash browns, and use the skins for tasty hors d'oeuvres.

4 large Idaho potatoes, baked
Oil, butter, or bacon grease
Salt and pepper
Butter
Parmesan cheese

Split potatoes and empty the shells. Put potatoes in frying pan with oil, butter, or bacon grease. Season with salt and pepper to taste. Cook over low heat for 45 minutes, keeping oil at a level so potatoes do not stick. Flatten potatoes in pan just before serving. Turn upside down on a serving plate. Makes 4 servings.

Potato Skins: Butter insides of potato skins. Sprinkle with Parmesan cheese; cut in strips. Bake in preheated 350° oven until crisp.

– Carl and Eleanor Strauss

Double-spout bottle, Peru, Nazca, ca. 400-600 A.D.,
painted pottery, 1956.216. Gift of Harold Kaye.
This color reproduction donated by Cincinnati Microwave, Inc.

The fiercely bristling figures which circle the upper portion of this double-spouted water jar are highly stylized deities, probably associated with agriculture and fertility. The Nazca Indians of Peru made and used pottery of this type a thousand years before Europeans knew the Americas. The jar is dated 400 to 600 A.D. While we know little of the specific symbolism of the top figures, the frieze of cheerful faces below them may well allude to beans, the Nazcas' staple crop. The slip-painted decoration has the sophistication of several shades of brown on its pale ground as well as a creamy color for faces. The lower section and the bottom are unpainted. As broad as it is tall, the spherical container stands seven inches high.

» Feathery Potato Casserole «

This can be made a day ahead and refrigerated, unbaked. Bring to room temperature before baking.

6 medium size Idaho potatoes, peeled and quartered
Salt and white pepper
1 egg, well beaten
½ cup half and half cream
3 tablespoons butter, melted
1 cup whipping cream, whipped

Cook potatoes until tender; mash. Season with salt and white pepper to taste. Mix beaten egg, half and half, and 2 tablespoons melted butter. Fold into mashed potatoes. Fold whipped cream into potatoes; mix thoroughly but lightly. Place in buttered casserole. Bake in preheated 350° oven for about 45 minutes, or until heated through. Drizzle remaining melted butter over top and put under broiler for browning about 2 minutes. Makes 6 servings.

» Spinach Souffle «

This variation on classic spinach souffle is special because of the Parmesan and onion flavors. The souffle mixture is also good baked in vegetable containers, like firm tomato cups, zucchini boats, or acorn squash halves.

10 oz. pkg. frozen chopped spinach, or 1½ lb. fresh spinach, cooked, chopped, and drained
¼ cup butter
1 small onion, finely chopped
¼ cup flour
1 cup milk
4 eggs, separated
2 tablespoons Parmesan cheese, grated
½ teaspoon salt
Grinding of black pepper
Grating of nutmeg

Cook frozen spinach according to package directions; drain and press out excess liquid. If using fresh spinach, be sure to snip through it while in the colander. Melt butter in a large saucepan; add onion and sauté until tender. Blend in flour; let cook a minute or two. Remove from heat; gradually stir in the milk. Return to heat; stir and cook until sauce is thickened. Remove from heat. Beat egg yolks in a separate bowl until light-colored. Stir into the sauce after first stirring a bit of the warm sauce into the yolks. Add spinach, cheese, salt, pepper, and nutmeg. Set a shallow pan filled with water to the depth of 1″ on the center rack in a preheated 350° oven.

Meantime, in a small, clean, and grease-free mixing bowl, beat the egg whites at high speed until stiff. They should not slip when the bowl is tipped or inverted. Fold a third of the glossy whites into the spinach mixture to lighten it. Blend until very well mixed. More carefully, incorporate the remaining egg whites, trying to preserve as much air as possible. Cut through the mixture with a rubber scraper and turn the bowl by quarter turns in order to fold in the whites. Turn the spinach mixture into a well-buttered 1½-quart souffle baking dish; set in the water in the pan in the oven. Bake 40 to 45 minutes, or until puffed and lightly browned. Serve as soon as possible. Makes 4 servings.

*– Joyce Rosencrans
Food Editor, The Cincinnati Post*

» Spinach Strata Supreme «

72 butter crackers
2½ cups Muenster cheese, grated
2-10 oz. pkgs. frozen chopped spinach, thawed and well-drained
2½ cups milk
2 tablespoons Dijon mustard
Few drops Tabasco sauce
2 cloves garlic, chopped
5 eggs, beaten

In a 2-quart shallow baking dish, arrange 24 crackers, slightly overlapping in 3 long rows. Combine cheese and spinach; sprinkle ⅓ of the mixture over the crackers. Repeat with 2 additional layers of crackers, alternating with spinach and cheese mixture, using 24 crackers for each layer and making 3 rows each time. In a medium bowl, beat mustard, Tabasco, and garlic with the eggs. Pour evenly over the baking dish. Bake in a preheated 350° oven for 30 to 35 minutes, or until puffed and golden. Makes 6 to 8 servings.

– Nan Strubbe (Mrs. John L.)

» Espinacas Catalan «

In the Spanish restaurant where we enjoyed this unusual spinach dish, the final cooking was done in a chafing dish at the table.

2 lbs. fresh spinach,
    cooked, or 2-10 oz. pkgs.
    frozen spinach, cooked
½ cup seedless raisins
½ cup hot water
¼ cup pine nuts

2 tablespoons combined
    butter and olive oil
½ cup ham, coarsely
    chopped
Salt and pepper

Drain cooked spinach thoroughly and chop coarsely. Combine raisins and hot water; let stand 30 minutes to plump raisins. Drain; stir-fry raisins and pine nuts in butter and oil in a heavy pan until nuts are golden brown. Add chopped ham and fry lightly. Add spinach and fry for two minutes, tossing constantly. Season with salt and pepper to taste; serve immediately.
Makes 4 servings.

– Beverly Mourning (Mrs. Marion P.)

» Spinach Artichoke Casserole «

This casserole may be made ahead and heated when you're ready to serve. It also freezes very well.

4 10 oz. pkgs. frozen
    chopped spinach
½ cup butter, melted
2-8 oz. pkgs. cream
    cheese, softened
8 oz. can artichoke hearts,
    drained and quartered
6 oz. can water chestnuts,
    drained and sliced

2 teaspoons onion powder
Cayenne and black
    pepper
½ cup herb dressing
    crumbs
½ cup Parmesan cheese,
    freshly grated

Thaw and drain spinach well, squeezing to remove all water. Add butter, cream cheese, artichoke hearts, water chestnuts, and onion powder. Season with cayenne and black pepper to taste and mix thoroughly. Place in a 2 quart casserole. Cover with herb crumbs and sprinkle with Parmesan cheese. Bake 30 to 40 minutes in preheated 350° oven, or until browned on top.
Makes 12 servings.

– Lucy Wagner (Mrs. Richard)

» Les Tomates Françaises «

The colorful contrast of these vegetables makes this a striking as well as tasty dish.

4 ripe medium tomatoes
Olive oil
White wine vinegar

Basil, fresh or ground dried
Salt and pepper
½ lb. snow pea pods,
    trimmed

Cut tops off tomatoes; scoop out the pulp and seeds. Remove seeds and mash pulp with a little oil, vinegar, and basil; season with salt and pepper to taste. Spoon pulp back into hollowed tomatoes and divide pea pods among tomatoes, placing in an upright position. Sprinkle with additional oil, vinegar, and basil. Place in a buttered baking dish and cook in preheated 350° oven until heated through and tender – about 20 minutes.
Makes 4 servings.

– Spencer Kuhn

» Stewed Tomatoes, Beans, and Artichokes «

Artichokes are a favorite Greek vegetable; here they are combined with some more familiar ones to come up with an uncommon dish.

2 onions, finely chopped
½ cup olive oil
1 lb., 14 oz., can tomatoes,
    or 2 lbs. fresh tomatoes
1 clove garlic, crushed
½ teaspoon dill

½ teaspoon basil
2 lbs. green beans, fresh
    or canned
8½ oz. can artichoke
    hearts

Sauté onions in olive oil until transparent. Remove seeds and skin from tomatoes by putting through a ricer, food mill, or colander. Add the tomato pulp to the onions and simmer over low heat for 30 minutes. Add the garlic, dill, and basil. If using fresh beans, boil in salted water to cover, until just tender; drain. Add drained beans to tomato sauce and simmer for 30 minutes. Add artichoke hearts and simmer for another 15 minutes. Serve warm.
Makes 8 servings.

– Cleo Seremetis (Mrs. Wm. G.)

» Tomato Pudding «

6 slices bread, crusts
   removed and diced
½ cup butter, melted
10½ oz. can tomato purée
¼ cup boiling water
¾ cup dark brown sugar,
   firmly packed

Mix together the bread and butter in a 1 quart glass casserole dish. In a small saucepan, bring the tomato purée and water to a boil; remove from heat and stir in sugar. Add to bread and butter mixture; mix well. Bake, covered, in a preheated 350° oven 1 hour. Remove cover and let stand 5 minutes before serving. Edge of pudding will be a very dark brown, but it will not taste scorched. For larger quantity, make two separate recipes instead of doubling. Makes 8 servings.

– Jane Sweeder (Mrs. Willard C.)

» Aunt Dannie's
Baked Tomatoes and
Artichoke Hearts «

This is a side dish my Aunt Dannie in Jackson, Mississippi, always served with perfectly broiled steaks. I never had it served anywhere else, so I think it was an original of hers.

2-16 oz. cans whole peeled
   tomatoes, drained
1 teaspoon salt
¼ teaspoon pepper,
   freshly ground
½ teaspoon sugar
¼ teaspoon sweet basil
16 oz. can artichoke hearts,
   drained and rinsed
4 tablespoons butter
1 cup bread crumbs,
   toasted
½ cup Parmesan cheese,
   grated

Butter your favorite casserole. Cross-cut the tomatoes so they can hold an artichoke heart. Place tomatoes properly spaced in casserole. Blend salt, black pepper, sugar, and basil; sprinkle over top and sides of tomatoes. Allow tomatoes to stand for 15 minutes. Place 1 artichoke heart in the center of each tomato; top with a pat of butter. Combine bread crumbs and Parmesan cheese. Sprinkle half the crumb mixture over tops and sides of tomatoes; bake in a preheated 400° oven for 10 minutes. Sprinkle with remaining crumb mixture, then

turn oven to broil. Cook on middle oven shelf for 2 to 3 minutes, or until golden brown. May be cooked ahead and broiled just before serving. Makes 6 to 8 servings.

– Jessie Mae Helms (Mrs. J. A.)

» Navets à l'Orange «

If you have always thought of turnips as a rather pedestrian vegetable, these turnips in orange sauce will be a delightful surprise. They make a perfect French complement to any rich meat course, such as duck, pork, or ham.

Juice of 2 oranges
1½ lbs. turnips, peeled
   and cut into even cubes
Chicken stock or bouillon
Coarse salt
Freshly ground pepper
Zest of 1 orange, grated

Combine orange juice, turnips, and enough stock or bouillon to cover. Season to taste, cover, and simmer for 20 to 30 minutes, or until tender. Drain and reserve liquid. Boil liquid rapidly until reduced by half; correct seasoning. Place turnips in serving dish, sprinkle with grated orange zest, and pour sauce over. Makes 4 to 6 servings.

– Winnie Love (Mrs. Wesley)

» Zucchini Casserole «

8 to 10 medium zucchini,
   diced
1 onion, chopped
5 eggs, beaten
3 tablespoons
   Worcestershire sauce
2-10¾ oz. cans cream of
   mushroom soup
Salt and pepper
1 cup butter cracker
   crumbs
3 tablespoons butter,
   melted

Cook zucchini in small amount of water, or steam until tender, but not soft, about 8 to 10 minutes. Mix in a bowl with onion, eggs, Worcestershire sauce, and mushroom soup; season with salt and pepper to taste. Place in buttered casserole. Top with cracker crumbs and melted butter. Bake in a preheated 350° oven for 1 hour. Makes 3-quart casserole.

– Davis Catering

» Zucchini Puffs «

Feta is a salty, crumbly white cheese made from goat's milk. Here the Turks combine it with zucchini to create a feathery delight.

1 lb. small zucchini, coarsely grated	2 tablespoons parsley, chopped
½ teaspoon salt	Dash of pepper
¼ lb. feta cheese, crumbled	2 eggs, beaten
½ cup fresh dill, chopped	1 cup flour
¼ cup mint, chopped	Peanut or vegetable oil
	Endive
	Tomato wedges

Sprinkle zucchini with salt and let stand in a colander to drain for 30 minutes; pat dry with paper towels to remove as much moisture as possible. Combine zucchini, feta cheese, dill, mint, parsley, and pepper in a large bowl; stir in eggs and flour. In a large heavy pan, heat 1″ oil to 400°. Drop mixture by rounded tablespoons into hot oil. Fry until golden brown, about 2 minutes on each side. Drain on paper towels and serve on plates lined with endive or lettuce, garnished with tomato wedges. For appetizers, use a rounded teaspoon of mixture. Makes 12 vegetable puffs, or 18 appetizers.

— Anne Seasholes Cozlu (Mrs. Cem)

» Zucchine Ripiene «
Stuffed Zucchini

6 to 8 medium-sized zucchini	⅓ cup wheat germ
6 slices bacon	2 tablespoons Parmesan cheese, grated
¾ cup onion, chopped	1 tablespoon catsup
1 clove garlic, minced	¾ teaspoon basil
4 oz. can sliced mushrooms, drained, or ¼ lb. fresh mushrooms, sliced	½ teaspoon salt
	⅛ teaspoon pepper
⅔ cup seasoned stuffing mix	1 to 2 tablespoons water, if needed

Cook whole zucchini in boiling water for 5 to 10 minutes, or until tender. Drain and cool. Cook bacon until crisp; drain, crumble, and set aside, reserving 3 tablespoons drippings. Sauté onion and garlic in drippings. Add mushrooms and cook 5 minutes, stirring often. Slice zucchini lengthwise. Scoop out to make boat shape.

Chop centers and add with all other ingredients, except bacon, to mushroom mixture. Mix well. If mixture is too dry, add 1 to 2 tablespoons water. Fill zucchini shells with mixture. Sprinkle bacon over top. Bake in large shallow pan in a preheated 400° oven for 15 to 20 minutes. Makes 6 to 8 servings.

— Peggy Andre (Mrs. J. Richard)

» Parmesan Zucchini «

Origano, as the Italians spell it, is a perfect partner to zucchini and Parmesan cheese.

6 zucchini, small or medium, sliced	canned tomatoes, drained and chopped
¼ cup onion, chopped	1 teaspoon oregano, dried
2 tablespoons butter or olive oil	½ teaspoon sugar
	Salt and pepper
1 large fresh tomato, chopped, or 1 cup	Parmesan cheese

Sauté zucchini and onion in butter or oil for 3 minutes. Add tomato, oregano, sugar, and salt and pepper to taste. Cover and cook for 5 to 10 minutes, until zucchini is tender but not mushy. Serve sprinkled generously with freshly grated Parmesan cheese. Makes 4 to 6 servings.

— Carolyn Kuderer (Mrs. Vernon)

» Zucchini Parmesan «

This Italian omelette can be served alone as a luncheon dish or as an accompaniment to a meat entree.

¼ cup olive oil	1 lb. zucchini, sliced
1 to 2 large onions, chopped	2 eggs, beaten
1 green pepper, chopped	1 cup Parmesan cheese, freshly grated
1 cup parsley, chopped	

Heat olive oil in a heavy skillet. Sauté onions, pepper, and parsley until onion is transparent. Add zucchini; sauté for about 10 minutes, or until zucchini is tender but not mushy. Pour eggs over zucchini and sprinkle Parmesan cheese over eggs. Cook until eggs are just set; serve immediately. Makes 6 servings.

— Giulia Kinneary (Mrs. William R.)

» Courgettes à la Crème «

The light touch of this zucchini with cream sauce has a decidedly French flavor. Use the smallest zucchini that you can find or grow.

½ cup onions, thinly sliced
1 or 2 cloves garlic, minced
1 tablespoon butter
1 tablespoon oil

1 lb. zucchini, sliced in ¾" rounds
½ cup whipping cream
Salt
Parsley, minced

Sauté onions and garlic in butter and oil in a heavy pan until onion is transparent. Add zucchini and cook until soft but not mushy. Stir frequently to prevent garlic and onion from browning. Add cream and heat just to boiling. Salt to taste, sprinkle with parsley, and serve at once. Makes 6 to 8 servings.

– Mme. M. Preston Jones
Roquefort-les-Pois, France

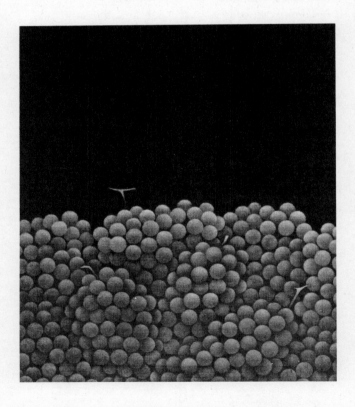

Hamaguchi Yozo, Japanese 1909-, "Grapes on a Black Ground,"
1961, color mezzotint,
108.1968. The Howard and Caroline Porter Collection

» Frosted Zucchini or Potato Rounds «

3 medium-size zucchini or thin-skinned potatoes
½ cup mayonnaise
¼ cup green onion, finely minced
3 tablespoons Parmesan cheese, grated

⅛ teaspoon garlic powder
½ teaspoon oregano leaves
Dash of pepper
¼ cup fine, dry cracker crumbs

Cut zucchini or potatoes crosswise into ¾" slices (about 24 zucchini slices or 12 potato pieces). Arrange slices in a single layer in a vegetable steamer. Cover and steam over boiling water about 5 minutes for zucchini, or 12 minutes for potatoes. Drain, cool, and blot dry. Meanwhile, mix mayonnaise, green onion, Parmesan cheese, garlic, oregano, and pepper. Frost 1 side of each zucchini or potato slice with mayonnaise mixture, then dip top in cracker crumbs. Place on cookie sheet, top side up. Broil about 4" from heat until lightly browned. Makes 3 to 4 servings.

– Toni Eyrich (Mrs. David J.)

» Squash Casserole «

1½ lbs. summer or zucchini squash, sliced ¼" thick
10¾ oz. can cream of chicken soup
8 oz. can water chestnuts, sliced

3 oz. jar pimientos, diced
2 medium onions, finely chopped
½ cup sour cream
½ cup butter
8 oz. pkg. herb stuffing, crumbled

Cook sliced squash in salt water for 8 minutes. Drain. Add all ingredients except butter and stuffing. Melt butter in skillet; add stuffing. Pack ¾ of the herb stuffing mix in bottom of 2-quart baking dish. Pour squash mixture over the top. Then add the remaining stuffing. Bake 30 minutes, until bubbly, in a preheated 350° oven. Makes 8 servings.

– Dot Hill (Mrs. Tom)

» Mystras Style Greek Vegetable Casserole «

1½ lbs. potatoes, peeled
 and sliced
1½ lbs. zucchini, peeled
 and sliced
16 oz. can tomatoes, sliced
Salt and pepper
½ cup parsley, chopped
½ cup fresh dill, or 1
 tablespoon dried dill

½ cup olive oil
5 whole green onions,
 chopped
3 cloves garlic, chopped
2 fresh tomatoes, chopped
1 medium size eggplant,
 sliced and salted
2-9 oz. pkgs. frozen okra
¼ cup bread crumbs

Mix potatoes, zucchini, and tomatoes together. Sprinkle with salt, pepper, parsley, and dill. Heat olive oil and add green onions, garlic, and fresh tomatoes. Sauté for 10 minutes. Rinse sliced eggplant in cold water and pat dry. In a 4-quart casserole, layer the vegetables as follows: potato, zucchini, tomato mixture, eggplant, and okra. Alternate vegetables as much as possible. Spoon the sauteed onions, garlic, and fresh tomatoes over the top. Sprinkle bread crumbs over casserole. Bake in a preheated 350° oven for 1 hour. This may be served warm or cold. Makes 6 to 8 servings.

– Zell Schulman (Mrs. Melvin)
From her book, "Something Different for Passover"

» Crustless Vegetable Pie «

1 medium eggplant,
 peeled and cubed
2 medium zucchini, cubed
1 large onion, chopped
¼ cup oil
4 medium tomatoes,
 peeled and chopped
3 eggs

¾ cup Parmesan cheese,
 grated
1 tablespoon parsley
½ teaspoon basil
½ teaspoon oregano
Salt and pepper
¼ lb. Mozzarella cheese,
 thinly sliced

Sauté eggplant, zucchini, and onion in oil until softened, about 10 minutes. Add tomatoes, cover, and simmer 20 to 25 minutes. Transfer to mixing bowl; cool and drain off most of the liquid. Beat eggs with ¼ cup Parmesan cheese, parsley, basil, and oregano; add to vegetables. Season with salt and pepper to taste. Pour half of mixture into greased 9" pie pan and top with ¼ cup Parmesan cheese. Layer remaining vegetables and top with Parmesan cheese and Mozzarella. Bake in preheated 350° oven for 40 to 45 minutes, until set and golden brown. Cool 10 minutes before serving. Makes 8 servings.

– Susan Pfau (Mrs. Daniel A.)

» Marinated Mixed Vegetables «

Chef Jim Gregory inspired many Cincinnati cooks with the gourmet cooking lessons he held at his lovely Victorian home in Hyde Park. The lesson started with aperitifs in the walled garden, and ended with the pupils consuming the mouthwatering concoctions. This dish may be served hot or cold. Use more seasoning if serving cold.

2 to 3 tablespoons olive oil
2 or 3 leeks, chopped
1 red onion, sliced thin
6 or 8 green onions,
 chopped, white part
 only
1 garlic clove, chopped
6 small zucchini, thinly
 sliced
2 tablespoons parsley,
 chopped

2½ tablespoons tarragon
 vinegar
Salt and pepper
2 tablespoons Dijon
 mustard with herbs
¼ cup dry white wine
1 lb. small mushrooms,
 whole
6 artichoke hearts and
 stems, cooked and
 sliced

Heat oil in a large skillet. Sauté leeks, red onion, and green onion. Keep them crisp, do not overcook. Add garlic, zucchini, parsley, tarragon vinegar, and salt and pepper to taste. Cook for a few minutes to reduce vinegar; add mustard, wine, and mushrooms. Stir well and cook, covered, for about 5 minutes over low heat. Add artichokes. Taste for seasoning.
Makes 4 to 6 servings.

– Chef Jim Gregory
From "Chef Gregory Cookbook"

Bowl of Darius the Great, gold, Iran, 522-485 B.C.,
1963.31. Museum Purchase.
This color reproduction donated by Mrs. James L. Magrish

Ancient splendor assumes tangible form in a superb dish of pure gold, fashioned 2,500 years ago. Beneath the rim appears an inscription, "Darius Great King," in three cuneiform languages: Old Persian, Elamite, and Babylonian. The king whose vessels bore his name was the first and mightiest of the three Persian rulers named Darius. During his thirty-seven-year reign (522 - 485 B.C.), he proved a formidable military commander as well as an innovative administrator for the powerful Persian Empire.

When red wine fills this shallow golden bowl, which measures twelve inches from edge to edge, its recessed flutes and lobes radiating from a convex center take on the look of a cross-sectioned pomegranate. Twenty-five-hundred years ago, the dish would perhaps have held red pomegranate wine for great state ceremonies or religious festivals.

Breads, Cakes, and Pastries

» English Muffin Bread «

This bread has the same texture and flavor as the traditional yeast-raised muffins which were sold by the wandering muffin man through the streets of Edwardian England.

2¼ oz. packages dry yeast
6 cups flour, divided
1 tablespoon sugar
1 teaspoon salt

¼ teaspoon baking soda
2 cups milk
½ cup water
White cornmeal

Combine yeast, 3 cups flour, sugar, salt, and baking soda. Heat milk and water until very warm (110°) and add to the dry mixture; stir in the remaining flour to make a very stiff batter. Grease two 8"x4" loaf pans and sprinkle with white cornmeal. Spoon batter into the pans and sprinkle with additional cornmeal. Cover loosely, set in a warm place, and let rise for 45 minutes. Bake in a preheated 400° oven for 35 to 40 minutes, or until lightly browned. Makes 2 loaves. This bread is best served warm.

– Marie Clift (Mrs. Robert G.)

» Honey Yeast Bread «

2 packets dry yeast
½ cup lukewarm water
1⅞ cups milk
½ tablespoon salt

1 tablespoon shortening
1½ tablespoons honey
6 cups flour

Dissolve yeast in lukewarm water and set aside to rise. Heat milk and add salt, shortening, and honey. Set aside and cool until lukewarm. Combine risen yeast and lukewarm milk mixture. Add 3 cups flour and mix well. Add 1 to 2 cups more flour, mixing slowly until mixture is too thick to stir. Sprinkle some of the remaining flour on a board and place entire mixture on it. Knead about 100 times, adding flour gradually until mixture is just tacky and has resilience like a sponge. Add only enough flour to obtain results. The less flour, the lighter the bread. Place in a greased receptacle for rising. Place in a cold oven along with a pan of water and allow the sponge to rise until it is twice its original size. By using a cold oven and a pan of water, you are making your own bread "proofer." Punch sponge down and turn it out onto table. Cut in half and shape each into a ball. Allow them to rest for 10 minutes. Roll ball into an 8"x16" rectangle. Loosen from table (may be a little sticky but don't be concerned), and fold edges together lengthwise. Roll this lengthwise and fold over one end a third and the other end on it. Hand roll this and place in greased standard-size bread pans with seam down. Place loaves again in cold oven with pan of water and allow to rise to at least double in size. Remove loaves and pan of water. Bake in preheated 400° oven for 35 minutes. After first 15 to 20 minutes, cover loaves with foil so bread won't darken too much. When baked, immediately remove bread from pans and brush tops with butter, if you prefer a soft crust. Makes 2 loaves.

– Jane S. Wulsin (Mrs. Eugene)

» Variations on Honey Yeast Bread «

Whole or Cracked Wheat
Use same basic recipe, but substitute 2 cups whole or cracked wheat for 2 cups of the all purpose flour. The more wheat you use, the heavier the bread will be.

Raisin

Use same basic recipe, but add, while mixing, raisins which have been soaked in hot water to puff, 1 tablespoon cinnamon, and 1 tablespoon nutmeg.

French or Italian

Use same basic recipe, but substitute water for milk and eliminate shortening and honey. Hand-roll into French loaf shapes and make 3 or 4 diagonal slits on top of loaves. Brush with water or egg whites 2 or 3 times during baking; do not cover with foil. Allow loaves to rise in French loaf pans or on a flat pan, such as a cookie sheet, lightly greased or dusted with cornmeal.

Herbal

Prepare as for French bread mixture, adding 1 tablespoon parsley flakes, 1 teaspoon tarragon, and ½ teaspoon celery seed.

– Jane S. Wulsin (Mrs. Eugene)

» Irish Soda Bread «

This is the wonderful bread you get throughout Ireland – light and hearty at the same time. The recipe was given to me by my cousin, who grew up in Ireland. It can be frozen. For a change, try using 2 cups white flour and 2 cups whole wheat flour.

3 cups white flour
1 cup graham or wheat
*   flour*
4 level teaspoons baking
*   powder*
1 heaped teaspoon baking
*   soda*
2 teaspoons salt
2 cups buttermilk

Mix dry ingredients together, using a wire whisk. Pour in buttermilk and mix well with a fork. Place on a well-floured board. It is quite sticky, so flour your hands well. Knead gently and quickly for about 2 minutes, just until the dough is no longer sticky and is smooth, and the dry ingredients are well distributed. Cut in half and form into 2 rounds. Place in 2 well-floured, but not greased, 9″ round pie tins. Cut across the top about ¼″ deep in the form of a cross. Bake in a preheated 450° oven for 30 to 40 minutes. Makes two 9″ loaves.

– Barbara McDonald (Mrs. John C.)

» Mexican Corn Bread «

⅓ cup butter
8 oz. can creamed corn
1 teaspoon salt
2 eggs
1 cup yellow cornmeal
½ teaspoon soda
¾ cup milk
4 oz. can mild green
*   chilies, chopped*
½ cup sharp Cheddar
*   cheese, shredded*

Melt butter in 9″ square pan. Combine the rest of the ingredients except cheese. Pour into pan, and sprinkle cheese on top. Bake in a preheated 400° oven for 30 to 35 minutes. Makes 12 servings.

– Mary Wydman (Mrs. Robert)

» Flour Tortillas «

These homemade tortillas are more pliable and thicker than store-bought ones. Use in making burritos, quesadillas, or eat with meals like bread.

4 to 6 cups white flour,
*   more if needed*
1 tablespoon salt
1 tablespoon baking
*   powder*
1 tablespoon cooking oil
Warm water

Combine flour, salt, and baking powder in a medium bowl, mixing well with hands. Mix in cooking oil. Gradually add warm water, continuing to mix and knead. Remove from bowl to wooden cutting board, and gradually add extra flour as you need to keep dough from sticking to fingers. When dough is smooth and elastic, make into small palm-size balls and put into bowl to keep out of your way while you work. Heat a cast-iron griddle on range burner; it is ready when a drop of water dances on hot surface. As griddle is heating, lightly flour cutting board and rolling pin. Place some extra flour in a plate to flatten dough ball just before rolling out. As dough is rolled out, turn it around ¼-turn and turn it over with every pass of the rolling pin; this helps to make tortilla round in shape. Roll until flat and thin. Lift edges at 11:00 and 2:00 (the area points on a clock), and support side edges with splayed fingers as you place it flat onto hot griddle. After a few seconds, turn over with a metal spatula. Pat bubbles down with spatula and turn over again. Place cooked tortilla on a plate draped with dish towel, cover to keep warm. Repeat procedure. Stack tortillas as each is cooked. Makes 36-8″ to 10″ tortillas.

– Lupe Gonzales-Hoyt

» Scandinavian Sampler Loaves «

This version of Swedish limpa bread is good enough to eat for dessert, but makes a hearty addition to any meal.

2 tablespoons orange
   rind, grated
2 cups water
½ cup honey
2 teaspoons caraway
   seeds
1 teaspoon anise seeds
1 teaspoon fennel seeds

2 tablespoons shortening
2 pkgs. dry yeast or 2
   cakes compressed yeast
¼ cup lukewarm water
2 teaspoons salt
2 cups rye flour, sifted
4 cups flour, sifted

Combine orange rind, water, honey, seeds, and shortening in a medium saucepan. Boil 5 minutes; cool to lukewarm. Dissolve yeast in ¼ cup lukewarm water; add to cooled honey mixture. Stir in remaining ingredients; knead until smooth. Cover; let rise in warm place until double in bulk. Knead on a lightly floured board; divide in half, and shape into 2 loaves. Place in greased 9"x5" loaf pans. Let rise until double in bulk. Bake in a preheated 350° oven for 1 hour, or until golden brown. Makes two 9"x5" loaves.

– Audrey McCafferty

» Whole Wheat Bread «

Reversing the usual procedure, I received this great recipe from my daughter, Randy.

4 to 4½ cups flour
2 cups whole wheat flour
2 pkgs. yeast
1 tablespoon salt
1½ cups milk
½ cup water

½ cup small-curd cottage
   cheese
¼ cup honey
¼ cup butter
Additional melted butter

Combine 1 cup flour, whole wheat flour, yeast, and salt in large mixer bowl; stir. Heat milk, water, cottage cheese, honey, and butter to 120° to 130°. Add to dry ingredients. In an electric mixer, beat at low speed until moist, then 3 minutes at medium speed. By hand, gradually stir in remaining flour. Knead until smooth. Place in a greased bowl, turn to grease dough all over, cover with damp cloth, and let rise until double. Divide into two loaves,

place in 2 greased 3"x9"x5" loaf pans; let rise until double. This will take 45 minutes to 1 hour. Bake in a preheated 375° oven for 35 to 40 minutes. Brush top with melted butter during last 5 minutes of baking. Remove from pans and cool. Makes 2 loaves.

– Ruth Upson (Mrs. Mark, Jr.)

» Chocolate Potato Torte «

⅔ cup butter, softened
2 cups sugar
4 egg yolks
1 cup potatoes, cooked
   and mashed
1 cup walnuts or pecans,
   chopped
½ cup milk

½ cup unsweetened
   chocolate, grated
2 cups flour
1 teaspoon cloves
1 teaspoon nutmeg
1 teaspoon cinnamon
2 teaspoons baking
   powder
4 egg whites, stiffly beaten

Cream butter and sugar together. Add egg yolks, potatoes, nuts, milk, and chocolate; blend well. Sift dry ingredients together and fold in well. Fold egg whites in completely; pour into greased 9"x5"x3" loaf pan. Bake 1 hour in a preheated 350° oven or until a toothpick inserted in the center comes out clean. Makes 1 loaf.

– Marjorie Mansell (Mrs. Sydney)
Magalia, California

» Chocolate Walnut Date Loaf «

6 oz. pkg. semi-sweet
   chocolate pieces
¼ cup butter
⅓ cup sugar
¾ cup boiling water
1 cup pitted dates, sliced
1 egg, beaten
1 teaspoon vanilla

¾ cup milk
2¾ cups flour, sifted
1½ teaspoons salt
1 teaspoon baking powder
1 teaspoon baking soda
1 cup walnuts, chopped
   coarsely

Melt chocolate and butter over hot water. Add sugar, mix well. Set aside to cool. Pour boiling water over dates, cool. Stir egg and vanilla into cooled chocolate mixture. Add milk and dates with water. Sift flour, salt, baking powder, and baking soda together. Add to chocolate mixture, stirring just until flour is moistened. Add walnuts and mix lightly. Turn into greased 9"x5"x3" loaf pan. Let stand for 20 minutes. Bake in preheated 350° oven for 65 to 75 minutes. Loaf is done when toothpick inserted in center comes out clean. Cool 5 to 10 minutes, then turn out on wire rack. Cool completely before serving. Makes 9"x5" loaf.

– Helen Voelkerding

» New England Blueberry Spice Bread «

This is good enough to serve in place of cake for dessert. It may be served warm or cold.

⅓ cup butter	¼ teaspoon cinnamon
1 cup sugar	⅛ teaspoon allspice
1 egg, well beaten	¼ teaspoon cloves
2½ cups flour, sifted	1 cup milk
½ teaspoon salt	1 pint blueberries
4 teaspoons baking powder	¼ cup flour

Cream butter and sugar until light. Add egg and beat until fluffy. Sift together 2½ cups flour, salt, baking powder, cinnamon, allspice, and cloves. Add milk, alternately with the dry ingredients. Beat until very light. Toss blueberries with ¼ cup flour; fold into batter. Place in a well-greased and floured 3"x9"x5" loaf pan, or a bundt or tube pan. Bake in a preheated 375° oven for 45 minutes. The bread is done when a toothpick inserted in the center of the loaf comes out clean. Makes 1 loaf.

– Dottie Jacobs (Mrs. Donald L.)

» Orange Waffles «

Among the most popular foods at the World's Fair in Knoxville were the sinfully-good Belgian waffles, which are that country's version of the typically northern European crisp cake. The Danes have their aebleskiver and the Norwegians their krumkakes. They're all wonderful, especially when topped with orange slices and whipped cream as in this version.

4 oranges	3 eggs, separated
1¾ cups cake flour	¼ cup butter, melted
2 teaspoons baking powder	1½ cups whipping cream
½ teaspoon salt	Additional whipped cream
1 tablespoon sugar	

Peel oranges carefully, removing colored part only with vegetable peeler or sharp knife. Grate or finely chop this orange zest. Remove remaining white part of orange peels, cut oranges into thin slices, and remove seeds, if necessary; set aside. Mix orange zest, flour, baking powder, salt, sugar, egg yolks, butter, and whipping cream in a blender or food processor. Beat egg whites until stiff but not dry; fold into flour mixture. Bake in a Belgian waffle iron, following manufacturer's directions. Serve topped with reserved orange slices and whipped cream. Makes 8 waffles.

» Peanut Butter Balls «

This is a nutritious snack that is fun for young children to make.

½ cup peanut butter	2 tablespoons instant non-fat dry milk
½ cup honey	
1 cup toasted wheat germ	

Mix ingredients well. Roll into small balls or pat flat in a pan as for fudge. Refrigerate. Makes 18 balls.

– Marcia Shortt (Mrs. Paul)

» Puffy German Pancakes «

This recipe may be doubled. In that case, a little longer baking time will be required.

½ cup flour, sifted	¼ teaspoon salt
3 eggs, slightly beaten	Melted butter
½ cup plus 1 tablespoon milk	Confectioners' sugar
2 tablespoons butter, melted	Fresh lemon juice, optional

Beat flour and eggs together with a rotary beater or electric mixer. Stir in milk, melted butter, and salt. Pour batter into a buttered, cold 9" or 10" skillet that may be used in an oven. Bake in preheated 450° oven for 20

minutes, or until golden brown and dry on top. Cut into wedges and serve topped with melted butter, confectioners' sugar, and lemon juice. These pancakes are also good with maple syrup. Makes 2 servings.

– *Dottie Jacobs (Mrs. Donald L.)*

» Coffee Kuchen «

2-¼ oz. pkgs. active dry
   yeast
¼ cup warm water
1 cup evaporated milk
1 cup water
½ cup butter
7 cups flour, sifted
1¼ cups sugar

1 teaspoon salt
2 beaten eggs
2 teaspoons lemon zest,
   grated
1 cup raisins
6 tablespoons sugar
¼ cup flour
2 tablespoons butter

Dissolve yeast in warm water. Heat milk, water, and butter together; cool to lukewarm. Sift flour, sugar, and salt into a large bowl. Combine yeast, milk mixture, eggs, lemon zest, and raisins. Add to sifted dry ingredients; mix thoroughly. Cover bowl. Let rise in warm place until

doubled in bulk, about 2 hours. Punch down and spread into 2-9″x13″x2″ greased baking pans. Combine sugar and flour; cut in butter until mixture resembles coarse crumbs; sprinkle over dough. Cover and let rise in a warm place until double in bulk, about 45 minutes to 1 hour. Bake in a preheated 375° oven for 25 to 30 minutes. Makes 2 cakes.

» Cinnamon Nut Coffee Cake «

This old family recipe for streusel coffee cake is a favorite of ours for Sunday morning breakfast or brunch. It can be made ahead; just reheat before serving.

1½ cups flour
3 teaspoons baking
   powder
½ teaspoon salt
¾ cup sugar
¼ cup butter, melted
1 egg
½ cup milk

1 teaspoon vanilla
½ cup brown or
   granulated sugar
2 tablespoons flour
2 teaspoons cinnamon
2 tablespoons butter,
   melted
½ cup nuts, chopped

Sift the first four ingredients together and add melted butter. Combine until the mixture resembles coarse meal. Thoroughly beat egg, milk, and vanilla; blend into sifted mixture, beating well. Pour ½ of mixture into buttered 8″x8″x2″ pan. Mix remaining ingredients together well, and sprinkle ½ of topping mixture over the first layer of batter. Repeat batter/topping layer. Bake in a preheated 375° oven for 25 minutes. Makes 16-2″ squares.

– Marilyn Krehbiel (Mrs. Charles, Sr.)

» Streusel Napfkuchen «

¾ cup butter, softened
1½ cups sugar
3 eggs
Zest of 1 lemon, grated
3 cups flour, sifted
2 teaspoons baking
   powder
1 teaspoon baking soda
1 teaspoon salt
1 cup buttermilk
½ cup raisins
½ cup apples, chopped
¼ cup butter
½ cup brown sugar,
   packed
⅓ cup flour
2 teaspoons cinnamon
1 cup confectioners' sugar
2 tablespoons lemon juice

Oil and flour a 10″ bundt or tube pan. Cream together the butter, sugar, eggs, and lemon rind until they are light and fluffy. Add flour, baking powder, baking soda, salt, and buttermilk; continue beating for 3 minutes. Fold in fruit and pour ½ of the mixture into prepared pan. Mix the butter, brown sugar, flour, and cinnamon together, cutting with a knife, pastry blender, or processor until the mixture resembles coarse meal. Sprinkle over the batter and cover with the remaining half of batter. Bake in a preheated 350° oven for 50 to 60 minutes, or until a cake tester inserted in the center comes out clean. Cool the cake on a rack for 15 minutes; remove the cake from the pan and prick it all over with a fork or toothpick. Combine sugar and lemon juice; drizzle over the warm cake. Makes 10″ bundt cake.

» Äpfelstrudel «

Apple strudel, called in Europe the "king of pastries," is probably the most well-known German confection in the United States. Phyllo or strudel leaves may be used in place of the puff pastry.

1½ lbs. puff pastry dough
2 lbs. apples, peeled,
   cored, and diced
2 tablespoons raisins,
   chopped
2 tablespoons English
   walnuts, chopped
½ cup sugar
½ teaspoon cinnamon
1 tablespoon fresh lemon
   juice
1 egg, beaten
Confectioners' sugar

Using a lightly floured board or marble slab, roll puff pastry into a rectangle approximately 24″x12″. Combine apples, raisins, walnuts, sugar, cinnamon, and lemon juice; mix gently, being careful not to crush apples. Spoon this mixture along 1 long side of rectangle, 1″ from edges. Roll pastry and apples, jelly-roll fashion, to form a long roll. Tuck ends under and place on a greased baking sheet. To help with transfer, roll strudel onto a clean linen towel and slide off onto baking sheet. Using a sharp knife or single-edged razor blade, cut 6 evenly spaced slits in top of strudel to allow breathing and to prevent dough from breaking open. Brush dough with beaten egg, using a pastry brush. Bake in a preheated 400° oven until the pastry is a light golden brown, about 30 minutes. Reduce heat to 350° and continue to bake for another 25 to 30 minutes, or until well browned. Sprinkle with confectioners' sugar and serve warm. Makes 10 to 12 servings.

» Peach Strudel «

Strudel is the national confection of Bavaria. This slightly Americanized version is less complicated than the original and features some novel ingredients.

2¼ cups flour
1 cup sour cream
1 cup butter
2 cups peach preserves
1 cup coconut, shredded
½ cup pecans, finely
   chopped, optional
Confectioners' sugar

Combine flour, sour cream, and butter in mixing bowl; blend well. Cover; chill at least 1 hour. Roll out the chilled dough on a well-floured surface, ½ at a time, to a 6″x12″ rectangle. Spread ½ of the peach preserves on the rectangle to within ½″ from the edges. Sprinkle ½ of the coconut and pecans over the preserves. Starting with the long side of the rectangle, roll up jelly roll fashion. Seal edges and ends. Repeat with rest of dough, peach preserves, coconut, and pecans. Place seam side down on ungreased cookie sheet. Bake in preheated 450° oven for 20 to 25 minutes, until lightly browned. Cool. Sprinkle with confectioners' sugar. Cut into slices. Makes 2 strudel rolls.

— Brenda Martin (Mrs. F. Gary)
Morgan City, Louisiana

» Zucchini Nut Muffins «

These muffins freeze well. Thaw and serve at room temperature, or reheat.

2 eggs, lightly beaten
½ cup brown sugar,
* packed*
½ cup honey
½ cup butter, melted
1 teaspoon vanilla
1¾ cups flour
1 teaspoon baking soda
1 teaspoon salt
½ teaspoon baking
* powder*
½ teaspoon ground
* nutmeg*
1½ teaspoons ground
* cinnamon*
1 cup granola-type cereal
½ cup pecans or walnuts,
* chopped*
1 cup zucchini, shredded

In large bowl, beat eggs lightly; then beat in brown sugar, honey, butter, and vanilla. In another bowl, stir together the flour, soda, salt, baking powder, nutmeg, and cinnamon. Add the dry ingredients to the egg mixture and stir until just evenly moistened. Stir in granola, nuts, and zucchini. Spoon into 18 well-greased muffin cups. Bake in preheated 350° oven for about 25 minutes. Serve warm. Makes 18 muffins.

— Toni Eyrich (Mrs. David J.)

» Cinnamon Apple Tart «

This Irish version of apple pie is made even more unusual by the addition of plump prunes, and the double infusion of cinnamon in the filling and crust.

1½ lbs. apples, peeled
* and sliced, or 1 lb.*
* apples and ½ lb. prunes*
1 teaspoon cinnamon
4½ tablespoons sugar
1½ cups flour
Pinch of salt
½ teaspoon baking
* powder*
6 tablespoons butter
1 teaspoon cinnamon
1 teaspoon sugar
1 egg yolk
Ice water

If using prunes, stew them with just enough water to cover until they are tender, remove pits, and chop coarsely. Mix apples, prunes, cinnamon, and sugar. Mix flour, salt, and baking powder and blend with butter until mixture resembles coarse meal. Add cinnamon, sugar, egg yolk, and just enough water to make mixture hold together. Don't use excessive water or overwork pastry. Using ⅔ of pastry mixture, roll on a floured board until large enough to fill a 9″ pie pan. Place pastry in pan and fill with apple mixture. Roll out remaining pastry and fit over the apples, pressing edge down to seal tart. Cut decorative slits in the top crust to allow steam to escape. Bake in a preheated 400° oven for 10 minutes; reduce heat to 350° and continue baking for 45 minutes, or until crust is crisp and nicely browned. Makes 6 to 8 servings.

» Black and White Ice Cream Pie «

9″ pie shell, baked
1 pint vanilla ice cream,
* softened*
1 pint chocolate ice cream,
* softened*
5 egg whites
1½ teaspoons vanilla
¼ teaspoon cream of
* tartar*
½ cup sugar
Chocolate Sauce

Spread softened vanilla ice cream over cooled pie shell; freeze. Spread softened chocolate ice cream over vanilla; freeze. Beat together egg whites, vanilla, and cream of tartar until soft peaks form. Then add sugar, gradually beating until stiff. Spread meringue on top of pie, sealing edges; freeze. Place under broiler until meringue browns, watching closely. Serve with warm Chocolate Sauce. Makes 8 to 10 servings.

Chocolate Sauce

2 ozs. unsweetened
* chocolate*
2 tablespoons butter
1 cup evaporated milk
1 cup sugar
1½ teaspoons vanilla

In a double boiler, melt the chocolate and butter. Slowly stir in the milk. Add the sugar. Cook over low heat and beat with electric mixer or stir often with wooden spoon until thickened. Add vanilla. Serve warm over pie.

— Ann Hinckley (Mrs. Charles C.)

» Brown Sugar Apple Pie «

10 baking apples, peeled, cored, and thinly sliced
½ cup brown sugar
2 tablespoons flour
1 teaspoon cinnamon
¼ cup lemon juice
9" pie shell, unbaked
¾ cup brown sugar
1 cup flour, sifted
½ teaspoon nutmeg
½ cup butter

Combine apples with brown sugar, flour, cinnamon, and lemon juice. Place in pie shell. Combine brown sugar, flour, and nutmeg; cut in butter until crumbly. Before baking, top apples with sugar mixture. This may seem like a tall pie, but it should be. Bake in preheated 400° oven for 45 minutes. Makes 8 servings.

— Ann Hinckley (Mrs. Charles)

» German Chocolate Pie «

4 oz. pkg. sweet cooking chocolate
¼ cup butter
13 oz. can evaporated milk
1½ cups sugar
3 tablespoons cornstarch
⅛ teaspoon salt
2 eggs
1 teaspoon vanilla
1 unbaked 10" pie shell
1⅓ cups flaked coconut
½ cup pecans, chopped

Melt chocolate with butter in saucepan over low heat; stir until blended. Remove from heat. Gradually blend in milk. Mix sugar, cornstarch, and salt; add eggs and vanilla. Gradually blend in chocolate mixture and pour into pie shell. Combine coconut and nuts; sprinkle over filling. Bake in a preheated 375° oven for 45 to 50 minutes, or until top is puffed and brown. Cool 4 hours before serving. Makes 8 to 10 servings.

» Butter Tarts «

These Canadian tarts are a nice addition to a picnic hamper or tea tray.

½ cup butter, melted
½ cup light corn syrup
½ cup brown sugar
¼ teaspoon nutmeg
¼ teaspoon salt
⅔ cup raisins, or ½ cup coconut
2 eggs, beaten
Pastry for 24 miniature tart shells

Mix butter, corn syrup, sugar, nutmeg, salt, and raisins or coconut. Add eggs and spoon into unbaked tart shells. Bake in preheated 450° oven for 15 to 20 minutes, until light brown on top. Remove from oven and cool 10 minutes before removing from tins. Makes 2 dozen tarts.

— Anne Nethercott (Mrs. J. W.)

» Damson Plum Pie «

The Scots are partial to these small dark-blue plums whose high acid and pectin content lends itself so well to pies and tarts.

Pastry for a 9" pie, unbaked
3 eggs
¼ cup butter, melted
1 cup seedless damson plum jam
2 tablespoons rum

Beat eggs until thick and light yellow. Fold in butter, plum jam, and rum. Pour into pastry crust. Bake in a preheated 400° oven for 10 minutes; reduce heat to 300° and bake for another 25 minutes. Makes 6 to 8 servings.

— Karen Rafuse (Mrs. Peter B.)

» Frozen Lemon Meringue Pie «

½ cup butter
½ cup lemon juice
3 tablespoons lemon zest
Pinch of salt
1½ cups sugar, divided
2 eggs
3 egg yolks
2 pints vanilla ice cream
9" pie shell, baked
6 egg whites

Melt butter in top of double boiler. Add juice, lemon zest, salt, and 1 cup sugar. Beat eggs and yolks. Gradually stir into butter mixture; cook over hot water, stirring constantly, until thick and smooth. Cool. Press 1 pint softened ice cream into baked pie shell. Freeze. Spread all the lemon filling over this and freeze again. Press 1 pint of softened ice cream over lemon filling; freeze. Beat egg whites until foamy; add ½ cup sugar gradually, continuing to beat until stiff. Spread meringue on pie, sealing edges. Freeze. Just before serving, place in preheated 475° oven until lightly browned, about 3 to 4 minutes. Dip knife into warm water to facilitate cutting of pie. Makes 8 servings.

— Ann Hinckley (Mrs. Charles)

» Grasshopper Pie «

1 cup chocolate wafer
   crumbs
¼ cup sugar
2 tablespoons butter,
   melted
2 tablespoons milk
3¼ cups miniature
   marshmallows
3 tablespoons white
   crème de cacao
¼ cup green crème de
   menthe
1 cup whipping cream,
   whipped and chilled
1 pint vanilla ice cream,
   softened slightly
Whipped cream,
   chocolate curls, or
   strawberries for
   garnish

Combine chocolate wafer crumbs, sugar, and butter in medium bowl. Press mixture along sides and bottom of a 9″ pie tin; chill. In top of double boiler, combine milk and miniature marshmallows. Heat over boiling water, stirring occasionally. Add crème de cacao and crème de menthe, and fold mixture into whipped cream. Spread softened vanilla ice cream over pie crust to form an even layer. Pour marshmallow mixture over ice cream; freeze for 6 hours or overnight. If desired, garnish with more whipped cream, chocolate curls, or strawberries. Makes 9″ pie.

– Mary C. Harness (Mrs. Edward G.)

» Lemon Butter «

In England, lemon butter or lemon curd is used as a spread on toast, between layers of light cakes, or as a filling for small tarts.

2 tablespoons butter
2 eggs
1 cup sugar
2 lemons

Mix butter, eggs, and sugar in top of double boiler. Remove only colored part of rind from lemons. A swiveled vegetable peeler works very well for this. Mince this zest finely and add to the egg mixture, along with the juice from the lemons. Cook over boiling water until mixture thickens. Cool and refrigerate until used. Makes about 1 cup.

– Anne Nethercott (Mrs. James)

» Mom's Lemon Pie «

My mother always served this as a special treat when I came home for a visit, even after I was married. The crispness of the almond-flavored meringue is a delicious contrast to the tart lemon filling.

1 cup sugar
3 tablespoons cornstarch
1 cup boiling water
2 teaspoons butter
2 eggs, separated
Juice of 1 lemon
Zest of ½ lemon, grated
9″ pie shell, baked until
   light brown
1 cup confectioners' sugar
¼ teaspoon almond
   extract

Mix sugar and cornstarch, add boiling water slowly, and cook about 4 minutes, or until clear. Mix in the butter, 2 beaten egg yolks, and lemon juice and zest; cool. Pour lemon mixture into baked pie shell. Whip the 2 egg whites very stiff, add confectioners' sugar and almond extract; spread over pie, sealing edges. Bake in a preheated 350° oven about 10 minutes, until meringue is a delicate tan. Makes 6 servings.

– Betsy Padgett (Mrs. Edward R.)

» Peanut Streusel Pie «

This pie won $5,000 and a trip to Europe for 17-year-old Bettijean Jeska and her home economics teacher from Swanton, Ohio, in the Kroger-Westinghouse Junior Cook of the Year contest in 1961.

⅓ cup peanut butter
¾ cup confectioners'
   sugar, sifted
9″ pie shell, baked
½ cup sugar
⅓ cup flour
⅛ teaspoon salt
2 cups milk, scalded
3 egg yolks, slightly beaten
2 tablespoons butter
½ teaspoon vanilla
3 egg whites
¼ teaspoon cream of
   tartar
½ cup sugar
1 teaspoon cornstarch

Blend peanut butter with confectioners' sugar until mealy; sprinkle ⅔ of mixture over baked pie shell. Combine ½ cup sugar, flour, and salt in the top of a double boiler; stir in scalded milk. Cook over boiling water, stirring constantly, until thickened. Stir a small amount of the cooked filling into the egg yolks, then stir back into hot mixture. Cook, stirring constantly, 2 to 3 minutes longer. Blend in butter and vanilla. Pour into pie shell. To make meringue, beat egg whites until stiff in medium size bowl; beat in cream of tartar. Gradually add sugar mixed with cornstarch. Beat until stiff and shiny. Swirl on top of filling in pie and sprinkle with remaining peanut butter mixture. Bake 15 to 20 minutes in preheated 350° oven, until meringue is golden. Chill before serving. Makes 6 to 8 servings.

– Audrey McCafferty

» Short-Crust Pastry «

½ cup butter, chilled, or 6 tablespoons butter and 2 tablespoons lard, chilled

1½ cups unbleached flour

2 teaspoons sugar, or ¼ teaspoon salt

3 to 4 tablespoons ice water

Cut butter and lard into ½" pieces. In a large chilled bowl or food processor, combine shortening, flour, salt, and sugar. Process in blender or food processor, or use your fingertips to rub together quickly until the mixture resembles coarse meal. Work quickly so mixture does not become warm. Add 3 tablespoons of water all at once, toss or process lightly, and gather dough into a ball. If dough crumbles, you may add more water by drops until a ball forms. Don't add any more than just necessary for tender, flaky crust. Wrap in waxed paper and refrigerate for at least 1 hour before using. Dough may be frozen before or after pie or tart shells are made. If dough is to be used for a savory or meat pie, add salt and omit sugar. Makes pastry for 9" pie or 12 tarts.

» Mother's Amalgamation Cake «

This wonderfully moist and rich cake of my mother's could be made at other times, but it could always be counted on for Christmas, as well as a fresh white coconut cake. Mother said that as long as all that fresh coconut had to be grated, she might as well have both kinds of cake, and anyone caught in the kitchen was expected to do "grating" duty. Use any good 3-layer white cake recipe for the base. The filling of the cake is the delicious part, and it's as thick as the cake itself. This cake is even better the second or third day. All five

children liked to sneak in and get teaspoons of the filling before it got to the cake. It may have been our introduction to bourbon.

3-layer white cake
8 egg yolks, beaten
2 cups sugar
1 cup butter, melted
2 cups pecans or walnuts, chopped
1 cup raisins, soaked in the whiskey

1 jigger good bourbon whiskey
2 cups fresh coconut, grated
White frosting
Additional coconut for topping

Prepare cake; set layers aside to cool. Mix the eggs, sugar, and butter in the top of a double boiler, and cook until the mixture will form a soft ball when dropped by a teaspoon in a cup of cold water. Stir the nuts, raisins, and whiskey into the filling, adding the coconut last. When cake is cooled sufficiently, cover each layer with filling, leaving top of last layer bare. Make any good white icing – mother used a Divinity one. Cover the cake and sprinkle coconut over the entire top. Makes 1 cake.

– Jessie Mae Helms (Mrs. J. A.)

» Applesauce Cake with Seafoam Icing «

½ cup oil
2 cups sugar
1 egg
2½ cups flour
¼ teaspoon salt
½ teaspoon cinnamon
½ teaspoon ground cloves

½ teaspoon allspice
2 teaspoons baking soda
½ cup boiling water
1½ cups applesauce
1 cup raisins or currants
½ cup nuts, chopped
Seafoam Icing

Mix oil with sugar; add egg. Sift flour with salt, cinnamon, cloves, and allspice; add to sugar mixture. Dissolve soda in water and add to mixture. Stir in applesauce, raisins, and nuts. Pour batter into 2 greased and floured 9" round cake pans; bake in a preheated 350° oven for 1 hour. Cool; frost with Seafoam Icing. Makes 8 servings.

Seafoam Icing

2 egg whites, unbeaten
1½ cups brown sugar, firmly packed
5 tablespoons water

1 teaspoon light corn syrup
1 teaspoon vanilla

Combine egg whites, sugar, water, and corn syrup in the top of a double boiler; heat and beat constantly with a hand mixer until mixture holds up in peaks, about 7 minutes. Remove from heat; add vanilla and beat until cool and thick enough to spread.

— Kathie Droesch (Mrs. David W.)

» Spirited Angel Food Cake «

This is a real fooler when you haven't much time but want to make a grand impression.

1 angel food cake	1 cup whipping cream,
1 cup crème de cacao, or	whipped
liqueur of your choice	Chocolate shavings

Poke about 60 holes of varying depth into top of cake and pour liqueur over it gradually. Cover and refrigerate overnight. Frost with whipped cream and garnish with chocolate shavings.

For an interesting variation, use melon liqueur and garnish with kiwi fruit slices. Makes 10 servings.

— Elaine Hocks (Mrs. Harry J.)

» German Apple Cake «

4 cups apples, peeled, cored, and coarsely chopped	2 teaspoons cinnamon
	1 cup English walnuts, chopped
2 cups sugar	8 oz. pkg. cream cheese, softened
2 eggs	
½ cup oil	4 tablespoons butter, softened
2 teaspoons vanilla	
2 cups flour, sifted	1 lb. confectioners' sugar
2 teaspoons baking soda	2 teaspoons vanilla, or 2 teaspoons orange juice
1 teaspoon salt	

Mix apples with sugar and let stand for a few minutes. In large mixing bowl, beat eggs slightly, then beat in oil and vanilla. Sift flour with baking soda, salt, and cinnamon. Stir into egg mixture alternately with apple mixture. Stir in walnuts. Pour into a greased 9"x13" pan. Bake in a preheated 325° oven for about 50 minutes, or until cake tests done. Cool. To make cream cheese frosting, cream

cheese, butter, and sugar together until smooth and fluffy. Add vanilla or orange juice and mix well. Ice cake with this frosting, or cut in squares and serve with hard sauce. Makes 10 to 12 servings.

— Marie Clift (Mrs. Robert G.)

» Apple Dapple Cake «

1½ cups oil	2 teaspoons vanilla
2 cups sugar	6 oz. package butterscotch chips
3 eggs	
3 cups flour	1½ cups walnuts, chopped
1 tablespoon salt	1 cup brown sugar
1 teaspoon baking soda	½ cup butter
3 cups tart apples	¼ cup milk

Combine oil and sugar; mix well. Stir in eggs and beat thoroughly. Add flour, salt, and soda. Peel, core, and finely chop apples; add along with vanilla, butterscotch chips, and walnuts; blend thoroughly. Pour batter into a greased and floured 10" tube or bundt pan; bake in a preheated 350° oven for 1 hour, 15 minutes, or until cake tests done. While cake is baking, combine brown sugar, butter, and milk in saucepan; cook for 3 minutes. Pour over cake while both are warm. Cool at least 3 hours before removing from pan. Makes 10" tube cake.

— Anita Ellis

» Blueberry-Peach Batter Cake «

2 cups blueberries	1 teaspoon baking powder
4 ripe peaches, peeled and sliced	¼ teaspoon salt
	¾ cup milk
Juice of ½ lemon	½ cup sugar
¾ cup sugar	1 tablespoon cornstarch
¼ cup butter, softened	¼ teaspoon salt
1 cup flour, sifted	1 cup boiling water

Line a greased 8" square pan with berries and peaches. Sprinkle lemon juice on top. Cream sugar and butter. Sift flour, baking powder, and salt together; add alternately with milk to creamed sugar and butter, beating well. Spread batter over fruit. Combine sugar, cornstarch, and salt; sprinkle over batter. Pour boiling water over all. Bake in preheated 350° oven for 1 hour. Makes 8 servings.

– Ann Hinckley (Mrs. Charles)

» Sour Cream Chocolate Cake «

¾ cup instant cocoa mix
¾ cup boiling water
½ teaspoon baking soda
1 cup sour cream
½ cup butter, softened
2 cups sugar

2 cups cake flour, measured after 2 siftings
3 egg whites, beaten until stiff
2 teaspoons vanilla

Mix together cocoa and water. Combine with baking soda mixed with sour cream. Cream butter and sugar. Alternately add the sifted flour and cocoa mixture to the creamed butter. Beat until fluffy. Fold in egg whites and vanilla. Pour into a greased 9"x13" pan and bake in preheated 300° oven for 50 minutes. Cool in pan. Ice with chocolate frosting or 7-minute white frosting. Makes 12 servings.

– Ann Hinckley (Mrs. Charles)

» Grandmother's Best Chocolate Cake «

This very special chocolate cake was inherited from my grandmother. It has been delighting our family for 75 years.

½ lb. sweet butter, softened
2 cups confectioners' sugar
1 teaspoon vanilla
8 eggs, separated
½ lb. almonds, chopped
½ lb. Maillard's or Belgian Callebaut chocolate, melted

1 tablespoon bread crumbs
½ lb. sweet German chocolate
1 cup light brown sugar
½ cup plus 2 tablespoons whipping cream
1 tablespoon sweet butter
1 teaspoon vanilla

Cream butter, confectioners' sugar, and vanilla. Add egg yolks, one at a time, beating after each addition. Mix in

almonds, chocolate, and bread crumbs. Beat egg whites until stiff and fold into mixture. Grease and flour 3-3"x9" round cake pans. Divide ¾ of the chocolate mixture among the 3 pans. Bake in a preheated 425° oven for 15 minutes. Let cool and remove from tins. Spread the reserved ¼ of the uncooked mixture between the cake layers in order to keep the cake moist. Combine German chocolate, brown sugar, and cream in the top of a double boiler; cook, stirring, until thickened and smooth. Add butter and vanilla; beat until creamy. Ice the top and sides of the cake with the frosting. Makes 10 to 12 servings.

– Amy J. Trounstine (Mrs. Henry)

» Taft Fruit Cake «

In 1927, Mr. and Mrs. Charles Phelps Taft gave one million dollars, their home, the land on which it stood, and their fine collection of paintings, porcelains, and jewelry to the Cincinnati Institute of Fine Arts. With additional funds donated by the people of Cincinnati, the Taft Museum was opened in 1932. This recipe was found in the archives of the Taft Museum and is presented as used by the Tafts' cook, Mrs. McQuain.

1 lb. butter
1 lb. confectioners' sugar
1 lb. flour
1½ lbs. raisins
1 lb. currants
½ lb. citron, finely chopped
8 eggs
1 cup brandy

1 cup milk
1 teaspoon cinnamon
1 scant teaspoon allspice
1 whole nutmeg, grated
1 scant teaspoon mace
1 teaspoon baking soda
4 teaspoons baking powder

Beat yolks of eggs and sugar to a light cream in separate dish. Then cream the butter, gradually add flour and milk, then the eggs and sugar. Add whites of eggs which have been beaten up stiff; add spices, raisins, currants, and citron. Roll fruit in flour before adding. Add baking powder and baking soda. Dissolve soda in a little boiling water and add to mixture. Put baking powder in dry before soda; don't mix with flour. The mixture is rather stiff. Bake in 2 deep granite pudding pans in a preheated 275° oven for 2¾ hours. Put paper over cake if it gets too brown. Try if done with a straw. Put greased paper in bottom of pans. Let stand in pan for a while after done.

» Flourless Chocolate Cake with Chocolate Mousse «

In 1830, Laura O'Bryon, age 19 years, began constructing the building that now houses her namesake restaurant. Other settlers followed and the area was named O'Bryonville after Laura. In 1982, the original building was restored keeping the early architecture and ambiance.

½ cup unsalted butter	Chocolate Mousse
8 oz. semi-sweet chocolate	Whipped cream
⅔ cup sugar	4 large strawberries,
5 eggs, separated	halved

Melt butter and chocolate in double boiler over hot water. Whip half of the sugar and 5 egg yolks together, until pale in color and fluffy. Whip egg whites and balance of sugar in a mixer until the mixture forms stiff peaks. Gently fold chocolate mixture into the yolk mixture. Then fold into egg whites with wire whisk, pulling from bottom to top and letting the mixture drop through the whisk gently. When all is incorporated, pour into a 9″ greased and floured cake pan. Bake for 1 hour, 15 minutes, in preheated 325° oven. Turn out immediately on cake rack to cool, letting it rest for about 2 hours. To serve, cut cake into eighths; top each with a large scoop of Chocolate Mousse. Garnish with a large scoop of whipped cream and half a strawberry. Makes 8 servings.

Chocolate Mousse

4 ozs. chocolate	2 cups whipping cream
¼ cup butter	2 egg whites
⅔ cup sugar	

Melt chocolate and butter in double boiler over hot water. Beat half the sugar and cream until stiff peaks are formed. Beat remaining sugar with egg whites until stiff peaks are formed. Fold chocolate gently into egg whites; fold that mixture into whipped cream. Refrigerate for 1 hour or more.

– Chef Eugene Quinn
Laura O'Bryon's Restaurant

Mary Cassatt, 1844-1926, American, "Tea," ca. 1890, drypoint, 1940.159. Gift of Herbert Greer French

» Guinness Cake «

This is a spicy, moist cake from the Emerald Isle. It is similar to our fruit cake, but with a special Irish flavor from the dark creamy stout, a staple of any Irish pub.

1 cup butter
1⅛ cups brown sugar
4 eggs
2½ cups flour
1 teaspoon cinnamon
½ teaspoon nutmeg
½ teaspoon allspice
1¾ cups seedless raisins
1¾ cups currants
¼ lb. mixed candied fruit, chopped
¾ cup walnuts, chopped
½ cup Guinness stout, or more if needed

Cream the butter and sugar until fluffy. Add the eggs, one at a time, mixing well after each addition. Fold in flour and spices. Add fruit and nuts; mix well. Add ¼ cup stout, or more as needed, to achieve a soft dropping consistency. Turn the mixture into a greased and floured 8″ cake pan. Bake in a preheated 325° oven for 1 hour, reduce heat to 300°, and continue baking for an additional 1½ hours. Cool the cake and remove from cake pan. Prick the cake with a skewer; spoon an additional ¼ cup of Guinness stout over the cake. Allow to soak in overnight. Wrap in foil and keep for at least 1 week before serving.
Makes 8″ cake.

» Orange Nut Cake «

½ cup butter, softened
1 cup sugar
1 egg, beaten
1 teaspoon baking soda
¼ teaspoon salt
1½ cups flour
1 cup sour cream
1 cup raisins
½ cup pecans or walnuts, chopped
Juice of 1 orange
Grated zest of 1 orange
½ cup sugar
Juice of 1 lemon
Juice of 1 orange

Cream butter and sugar; add egg. Sift baking soda, salt, and flour together; add to butter mixture. Stir in sour cream, raisins, nuts, and orange juice and zest. Pour into a greased 8″ square pan. Bake in preheated 350° oven for 50 minutes. Meanwhile, dissolve sugar in heated lemon and orange juices. Pour over cake after removing from oven. Makes 8 servings.

– Ann Hinckley (Mrs. Charles)

» Orange Pecan Loaf Cake «

If you can wait, this cake is even better the next day.

1½ cups flour
1 teaspoon baking powder
1 teaspoon salt
⅓ cup butter, softened
1 cup sugar
2 eggs, beaten
½ cup milk
2 teaspoons orange zest, grated
3 tablespoons fresh orange juice
½ cup pecans, toasted and chopped
3 tablespoons fresh orange juice
½ cup sugar

Sift flour, baking powder, and salt. Mix butter with sugar and eggs; beat well until fluffy. Stir flour mixture alternately with milk into egg mixture. Beat until batter is of a smooth consistency. Add orange zest, orange juice, and pecans. Pour into a greased 3″x5″x9″ loaf pan. Bake in a preheated 350° oven for about 1 hour. Cake is done when a toothpick inserted in the center of the loaf comes out clean. Cool for 10 minutes, loosen sides, and turn out on a wire rack. As cake cools, make orange glaze. Mix orange juice with sugar. Do not dissolve sugar since it makes for a crustier frosting. After the 10-minute cooling period, sprinkle orange-sugar mixture over the cake slowly, allowing it to be absorbed in the cake. When cake is cool, cover lightly with plastic wrap or aluminum foil. Makes 1 loaf.

– Anne Carson (Mrs. Robert)

» Seed Cake «

Caraway seeds are a favorite Scotch seasoning in cakes, cookies, and biscuits. The Scots also sugar the seeds to make a confection called carvies.

½ cup butter
½ cup sugar
3 eggs
2 cups flour
2 teaspoons baking powder
1 teaspoon cinnamon
1 teaspoon nutmeg
⅓ cup milk
2 teaspoons orange zest, minced
2 teaspoons lemon zest, minced
¼ cup candied citron, minced
⅓ cup almonds, chopped
2 teaspoons caraway seeds

Cream butter and sugar until fluffy, beat in eggs, and mix well. Lightly mix flour, baking powder, cinnamon, and nutmeg. Add to butter and egg mixture alternately with milk, mixing well each time. Add remaining ingredients and mix thoroughly. Prepare a greased pan lined with greased wax paper; you may use either a 9″ round or square or a loaf pan. Bake in a preheated 350° oven for 30 minutes. Makes 1 cake.

» Erdbeer Schaum Torte «

This ambrosial Austrian dessert is from Schloss Fuschl, a former archbishop's hunting lodge that is now a lovely inn, located outside Salzburg, overlooking a beautiful lake. This torte takes time to make, but is worth it for special occasions.

Pinch of salt	8 oz. package semi-sweet
4 egg whites	chocolate
¼ teaspoon cream of	3 tablespoons brandy
tartar	3 cups whipping cream
1 cup sugar	⅓ cup sugar
½ teaspoon vanilla	1 teaspoon vanilla
	3 cups strawberries

Add salt to egg whites and beat until fluffy. Add cream of tartar and continue beating, adding sugar gradually, until the mixture is stiff and glossy; stir in vanilla. Grease and flour 3-9″ round cake pans; divide mixture among pans. Bake in a preheated 275° oven for 45 minutes; turn heat off and let meringues remain in the closed oven for another 45 minutes. Meanwhile, combine chocolate and brandy in a double boiler; heat over boiling water until completely melted. Set aside to cool slightly. Whip cream until stiff; add sugar and vanilla. Slice strawberries, reserving 8 perfect ones for decoration. Place 1 layer of meringue on serving plate and drizzle with ⅓ of chocolate. Spread with a ¾″ layer of whipped cream and a layer of sliced strawberries. Place another layer of meringue on top; repeat procedure. Top this with the last layer of meringue. Frost the sides of the torte with whipped cream and drizzle the remaining chocolate decoratively over the top of the meringue. Place 8 mounds of whipped cream around top edge of torte and top with whole strawberries. Chill for 2 to 5 hours, and then serve immediately. Slice with a sharp, pointed knife. Makes 8 to 10 servings.

– Frances McClure (Mrs. George H.)

» Aunt Rosella's Sponge Cake «

This feathery light cake is great alone or with berries and whipped cream. Aunt Rosella guarded her recipe, but I persuaded her daughter-in-law that it was too good not to share.

7 eggs, separated	Juice of ½ lemon
½ teaspoon salt	½ teaspoon lemon zest,
1 teaspoon cream of tartar	grated
1 teaspoon vanilla	1¾ cups sugar
¼ teaspoon almond	2 whole eggs
extract	1 scant cup flour

Beat 7 egg whites until foamy. Add salt, cream of tartar, vanilla, almond extract, juice and zest of lemon. Continue beating while mixing in ¾ cup sugar; beat until glossy peaks form. In separate bowl, beat egg yolks with 2 whole eggs, gradually adding remaining sugar. Add flour and blend. Gently fold in egg whites. Pour into an ungreased 9″ tube pan and bake in a preheated 350° oven for 50 to 60 minutes. Cool upside down for 1 hour, or until cool. Remove from pan. Makes 9″ cake.

– Toody Kaplan (Mrs. Arthur)

» Amaretto Cheesecake «

Amaretto is one of America's favorite liqueurs that originated in the Italian town of Saronno, near Milan. It has a slightly bitter almond flavor, but does not contain almonds and, in fact, is made from apricot pits, alcohol, and aromatic herbs.

1½ cups graham cracker	5 tablespoons Amaretto
crumbs	liqueur
1 cup roasted pecans,	Juice of 1 lemon
chopped	Zest of 1 lemon, chopped
½ cup sugar	3 ozs. ricotta cheese
¼ cup butter	2 oz. cream cheese,
1 tablespoon water	softened
6 oz. almond paste	1¼ cups sour cream
1½ lbs. cream cheese,	2 tablespoons brown
softened	sugar
1 cup sugar	1½ teaspoons vanilla
5 eggs	1 tablespoon Amaretto
⅓ cup whipping cream	liqueur
1 teaspoon almond extract	½ teaspoon cinnamon

· 155 ·

Mix crumbs, pecans, sugar, butter, and water. Press into the bottom of a 9″ springform pan; spread almond paste over crust. Cream the softened cream cheese; add sugar and the eggs, one at a time, beating after each addition. Add cream, almond extract, Amaretto, lemon, zest, and ricotta cheese; mix well. Pour into crust and bake in a preheated 350° oven for 1 hour. Meanwhile, mix cream cheese, sour cream, brown sugar, vanilla, Amaretto, and cinnamon. Pour over cheesecake and bake for an additional 20 minutes. Cool overnight, unmold, and refrigerate until serving. Makes 12 servings.

– Rob Fogel
Edwards Under 5th Cafe

» Cheese Cake Deluxe «

This makes a very light, fresh, and delicious cake, not too heavy and not too cheesy.

8 oz. pkg. cream cheese	1 cup sour cream
3 eggs	2 tablespoons sugar
⅔ cup sugar	Several drops vanilla
Several drops almond extract	

Mix cream cheese, eggs, sugar, and almond extract in an electric mixer or blender. Place in a 9″ springform pan. Bake 30 to 35 minutes in preheated 350° oven; cool for 10 minutes. Mix sour cream, 2 tablespoons sugar, and vanilla extract. Stir well and pour over cheesecake. Bake 10 minutes. Cool and serve. Makes 8 servings.

– Anne Rittershofer Neumann

» Cream Cheese Pie «

For a really special treat, serve this with fresh strawberries or peaches.

24 ozs. cream cheese, softened	¾ cup confectioners' sugar
3 eggs	½ pint sour cream
2 tablespoons vanilla	3 tablespoons confectioners' sugar
1 teaspoon almond extract or Amaretto liqueur	½ teaspoon vanilla

Cream cheese, add eggs, and beat well. Add vanilla, almond extract or Amaretto, and confectioners' sugar; beat well. Pour into a buttered 9″ pie pan. Bake in

preheated 350° oven for 30 to 35 minutes. Cool for 15 minutes. Mix sour cream, confectioners' sugar, and vanilla. Spread over cheese pie, not quite to the edge. Bake 5 minutes more to set; cool and refrigerate. Makes 6 to 8 servings.

– Gayle Mahler

» Walnut Wonder Cake «

This is a very rich cake, not too sweet, and worth every calorie. It was a contest prizewinner in Cincinnati about 25 years ago.

2 cups flour, sifted	1 teaspoon vanilla
1 teaspoon baking powder	1 cup sour cream
1 teaspoon baking soda	⅓ cup brown sugar, firmly
½ teaspoon salt	packed
1 cup butter	¼ cup sugar
1 cup sugar	1 teaspoon cinnamon
2 eggs	1 cup walnuts, chopped

Sift flour, baking powder, soda, and salt together. Cream butter with 1 cup sugar until light and fluffy. Add eggs and vanilla; beat thoroughly. Blend in sour cream alternately with sifted dry ingredients. Spread half the batter in greased and floured 9″x13″x2″ pan. Combine remaining ingredients and sprinkle ½ of mixture over first layer of batter. Repeat layer of batter and topping. Bake 35 minutes in preheated 350° oven. Cut in squares; serve warm as coffee cake or dessert.
Makes 12 to 16 servings.

– Audrey McCafferty

» Chocolate Almond Cheesecake «

1½ cups graham cracker crumbs	4 eggs
	⅓ cup Amaretto liqueur
2 tablespoons sugar	1 cup sour cream
1 teaspoon ground cinnamon	1½ tablespoons sugar
6 tablespoons butter, melted	1 tablespoon Amaretto liqueur
3-8 oz. pkgs. cream cheese, softened	¼ cup almonds, toasted and sliced
1 cup sugar	12 ozs. semi-sweet chocolate, grated

Combine graham cracker crumbs, 2 tablespoons sugar, cinnamon, and butter; mix well. Firmly press mixture into bottom and ½" up on sides of a 9" springform pan. Beat cream cheese with electric mixer until light and fluffy. Gradually add l cup sugar, mixing well. Add eggs, one at a time, beating well after each one. Stir in Amaretto. Pour into prepared pan. Bake in preheated 375° oven for 40 to 50 minutes, or until set. Combine sour cream, sugar, and Amaretto; stir well and spoon over cheesecake. Return to oven and bake at 500° for 5 minutes. Let cool to room temperature; refrigerate 24 to 48 hours. Garnish with almonds and grated chocolate. Makes 12 servings.

— *Susie Mc Beath (Mrs. Walter)*

» Baklava Rolls «

3⅓ cups walnuts, finely chopped
¼ cup brown sugar, firmly packed
½ teaspoon cinnamon
1 lb. frozen phyllo leaves, thawed
1½ cups sweet butter, melted
1 lemon
3 cups sugar
2½ cups water
¼ cup pistachio nuts, chopped

Mix walnuts, brown sugar, and cinnamon; set aside. Remove phyllo leaves from package and place between barely dampened towels to prevent drying while assembling rolls. Place a phyllo leaf on a sheet of waxed paper and brush with melted butter. Top with 9 additional leaves, brushing each with butter. Sprinkle evenly with ½ of the walnut mixture. Top with remaining phyllo leaves, brushing each with butter. Starting with long edge, roll phyllo leaves jelly roll fashion. Using a sharp knife, cut into 1" slices and place cut-side-up in 16 paper-lined muffin tins. Sprinkle each with remaining walnut filling. Bake in preheated 300° oven until golden brown, about 1 hour. While pastries are baking, cut zest from lemon. Cut into very thin julienne strips, 1"x⅛" each. Remove juice from lemon. Simmer julienne strips, juice, sugar, and water, stirring occasionally, for 10 minutes. Pour syrup over hot pastries as they are removed from oven. Sprinkle with pistachio nuts and cool completely. Remove from paper to serve. Makes 16 pastries.

— *Anne Seasholes Cozlu (Mrs. Cem)*

» Boccinotti «

I have never found these Italian filled pastries in the United States except in the homes of my mother-in-law's contemporaries — who taught me how to make them — and then only at Christmas time. However, I did find them in a bakery in a small town near Pisa, Italy, where they were filled with rice pudding. Delicious! These will keep a week or more when refrigerated.

1 lb. flour
1 lb. sugar
1 lb. vegetable shortening, or ⅔ lb. vegetable shortening plus ⅓ lb. margarine
10 large egg yolks, or 12 small egg yolks
1 lb. dried fruit — apricots,
peaches, or a combination of apricot, peach, pear, and prune or apricot preserves
Water
Confectioners' sugar
Maraschino cherries, cut into crescent shaped pieces

Combine flour and sugar; cream with shortening until well blended. Add egg yolks one at a time, beating well after each addition. The dough may be frozen at this point for up to a month. Pinch off golf ball-sized pieces of dough and press into well-greased muffin pans, lining bottom and sides of tins. Cut fruit into small pieces and stew with a small amount of water until soft, adding a little sugar if desired. Purée with a fork or in a food processor or blender. Cool and drop a heaping teaspoonful into each muffin tin. Pinch off a piece of dough a bit smaller than a golf ball and press over the top of each pastry, sealing around the edges. When baked they will look like cupcakes. Bake in a preheated 350° oven for 15 to 20 minutes or until golden brown. Because these pastries are so rich, they are sometimes difficult to remove from the pan. Run a knife around the edge of each cake. Fold a dish towel into thirds and stretch across the top of the pastries. Holding the sides of the pan firmly, flip it over, emptying the cakes onto the towel. If cakes stick in the tins, pry them out quickly with a knife and press together. They become firm when they cool and will meld together. When cool, sprinkle lightly with confectioners' sugar and decorate with Maraschino cherries. Makes 36 pastries.

— *Mrs. Ruth Rotunno*

Giorgio Morandi, 1890-1964, Italian, "Still Life," 1956, etching, 1957.276. Gift of Albert P. Strietmann

» Lebanese Baklava Rolls «

This recipe came from my mother – Marie Sfire Kraus. It's a very rich and ambrosial pastry.

2 lbs. sugar
1½ cups water
Juice and zest of 1 lemon, grated
Few drops of rose water

1 lb. box phyllo dough
1¼ lb. clarified butter
1¼ lb. walnuts, ground
½ cup sugar

Make the syrup for the rolls 1 day ahead. Combine sugar and water; simmer for 10 to 15 minutes. Add lemon juice and zest; simmer an additional 5 minutes. Remove from heat and add rose water. Cool and refrigerate overnight. Spread 3 sheets of phyllo dough with melted butter; stack 3 layers deep. Combine walnuts and sugar; spread on the top layer of phyllo to the thickness of a fat cigar. Starting along long edge of dough, roll very tightly. Place roll in a greased 10″x17″x1½″ pan. Continue making rolls until pan is full. Before baking, use a very sharp knife and cut rolls into 3″ pieces. Bake in a preheated 350° oven for 30 minutes. Remove from oven; immediately pour prepared syrup over rolls. Makes 20 rolls.

– Marcia Joseph (Mrs. Ronald G.)

» Butterscotch Bars «

⅓ cup butter
½ cup Grapenuts cereal
¾ cup brown sugar, packed
1 egg, well beaten
1 teaspoon vanilla

¾ cup flour
½ teaspoon baking powder
⅛ teaspoon baking soda
¼ teaspoon salt
½ cup dates, chopped

Melt butter in a saucepan. Add Grapenuts and cook about 2 minutes, until cereal is softened. Remove from heat and stir in sugar. Cool slightly and stir in egg and vanilla. Sift together flour, baking powder, baking soda, and salt. Add to cereal mixture, a little at a time. Mix well after each addition. Stir in the dates. Spoon into a greased 8″x8″x2″ pan. Press down evenly. Bake in preheated 350° oven 20 to 30 minutes, or until golden brown. Cool and cut into bars. Makes 20 bars.

– Gladys Orton (Mrs. Robert)

» Mint Brownies «

4 eggs, beaten	¼ teaspoon vanilla
2 cups sugar	½ teaspoon peppermint
1 cup flour	extract
1 cup butter	2 to 3 drops green food
4 ozs. unsweetened	coloring
chocolate	Milk, if needed
3 cups confectioners'	3 tablespoons butter
sugar	3 ozs. semi-sweet
3 tablespoons butter,	chocolate
softened	

Beat eggs and sugar together. Add flour. Melt butter and chocolate together; add to flour mixture. Spread in greased jelly roll pan. Bake in preheated 350° oven for 15 minutes on middle rack. Cool. Mix confectioners' sugar, butter, vanilla, peppermint extract, and green food coloring together. If needed to obtain a spreading consistency, add a small amount of milk. Spread over cake and refrigerate. Melt remaining butter and chocolate together; drizzle on cake. Make wave design with knife. Refrigerate. Cut into squares to serve. Makes about 40 brownies.

– Kathie Droesch (Mrs. David)

» Cincinnati Saucepan Butterscotch Sticks «

These moist cookie bars are wonderful for brown bag lunches, or picnic suppers at Riverbend, where summer concerts are held under Cincinnati stars.

½ cup butter	1 tablespoon baking
1 cup brown sugar	powder
1 egg	1 teaspoon vanilla
1 cup flour, sifted	¼ cup walnuts or pecans,
¼ teaspoon salt	chopped

Melt butter in saucepan; add brown sugar, stirring until melted. Cool and beat in egg. Add flour, salt, and baking powder. Add vanilla and nuts. Spread in 8″ square pan. Bake in preheated 400° oven about 10 minutes. While still hot, cut into finger lengths. Makes 20 cookie bars.

– Jean L. Hait (Mrs. Richard)

» Nutty Currant Cheesecake Squares «

½ cup butter, softened	8 oz. pkg. cream cheese,
⅔ cup brown sugar,	softened
packed	¼ cup sugar
1 cup Passover cake meal	1 egg, beaten
1 cup matzo meal	2 tablespoons milk
1 cup nuts, chopped	2 tablespoons lemon juice
½ cup currant jelly	½ teaspoon vanilla

Cream the butter and brown sugar. Add cake meal and matzo meal; stir in the nuts. Reserve 1 cup of mixture for topping and press remainder into bottom of 9″x13″ baking pan. Bake in a preheated 350° oven for 15 minutes. Cool and then spread jelly over the cooled crust. To prepare the filling, beat the cream cheese and sugar together well. Add the egg, milk, lemon juice, and vanilla; mix well. Pour onto the baked crust and sprinkle with the remaining crumb mixture. Bake 30 minutes more. Cool; cut into squares. Makes 20 squares.

– Dottie Borstein

» Lirios de Queijo-Creme «
Brazilian Cream Cheese Lily Cookies

8 oz. package cream	2 cups flour, sifted
cheese	Raspberry jam
1 cup butter	Confectioners' sugar

Blend cream cheese and butter. Add flour and mix well. On a floured cloth, roll dough to about ⅛″-thickness and cut with floured 2″-round biscuit cutter. Fold into a cornucopia shape and fill each with about ¼ teaspoon raspberry jam. Bake in a preheated 375° oven for about 12 to 15 minutes, or until very lightly browned. Sprinkle with confectioners' sugar while hot.
Makes 5 to 6 dozen cookies.

– Peggy Andre (Mrs. J. Richard)

» Double Chocolate Oatmeal Cookies «

2 cups semi-sweet
　chocolate pieces,
　divided
¾ cup flour
¾ cup oats, uncooked
l teaspoon baking powder
l teaspoon ground

cinnamon
¼ teaspoon salt
¼ teaspoon baking soda
½ cup butter, softened
½ cup sugar
l egg
½ teaspoon vanilla

In a heavy saucepan, melt l cup chocolate pieces. Cool slightly. In small bowl, combine flour, oats, baking powder, cinnamon, salt, and baking soda. In a medium bowl, beat together butter and sugar until light and fluffy. Blend in egg and vanilla; stir in melted chocolate. Gradually add dry ingredients. Mix well. Stir remaining cup of chocolate pieces into batter. Drop by rounded spoonfuls onto ungreased baking sheet. Bake in preheated 375° oven about 8 minutes. Cool l minute on baking sheet, then remove to wire cooling rack. Makes 3 dozen.

— Nan Strubbe (Mrs. John L.)

» Chocolate Walnut Bars «

1½ cups flour
½ teaspoon cinnamon
¼ teaspoon baking
　powder
½ cup brown sugar, firmly
　packed
¾ cup butter, softened
3 eggs
½ cup brown sugar, firmly
　packed

1 cup dark corn syrup
¼ cup flour
2 ozs. semi-sweet
　chocolate, melted and
　cooled
1½ teaspoons vanilla
¼ teaspoon salt
1½ cups walnuts, coarsely
　chopped

Sift flour, cinnamon, and baking powder into large bowl. Stir in brown sugar. Cut in butter with a pastry blender until crumbly. Pat into greased 9"x13"x2" pan. Bake in preheated 350° oven for 10 minutes. Remove to a rack and leave the oven on. Beat eggs, brown sugar, syrup, flour, chocolate, vanilla, and salt together until blended. Pour over dough layer in pan and sprinkle with nuts. Return to oven and bake 30 minutes longer. Cool on a wire rack and cut into bars. Makes 24 bars.

— Lois Monterosso (Mrs. John)

» Florentines «

These attractive crisp wafer-like cookies may be served by themselves or with a fruit mousse or sorbet.

½ cup sugar
⅓ cup whipping cream
⅓ cup light corn syrup
2 tablespoons butter
¼ cup flour, sifted
1 cup blanched almonds,
　sliced

⅓ cup mixed candied
　fruit, finely chopped
3 ozs. semi-sweet
　chocolate
2 teaspoons instant coffee
1 tablespoon butter

Combine sugar, cream, corn syrup, and butter in a heavy saucepan. Place over low heat and cook, stirring, until sugar is dissolved. Increase heat to moderate and cook until the mixture registers 238° on a candy thermometer. Remove from heat and add flour, almonds, and candied fruit. Mix well and drop by rounded teaspoonful onto a greased or foil-covered baking sheet, 2" apart. Bake in a preheated 375° oven for 8 to 10 minutes, or until cookies are lightly browned. Cool slightly while still on cookie sheet; remove carefully to a surface covered with waxed paper to continue cooling. Meanwhile, melt chocolate, instant coffee, and butter in a heavy pan over low heat, until the mixture is thick and smooth. Brush the chocolate over the tops of the cooled cookies with a pastry brush. Makes 6 dozen cookies.

— Betty S. Graf (Mrs. Douglas P.)

» Galaktobouriko «

In Greece, this rich custard pie is made with sheep or goat's milk. With a phyllo crust, it is a delicate, exquisite dessert.

4¼ cups milk
1 cup sugar
Zest of one lemon or
　orange, grated
1 cup semolina flour
6 eggs, beaten

1 lb. phyllo dough
Melted butter
4 cups sugar
2 cups water
Juice of ½ lemon
½ cup brandy

Combine milk and sugar in a heavy saucepan and bring just to a boil over low heat. Remove from heat and add grated rind. Gradually add semolina, stirring constantly. Return pan to heat, stirring constantly, until mixture thickens slightly. Add a small amount of the hot mixture to the beaten eggs and then add the eggs to the hot mixture. Continue stirring over heat until mixture is thick and smooth; cool. Spread 10 layers of phyllo in a 9"x13" pan. Brush every other layer with melted butter. Spread the cooled cream evenly over the 10th layer. Spread remaining layers of phyllo in pan, brushing every other layer with melted butter and ending with buttered layer. With a very sharp knife cut the top layers into squares, being careful not to cut into the cream layer. Bake in a preheated 375° oven for 40 to 45 minutes. Meanwhile, combine remaining sugar, water, and lemon juice in a heavy pan and simmer over low heat for 5 minutes. When galaktobouriko has baked for 40 to 45 minutes, remove syrup from heat; add brandy and pour syrup over galaktobouriko as it is removed from oven. Makes 20 to 24 squares.

» Ginger Snaps «

This typically American cookie actually originated in Edinburgh. The Scots have always been fond of ginger cakes in various forms and thicknesses. Snaps are slightly thicker than parlies, but still have the crisp crunchiness that gives them their name.

1 cup sugar	*3 cups flour*
1 cup butter, softened	*1½ teaspoons baking soda*
¾ cup dark molasses	*2 teaspoons ginger*
1 egg	*⅛ teaspoon white pepper*
1½ teaspoons vinegar	

Cream sugar and butter together until fluffy. Add molasses, egg, and vinegar; blend well. Stir in remaining ingredients. Using a teaspoon, drop cookies onto a greased baking sheet. Bake in a preheated 350° oven for 7 to 10 minutes. Makes 100 cookies.

» Kadaifi «

This shredded wheat pastry, a classic Lebanese sweet, lends new life to an old American breakfast cereal.

10 oz. package shredded wheat biscuits	*¼ cup sugar*
½ cup butter, melted	*½ cup butter, melted*
1 cup walnuts, ground	*1½ cups milk*
	1½ cups sugar

Dip ½ of the wheat biscuits quickly into hot water, one at a time. Split biscuits along seam with a fork; arrange in one layer in a greased 9"x13"x2" pan. Spoon ½ cup butter over and bake in a preheated 400° oven until golden, about 15 minutes. Sprinkle walnuts and sugar over hot biscuits. Dip remaining biscuits into hot water, one at a time. Split biscuits along seam with a fork; arrange on top of walnuts. Spoon remaining butter over biscuits and bake until golden and crisp, about 30 minutes. Meanwhile, heat milk and sugar in a heavy saucepan over medium heat; stir constantly until milk begins to boil. Remove from heat and pour over hot pastry. Cool completely and allow all of milk to absorb, about 8 hours. Cut into squares. Makes 12 to 14 pastries.

– Anne Seasholes Cozlu (Mrs. Cem)

» Lebkuchen «

The lebkuchen is a traditional German Christmas cake; these are cut into squares before baking.

6 eggs	*1 teaspoon salt*
1 lb. light or dark brown sugar	*1 teaspoon baking powder*
5 cups flour, more if needed	*1 cup pecans, chopped*
1 teaspoon cinnamon	*1 cup candied fruit, chopped, optional*
½ teaspoon cloves	*½ cup confectioners' sugar*
½ teaspoon baking soda	

Reserve 1½ egg whites for the icing. Beat remaining egg whites and yolks with the brown sugar until light and fluffy. Sift the flour, cinnamon, cloves, baking soda, salt, and baking powder together. Mix well with the egg mixture; add pecans and candied fruit. The resulting dough should be quite thick. Add more flour, if necessary. Divide dough into 6 equal parts. Roll each part into a rectangle ⅜" thick. Beat the reserved egg whites until they are stiff and add confectioners' sugar. Frost the dough with this icing; cut the rectangles into smaller 2"x3" rectangles. Place on a greased cookie sheet; bake in a preheated 350° oven for 12 to 15 minutes. Makes 6 dozen cookies.

» Lemon Squares «

1 cup butter
½ cup confectioners'
  sugar
¼ teaspoon salt
2 cups flour
4 eggs, beaten

2 cups sugar
6 tablespoons lemon juice
Grated zest of 1 lemon
2 tablespoons
  confectioners' sugar for
  topping

Make pastry by cutting butter, confectioners' sugar, and salt into flour. Pat pastry into an 9"x13" pan and bake in a preheated 350° oven for 20 minutes. Mix together eggs, sugar, lemon juice, and grated lemon zest. Spread this mixture over pastry. Bake for 25 minutes. Cool and sprinkle with powdered sugar. Cut in bars.
Makes about 36 bar cookies.

– Eleanor Dwyer
Contributed by John Costello, S.J.

» Mandelbrot «

Mandel means almond, and brot means bread. These German almond pastries are very tasty dunked in coffee.

3 eggs, beaten
1 cup oil
1 cup sugar
1 teaspoon vanilla
1 cup almonds, chopped
1 cup chocolate chips,
  optional

3 cups flour
Pinch of salt
2 teaspoons baking
  powder
½ cup sugar
1 teaspoon cinnamon

Add oil to eggs, beating slowly. Add sugar and beat gently. Add vanilla; fold in almonds and chocolate chips, if desired. Sift flour, salt, and baking powder together. Fold flour into eggs. The dough should come away from the sides of the bowl: add additional flour, if needed. Divide the dough mixture into 6 equal parts. Form each part into a strip, approximately 12" long and 2" wide. Place strips on a greased cookie sheet. Slice diagonally ¾ of the way down and 1" apart. Before baking, sprinkle with sugar and cinnamon mixture. Bake in a preheated 350° oven for 30 minutes. Remove from oven and finish cutting each strip into 12 pieces. Makes 72 pieces.

– Bonnie Warton

» Frappe «
Lover's Knots

Italians serve these crisp sweets at the end of a hearty meal or with a glass of sweet dessert wine at any time.

1¾ cups flour
½ teaspoon baking
  powder
Pinch of salt
2 tablespoons butter, at
  room temperature
2 eggs, slightly beaten

1 tablespoon rum
1 tablespoon anisette
1 tablespoon vanilla
4 teaspoons sugar
Oil for deep frying
Confectioners' sugar

Sift flour, baking powder, and salt together. Add butter and blend thoroughly. Add eggs, rum, anisette, vanilla, and sugar. Knead well. Wrap in a cloth and place in a cool place for 1 hour. On a floured board, roll out dough into a thin sheet. Cut into strips about 1" wide and 6" long. Gently tie each strip into a loose knot. Fry the knots, a few at a time, in sufficient oil to permit them to puff up. When golden brown, remove immediately. Drain on paper towels, and when cooled, sprinkle with confectioners' sugar. Makes 4 dozen pastries.

– Bertha Benigni Galvin (Mrs. John J.)

» Paxemadia «

These crisp, anise-flavored biscuits are served with coffee in Greek coffee houses and at the yearly Panegyri Greek Festival at Holy Trinity-St. Nicholas Church in Cincinnati.

1½ cups sugar
4 eggs
1 cup oil
5 cups flour
½ teaspoon baking soda

2½ teaspoons baking
  powder
2 teaspoons vanilla
2 teaspoons ground anise
  seeds
¼ cup sesame seeds

Beat sugar and eggs together until they are light and lemon-colored, about 5 minutes; add oil and beat another 10 minutes. Add flour, soda, baking powder, vanilla, and ground anise; mix well and refrigerate 20 minutes. Shape five 4"x10" loaves on greased cookie sheets. Pat sesame seeds on top and score the loaves diagonally with a very sharp knife or razor blade. Bake in a preheated 350° oven for 30 minutes, or until browned; cool. To serve, slice loaves where scored, and toast in oven on each side until brown. Makes five 4"x10" loaves.

– Sophia Georges (Mrs. Charlie)

Claude Michel (Clodion), 1738-1814, French, "Bacchant and Bacchante with Cupid," 1799, terra cotta. 1975.74. J.J. Emery Fund

» Pepparkakor «

These crisp, thin gingersnaps are a Swedish Christmas tradition found in every home. At Christmas time, the cookies are often cut into animal shapes and decorated with confectioners' sugar frosting.

½ cup butter, softened
¾ cup sugar
1 egg
¾ cup dark corn syrup
2 teaspoons orange zest, grated
3½ cups flour, sifted

1 teaspoon baking soda
1 tablespoon ginger
1 tablespoon cinnamon
2 teaspoons ground cloves
1 teaspoon ground cardamom
Almond halves

Cream butter and sugar thoroughly; add egg and beat until light and fluffy. Add corn syrup and orange zest; beat well. Sift flour with baking soda and spices. Stir into creamed mixture a little at a time. Blend well. Cover; chill overnight. Roll out on well-floured pastry cloth or board to ⅛" thickness. Cut into a variety of shapes with cookie cutters. Place on greased baking sheets. Place a blanched almond half in center of each cookie. Bake in a preheated 350° oven for 8 to 10 minutes. Makes 10 to 12 dozen cookies. The baked cookies store well. Dough may be used in small amounts, if desired, and will keep one week.

– Audrey McCafferty

» Sesame Seed Twists «

These delicate Greek confections are a marvelous and not-too-sweet end to a rich dinner.

¾ cup butter, softened	2 eggs
1 cup sugar	3 cups flour
1 tablespoon baking powder	1 egg white
1 teaspoon vanilla	3 tablespoons sesame seeds
½ teaspoon salt	

Combine butter, sugar, baking powder, vanilla, salt, eggs, and 2 cups of flour. Beat with mixer at low speed until well blended, scraping bowl constantly with rubber spatula. Stir remaining 1 cup of flour in with a wooden spoon; mix until smooth. Chill in refrigerator for several hours. With hands, roll 1 tablespoon of dough into a 6″ long rope; twist rope around finger to form a coil and place coils 1″ apart on buttered baking sheet. Brush with egg white and sprinkle with sesame seeds. Bake in a preheated 350° oven for 20 minutes or until lightly browned. Remove cookies to a rack to cool; store in a tightly covered container. May be stored up to 2 weeks. Makes 24 cookies.

– Jean L. Hait (Mrs. Richard J.)

» Shortbread Fingers «

This is a Scottish recipe handed down through the years in the MacMillan clan.

1 cup butter, softened	1½ cups flour, sifted
⅔ cup sugar	Granulated sugar

Cream butter and sugar until light and fluffy. Add ¾ cup of flour and mix well. Add remaining flour and mix in – mixture will be very stiff. Knead on a lightly floured board until soft and pliable. This will take some time and energy, but is the secret to good shortbread. Spread smoothly on a large ungreased cookie sheet and score into 64 fingers – 4 across and 16 down. Prick all over with a fork. Bake on the top shelf of a preheated 325° oven for 40 minutes or until pale golden; do not overbake. Dust with granulated sugar and cool on a rack. Makes 64 bar cookies.

– Ann Gebbie (Mrs. Douglas)

» Shortbread «

Although the Scots are known for their thriftiness, please don't skimp with this recipe. Use only the freshest, sweetest butter obtainable.

1 cup sweet butter, room temperature	½ cup plus 1 tablespoon sugar
½ teaspoon vanilla extract	2¾ cups flour

In a large bowl, beat the butter with the vanilla until smooth. Gradually add the sugar and beat for about 5 minutes, until smooth and light-colored. Continue beating, gradually adding the flour, about ¼ cup at a time, until completely incorporated. Turn out onto a lightly floured surface and knead for about 3 minutes, until a smooth ball forms. Place the dough between two sheets of waxed paper and roll into a 10″ round. Remove the top sheet of waxed paper and invert the dough onto a lightly buttered baking sheet. Remove the waxed paper; prick the dough all over with a fork and score lightly into 8 equal wedges. Bake in a preheated 350° oven for 30 to 40 minutes, lowering the heat to 300° after 20 minutes. The shortbread should be golden when finished. Remove from the oven, sprinkle with sugar, and cut into wedges while still warm. Store in an airtight tin. The dough can also be cut in fingers about ½″ thick and baked for 20 to 25 minutes. Lower the heat after 15 minutes. Makes 8 wedges.

– Margaret Macpherson (Mrs. Colin R.)

Ceremonial Vessel, Type Fangyi, cast bronze,
China, late Shang Dynasty, 13th-11th century B.C., 1948.75.
Given in honor of Mr. and Mrs. Charles F. Williams
by their children. This color reproduction
donated by Mr. and Mrs. John Z. Herschede

More than three thousand years ago, a skilled Chinese metal craftsman cast this square bronze vessel, meant for ceremonial use by Shang Dynasty aristocrats to provide offerings of food for their deceased ancestors. Because its shape, with the lid suggesting a roof, imitates a granery it is likely that the ritual food it held was millet.

China's ancient bronzes were unknown until the early 20th century, when their discovery prompted the immediate interest of archaeologists and art historians. This handsome example, its surface rich with decorations whose meanings can only be guessed at, is a splendid piece of sculpture in its own right and also suggests the timeless symbolic importance of matters relating to nourishment.

Desserts

» Baked Spiced Apples «

6 large baking apples,
    peeled and cored
⅓ cup butter, melted
⅓ cup fine dry bread
    crumbs
½ teaspoon ground cloves
½ cup sugar
1 teaspoon cinnamon

2 tablespoons sugar
½ cup almonds, ground
2 tablespoons water, or
    1 egg white
3 tablespoons water,
    cider, fruit juice, or
    white wine
Thick cream, sour cream,
    or vanilla sauce

Roll apples in butter. Mix crumbs, cloves, sugar, and cinnamon; roll buttered apples in mixture. Mix sugar, almonds, and 2 tablespoons water or egg white; stuff into cored apples. Place apples in a greased ovenproof casserole, place 3 tablespoons water, cider, apple juice, or other liquid around the apples, and bake in a preheated 350° oven for 30 minutes, or until tender. Serve warm with thick cream, sour cream, or vanilla sauce. Makes 6 servings.

– Sally Brown (Mrs. Fred I., Jr.)

» Apple Crisp «

McIntosh apples are best for this recipe. It's extra delicious with vanilla ice cream or sweetened cream over the top.

3 lbs. cooking apples
Water
Lemon juice
Cinnamon

1 cup flour
1 cup sugar
½ cup butter

Pare, core, and dice apples into an ungreased 9″x9″ pan. Add a small amount of water, sprinkle with lemon juice if apples are not tart, and sprinkle with cinnamon. Work flour, sugar, and butter into crumb texture with hands. Sprinkle over apples. Bake in preheated 375° oven for 40 to 50 minutes, until apples have cooked down. Serve warm. Makes 8 servings.

– Mary Pease (Mrs. James L.)

» Apple Clafouti «

This is an interesting variation of the thick fruit pancake of France, which is most often made with black cherries from the Limousin region.

3½ cups cooking apples,
    peeled, cored, and
    sliced
¼ cup butter, melted
4 eggs
1 cup milk
¼ cup cream
Pinch salt
¼ teaspoon nutmeg
½ teaspoon cinnamon
1 teaspoon lemon juice

1 tablespoon vanilla
2 tablespoons almond
    extract
1¼ cups flour, sifted
½ cup sugar
2 tablespoons almonds,
    toasted and sliced
Confectioners' sugar
Whipped cream or vanilla
    ice cream, optional

Grease a 10″ quiche dish. Arrange the apple slices on the bottom in a neat layer. Place the butter, eggs, milk, cream, salt, nutmeg, cinnamon, lemon juice, vanilla, and almond extract in a mixer or food processor; blend until smooth. Beat in flour and sugar with a wooden spoon. Pour over apples. Bake in a preheated 350° oven for 40 to 45 minutes, or until batter rises and puffs, and a knife inserted in the center comes out clean. Serve warm, sprinkled with almonds and confectioners' sugar. If desired, pass a bowl of whipped cream or vanilla ice cream. Makes 6 servings.

– Barbara Lauterbach (Mrs. Peter)

» Old Fashioned Apple Dumplings «

The secret of these apple dumplings is the freshly grated nutmeg and cooking the dumplings in the syrup. The size of the pan is very important – it should be small enough so there is no space between the dumplings and deep enough that the syrup can boil up around them while they are baking.

5 tart cooking apples	4 teaspoons baking
2 cups sugar	powder
1 teaspoon cinnamon	¾ teaspoon salt
¼ teaspoon nutmeg,	½ cup shortening
freshly grated	¾ cup milk
2 cups water	2 tablespoons sugar
2 tablespoons butter	Cinnamon
2½ cups flour, sifted	Butter

Pare, core, and slice apples; set aside. Combine sugar, cinnamon, nutmeg, water, and butter; simmer together for 5 minutes to make a thin syrup. Reduce heat and keep hot. Sift together flour, baking powder, and salt. Cut shortening into the dry ingredients until the mixture is as fine as cornmeal. Stir in just enough milk to make a rather soft dough. Turn out on a floured board and knead lightly about ½ minute. Roll out ½" thick in a rectangle shape; cut into 6 squares, each about 5"x5". Divide apples into six portions, mounding slices in the center of each square; top each with 1 teaspoon sugar, a dash of cinnamon, and a dot of butter. Bring corners up over the apples and pinch together; place smooth side up in a large buttered baking dish or pan, about 12" across and 4" to 5" deep. Pour hot syrup over the dumplings, cut a slit in the top of each, and bake in a preheated 425° oven for 10 minutes; reduce heat to 375° and continue baking for 30 to 35 minutes, or until dumplings are lightly browned. Serve warm with their own syrup as sauce. Makes 6 dumplings.

– Marjory Van Lieu

» Angel Mousse «

9" angel food cake	2-¼ oz. pkgs. unflavored
4 egg yolks, beaten	gelatin
¾ cup sugar	½ cup cold water
2 tablespoons flour	3 cups whipping cream
¼ teaspoon salt	4 egg whites
2 cups milk, scalded	¼ cup sugar
1 tablespoon vanilla	1 cup shredded coconut

Remove any brown crust from cake. Cut remainder into cubes and place in a large bowl. To make custard, place egg yolks, sugar, flour, and salt in top of double boiler over hot water; beat well with a wire whisk; add scalded milk slowly, mixing constantly until custard thickens; add vanilla. Mix gelatin with cold water, stir well, add to custard, mix, and let cool. Beat whipping cream until stiff; reserve 1 cup for frosting. Beat egg whites until stiff, adding sugar gradually. Fold whipped cream and egg whites into cooled custard. Pour over cubed cake. Mix ever so slightly. Spoon into a springform pan and refrigerate overnight. When ready to serve, turn out onto a large plate. Frost with remainder of whipped cream. Sprinkle with coconut. Makes 10 to 12 servings.

– Roma Ervin (Mrs. W. J.)

» Golden Globes «

½ lb. dried whole pitted	1 cup whipping cream,
apricots	whipped
1 cup sugar	Blanched whole almonds
2 teaspoons lemon juice	

Soak apricots in cold water to cover overnight; drain, reserving ¼ cup water. Heat apricots, reserved water, sugar, and lemon juice in a small heavy saucepan. Bring to a boil, stirring constantly. Simmer, covered, over low heat until syrup thickens, about 30 minutes. Watch very carefully during final cooking time, so that mixture does not scorch. Remove apricots from syrup; cover and refrigerate. Using a pastry tube fitted with a large tip, pipe whipped cream into each apricot. Insert 1 almond into each apricot and arrange apricots, open side down, in a shallow serving dish. Pour syrup over apricots, reheating if necessary to pour. Serve at room temperature. May be stored, covered, in refrigerator.

Dried apricot halves may be substituted for whole apricots, pressing 2 halves together for each portion. Makes 6 servings.

— Anne Seasholes Cozlu (Mrs. Cem)

» Crema de Aguacate «

This is a not sweet but satisfying dessert to follow a fiery or rich south-of-the-border meal.

4 ripe avocados	*2 tablespoons Curacao*
1 tablespoon lime juice	*liqueur, if desired*
¼ cup sugar	

Combine all ingredients in a blender or food processor; blend until smooth. Pour into a shallow tray and place in freezer until icy cold but not frozen. Serve in individual dessert bowls or stemmed glasses. Makes 6 servings.

» Jamaican Bananas «

4 firm ripe bananas,	*⅓ cup freshly grated*
peeled	*coconut*
¼ cup butter	*¼ cup rum*
¼ cup brown sugar	*Pinch of cinnamon*
Zest of 1 orange, grated	*Ice cream*
Juice of 1 orange	

Sauté bananas in butter for one minute in a heavy pan. Add sugar, orange zest, orange juice, coconut, 2 tablespoons rum, and cinnamon. Sauté, turning to brown on all sides, until bananas are tender, 4 to 6 minutes. Add remaining rum and ignite carefully with a match. Serve with ice cream. Makes 4 servings.

» Blueberry Pudding «

1 quart blueberries,	*1 cup sugar*
washed	*½ teaspoon cinnamon*
1 cup flour	*Juice of ½ lemon*
1 cup butter, melted	

Place blueberries in ovenproof casserole. Mix all other ingredients and toss lightly with blueberries. Bake in preheated 350° oven for 45 minutes. Makes 4 to 6 servings.

— Hilda Timmerman

» Bakewell Tart «

This delicious dessert is a cross between a tart and a pudding. Bakewell refers not to the cooking process but to the geographic origin of the recipe, a village in Derbyshire, England.

Short crust pastry	*Almond extract*
for a 9" pie	*½ cup blanched almonds,*
¼ cup butter	*ground*
⅓ cup sugar	*½ cup raspberry jam*
1 egg, well beaten	

Line a 9" tin with the pastry. Cream butter and sugar until light and fluffy. Stir in egg, a few drops of almond extract, and the ground almonds; mix well. Spread jam over pastry and pour butter mixture over. Bake in a preheated 400° oven until well risen and set and lightly browned — about 30 to 40 minutes. Cool completely before serving. Makes 9" tart.

— Jeanna Horwitz (Mrs. Harry)

» Brandy Bread Pudding «

6-⅜" thick slices stale	*3 eggs*
white bread, cut into	*⅔ cup sugar*
½" cubes	*¼ teaspoon salt*
¼ cup butter	*2 tablespoons brown*
2½ cups milk	*sugar, firmly packed*
⅓ cup cognac or brandy	*Cream for topping*
2 tablespoons butter	

In a heavy skillet, sauté the bread in batches in ¼ cup butter over medium high heat, until golden. Transfer to a buttered, shallow, 1-quart baking dish. In a saucepan, scald milk with cognac or brandy and butter; let cool. In a bowl, mix eggs, sugar, and salt, and then add milk mixture in a stream, beating. Pour over bread and let stand, stirring occasionally, until bread is very soft, about 2 hours. Place the pudding dish in a baking pan with hot water halfway up sides. Bake in a preheated 350° oven for 45 minutes, until the pudding is puffed and knife inserted in center comes out clean. Remove dish from pan and force the brown sugar through sieve over pudding; broil under preheated broiler 2" from heat for 1 minutes, until sugar is caramelized. Let cool for 30 minutes and serve topped with cream. Makes 4 servings.

— Hermine Wirthlin (Mrs. C. Ray)

» Budino di Amaretto «

This rich Italian pudding may be decorated with glacéed fruit or marrons to give it an especially festive touch.

1 tablespoon unflavored gelatin
2 cups milk
3 egg yolks
½ cup sugar
1 tablespoon flour
1 cup macaroons, finely chopped
3 egg whites, beaten until stiff but not dry
1 teaspoon Amaretto liqueur
1 cup whipping cream, beaten until stiff and sweetened to taste

Sprinkle gelatin over milk and let stand 20 minutes. Combine egg yolks, sugar, and flour and beat until well blended. Mix well with gelatin mixture; cook over boiling water until the mixture is thick enough to coat the back of a metal spoon. Add macaroons, cool, and then refrigerate until mixture is syrupy and beginning to set. Fold in stiffly beaten egg whites and liqueur. Place in mold and chill for 4 to 6 hours. Unmold and serve with a generous amount of whipped cream. Makes 8 servings.

– Joan M. Rust (Mrs. Richard S., Jr.)

» Zurich Cherries Jubilee «

The Swiss say, "es isch usgezeichnet" – meaning "it is excellent." This dessert is simple to make, but looks complicated and impressive as you flambé it for your guests at the table. Vanilla sugar can be made by placing a vanilla bean in a tightly covered container with granulated sugar.

¼ cup butter
2 tablespoons sugar, vanilla sugar if available
16 oz. can dark sweet cherries, drained
2 ozs. Grand Marnier liqueur
1 oz. Kirsch
4 large scoops of vanilla ice cream

Melt butter in a flambé pan. Add sugar and stir over flames with a wooden spoon until dissolved. Add cherries and cook for a few minutes. Add Grand Marnier and Kirsch and light carefully with a match. When flames die, ladle cherries and liquid over ice cream. Makes 4 servings.

– Barbara Eveland (Mrs. Joseph)

» Muthries Mousse au Chocolat «

What could be simpler or richer than this elegant French confection? It is especially attractive served in pots de creme containers or stemmed glasses.

8 oz. pkg. semi-sweet chocolate morsels
4 tablespoons hot, but not boiling, water
5 eggs, separated

Melt chocolate in double boiler with water. Stir in 5 egg yolks. Remove from stove and when a bit cool, fold in the well-beaten egg whites. Chill in refrigerator for at least 3 hours. Makes 4 servings.

– Bee Herschede (Mrs. John Z.)

» Chocolate Mousse Gâteau «

This chocolate mousse centered in chocolate meringue layers is very rich, looks impressive, and is not difficult.

4 egg whites
¼ teaspoon salt
¼ teaspoon cream of tartar
1½ cups sugar
3 tablespoons unsweetened cocoa
6 ozs. semi-sweet chocolate
½ teaspoon salt
2 tablespoons water
4 eggs, separated
2 teaspoons instant coffee
2 teaspoons vanilla
1 cup whipping cream, whipped
Sweetened cocoa or chocolate curls

Beat egg whites until frothy. Add salt, cream of tartar, sugar, and cocoa while continuing to beat until very stiff. Grease and flour a large cookie sheet. Mark 2-8"-circles by pressing an inverted 8"-bowl on the sheet. Spread the meringue on these circles, being careful that the edges are well covered, so the meringue won't break while being lifted off. Bake in a preheated 250° oven for one hour. Leave in oven 1 hour with door closed, or preheat oven to 400°, put meringue in, close door, turn off the heat, and leave 12 hours. Melt chocolate, salt, and water in the top of a double boiler. Beat egg yolks, add to chocolate along with coffee and vanilla. Beat egg whites until stiff and fold into chocolate mixture. Fold in whipped cream. Chill mousse in refrigerator several hours. Spread between meringue layers, leaving smooth sides outside. Sprinkle with sweetened cocoa or chocolate curls. Makes 8 servings.

– Mme. M. Preston Jones
Roquefort-les-Pins, France

» Cocada Leticia «

This is an unusual South American dessert from a Brazilian friend, Heloisa Prazares.

3-14 oz. cans sweetened condensed milk	1 cup plus 2 tablespoons Parmesan cheese
6 egg yolks	½ teaspoon vanilla
3 cups coconut flakes	Fresh fruit

Mix all ingredients well. Place in 9"x13" greased pan. Bake in preheated 350° oven for 20 minutes, or until the surface is golden brown; cut into bars, approximately 1"x2½" each. Serve with fresh fruit. Makes 40 bars.

– Mary Courter (Mrs. Sanford)

» Crème Brûlée a l'Orange «

This recipe for "burnt cream" is actually a Creole one, although many think it French. The addition of orange flavorings gives it a distinctive dimension.

3 cups whipping cream	1 tablespoon orange zest, grated
6 egg yolks	
6 tablespoons sugar	1 cup light brown sugar
2 tablespoons Grand Marnier liqueur	

In top part of double boiler over direct heat, scald cream. Beat egg yolks in bowl and slowly add sugar while continuing to beat. Beat until light and creamy. Slowly add scalded cream to egg yolks, beating rapidly. Add liqueur and grated orange zest. Return mixture to double boiler and cook over hot, not boiling, water until mixture thickens and coats a metal spoon. Pour into a shallow serving bowl and chill thoroughly. Cut a piece of aluminum foil exactly the size of the dish into which you have poured the crème brûlée. Trace the outline with the point of a knife and cut with scissors. Grease foil with

butter and cover with ¼" layer of brown sugar, patting down to pack well. Broil on cookie sheet under preheated broiler until sugar is caramelized. Watch carefully – do not burn. Put on top of cooled custard and peel paper off carefully. Makes 8 servings.

– Jo Steman (Mrs. Robert)

» Crème au Rhum «

This elegant French confection is a perfect ending for a rich meal.

3 egg yolks	2 cups whipping cream, whipped
¼ cup sugar	
1 tablespoon lemon juice	Grated nutmeg or semi-sweet chocolate
2 tablespoons dark rum, or more to taste	

Beat together egg yolks, sugar, and lemon juice for about 5 minutes, or until thick and lemon colored. Add rum gradually while continuing to beat. Fold whipped cream into egg mixture, reserving some for garnish. Spoon into 6 stemmed glasses, cover and chill for 4 hours or overnight. To serve, garnish with reserved whipped cream and grated nutmeg or semi-sweet chocolate. Makes 6 servings.

– Retta Traquair (Mrs. James)

» Crema de Coconut «

2 tablespoons unflavored gelatin	2 cups whipping cream
	2 cups freshly grated coconut
2 cups milk	
¼ teaspoon salt	Chocolate sauce or fresh fruit
⅓ cup sugar	

Soften gelatin by sprinkling over ¼ cup of cold milk. Combine remaining 1¾ cups of milk with salt and sugar; heat just to the boiling point. Add gelatin mixture and stir well to dissolve gelatin. Cool until slightly thickened. Beat whipping cream until stiff. Fold into milk mixture along with coconut. Pour into 10-cup mold which has been rinsed in cold water. Refrigerate overnight; serve with chocolate sauce or fresh fruit. Makes 10 servings.

» Crema Fritta «
Deep-Fried Cream

This luscious Italian dish requires patience in preparation, but the reward is more than satisfying. Prepare it in the morning, or even a day ahead, for best results.

3 eggs	*1 teaspoon water*
½ cup sugar	*Plain bread crumbs*
¾ cup unbleached flour	*Vegetable oil for frying,*
2 cups milk	*about 1″ deep*
Zest of 2 lemons, grated	*Marinated fruit*

In a copper Zabaglione pan or a double boiler, beat 2 eggs and the sugar together until sugar is partially dissolved. Add 2 tablespoons of flour to the mixture; stir until absorbed. Repeat until all flour has been used. Bring milk almost to a boil and add gradually to the egg mixture, beating with a wire whisk constantly. Add grated lemon. Place copper pan or double boiler over simmering water. Continue stirring with whisk for about 30 minutes, or until cream is thick and smooth. Pour cream into a buttered dish. Cream should be about ¾″ thick. Let cool. When cool, cut into desired size and shape (about the size of a generous saltine cracker). Beat the remaining egg together with about 1 teaspoon of water. Place each piece in crumbs, then egg wash, and again in crumbs. Fry in hot oil until golden brown on one side, then turn and fry until brown on the other side. Drain on paper towels. Serve hot with marinated fruit of the season. Makes 8 servings.

– Lu Dixon (Mrs. J. Gordon)

» Date Pudding «

½ lb. pitted dates	*3 rounded tablespoons*
¾ cup pecans or walnuts,	*confectioners' sugar*
coarsely chopped	*2 egg whites*
2 tablespoons flour	*1 pint whipping cream,*
1 teaspoon baking powder	*whipped*
2 egg yolks, beaten	

Mix dates and nuts with blended flour and baking powder. Add egg yolks; mix. Add confectioners' sugar to egg whites while beating; continue beating until soft peaks form. Fold carefully into flour mixture. Spread in a greased 9″x9″ pan. Bake in preheated 325° oven for 30 minutes. Invert on a rack to cool. Break into bite-size pieces and serve topped with whipped cream. Makes 6 servings.

– Mary Pease (Mrs. James L.)

» Old English Drunken Pudding «

This frothy pudding actually resembles a syllabub. The word derives from sille, a wine from Sillery in the Champagne district of France, and bub, Elizabethan slang for a bubbling drink – so it came to mean any dessert or drink of beaten cream flavored with wine.

½ cup white wine or	*Zest of 1 lemon, grated*
sherry	*4 tablespoons sugar*
2 tablespoons brandy	*1 cup whipping cream*
Juice of 1 lemon	*Pinch nutmeg*
Candied fruit, angelica, or twist of lemon peel, optional	

Combine wine, brandy, lemon juice, and lemon zest; let stand overnight. Strain; add sugar, stirring until dissolved. Add cream and nutmeg; beat with wire whisk, or rotary or electric beater until mixture is stiff and holds its shape. At this point, mixture may be refrigerated for several days. Serve in individual glass dishes or stemmed glasses. May be decorated with candied fruit, angelica, or a twist of lemon peel. Makes 4 to 6 servings.

– Hilary Smith
London, England

» Fresh Fruit with Ricotta Amaretto Sauce «

Amaretto is the almond-flavored Italian liqueur which does so much to enhance the flavor of fresh fruits.

3 cups fresh fruit –	*8 oz. package cream*
peaches, berries,	*cheese, softened*
figs, etc.	*½ cup sugar*
¼ cup Amaretto liqueur	*4 egg yolks*
¼ cup confectioners'	*2 tablespoons whipping*
sugar	*cream*
½ lb. ricotta cheese	*3 tablespoons Amaretto*
	liqueur

Toss the fruit with Amaretto and confectioners' sugar. Set aside and chill. Mix the ricotta and cream cheese in a blender or food processor. Add sugar, egg yolks, cream, and Amaretto; continue blending until very smooth and light. Pour into a serving dish and chill. Serve fruit chilled; pass sauce separately. Makes 4 to 6 servings.

– *Barbara Lauterbach (Mrs. Peter)*

» Soufflés aux Fruits Frais «

The Gourmet Room, atop the Terrace Hilton Hotel, is one of Cincinnati's four-star French restaurants. The spectacular mural by Joan Miró that formerly was the backdrop for the Gourmet Room is now on display at the Cincinnati Art Museum.

1 orange	*1 cup flour*
½ apple	*2 cups milk*
½ medium banana	*6 egg whites*
1 cup strawberries, sliced	*Butter*
1 cup raspberries	*Confectioners' sugar*
½ cup Cointreau liqueur	*4 egg yolks*
Juice of ½ lemon	*¼ cup sugar*
4 egg yolks	*¼ cup Cointreau liqueur*
½ cup sugar	*1 oz. Marsala wine*

Peel orange, apple, and banana; cut into small pieces. Mix gently with strawberries and raspberries. Place in a stainless steel or glass bowl and sprinkle with Cointreau and lemon juice. Mix gently. Beat egg yolks and sugar together until pale yellow, add flour and blend well; set aside. Heat milk just until it reaches the boiling point, watching it carefully. Pour over sugar and egg mixture; beat with a wire whip until cool. Fold fruit into mixture with a wooden spoon; set aside. Beat egg whites until stiff and gently fold into fruit mixture. Grease the insides of 4 small souffle cups with butter and sprinkle with confectioners' sugar. Fill to the top. Bake in a preheated 375° oven for 25 to 30 minutes. Serve with Sabayon Sauce. To make sauce, mix together in a stainless steel bowl egg yolks, sugar, Cointreau, and Marsala wine. Whip hard with a wire whip over warm water, until it is the consistency of cream. Makes 4 souffles.

– *Chef George Pulver*
Gourmet Room, Terrace Hilton Hotel

» Guard's Pudding «

This dessert, or sweet, as it is called in England, is traditionally served to the Guard's Officers on duty at Whitehall or St. James's Palace.

1 cup white bread crumbs	*6 tablespoons raspberry*
¾ cup sugar	*jam*
¾ cup butter	*Thin cream or 3 extra*
Pinch of baking soda	*tablespoons raspberry*
1 teaspoon water	*jam for sauce*
3 eggs, well beaten	*2 tablespoons water*
	Juice of ½ lemon

Mix bread crumbs with sugar and butter. Add baking soda dissolved in water. Mix eggs and raspberry jam. Mix all together vigorously. Put it all into a buttered mold or pudding dish. Cover mold with 3 or 4 layers of waxed paper, held in place with strong kitchen twine. Butter the first layer of waxed paper that is next to the pudding. Steam for 6 hours. To do this, stand the mold in a double boiler or a saucepan of boiling water, but be sure the water doesn't come more than halfway up the sides of the mold. Cover the saucepan tightly so water doesn't boil away. From time to time, add a little more, to keep it always at the same level. This pudding is served with either light cream, or a thin sauce made by boiling jam and water together for a few minutes; add the lemon juice and stir well. Makes 6 to 8 servings.

– *Jeanna Horwitz (Mrs. Harry)*

» Lemon Ice Cream «

Mexican ice cream is wonderful, with a taste that's close to homemade. This fresh lemon-flavored version is lovely as a light dessert or as a palate cleanser between courses.

3 tablespoons lemon juice	*2 cups whipping cream*
2 teaspoons lemon zest,	*2 drops yellow food*
grated	*coloring*
1 cup sugar	

Mix lemon juice, zest, and sugar well. Slowly stir in cream and food coloring. Pour into shallow tray and cover with aluminum foil. Set refrigerator freezer at lowest setting and place tray in freezer for three hours or longer. Do not stir; ice cream will freeze smoothly. Makes 6 servings.

– *Fanny Smith (Mrs. George R.)*

» Lemon Pudding «

1 lemon, seeded and
    sliced paper-thin
1½ cups sugar
1½ cups hot water
3 tablespoons butter
1½ cups sugar

½ cup water
3 eggs
1½ cups flour
1½ teaspoons baking
    powder
1 teaspoon vanilla

Arrange lemon slices in a greased 9"x9" pan. Mix sugar, hot water, and butter; pour carefully over lemon slices. Mix remaining sugar with water, eggs, flour, baking powder, and vanilla. Pour the batter over the sliced lemon mixture. Bake in a preheated 350° oven for 35 minutes. Let pudding cool in the pan for 5 minutes and then unmold onto a plate or platter, leaving lemon side up. Cool thoroughly and cut into squares.
Makes 8 servings.

– Karen Rafuse (Mrs. Peter B.)

» Frozen Mint Chocolates «

1 cup butter
2 cups confectioners'
    sugar, sifted
4 ozs. unsweetened
    chocolate, melted
4 eggs

2 teaspoons vanilla
2 teaspoons peppermint
    flavoring
2 cups vanilla wafer
    crumbs

Do not substitute margarine in this recipe. In an electric mixer or by hand, cream butter and sugar until light and fluffy. Add melted chocolate gradually. Add eggs, one at a time, beating thoroughly after each addition. Add vanilla and peppermint. Sprinkle ½ the crumbs into 24 small cupcake liners. Add filling; top with remaining crumbs. Freeze until firm. Serve frozen. Makes 24.

– Ann Hinckley (Mrs. Charles)

» Mint Mallow Dessert «

36 large marshmallows
1 cup crème de menthe

3 cups whipping cream,
    whipped
Hot chocolate sauce

Melt marshmallows in crème de menthe in top of double boiler. Cool slightly. Into this mixture, fold in whipped cream; mold in a 9" pie pan and freeze. Cut into wedges and serve with hot chocolate sauce.
Makes 8 to 10 servings.

Hot Chocolate Sauce

1 cup light corn syrup
1 teaspoon vanilla

2 ozs. unsweetened
    chocolate

Combine corn syrup and chocolate in a heavy saucepan or in a double boiler over hot water. Cook, stirring constantly, until the chocolate is melted. Remove from heat and beat with a rotary beater or electric mixer until the sauce is smooth and creamy. Add vanilla and reheat over hot water before serving. Makes 1 cup.

– Jane S. Wulsin (Mrs. Eugene)

» Orange Flan «

Strange as it seems today, Mexican cuisine did not include sugar and cream prior to the Spanish entry into their country. Without them, we could not enjoy one of Mexico's favorite desserts.

¾ cup sugar
2 cups half and half cream
6 whole eggs
2 egg yolks
⅔ cup sugar

1 tablespoon orange zest,
    grated
½ teaspoon lemon zest,
    grated
2 tablespoons orange
    liqueur

In a small, heavy pan, melt the sugar over moderate heat, shaking to stir. Cook until caramelized. Coat a 9" metal pie pan or cake pan with syrup. Scald cream, let cool a bit. Beat together all other ingredients just enough to blend. Stir in cream. Pour into caramel-coated pan. Put into a larger pan containing hot water that just barely comes up the sides of the smaller pan. Bake in in a preheated 350° oven for 30 to 35 minutes, or until completely set. Remove from oven and chill until completely cold. When cold, loosen the custard around the edges with a metal spatula; invert onto a rimmed serving plate. Cut into wedges to serve.
Makes 8 to 10 servings.

– Marilyn Harris
L.S. Ayres 4th Street Market

Paul Cézanne, 1839-1906, French, "Still Life with Bread
and Eggs," 1865, oil on canvas, 1955.73.
Gift of Mary E. Johnston. This color reproduction donated by
Mr. and Mrs. Warren R. Woodward

In 1865, the young Cézanne was pleased with a compliment on a new group of still lifes from a more established artist, Edouard Manet, who already was a leader of the avant-garde. This painting was among those that caught Manet's eye. Certainly Cézanne himself was proud of the work, for it is one of only half a dozen he both signed and dated.

In "Still Life with Bread and Eggs," Cézanne looks back to Chardin's authoritative handling of a few simple elements for his composition: the long horizontal of the bread is punctuated by a knife laid askew, by the verticals of a pewter pitcher and a drinking glass, and also by the varied roundnesses of the two red onions and two (possibly peeled?) eggs. He sets them off against a dark background and a white cloth, which has been tossed down with deceptive carelessness, and throughout the work exhibits a painterly delight in texture.

Impressionism would later lighten Cézanne's palette, although his work never fell precisely within that movement. His examination of form, however, developed so significantly that several generations of painters have explored directions suggested by his canvasses.

» Macaroon Custard St. Nicholas «

This recipe from the elegant old St. Nicholas Hotel appeared in Anita Auch's column in the Cincinnati Enquirer in 1932.

2 cups milk	1 teaspoon vanilla
4 eggs	8 macaroons
⅔ cup sugar	Jelly cubes

Scald the milk in a double boiler. Beat the eggs and sugar together lightly. Add a little of the hot milk and then return all to the double boiler and cook until the mixture coats a clean, cold spoon. Stir constantly. Remove from the heat just as soon as the custard coats the spoon. Add the vanilla and when cool, chill the custard. Dry the macaroons in a warm oven, just as slowly as possible, and then crumble and roll. Add to the chilled custard and serve in glasses topped with cubes of jelly. Makes 6 servings.

» Oranges à l'Indienne «

This is a simple but elegant dessert that is a perfect ending to a rich meal.

2 to 4 tablespoons brown sugar	6 navel oranges, peeled and cut into ½" cartwheels
¼ teaspoon curry powder	Sour cream

Combine sugar and curry powder; add oranges. Chill; serve garnished with sour cream. Makes 6 servings.

– Mary Wydman (Mrs. Robert)

» Aranci Orientali «
Oriental Oranges

This elegant dessert is made even more so if served with a small chocolate truffle or an imported chocolate.

8 large seedless oranges	¼ teaspoon cream of tartar
⅔ cup water	Juice of 1 lemon
⅔ cup Marsala wine	
1 cup sugar	

Peel zest from oranges, using a vegetable peeler. Cut the zest into julienne strips and combine with water, Marsala, sugar, cream of tartar, and lemon juice. Bring to a boil and simmer until syrup is reduced by ⅓; cool. Remove all of the white pulp from oranges and cut crosswise into thin slices. Reserve juice and add to syrup. Arrange slices in a clear glass bowl or reassemble into whole oranges. Decorate with caramelized peel and spoon syrup over. Chill until serving. Makes 8 servings.

» Poached Pears with Crème Anglaise «

Crème Anglaise is a light cream sauce which is the basis of many French desserts and pastries.

6 Bosc or Anjou pears	1 cup milk
4 cups water	½ cup whipping cream
2 cups sugar	1" piece of vanilla bean, or 1 teaspoon vanilla
Juice of 1 fresh lemon	6 tablespoons sugar
Zest of 1 lemon, grated	4 egg yolks
Cinnamon stick	2 teaspoons cornstarch
3 cloves	

Peel pears, leaving stems on, if desired. Drop into water combined with sugar and lemon juice. Add zest of lemon, cinnamon stick, and cloves; bring to a boil. Cover and keep the syrup at a rolling boil until pears are tender – about 30 minutes. They should pierce easily with a knife tip and be slightly translucent. Transfer carefully to a shallow platter. Stand on bottom until cool; if necessary, cut flat bottom with knife after pears have cooled. Pour a little of the syrup over pears, cover, and refrigerate several hours. Combine milk, cream, and vanilla bean. If using vanilla extract, add later. Bring just to a boil and let stand 10 minutes to absorb the flavor of the vanilla bean. Beat sugar and egg yolks together until mixture is pale yellow and creamy. Beat in cornstarch and add milk and cream mixture. Cook over low heat, stirring vigorously, until mixture is quite thick; do not boil. Remove from heat and cool, stirring frequently. Remove vanilla bean or add vanilla extract. Chill the sauce thoroughly and serve over poached pears. Makes 6 servings.

– Pam Kneer (Mrs. Tom)

» Poires au Vin Rouge «

The French love of pears and red wine is combined in this recipe to produce an extraordinary culinary treat.

4 pears, preferably Bartlett, Bosc, or Anjou	1 bay leaf
2 cups dry red wine	¼ teaspoon peppercorns
1 cup water	6 whole allspice
½ cup sugar	5 whole cloves
	½" cinnamon stick

Peel pears, leaving stem on. Using an apple corer, core pear from the bottom, but do not cut all the way to the stem end. Combine the remaining ingredients in a saucepan and add pears. Bring to a boil and simmer 10 minutes, turning pears occasionally in the syrup, so that they cook evenly. Remove pears from the syrup, and reduce syrup to about one half of volume. Remove from heat, return pears to syrup, and let stand in syrup until cooled. May be served at room temperature or refrigerated. Makes 4 servings.

– Barbara Lauterbach (Mrs. Peter)

» Pineapple Flan «

The pineapple in Mexico is delightful – sweet and dripping with juice. It blends tastefully with the creamy smoothness of the custard.

1 large fresh pineapple	7 large eggs, lightly beaten
1½ cups sugar	¾ cup sugar

Peel and core pineapple. Purée pineapple chunks in blender or food processor and drain through a triple thickness of cheesecloth. You will need 3 cups of juice for the recipe. If this is not accomplished with the first draining, add water to the leftover pineapple pulp and purée again. Drain through the cheesecloth. Use canned pineapple juice only in an emergency situation, as it will alter the flavor. Heat the pineapple juice with sugar until sugar dissolves; cool. Add eggs to the cooled pineapple-sugar mixture. Heat ¾ cup sugar in a skillet over medium high heat. When sugar begins to melt, reduce heat to medium. Continue to cook sugar, stirring occasionally. When sugar is melted and browned, spoon over bottom and sides of a shallow 1½-quart baking dish. Work quickly – caramel hardens very fast at this point. Set aside to cool a minute or two. Pour pineapple mixture into baking dish lined with caramelized sugar. Place baking dish in a pan; pour hot water into the pan halfway up the sides of the baking dish. Bake in preheated 325° oven about 1½ hours, or until a knife inserted comes out clean. If necessary, cover flan loosely with foil to prevent excessive browning. Remove baking dish from pan of hot water. Cool, then refrigerate at least 3 hours. To serve, run a knife around top edge and invert flan onto a serving plate. Makes 6 to 8 servings.

– Jan Denton (Mrs. M. Drue)

» Pineapple Delight «

1 cup sugar	1 teaspoon vanilla
½ cup butter, softened	2 egg whites, beaten until stiff
2 egg yolks, beaten lightly	
2½ cups crushed pineapple, well drained	9 oz. box vanilla wafers
	1 cup whipping cream
1 cup walnuts or pecans, finely chopped, measure before chopping	2 tablespoons sugar
	1 teaspoon vanilla
	Nonpareils, colored sugar, or chocolate jimmies

Cream sugar and butter together. Add beaten egg yolks, pineapple, and nuts. Beat well after each addition. Add vanilla. Then gently fold in beaten egg whites. Line the bottom of a square 9"x9" or 8"x8" dish or pan with a layer of vanilla wafers. Use broken pieces to fill in little spots. Spread ½ of the pineapple mixture on the wafers. Repeat the layers of vanilla wafers and the pineapple mixture. Refrigerate overnight. To serve, cut into 9 or 12 pieces. Whip the cream in a chilled bowl with chilled beaters. Add sugar and vanilla. Put a dollop of cream on each serving, sprinkle with nonpareils, colored sugar, or chocolate jimmies. Makes 9 to 12 servings.

– Jane Sweeder (Mrs. Willard C.)

» Hard Sauce «

⅓ cup sweet butter, softened	1 tablespoon brandy
	Pinch nutmeg
1 cup confectioners' sugar	

Cream butter and add sugar gradually until fluffy and thoroughly blended. Add brandy gradually and continue beating. Add nutmeg; chill. Makes 1½ cups.

– Sallie Wadsworth (Mrs. Randolph)

*Georges Braque, 1882-1963, French, "Compote, Bread and Cheese,"
1941, oil and sand on canvas, 1967.1317. Bequest of Mary E. Johnston*

» Plum Pudding «

Plum pudding began in the Middle Ages as a porridge served with meats. The recipe gradually evolved to the fruit-filled treat we know today, and only the suet remains from the original recipe. The largest pudding known was 900 pounds; it was created by adventurous villagers in Devon in 1819, long before the Guinness Book of Records.

5 cups raisins	1 teaspoon nutmeg
2 cups currants	8 eggs
2 cups citron	2½ cups light brown
1 cup candied cherries	sugar, packed
1 cup candied orange peel	4 cups beef suet, finely
1 cup brandy	chopped
2 cups almonds, toasted	3 cups apples, finely
2 cups flour	chopped
2 teaspoons cinnamon	2 cups fine bread crumbs
2 teaspoons allspice	Additional brandy
1 teaspoon salt	Hard Sauce, optional
1 teaspoon cloves	

Put raisins, currants, citron, candied cherries, and orange peel through a food grinder, or chop coarsely in a food processor. Add brandy and almonds. Sift together dry ingredients. Beat eggs until light, add brown sugar, suet, apples, and bread crumbs; mix well. Stir in dry ingredients and fruit. Mix well, using hands for best results. Place mixture in greased molds and cover with lids or layers of cheesecloth tied on. Set on a rack in a pan and add water halfway up mold – a turkey roaster works well. Cover, bring water to a simmer, and steam at least 6 hours. Check on water level occasionally; add additional hot water, if necessary. Cool and remove from molds. Brush with brandy and place in plastic wrap or bags. Store in a cool place. To serve, wrap in foil and place in a preheated 300° oven until heated through. Serve with Hard Sauce, if desired. Makes 10 lbs.

– Sallie Wadsworth (Mrs. Randolph)

» Raspberry Fluff «

10 oz. package frozen	2 egg whites
raspberries, thawed, or	1 cup whipping cream,
2 cups fresh raspberries	beaten until stiff
½ cup sugar	

Purée berries; force through a sieve to remove seeds, if desired. Using a large mixing bowl, beat raspberries, sugar, and egg whites for about 5 minutes, or until very stiff. Fold in whipped cream very gently; chill. Serve in stemmed glasses with a crisp cookie. This dessert is best when served within 2 hours of preparation. Makes 8 to 12 servings.

– Anne Nethercott (Mrs. J. W.)

» Arroz con Leche «

In Spain, the caramelized topping of this rice pudding is made by using a red-hot bar to burn the sugar into decorative designs.

1 cup rice
6 tablespoons water
3 tablespoons butter
1 stick cinnamon
Lemon slice
2 cups milk
Sugar

Rinse rice well and drain. Boil water, add rice, and cook for a few minutes. Add butter, cinnamon to taste, slice of lemon, and part of the milk. Continue cooking over low heat, adding milk to keep moist. Amount of milk used is determined by the type of rice being used. Total cooking time should be about 20 minutes, or until rice is tender. Add sugar to taste, pour rice on a shallow platter, and pat down to flatten. When surface is slightly cooled and beginning to solidify, sprinkle generously with sugar. Place it under a broiler, 3″ from heat source, and quickly caramelize the sugar. Serve warm. Makes 6 servings.

– Carlos Casariego

» Savarin «

Jean Anthelme Brillat-Savarin, the noted French gastronome who wrote La Physiologie du Gout – The Physiology of Taste – was the inspiration for this classic dessert.

1 cup flour
2/3 cup sugar
2 teaspoons baking
   powder
2 eggs, beaten
Dash salt
1/4 cup milk
1/2 cup sugar
3/4 cup water
1/4 cup rum
Flavored whipped cream
   or fruit salad

Mix flour, sugar, and baking powder. Add eggs, salt, and milk; mix well. Pour mixture into greased 9″ round pan and bake in a preheated 350° oven for 25-30 minutes, until cake is set and top is lightly browned. Unmold while warm and then return to pan. While cake is baking, combine sugar and water and simmer for 10 minutes or until thick. Remove from heat and add rum. Pour at once over still warm cake, so syrup is absorbed. Unmold cake and serve with flavored whipped cream or fruit salad. Makes 8 servings.

– Sarah Headley (Mrs. Grant)

» Strawberry Cloud «

This dessert is served during the annual Rose Festival in the City of Roses – Portland, Oregon – my home town. Strawberry time in the Pacific Northwest magically coincides with the Rose Festival, largest festival of its kind in that part of the country.

1/2 cup butter, melted
1/4 cup brown sugar, firmly
   packed
1 cup flour
1/2 cup walnuts or pecans,
   chopped
2 egg whites
1 cup sugar
2 cups strawberries,
   sliced
1 tablespoon lemon juice
1 teaspoon vanilla
1 cup whipping cream,
   whipped
Whole strawberries for
   garnish

In a jelly roll pan, stir melted butter and brown sugar together. With a fork, mix in flour and nuts. Distribute over bottom of pan. Bake in preheated 400° oven for 15 to 20 minutes, stirring occasionally. Set crumb mixture aside to cool. In a large mixing bowl, beat egg whites to soft peaks, gradually adding sugar. Add berries, lemon juice, and vanilla. Beat on high speed until mixture triples in volume and forms stiff peaks. Fold in whipped cream. Spread all but 1/2 cup of the crumb mixture in the bottom of a 9″ springform pan. Top with the egg white mixture, then remaining crumbs. Freeze. To serve, remove ring of pan, transfer to serving platter, and garnish with fresh berries. Makes 12 servings.

– Naomi Bergert (Mrs. Jack R.)

» Strawberries Elizabeth Nourse «

This festive dessert was created to celebrate the opening of "Elizabeth Nourse 1859-1938: A Salon Career" at the Cincinnati Art Museum on May 12, 1983.

1 quart strawberries
1 cup rosé wine
1/2 cup honey
Whipped cream, sour
cream, or vanilla ice
cream, softened
Grand Marnier liqueur,
optional

Hull and wash berries; cut in half. Combine rosé wine and honey; gently heat to mix. Let cool before pouring over berries. Depending upon personal taste, the mixture of rosé wine and honey can be varied to allow for variations in sweetness. Marinate berries about 6 hours in the refrigerator. Be certain to turn the berries at least once. This is best done by transferring the top berries to another bowl so they will be at the bottom, and then pouring the rosé wine-honey mixture over the berries again; reserve liquid. Serve berries on chilled plates or in bowls; pour reserved liquid over berries. Top with whipped cream, sour cream, or a softened vanilla ice cream. For a variation, add a splash of Grand Marnier liqueur to the whipped cream before it is prepared. Makes 3 to 4 servings.

– Kenneth R. Trapp

» Charlotte aux Fraises «

A traditional French charlotte mold is a tinned cylindrical mold with two distinctive ears protruding from its sides. A souffle dish or ceramic mold may be substituted in this recipe.

⅓ cup sugar	40 ladyfingers
½ cup sweet butter, softened	4 cups strawberries, halved
5 tablespoons Grand Marnier liqueur	1 cup whipping cream, whipped
3 ozs. blanched almonds, grated	Whole strawberries, for garnish
⅔ cup whipping cream, whipped	

Beat sugar and butter until light and fluffy. Stir in Grand Marnier a little at a time. Add almonds and fold in whipped cream. Cut 24 ladyfingers in half on the diagonal. Line the base of an oiled 1½-quart charlotte mold with waxed paper and cover with the lady fingers with rounded side down. Line sides of mold with upright ladyfingers rounded side out. Put ⅓ of almond cream mixture over ladyfingers. Put ½ of strawberries on top and cover with another layer of ladyfingers. Repeat process until mold is filled, ending with ladyfingers. Cover with plate to weight down; refrigerate several hours or overnight. Run sharp knife around mold, invert onto a serving plate. Cover with remaining whipped cream and decorate with strawberries.
Makes 10 to 12 servings.

– Winnie Love (Mrs. Wesley)

» Strawberry Mousse «

2 quarts strawberries, washed and hulled	½ cup boiling water
½ cup dry white wine	2 cups whipping cream, beaten until soft peaks form
½ cup sugar	
½ cup cold water	Additional whipped cream
2 envelopes unflavored gelatin	

Save 1 quart of the prettiest berries for garnish. Put other quart of berries in food processor with chopping blade. Add wine and blend until smooth. Pour into a large bowl; add sugar. Stir well, then chill. Put cold water in a small bowl and sprinkle gelatin over it. Add boiling water and stir until dissolved. Cool. Combine with berry mixture and beat until fluffy. Fold whipped cream into berry mixture, mixing well. Pour into lightly oiled 2-quart ring mold, or other shape; chill 3 to 4 hours. Unmold and heap reserved berries in center of ring or around other mold. Garnish with additional whipped cream.
Makes 8 to 10 servings.

– Christine Evans (Mrs. Nicholas M.)

» Strawberry Sabayon «

From Restaurant Review by Ken Neuhauser: "The Coach and Four's Strawberry Sabayon is a combination of berries and frothy custard, neatly packaged in a tulip glass — nothing short of heaven."

8 egg yolks	1 quart fresh strawberries, washed and hulled
¼ cup sugar	
¾ cup white rum	
2 cups whipping cream, whipped	

Mix egg yolks, sugar, and white rum in a double boiler over boiling water at low heat. Whip until mixture thickens to a light yellow color. Remove from stove and continue to whip for about 10 minutes, or until mixture returns to room temperature. Fold in whipped cream. Place 2 tablespoons of sabayon in each parfait glass, add strawberries, and top with more sabayon.
Makes 6 to 8 servings.

– Coach and Four Restaurant
Covington, Kentucky

» Strawberry Souffle «

2 cups fresh or frozen
   strawberries
1 cup sugar
1 tablespoon lemon juice

1⅛ teaspoons vanilla
2 egg whites
Whole strawberries for
   garnish

Combine berries, sugar, lemon juice, vanilla, and egg whites. Beat at medium speed until mixture is quite stiff and shining; or beat egg whites first and then fold in the rest of the mixture, which has been blended together in a blender until fairly smooth. Pour into a lightly greased 9″ springform pan and freeze at least 4 hours, preferably overnight. Remove from pan 5 to 7 minutes before serving; garnish with whole strawberries. Makes 10 servings.

– Jane Jacobs (Mrs. Brent A.)

» Chocolate Rum Truffles «

The praline powder gives these truffles a nutty texture and richness that justifies extra preparation time.

Butter
2¼ cups brown sugar,
   firmly packed
¾ cup water
¾ cup rum
2 cups salted cashews,
   English walnuts, or
   pecans
7 oz. unsweetened
   chocolate

¼ cup butter
¼ cup light corn syrup
1 tablespoon creme de
   cocoa or almond
   liqueur
½ cup cocoa
½ cup confectioners'
   sugar
¼ teaspoon cinnamon

Butter the sides of a heavy saucepan; this will prevent the sugar from crystallizing while cooking. Add sugar, water, and rum; cook over high heat, stirring occasionally, until mixture reaches 295°F. on a candy thermometer. Spread nuts on a buttered or foil-covered baking sheet and pour the boiling syrup over the nuts. Let the mixture harden and then crack it into small pieces. Grind the pieces, a few at a time, in a blender until they are a fine powder. Discard any unpowdered bits. Meanwhile, melt chocolate, butter, corn syrup, and liqueur in a heavy pan over low heat until smooth and thick. Remove from heat and combine thoroughly with praline powder. When mixture has cooled, shape into walnut-sized balls with a greased teaspoon or ice cream scoop. Mix cocoa, confectioners' sugar, and cinnamon on a piece of waxed paper. Roll the balls in this mixture until thoroughly coated. Store in refrigerated airtight container until used. Makes 4 dozen.

» Chocolate Velvet Truffles «

Truffles, long a delight of chocoholics, have become so popular in recent years that stores selling nothing but this confection have been opened. A simple dessert of fresh fruit becomes special when accompanied by chocolate truffles.

¼ cup whipping cream
2 tablespoons Curacao or
   Grand Marnier liqueur

6 ozs. semi-sweet
   chocolate, grated
¼ cup butter, softened
¼ cup cocoa

Place the whipping cream in a heavy saucepan; boil over low heat until the cream is reduced by half. Remove from heat and add liqueur and chocolate; return to heat and continue cooking, stirring constantly, until the mixture is thick and smooth. Remove from heat and whisk in butter, a little at a time, until all is incorporated. The more the mixture is beaten with a whisk or beater, the smoother and lighter the truffles. Refrigerate the mixture until it is firm enough to shape into walnut-sized balls with a greased teaspoon or ice cream scoop. Place cocoa on waxed paper and roll the truffles in it until they are well coated. Store in an airtight container in the refrigerator until 1 hour before serving. Makes 2 dozen.

» Chocolate Truffles «

These are easy to make and will store in the freezer, well wrapped, up to a month.

1½ cups whipping cream
½ cup unsalted butter
1 lb. plus 3 oz. semi-sweet
   chocolate, broken into
   pieces

6 tablespoons sugar
Pinch of salt
¼ cup Cognac brandy
½ cup unsweetened cocoa

Butter three l7″xl4″ baking sheets. Set aside. In a 1-quart saucepan, bring cream and butter to a simmer. Using a food processor, or blender in small batches, chop chocolate, sugar, and salt finely. Add simmering cream slowly, processing until mixture is smooth and chocolate is melted. Add Cognac, blending thoroughly. Transfer mixture to a bowl and place it in a pan of ice water. Beat with spoon until mixture is thick enough to hold shape. Spoon into pastry bag fitted with ½″ plain tip; pipe 1″ rounds on baking sheets, or use a small, chilled ice cream scoop to make truffles of the desired size. Place in freezer until firm. Put cocoa in bag, add batches of frozen truffles, shaking to coat. Remove and tap off excess cocoa. Makes about 175 candies.

— Mrs. Molly Fox

» Nut Truffles «

A blender or food processor may be used to grate the chocolate for these elegant confections. They should be refrigerated until about 2 hours before serving.

*3 ozs. semi-sweet
    chocolate, grated
¼ cup butter
2 tablespoons whipping
    cream
7 tablespoons confectioners'
    sugar, sifted*

*2 tablespoons walnuts,
    almonds, or hazelnuts,
    grated
¼ cup cocoa
¼ teaspoon cinnamon*

Place chocolate, butter, and whipping cream in a heavy saucepan; cook over low heat, stirring, until chocolate is melted and the mixture is smooth. Remove from heat and add the confectioners' sugar and nuts; mix well. Cool and shape into walnut-sized balls with greased hands or an ice cream scoop. Place the truffles in the refrigerator for a few minutes. Meanwhile, mix the cocoa and cinnamon on a sheet of waxed paper. Roll the truffles in this mixture until they are thoroughly coated. Store in an airtight container in the refrigerator. Makes 2 dozen.

» Brandied Caramel Sauce «

This is a marvelous sauce for holiday pies or puddings. It also stores well, although it becomes less fluffy.

*¼ cup butter, softened
1 cup brown sugar
2 tablespoons brandy,
    rum, or bourbon*

*2 egg yolks, well beaten
½ cup cream
3 egg whites, stiffly beaten*

Cream butter. Add sugar gradually, then brandy, rum or bourbon very slowly. Add egg yolks and cream. Cook over hot water until the mixture thickens, as a custard. Fold into egg whites just before serving.
Makes about 2 cups.

— Phyllis Hopple (Mrs. William)

*Block from Right Pilaster of Shrine III Atargatis as
Grain Goddess, early 2nd century A.D., Nabataean, limestone,
1939.238. Gift by subscription*

BEER STREET.

Glossary

For your guidance in using the recipes in this cookbook, the following rules apply to some basic ingredients:

"Eggs" are large unless otherwise specified.

"Sugar" is granulated unless otherwise specified.

"Brown sugar" is light brown unless dark is specified, and it is firmly packed.

"Flour" is all purpose unless otherwise specified.

"Oil" refers to vegetable oils such as corn, peanut, safflower, soybean, or whatever light oil you prefer. Olive oil or sesame oil will be specified if it can or should be used.

"Butter" is used throughout the recipes. Regular margarine may be substituted.

"Whipping cream" is used where heavy cream is called for; "half and half" is called for when light cream is specified. Other creams of comparable butterfat may be substituted.

Servings are given as an average portion. If your guests are either hearty or light eaters, you can easily alter your estimates of the number the recipe will serve.

Measurements are level unless otherwise specified.

Because friends of the Cincinnati Art Museum who purchase this cookbook may be located in many other cities than Cincinnati, we have not provided specific local sources for some of the unusual products. We hope that the following general directions may be helpful to our readers. Also included in the following list are some cooking terms that are used in these recipes:

Al dente – An Italian term used to describe pasta or vegetables cooked until tender but still firm. Its literal meaning is "to the tooth," meaning that it offers some resistance to the bite.

Arrowroot – A thickening flour made from the roots of a tropical plant. Used in sauces and desserts.

Basmati Rice – A superior long-grain rice. Available in gourmet food sections or in Oriental or Indian food stores.

Bechamel Sauce – French term for a basic white sauce made by cooking together flour and butter and adding milk and seasonings.

Bordelaise Sauce – A French brown sauce made with red wine and beef marrow.

Dry Black Beans – Small, richly flavorful beans sometimes called Cuban or turtle beans. Used for soup and with rice. Available in specialty stores and supermarkets.

Fermented Black Beans – Small black beans preserved in salt. Used in Oriental cooking. Rinse with warm water and mash before using. Available in Oriental markets.

Bok Choy – Also known as Chinese chard and white mustard cabbage. Leafy green vegetable with white stems and dark green leaves. Used in chop suey, chow mein, and other Oriental-type dishes. Excellent in chicken soup. Available in supermarket produce departments and in specialty stores.

Bouquet garni – A bunch of herbs usually tied in a cheesecloth bag and cooked with a soup or stew. Most often parsley, thyme, bayleaf, and selected other herbs.

Bulgur – Cracked wheat that has been hulled and parboiled so that it is easier to cook and of a lighter texture. Available in Middle Eastern food markets and in some supermarkets.

Celeriac – Also called celery root. A turnip-shaped root which may be braised or served cold with a Dijon mayonnaise dressing.

Chiles:

Green Chiles (Far East) – Mild to slightly hot chiles. Available canned in supermarkets and specialty stores.

Poblano Chiles – The fresh version of the Ancho chile. Similar in size and flavor to green bell peppers. Usually mild but can vary to medium hot. Ideal for stuffing. Sold fresh and canned.

Anaheim Chiles – Also known as California green chiles. About 5″ to 8″ in length, bright green when fresh, and ranging from sweet and mild to mildly hot. Available fresh or canned.

Jalapeno Peppers – Small, hot chile; green in color and about 2½″ long. Sold fresh, canned, or pickled in supermarkets and specialty stores.

Ancho Chiles – Ripened, dried Poblano chile that is most commonly used in Mexican cooking. Deep reddish brown but turns brick red when softened in water.

Cilantro/coriander – Coriander is the term used to refer to the seeds and cilantro to the leaves of the coriander plant. The dried ripe coriander seeds or ground coriander have an aromatic taste described as a combination of lemon peel and sage. Cilantro, which is the Spanish name for coriander, also is known as Chinese or Mexican parsley, and resembles parsley in appearance. It may be used any place parsley is used, but has a stronger flavor and therefore should be used sparingly.

Chili oil – A spicy-hot oil used in Oriental cooking, often flavored with garlic. Available in Oriental stores.

Coconut cream – A smooth, creamy paste of coconut. Available in cans in supermarkets and specialty stores.

Creole mustard – A mellow, slightly tart, brown mustard which contains mustard seeds. Used in Cajun cooking. Available in most larger supermarkets.

Daikon radish – A crisp, long white radish used in Japanese cookery. Available in specialty stores and supermarket produce departments.

Fennel – An aromatic Mediterranean plant with a faintly anise flavor. The shoots are eaten raw or cooked, the leaves are used as salad or seasoning, and the seeds as a spice in cooking. The dried stalks may be burned to aromatically fume fish or grilled meats.

Fenugreek seeds – Floury, somewhat bitter seeds which may be ground after roasting. Used in curries, chutneys, and stews.

Finnan Haddie – Smoked salt water haddock, usually split with part of the backbone removed and the head cut off.

Five-spice powder – A fragrant and pungent mixture of spices ground together into a powder, usually anise seed, cinnamon, licorice, cloves, and ginger, or a mixture of star anise, Szechwan peppercorns, fennel, cloves, and cinnamon. Available in Oriental markets and some supermarkets.

Foie gras – Literally, fat goose liver, usually in the form of a pâté, purée, or terrine.

Fontina cheese – A soft Italian goat's milk cream cheese.

Garam Masala – A mixture of ground spices and herbs – usually ground cardamom, cinnamon, and cloves. Used in Indian cooking. Available at specialty food stores.

Ghee – Butter from which all the milk solid deposits have been removed by clarifying. In India, it is favored for frying very delicate foods. Available in specialty food stores.

Ginger root – A pungent, aromatic, knobby root sold in supermarket produce departments and in Oriental food stores. It may be sliced, shredded, or grated, and is used in Chinese meat and vegetable dishes, in desserts, and in Indian curries.

Goat cheese – "Chevre" is the term often used almost generically to describe any cheese made from goat's milk, although it specifically refers to a type from France. Many countries produce their own versions of goat cheese – among the best known are feta from Greece and fontina from Italy. Available in specialty food markets and in supermarkets.

Greek seasoning – A mixture usually of garlic, oregano, basil, and pepper.

Fresh horseradish – A large, fleshy, pungent white root which may be peeled and grated. Served as a condiment with roasted meats, fish, and in sauces. It may also be purchased grated and preserved in vinegar in a bottle in many stores. Dried horseradish is also available, but is not as strong as the fresh root.

Juniper berries – While more familiar as the base for gin, these hard, blue-purple berries lend a spicy background flavor to many meat dishes. Available in spice sections of some supermarkets and in specialty food stores.

Dried lily pods – The pods of the lily flower which are softened in very hot water and added to soups. Available in Oriental groceries.

Mai Fun (see Noodles)

Maillard's or Belgian Callebaut chocolate – Fine, intensely flavored imported chocolate available in specialty stores.

Mace blades – The arillode or false aril that covers the seed of the nutmeg and is used in Indian cooking primarily. Powdered mace may be substituted. Available in Indian food stores.

Morels (see Mushrooms)

Mushrooms:

Dried black Chinese Mushrooms – These dark-colored dried mushrooms must be soaked in water for at least one-half hour to revive the meaty texture – the tough stems are discarded. Available in Oriental food stores and some supermarkets.

Morels – A meaty-flavored mushroom that only grows in the wild and is treasured by many cooks. A morel is cone-shaped, and the cap has a spongelike appearance. Fresh morels are available in some supermarkets and produce stores for only about six weeks a year, from mid-April to the beginning of June. Canned freeze-dried morels are available in gourmet food departments. They should be soaked for about 10 minutes in water and then pressed dry before adding to soups or stews.

Porcini – This strong, meaty fungus is known to the French as cepe, to the Germans as steinpilze, and to the Italians as porcini. It keeps its texture in cooking. Also available dried.

Tree Ear Mushrooms – A kind of tree-growing fungus purchased dried and soaked in boiling water before using. The resulting gelatinous tree ears are added to Chinese dishes.

Nappa – Also known as Chinese cabbage. Has an elongated, crinkly leaf similar in shape to Romaine lettuce, but more creamy white than green. Has a light, crisp texture and *delicate flavor. Used in salads and stir-fry cooking. Available in supermarkets and specialty stores.*

Noodles:

Dried Oriental noodles – Chinese noodles may be made of wheat or rice flour, arrowroot, or pea starch. They come in a variety of sizes and shapes, and can usually be used interchangeably. Japanese noodles are made from buckwheat flour, pea starch, or white flour. Available in supermarkets and specialty stores.

Mai Fun/Rice Sticks – Delicate curled noodles made from rice flour. The unsoaked noodles have the dramatic ability, when fried in deep, hot fat, to puff up almost instantaneously. They make a crisp addition to salads and other dishes. May also be prepared like regular noodles. Available in supermarkets and in Oriental food stores.

Olives:

Black Greek – Oily, wrinkled olives available in specialty food shops and supermarkets.

Calamata – Salty oval black olives preserved in brine.

Nicoise – Smaller, pungent, salty Mediterranean olives.

Orzo – Small, rice-shaped pasta especially popular in the Middle East.

Oyster sauce – A salty, dark brown sauce made of fermented oysters and seasonings. Used in stir-fry dishes and as a dipping sauce. Available in specialty food stores and some supermarkets.

Pine nuts – Sometimes called pignolia. The edible seed of some pine cones, used as a substitute for nuts.

Prosciutto – A salted, air-dried ham, usually from the mountainous Parma region of Italy. Available at Italian and specialty stores.

Vinegar:

Raspberry vinegar – A mild wine vinegar flavored with the infusion of raspberries. Available at specialty food stores.

Champagne vinegar – A lively white vinegar from France. Available where imported goods are sold.

Rice vinegar – An Oriental vinegar, mild in flavor. Sold in Oriental groceries and supermarkets.

Rice sticks (see Noodles)

Rose water – A flavoring distilled from fresh rose petals. Available in specialty food stores and some pharmacies.

Saltpetre – Potassium nitrate which is used as a preservative and red coloring agent in cured meats. Curing salt is now often substituted. Available in specialty shops and supermarkets.

Semolina flour – Wheat particles of hard durum wheat, used to make pasta and puddings, and to thicken soups and sauces. Available in Italian specialty stores and some supermarkets.

Sesame seed paste (see Tahini)

Sesame oil – A nutty, flavorful oil derived from sesame seeds.

Used sparingly in Oriental cookery.

Star anise – A seed formation with eight cloves which resembles a star. It is available in Chinese groceries and specialty food stores. Anise seed may be used as a substitute.

Tahini – A nutty-flavored paste made from crushed sesame seeds. Available in specialty markets.

Tamarind – The fruity pod of the tropical tamarind tree; also known as Indian dates. The sharply sour juice is obtained by steeping the dried pod in hot water until the juice and pulp can be squeezed out. Used in much the same manner as lemons or limes to add acidic flavor to Indian dishes such as curries or chutneys; also used in Latin America to make a refreshing drink. Available in specialty food stores.

Terrine – The oblong earthernware dish in which pates are cooked. Also refers to the food cooked in this dish.

Tofu – Japanese bean curd cakes. Made of cooked, mashed soybeans, cultured much like cottage cheese and pressed into creamy-white cakes with a firm custard-like consistency. Called dow fu in Chinese. It is cut into strips or cubes, and deep-fried or incorporated into stir-fry dishes, soups, and cold dishes. Available in supermarket produce sections and Oriental food stores.

Tomatillos – Small, light-green, husk-covered vegetables that look like a baby green tomato, but taste somewhat like a plum when raw. Used in Mexican cooking. Available fresh and canned in specialty stores and some supermarkets.

Truffle – An edible fungus which grows below the ground, especially in France and Italy. They are black or white, and are valued for the flavor they impart to sauces and other savory dishes and are often used as a garnish. Available in cans in specialty food shops and occasionally, and expensively, fresh.

Zest – The colored, oily, outer peel of lemons and oranges, which has a strong, not bitter, fruit flavor. The white peel underneath should not be used for grating because it has a bitter flavor.

Equivalents

Dash = Less than 1/8 teaspoon

3 teaspoons = 1 tablespoon

2 tablespoons = 1 fluid ounce

4 tablespoons = 1/4 cup or 2 fluid ounces

5 tablespoons + 1 teaspoon = 1/3 cup

16 tablespoons = 1 cup or 8 fluid ounces

2 cups = 1 pint

2 pints = 1 quart

4 quarts = 1 gallon

1 stick butter = 8 tablespoons

1 pound butter = 4 sticks or 2 cups

1 pound American or Cheddar cheese = 4 cups grated

1 cup half and half = 1 cup whole milk plus 1½ tablespoons butter

1 cup whipping cream (for cooking purposes only) = ¾ cup whole milk plus ⅓ cup butter

1 cup whipping cream = 2 cups whipped cream

1 cup regular rice = 3 or more cups cooked rice

1 pound all purpose flour = 4 cups sifted

1 cup dry bread crumbs = 3 to 4 slices bread

1 slice bread = ¾ cup soft bread crumbs

1 medium yellow onion = ½ cup chopped

1 pound fresh mushrooms = 6 cups sliced raw or 3 cups sliced and sautéed

1 pound tomatoes = 3 large or medium, or 1½ cups chopped

1 pound fresh apples = 3 medium, or about 3 cups sliced or diced

1 pound lemons = 5 lemons, or 1 cup juice

1 medium lemon = 3 tablespoons juice and 2 teaspoons grated zest

1 pound oranges = 3 medium, or 1 cup juice

1 ounce unsweetened chocolate = 1 square, or 3 tablespoons dry cocoa plus 1 tablespoon fat

1 ounce unsweetened chocolate plus 4 tablespoons sugar = 1⅔ ounces semi-sweet chocolate

1 small garlic clove = ⅛ teaspoon garlic powder, or ½ teaspoon garlic salt (adjust recipe for salt content)

⅓ to ½ teaspoon dried herbs = 1 tablespoon fresh herbs

3 teaspoons chopped fresh parsley = 1 teaspoon dried parsley

1 pound brown sugar = 2¼ cups firmly-packed

1 pound confectioners' sugar = About 4 cups sifted

1 pound granulated sugar = 2¼ cups

1 pound marshmallows = About 90 large or 900 mini marshmallows

Stein, German, 19th century, 1937.36. Museum purchase

Index

In addition to alphabetical listings of recipes, special category listings are included for those recipes which do not appear in the expected section of this cookbook. For example, most Beef recipes are easily found in the Meats section – the special listing under Beef in this Index covers recipes from other sections which use beef (such as Carpaccio, which appears in the Appetizer section). For your convenience, major ingredients in recipes are also cross-referenced. And in case you'd like to plan a meal or a party using recipes from another country, we've also grouped those for you.

A

Aberdeen Carrot Puff (Scotland), 127
Africa
    Bobotie, 48
    Peach Chutney, 49
    Pork and Watercress, 65
    Zucchini and Cucumber Salad, 43
Agneau aux Petits Fruits (France), 60
Agneau sans Egal (France), 59
Ajiaco (Colombia), 25
Alouette's Cold Avocado Soup, 26
Amanda's French Dressing, 45
Amaretto Cheesecake, 155
Anchovy Eggs, 9
Angel Mousse, 166
Äpfelstrudel (Germany), 146
Apples
    Äpfelstrudel (Germany), 146
    Apple Clafouti (France), 165
    Apple Crisp, 165
    Apple Dapple Cake, 151
    Applesauce Cake with
      Seafoam Icing, 150

Baked Spiced Apples, 165
    Brown Sugar Apple Pie, 148
    Cinnamon Apple Salad, 37
    Cinnamon Apple Tart, 147
    German Apple Cake, 151
    Old Fashioned Apple Dumplings, 166
    Rotkohl mit Äpfeln (Germany), 126
    Streusel Napfkuchen, 146
    Weisswurst (Germany), 73
Apple Clafouti (France), 165
Apple Crisp, 165
Apple Dapple Cake, 151
Applesauce Cake with
    Seafoam Icing, 150
Apricots
    Chilled Essence of Apricot Soup, 26
    Golden Globes (Turkey), 166
    Lamb and Apricot Pilaf, 59
Aranci Orientali (Italy), 173
Arroz Mexicana (Mexico), 114
Arroz con Leche (Spain), 176
Artichokes
    Aunt Dannie's Baked Tomatoes and
      Artichoke Hearts, 137
    Artichoke Dip, 9
    Artichoke, Mushroom, and Pine Nut
      Casserole (Lebanon), 123
    Marinated Mixed Vegetables, 140
    Salade Elégante (France), 40
    Spinach Artichoke Casserole, 136
    Stewed Tomatoes, Beans, and
      Artichokes (Greece), 136
Asparagus
    Cream of Asparagus Soup, 25
    Ham and Asparagus Casserole, 64
    Spiced Beef with Fresh Asparagus
      (China), 54
Aunt Dannie's Baked Tomatoes and
    Artichoke Hearts, 137
Aunt Dannie's Sour Cream
    Hollandaise, 45

Aunt Rosella's Sponge Cake, 155
Austria
    Erdbeer Schaum Torte, 155
    Wiener Schnitzel, 74
Avocado
    Ajiaco (Colombia), 25
    Alouette's Cold Avocado Soup, 26
    Crema de Aguacate (Mexico), 167
    Curried Avocado Soup, 26
    Layered Guacamole Dip, 13
    Molded Avocado Salad, 37
    Medaillon de Veau au Beurre
      d'Avocat (France), 70
    Medallions of Veal Celestial, 71
    Pete's Guacamole, 13
Ayrshire Hot Pot (Scotland), 47

B

Baked Cheese Grits, 112
Baked Fish Mousse with Lobster Sauce
    (Sweden), 94
Baked Lamb with Feta, 58
Baked Red Snapper, 97
Baked Spiced Apples, 165
Baked Stuffed Red Snapper, 98
Bàkewell Tart (England), 167
Baklava Rolls (Greece), 157
Baklava Rolls, Lebanese, 158
Bananas
    Banana Fritters (India), 123
    Jamaican Bananas, 167
Banana Fritters (India), 123
Barbecued Spare Ribs (Appetizers), 21
Barbecued Spare Ribs, 66
Basmati Rice (India), 112
Baten Gen Mihshee (Lebanon), 61
Beans
    Clams in Black Bean Sauce, 99
    Creole Calico Bean Soup, 27
    Cuban Black Beans (Cuba), 29
    Estofado (Philippines), 75

Green Beans in Olive Oil
(Middle East), 125
Green Beans with Buttered
Breadcrumbs, 125
Haricots Verts au Gratin
(France), 125
Indian Beans (India), 125
Kentucky Baked Beans, 124
Kentucky Bean Bash Soup, 27
Mama's Frijoles (Mexico), 123
Mark's Lima Beans, 124
Puerto Rican Paella (Puerto Rico), 90
Red Beans and Rice, 112
Red Pottage, 35
Salade Elégante (France), 40
Schnitzel Beans, 124
Sesame Green Beans, 124
Stewed Tomatoes, Beans, and
Artichokes (Greece), 136
Western Style Baked Lima
Beans, 123
Bean Sprouts with Ginger, 125
Beef
*(Following cross-references are in
addition to Beef recipes in the Meats
section of this cookbook.)*
Burgoo, 26
Carpaccio (Italy), 10
Easy Mock Turtle Soup, 32
Frick-a-Dillers (Denmark), 12
Pasta Sauce with Beef and
Mushrooms (Italy), 119
Pirozhki (Russia), 19
Russian Cabbage Borscht
(Russia), 29
Samosas (India), 18
Sauerbraten Meat Balls with
Gingersnap Gravy, 21
Tagliarini con Carne (Italy), 122
Tostadas de Carne (Mexico), 22
Zucchini Stew, 77
Beef and Borscht Skillet, 47
Beef Olives (India), 48
Beef Rouladen (Germany), 53
Beef with Beer (Belgium), 74
Beet Salad Vinaigrette, 37
Belgium
Beef with Beer, 74
Brussels Endive Salad, 40
Endive en Casserole, 129
Endive, Orange, and

Walnut Salad, 41
Endive with Bacon Sauce, 40
Ham-Wrapped Endive with
Cheese Sauce, 129
Orange Waffles, 144
Salade Mignonne, 83
Black and White Ice Cream Pie, 147
Black Walnut Soup Chantilly, 36
Blueberries
Blueberry-Peach Batter Cake, 151
Blueberry Pudding, 167
New England Blueberry Spice
Bread, 144
Bobotie (Africa), 48
Boccinotti (Italy), 157
Braised Celery (England), 128
Brandied Braunschweiger, 9
Brandied Caramel Sauce, 179
Brandy Bread Pudding, 167
Brandy Steak, 54
Bread
English Muffin, 141
French, 142
Herb, 142
Honey Yeast, 141
Italian, 142
Raisin, 142
Whole or Cracked Wheat, 141
Whole Wheat, 143
Scandanavian Sampler Loaves, 143
Breakfast or Brunch Dishes
Banana Fritters (India), 123
Cardigan Savories (Scotland), 108
Cinnamon Nut Coffee Cake, 145
Coffee Kuchen, 145
Enchilada Breakfast
(Guatemala), 110
Goetta, 109
Orange Waffles, 144
Puffy German Pancakes, 144
Sausage Scrapple, 109
Streusel Napfkuchen, 146
Walnut Wonder Cake, 156
British Isles
Aberdeen Carrot Puff (Scotland), 127
Ayrshire Hot Pot (Scotland), 47
Bakewell Tart (England), 167
Braised Celery (England), 128
Cardigan Savories (Scotland), 108
Cinnamon Apple Tart (Ireland), 147
Clapshot (Scotland), 133

Claridge's Sauce Balmoral
(England), 45
Cock-A-Leekie Soup
(Scotland), 28
Colcannon (Ireland), 133
Cream of Almond Soup
(Scotland), 25
Creamed Finnan Haddie
(Scotland), 94
Damson Plum Pie (Scotland), 148
Dublin Coddle (Ireland), 67
Ginger Snaps (Scotland), 161
Guard's Pudding (England), 171
Guinness Cake (Ireland), 154
Hard Sauce (England), 174
Irish Coffee (Ireland), 24
Irish Soda Bread (Ireland), 142
Kidney and Mushroom Toast
(England), 78
Leek Pie (Scotland), 131
Leith's Restaurant Stilton Soup
(England), 35
Lemon Butter (England), 149
Old English Drunken Pudding
(England), 170
Plum Pudding (England), 175
Potato Cakes (Ireland), 134
Potted Herrings (Ireland), 94
Seed Cake (Scotland), 154
Shortbread (Scotland), 164
Shortbread Fingers (Scotland), 164
Smoored Pullets (Scotland), 91
Snaffles Mousse (England), 15
Spiced Beef (Ireland), 50
Stuffed Mushrooms (England), 15
Toad-in-the-Hole (England), 69
Trout and Bacon (Wales), 97
Yorkshire Pudding (England), 122
Individual Yorkshire Puddings
(England), 122
Broccoli
Broccoli Rice Casserole, 113
Fettuccine with Broccoli and
Mozzarella (Italy), 121
Brown Sugar Brisket, 49
Brown Sugar Apple Pie, 148
Brussels Endive Salad, 40
Budino di Amaretto (Italy), 168
Burgoo, 26
Butter Tarts, 148
Butterscotch Bars, 158

C

Cabbage
  Colcannon (Ireland), 133
  Croatian Stuffed Cabbage, 56
  Hot and Sour Cabbage (China), 126
  Indiana Cabbage and Lettuce
    Salad, 37
  Johanna's Red Cabbage (Russia), 126
  Lebanese Lamb-Stuffed Cabbage
    (Lebanon), 60
  Rotkohl mit Äpfeln (Germany), 126
  Russian Cabbage Borscht
    (Russia), 29
  Stuffed Cabbage, 57
  Stuffed Cabbage Roll with
    Sauerkraut, 56
Caesar Salad, Lookout House, 38
Cakes
  Apple Dapple Cake, 151
  Applesauce Cake with
    Seafoam Icing, 150
  Aunt Rosella's Sponge Cake, 155
  Blueberry-Peach Batter Cake, 151
  Erdbeer Schaum Torte (Austria), 155
  Flourless Chocolate Cake with
    Chocolate Mousse, 153
  German Apple Cake, 151
  Grandmother's Best Chocolate
    Cake, 152
  Guinness Cake (Ireland), 154
  Mother's Amalgamation Cake, 150
  Orange Nut Cake, 154
  Orange Pecan Loaf Cake, 154
  Seed Cake (Scotland), 154
  Sour Cream Chocolate Cake, 152
  Spirited Angel Food Cake, 151
  Taft Fruit Cake, 152
  Walnut Wonder Cake, 156
Camaron Rebosado (Philippines), 9
Canard en Civet aux Olives Noires
  (France), 92
Caraway Spread, 10
Cardigan Savories (Scotland), 108
Carpaccio (Italy), 10
Carre d'Agneau (France), 60
Carrots
  Aberdeen Carrot Puff (Scotland), 127
  Carrot Souffle (France), 127
  Peasant's Chicken in a Pot
    (France), 86
  Vichy Carrot Salad, 38

Cauliflower
  Soupe de Choux Fleur et Poireaux
    (France), 28
Caviar Appetizer, 10
Céleri Rémoulade (France), 10
Celery
  Braised Celery (England), 128
Cervelat Salad (France), 38
Ceviche (Mexico), 12
Charlotte aux Fraises (France), 177
Châteaubriand Farci (France), 48
Chawanmushi (Japan), 111
Cheddar Soup, 28
Cheese
*(Following cross-references are in
addition to Cheese recipes in the Eggs,
Cheese, Rice, and Pasta Section.)*
  Artichoke Dip, 9
  Baked Lamb with Feta, 58
  Caraway Spread, 10
  Carpaccio, 10
  Cheddar Soup, 28
  Cheese Fondue (Switzerland), 116
  Chicken and Cheese Enchiladas
    (Mexico), 87
  Chicken Cutlets with Swiss Cheese
    Crust, 86
  Chicken Parmesan, 82
  Chicken Saltimbocca, 83
  Chicken with Sherry Sauce, 80
  Chilaquiles (Mexico), 79
  Crustless Vegetable Pie, 140
  Crusty Luncheon Dish, 108
  Ham Wrapped Endive with Cheese
    Sauce (Belgium), 129
  Haricots Verts au Gratin
    (France), 125
  Herb Cheese, 14
  Hot Pepper Jelly with Cream
    Cheese, 18
  Lasagne Verdi (Italy), 84
  Leith's Restaurant Stilton Soup
    (England), 35
  Medallions of Veal Celestial, 71
  Pollo alla Margherita (Italy), 81
  Sausage and Cheese Casserole, 68
  Scallopini of Veal with Lemon Zest
    (Italy), 72
  Snaffles Mousse (Ireland), 15
  Spanakopita (Greece), 108
  Swiss Sausage Casserole, 69

  Tamale Pie (Mexico), 68
  Tangy Cheese Bread, 11
  Tiropita (Greece), 23
  Tomato Soup au Gratin, 35
  Veal Scallopini with Roquefort Sauce
    (France), 73
  Zucchini Parmesan, 138
  Zucchini Puffs, 138
  Zucchini Stew (Italy), 77
Cheesecakes
  Amaretto Cheesecake, 155
  Cheesecake Deluxe, 156
  Chocolate Almond Cheesecake, 156
  Cream Cheese Pie, 156
Cheese Fondue (Switzerland), 116
Cheesecake Deluxe, 156
Cherries
  Chicken with Bing Cherries, 79
  Zürich Cherries Jubilee
    (Switzerland), 168
Chicken
*(Following cross-references are in
addition to Chicken recipes in the
Poultry and Seafood section.)*
  Ajiaco (Colombia), 25
  Burgoo, 26
  Chinese Chicken Fingers with Plum
    Sauce, 11
  Cock-A-Leekie Soup (Scotland), 28
  Oriental Chicken Sprout Salad, 39
  Pancit Cuisado (Philippines), 67
  Pennsylvania Dutch Chicken Rivel
    Soup, 27
  Salade Mignonne, 83
  Scalloped Chicken and Oysters, 102
  Sesame Chicken Salad, 39
  Velvet Sweet Corn Soup (China), 29
  Chicken Adobo (Philippines), 88
  Chicken and Cheese Enchiladas
    (Mexico), 87
  Chicken Breast for One, 79
  Chicken Breast with Herb
    Stuffing, 81
  Chicken Cacciatore, 80
  Chicken Cutlets with Swiss Cheese
    Crust, 86
  Chicken Saltimbocca (Italy), 80
  Chicken Stuffed with Pork, Spinach,
    and Pine Nuts, 89
  Chicken Teriyaki (Japan), 90
  Chicken Tikka Masala (India), 83

Chicken with Bing Cherries, 79
Chicken with Mole Sauce
(Mexico), 89
Chicken with Sherry Sauce, 80
Chicken Parmesan (Italy), 82
Chilaquiles (Mexico), 79
Chiles Rellenos con Queso
(Mexico), 109
Chilled Essence of Apricot Soup, 26
China
Chinese Chicken Fingers with Plum
Sauce, 11
Chinese Prawn and Bean Sprout
Omelette, 107
Clams in Black Bean Sauce, 99
Egg Flower Soup, 31
Hot and Sour Cabbage, 126
Hot and Sour Soup, 31
Hot Chinese Beef Shreds, 54
Ma Po Hot Tofu, 57
Marbled Tea Eggs, 13
Pecan Chicken, 82
Peking Duck, 92
Pork, Shrimp, and Mushroom Loo
Mein, 66
Princess Chicken, 82
Red Hot Spicy Tofu, 58
Shrimp and Snow Pea Pods, 106
Shrimp Fu Yung, 104
Shrimp with Cashews, 103
Spiced Beef with Fresh
Asparagus, 54
Stir-Fried Shrimp and Ham Rice, 105
Velvet Sweet Corn Soup, 29
Chinese Chicken Fingers with Plum
Sauce, 11
Chocolate
Black and White Ice Cream Pie, 147
Chicken with Mole Sauce, 89
Chocolate Almond Cheesecake, 156
Chocolate Mousse Gateau
(France), 168
Chocolate Potato Torte, 143
Chocolate Rum Truffles, 178
Chocolate Truffles, 178
Chocolate Velvet Truffles, 178
Chocolate Walnut Bars, 160
Chocolate Walnut Date Loaf, 143
Double Chocolate Oatmeal
Cookies, 160
Flourless Chocolate Cake with

Chocolate Mousse, 153
Frozen Mint Chocolates, 172
German Chocolate Pie, 148
Grandmother's Best Chocolate
Cake, 152
Mint Brownies, 159
Muthries Mousse au Chocolat, 168
Nut Truffles, 179
Sour Cream Chocolate Cake, 152
Chocolate Almond Cheesecake, 156
Chocolate Mousse Gateau (France), 168
Chocolate Potato Torte, 143
Chocolate Rum Truffles, 178
Chocolate Truffles, 178
Chocolate Velvet Truffles, 178
Chocolate Walnut Bars, 160
Chocolate Walnut Date Loaf, 143
Chuletas de Cerdo a la Madrileña
(Spain), 64
Cincinnati Herb Society's Saltless
Salt, 46
Cincinnati Saucepan Butterscotch
Sticks, 159
Cinnamon Apple Salad, 37
Cinnamon Apple Tart (Ireland), 147
Cinnamon Nut Coffee Cake, 145
Circassian Chicken with Walnuts
(Turkey), 91
Clams
Clams Casino, 11
Clams in Black Bean Sauce
(China),99
Hot Clam Dip, 12
Linguine with Clam Sauce (Italy), 99
Spaghetti alle Vongole (Italy), 100
Clapshot (Scotland), 133
Claridge's Sauce Balmoral (England), 45
Cocada Leticia (Brazil), 169
Coconut Rice (India), 113
Cock-A-Leekie Soup, 28
Coconut
Cocada Leticia (Brazil), 169
Coconut Rice (India), 113
Crema de Coconut, 169
Crispy Coconut Treats, 12
German Chocolate Pie, 148
Ginger Cream Cheese Ball, 12
Indian Beans (India), 125
Mother's Amalgamation Cake, 150
Coffee Kuchen, 145
Colcannon (Ireland), 133

Cold Cucumber and Yogurt Soup
(Turkey), 30
Cold Curried Chicken, 88
Cold Raspberry Soup, 33
Conchiglie e Luganegna (Italy), 119
Corn
Ajiaco (Colombia), 25
Green Corn Cakes, 128
Mexican Corn Bread (Mexico), 142
Spoonbread, 128
Tamale Pie (Mexico), 68
Velvet Sweet Corn Soup (China), 29
Corned Beef Salad, 53
Coq au Vin (France), 91
Coquilles à la Nage (France), 102
Country Cornish Hens, 92
Courgettes à la Crème (France), 139
Crab
(Following cross-references are in
addition to Crab recipes in the Poultry
and Seafood section.)
Longboat Key Salad, 40
Medallions of Veal Celestial, 71
Puerto Rican Paella (Puerto Rico), 90
Seafood Tartlets, 22
Crabmeat au Gratin, 100
Crabmeat Key West, 101
Cracked Wheat Pilaf (Middle East), 116
Cranberry Marble Mold, 39
Cranberry Nut Relish, 46
Crawfish Etouffée, 100
Cream Cheese Pie, 156
Cream Cucumber Soup, 30
Cream of Almond Soup (Scotland), 25
Cream of Asparagus Soup, 25
Cream of Lettuce Soup, 32
Creamed Finnan Haddie (Scotland), 94
Creamy Cheese Noodle Casserole, 121
Crema de Aguacate (Mexico), 167
Crema de Coconut, 169
Crema Fritta (Italy), 170
Crème au Rhum (France), 169
Crème Brulee à l'Orange, 169
Creole Calico Bean Soup, 27
Crepes aux Roquefort (France), 111
Crispy Coconut Treats, 12
Croatian Stuffed Cabbage, 56
Crunchy Noodles, 116
Crustless Vegetable Pie, 140
Crusty Luncheon Dish, 108
Cuban Black Beans (Cuba), 29

Cuban Picadillo, 53
Cuban Seafood Soup (Cuba), 33
Cucumbers
Cold Cucumber and Yogurt Soup
(Turkey), 30
Cream Cucumber Soup, 30
Cucumber Aspic, 106
Cucumbers with Yogurt, 39
Greek Summer Salad (Greece), 39
Sunomono (Japan), 44
Tzatziki (Greece), 24
Zucchini and Cucumber Salad
(Africa), 43
Cucumber and Chive Dressing, 96
Cucumbers with Yogurt, 39
Curried Avocado Soup, 26
Curried Beef, 50
Curried Chicken Breasts, 80

D

Damson Plum Pie, 148
Date Pudding, 170
Daube de Campagne (France), 49
Denmark
Frick-a-Dillers, 12
Dill Mayonnaise, 96
Double Chocolate Oatmeal Cookies, 160
Double Duty Potatoes, 134
Dublin Coddle (Ireland), 67
Duck
(Following cross-references are in
addition to Duck recipes in the Poultry
and Seafood section.)
Duck Pâté (France), 17
Terrine de Canard aux Raisins
(France), 23

E

East Indian Casserole (East Indies), 88
Easy Mock Turtle Soup, 32
Egg Curry (Malaysia), 108
Egg Dishes
(Following cross-references are in
addition to Egg recipes in the Eggs,
Cheese, Rice, and Pasta section.)
Anchovy Eggs, 9
Caviar Appetizer, 10
Chinese Prawn and Bean Sprout
Omelette (China), 107
Crusty Luncheon Dish, 108
Egg Curry (Malaysia), 108

Egg Flower Soup (China), 31
Marbled Tea Eggs (China), 13
Sausage 'n' Egg Casserole, 107
Tortilla de Patata (Spain), 107
Eggplant
Crustless Vegetable Pie, 140
Eggplant and Beef with Yogurt
(Turkey), 47
Japanese Eggplant Ratatouille
(France), 128
Mystras Style Greek Vegetable
Casserole, 140
Moussaka, 62
Eight-Boy Curry (Netherlands), 62
Enchilada Breakfast (Guatemala), 110
Endive, Belgian
Brussels Endive Salad (Belgium), 40
Endive en Casserole (Belgium), 129
Endive, Orange, and Walnut Salad
(Belgium), 41
Endive with Bacon Sauce
(Belgium), 40
Ham-Wrapped Endive with Cheese
Sauce (Belgium), 129
Salade Mignonne (Belgium), 83
English Muffin Bread, 141
Erdbeer Schaum Torte (Austria), 155
Espinacas Catalan (Spain), 136
Estofado (Philippines), 75

F

Family Style Onion Soup Metropole, 28
Far East
(See also China, India, and Japan)
Bean Sprouts with Ginger
(Singapore), 125
Camaron Rebosado (Philippines), 9
Chicken Adobo (Philippines), 88
Egg Curry (Malaysia), 108
Estofado (Philippines), 75
Frikedel Jagung, Shrimp
(Indonesia), 103
Korean Beef (Korea), 55
Nappa in Cream Sauce, 132
Pancit Cuisado (Philippines), 67
Philippine Pork Stew
(Philippines), 77
Nasi Minyak (Malaysia), 114
Serundeng (Indonesia), 58
Feathered Rice, 114
Feathery Potato Casserole, 135

Fettuccine with Broccoli and
Mozzarella (Italy), 121
Filet Mignon de Porc en Croute
(France), 64
Fish and Seafood
(Following cross-references are in
addition to Fish and Seafood recipes in
the Poultry and Seafood section.)
Ceviche (Mexico), 12
Cuban Seafood Soup, 33
Rainbow Pasta Salad, 42
Seafood Tartlets, 22
Sillsalad (Sweden), 42
Taramosalata (Greece), 22
Flamiche aux Poireaux
(France), 130
Florence Shullman's Famous Chopped
Liver, 14
Florentines, 160
Flour Tortillas (Mexico), 142
Flourless Chocolate Cake with
Chocolate Mousse, 153
France
Agneau aux Petits Fruits, 60
Agneau sans Egal, 59
Apple Clafouti, 165
Canard en Civet aux Olives
Noires, 92
Carre d'Agneau, 60
Carrot Souffle, 127
Céleri Rémoulade, 10
Cervelat Salad, 38
Charlotte aux Fraises, 177
Châteaubriand Farci, 48
Chocolate Mousse Gateau, 168
Coq au Vin, 91
Coquilles à la Nage, 102
Courgettes à la Crème, 139
Crème au Rhum, 169
Crepes aux Roquefort, 111
Daube de Campagne, 49
Duck Pâté, 17
Filet Mignon de Porc en Croute, 64
Flamiche aux Poureaux, 130
Garlic Soup, 30
Haricots Verts au Gratin, 125
Jambon au Saupiquet, 64
Jambon Veronique, 63
Japanese Eggplant Ratatouille, 128
Les Crevettes Gourmet, 103
Les Tomates Françaises, 136

Medaillon de Veau au Beurre d'Avocat, 70
Mushroom Roll with Pâté, 14
Navarin de Coquilles St. Jacques, 15
Navets a l'Orange, 137
Oignons à la Monegasque, 132
Pâté aux Champignons, 16
Pâté de Campagne, 16
Peasant's Chicken in a Pot, 86
Poached Pears with Crème Anglaise, 173
Poires au Vin Rouge, 174
Pommes Anna, 134
Poulet Dijonnais, 89
Quenelles de Poisson avec Sauce Normande, 101
Quiche Lorraine, 110
Ris de Veau, Madeira, 78
Riz au Four, 115
Roast Veal Dijon, 70
Salade des Lentilles, 41
Salade Elégante, 40
Salade Tiede St. Jacques, 103
Saumon Grillé, Flambé au Fenouil, 96
Sauté de Lapin au Vin, 76
Savarin, 176
Souffles aux Fruits Frais, 171
Soupe de Choux Fleur et Poireaux, 28
Terrine de Canard aux Raisins, 23
Veal Florentine with Sauce Choron, 70
Veal Morels, 71
Veal Scallopini with Roquefort Sauce, 73
Vichy Carrot Salad, 38
Frappe (Italy), 162
French Bread, 142
Fresh Fruit with Ricotta Amaretto Sauce (Italy), 170
Frick-a-Dillers (Denmark), 12
Frikedel Jagung, Shrimp (Indonesia), 103
Frosted Zucchini or Potato Rounds, 139
Frozen Lemon Meringue Pie, 148
Frozen Mint Chocolates, 172
Fruit Compote, 129
Fruit Melange, 129
Fruit Salad Dressing, 44

G

Galaktobouriko (Greece), 160
Garlic Soup (France), 30
Gazpacho el Bodegon (Spain), 30
Gazpacho Malaca (Spain), 31
Genoese Beef (Italy), 51
Germany
    Äpfelstrudel, 146
    Beef Rouladen, 53
    Crunchy Noodles, 116
    Kümmel Steak, 55
    Lebkuchen, 161
    Lentil Soup, 32
    Mandelbrot, 162
    New Year's Day Sauerkraut, 67
    Paprika Huhn, 90
    Peach Strudel, 146
    Potato Kugel, 134
    Puffy German Pancakes, 144
    Raspberry Champagne Cocktails, 23
    Rotkohl mit Äpfeln, 126
    Sauerbraten, 52
    Sauerbraten Meat Balls with Gingersnap Gravy, 21
    Sauerkraut Balls, 21
    Schwadenmagen, 21
    Spaetzle, 121
    Stuffed Pork Loin, 65
    Sweet and Sour Potato Salad, 42
    Weisswurst, 73
German Apple Cake, 151
German Chocolate Pie, 148
German Spaetzle, 121
Ginger Cream Cheese Ball, 12
Ginger Snaps (Scotland), 161
Gnocchi di Spinaci (Italy), 117
Goetta, 109
Golden Globes (Turkey), 166
Grandmother's Best Chocolate Cake, 152
Grasshopper Pie, 149
Greece
    Baked Lamb with Feta, 58
    Baklava Rolls, 157
    Galaktobouriko, 160
    Greek Potato Salad, 42
    Greek Summer Salad, 39
    Kadaifi, 161
    Keftedes, 51
    Moussaka, 62
    Pastitsio, 52

Paxemadia, 162
Roast Leg of Lamb, 61
Sesame Seed Twists, 164
Spanakopita, 108
Stewed Tomatoes, Beans, and Artichokes, 136
Stifado, 77
Taramosalata, 22
Tiropita, 23
Tzatziki, 24
Green Beans in Olive Oil (Middle East), 125
Green Beans with Buttered Breadcrumbs, 125
Green Corn Cakes, 128
Grilled Shark with Ripe Red Peppers, 97
Grilled Shrimp, 106
Guard's Pudding (England), 171
Guinness Cake (Ireland), 154

H

Hake à la Cazuela (Spain), 93
Ham
    Chicken Saltimbocca (Italy), 83
    Creole Calico Bean Soup, 27
    Ham and Asparagus Casserole, 64
    Ham-Wrapped Endive with Cheese Sauce (Belgium), 129
    Kentucky Bean Bash Soup, 27
    Piselli in Sugo Proprio con Prosciutto (Italy), 133
    Pollo alla Margherita (Italy), 81
    Sartu di Riso alla Napoletana (Italy), 114
    Sauerkraut Balls (Germany), 21
    Stir-Fried Shrimp and Ham Rice (China), 105
    Sweetbreads and Ham, 78
Hard Sauce (England), 174
Haricots Verts au Gratin (France), 125
Hawaiian Chicken Ono-Ono, 86
Herb Bread, 142
Herb Cheese, 14
Honey Yeast Bread, 141
Horseradish Sauce, 97
Hot and Sour Cabbage (China), 126
Hot and Sour Soup (China), 31
Hot Chinese Beef Shreds (China), 54
Hot Clam Dip, 12
Hot Fruit Compote, 129

Hot Mustard, 44
Hot Pepper Jelly with Cream Cheese, 18
Hummous Dip (Middle East), 13
Hungarian Goulash
   (Hungary), 75

I

India
   Banana Fritters, 123
   Basmati Rice, 112
   Beef Olives, 48
   Beet Salad Vinaigrette, 37
   Chicken Tikka Masala, 83
   Coconut Rice, 113
   Curried Chicken Breasts, 80
   East Indian Casserole, 88
   Indian Beans, 125
   Indian Cashews, 10
   Indian Fried Fish, 95
   Lamb Bhuna, 62
   Pork Vindalho, 66
   Samosas, 18
Indiana Cabbage and Lettuce
   Salad, 37
Indian Beans (India), 125
Indian Cashews, 10
Indian Fried Fish (India), 95
Individual Luncheon Sandwiches, 46
Irish Coffee (Ireland), 24
Irish Soda Bread (Ireland), 142
Italian Bread, 142
Italy
   Aranci Orientali, 173
   Boccinotti, 157
   Budino di Amaretto, 168
   Carpaccio, 10
   Chicken Parmesan, 82
   Chicken Saltimbocca, 83
   Conchiglie e Luganega, 119
   Crema Fritta, 170
   Fettuccine with Broccoli and
      Mozzarella, 121
   Frappe, 162
   Fresh Fruit with Ricotta Amaretto
      Sauce, 170
   Genoese Beef, 51
   Gnocci di Spinaci, 117
   Lasagne Verdi, 84
   Nona Sauce for Pasta, 87
   Ossobuco, 72
   Parmesan Zucchini, 138

Piccata di Vitello, 72
Piselli in Sugo Proprio con
   Prosciutto, 133
Pasta con Pesto, 118
Pasta Sauce with Beef and
   Mushrooms, 119
Pollo alla Margherita, 81
Risotto alla Milanese, 115
Sartu di Riso alla Napoletana, 114
Scallopini of Veal with
   Lemon Zest, 72
Spaghetti alla Bolognese, 118
Spaghetti alla Carbonara, 118
Spaghetti alle Vongole, 100
Spinach and Sausage Casserole, 69
Tagliarini con Carne, 122
Veal Scallopini with Mushrooms, 73
Vitello alla Fiorentina, 70
Zucchini Parmesan, 138
Zucchini Ripiene, 138
Zucchini Stew, 77

J

Jamaica Flower Water (Mexico), 24
Jamaican Bananas, 167
Jambon au Saupiquet (France), 64
Jambon Veronique (France), 63
Japan
   Chawanmushi, 111
   Chicken Teriyaki, 90
   Japanese Fruit Bowl, 130
   Japanese Sweet and Sour Pork, 65
   Sukiyaki, 57
   Sunomono, 44
   Teriyaki Roast Tenderloin, 56
   Yakitori, 87
Japanese Eggplant Ratatouille
   (France), 128
Johanna's Red Cabbage
   (Russia), 126

K

Kadaifi (Greece), 161
Keftedes (Greece), 53
Kentucky Baked Beans, 124
Kentucky Bean Bash Soup, 27
Kidney and Mushroom Toast
   (England), 78
Korean Beef (Korea), 55
Kumback Barbecue Sauce, 58
Kümmel Steak (Germany), 55

L

Lamb and Apricot Pilaf, 59
Lamb Bhuna (India), 62
Lamb-Stuffed Chicken, 84
Lasagne Verdi (Italy), 84
Latin America
   Ajiaco (Colombia), 25
   Cocada Leticia (Brazil), 169
   Cuban Black Beans (Cuba), 29
   Cuban Picadillo (Cuba), 53
   Cuban Seafood Soup (Cuba), 33
   Enchilada Breakfast, 110
   Lirios de Queijo Creme (Brazil), 159
   Pastel del Choclo (Chile), 82
   Puerto Rican Paella (Puerto Rico), 90
Layered Guacamole Dip, 13
Lebanese Baklava Rolls, 158
Lebanese Lamb-Stuffed Cabbage
   (Lebanon), 60
Lebkuchen (Germany), 161
Leeks
   Cock-A-Leekie Soup, 28
   Flamiche aux Poireaux (France), 130
   Leek Pie (Scotland), 131
   Soupe de Choux Fleur et Poireaux
      (France), 28
Leith's Restaurant Stilton Soup
   (England), 35
Lemon
   Frozen Lemon Meringue Pie, 148
   Lemon Butter (England), 149
   Lemon Ice Cream (Mexico), 171
   Lemon Pudding, 172
   Lemon Squares, 162
   Mom's Lemon Pie, 149
Lentil Soup (Germany), 32
Lentils and Rice, 113
Les Crevettes Gourmet
   (France), 103
Les Tomates Françaises, 136
Linguine with Clam Sauce, 99
Lirios de Queijo Creme (Brazil), 159
Liver
   Duck Pâté (France), 17
   Florence Shullman's Famous
      Chopped Liver, 14
   Liver Pâté, 17
   Liver Pâté (England), 17
   Pâté de Campagne (France), 16
   Philippine Pork Stew
      (Philippines), 77

Terrine de Canard aux Raisins
(France), 23
Lobster
Baked Fish Mousse with Lobster
Sauce (Sweden), 94
New England Clambake, 102
Longboat Key Salad, 40
Lookout House Caesar Salad, 38
Lube a fe Lahem (Lebanon), 60
Lukchen Kugel, 116
Luncheon Dishes
Chawanmushi (Japan), 111
Chinese Prawn and Bean Sprout
Omelette (China), 107
Corned Beef Salad, 53
Crepes aux Roquefort (France), 111
Crusty Luncheon Dish, 108
Curried Beef, 50
Egg Curry (Malaysia), 108
Ham and Asparagus Casserole, 64
Ham-Wrapped Endive with Cheese
Sauce (Belgium), 129
Individual Luncheon Sandwiches, 46
Mushroom Pie, 111
Mushrooms Supreme, 131
Onion Custard Pie, 111
Sausage 'n' Egg Casserole, 107
Tangy Cheese Bread, 11
Tortilla de Patata (Spain), 107

M

Ma Po Hot Tofu (China), 57
Macaroon Custard St. Nicholas, 173
Mackinac Broil, 52
Mama's Frijoles (Mexico), 123
Mandelbrot (Germany), 162
Marbled Tea Eggs (China), 13
Marinated Mixed Vegetables, 140
Mark's Lima Beans, 124
Maryland Crab Imperial, 100
Maurice Salad, 38
Medaillon de Veau au Beurre
d'Avocat (France), 70
Medallions of Veal Celestial, 71
Menudo Soup (Mexico), 33
Mexican Corn Bread (Mexico), 142
Mexico
Arroz Mexicana, 114
Chicken and Cheese Enchiladas, 87
Chicken with Mole Sauce, 89
Chilaquiles, 79

Chiles Rellenos con Queso, 109
Crema de Aguacate, 167
Flour Tortillas, 142
Jamaica Flower Water, 24
Lemon Ice Cream, 171
Mama's Frijoles, 123
Menudo Soup, 33
Mexican Corn Bread, 142
Orange Flan, 172
Pineapple Flan, 174
Tamale Pie, 68
Tostadas de Carne, 22
Middle East
Artichoke, Mushroom, and Pine Nut
Casserole (Lebanon), 123
Baklava Rolls (Lebanon), 158
Baten Gen Mihshee (Lebanon), 61
Circassian Chicken with Walnuts
(Turkey), 91
Cold Cucumber and Yogurt Soup
(Turkey), 30
Cracked Wheat Pilaf, 116
Cucumbers with Yogurt, 39
Eggplant and Beef with Yogurt
(Turkey), 47
Golden Globes (Turkey), 166
Green Beans in Olive Oil, 125
Hummous, 13
Lamb-Stuffed Chicken (Lebanon), 84
Lebanese Lamb-stuffed Cabbage, 60
Lentils and Rice, 113
Lube a fe Lahem (Lebanon), 60
Persian Leg of Lamb (Iran), 59
Rice Pilaf, 115
Skewered Chicken (Turkey), 84
Sultan Reshat Pilavi (Turkey), 63
Tabbouleh Salad (Lebanon), 43
Turkish Coffee (Turkey), 24
Turkish Lamb Kabobs (Turkey), 61
Zucchini Puffs (Turkey), 138
Mim's Easy Vegetable Soup, 36
Mint Brownies, 159
Mint Mallow Dessert, 172
Mock Turtle Soup, 32
Mom's Lemon Pie, 149
Mother's Amalgamation Cake, 150
Moussaka (Greece), 62
Mushrooms
Artichoke, Mushroom, and Pine Nut
Casserole (Lebanon), 123

Beef with Beer (Belgium), 74
Chicken Breast with Herb
Stuffing, 81
Chicken Cacciatore, 80
Chicken Saltimbocca (Italy), 83
Coq au Vin (France), 91
Hawaiian Chicken Ono-Ono, 86
Kidney and Mushroom Toast
(England), 78
Lasagne Verdi (Italy), 84
Marinated Mixed Vegetables, 140
Medaillon de Veau au Beurre
d'Avocat (France), 70
Mushroom Pie, 111
Mushroom Roll with Pâté
(France), 14
Mushrooms Supreme, 131
Pasta Sauce with Beef and
Mushrooms (Italy), 119
Pâté aux Champignons (France), 16
Peasant's Chicken in a Pot
(France), 86
Piccata di Vitello (Italy), 72
Pork, Shrimp, and Mushroom Loo
Mein (China), 86
Ris de Veau, Madeira, 78
Sartu di Riso alla Napoletana
(Italy), 114
Scalloped Chicken and Oysters, 102
Stuffed Mushrooms (England), 15
Stuffed Mushrooms with Bechamel
Sauce, 130
Sweetbreads and Ham, 78
Veal Florentine with Sauce Choron
(France), 70
Veal Morels (France), 71
Veal Patties with Mushroom Cream
Gravy, 72
Veal Scallopini with Mushrooms
(Italy), 73
Veal Stew, 77
Vitello alla Fiorentina (Italy), 70
Zucchine Ripiene (Italy), 138
Muthries Mousse au Chocolat, 168
Mystras Style Greek Vegetable
Casserole, 140

N

Nappa in Cream Sauce, 132
Nasi Minyak-Malaysian Rice
(Malaysia), 114

Navarin de Coquilles St. Jacques
(France), 15
Navets a l'Orange (France), 137
New England Blueberry Spice
Bread, 144
New England Clambake, 102
New Year's Day Sauerkraut
(Germany), 67
New Year's Stew, 74
Nona Sauce for Pasta (Italy), 87
Non-Irish Baked Corned Beef, 50
Nuts
Artichoke, Mushroom, and Pine Nut
Casserole (Lebanon), 123
Baklava Rolls (Greece), 157
Baklava Rolls (Lebanon), 158
Black Walnut Soup Chantilly, 36
Chicken Stuffed with Pork, Spinach,
and Pine Nuts, 89
Chicken with Mole Sauce
(Mexico), 89
Chocolate Almond Cheesecake, 156
Chocolate Potato Torte, 143
Chocolate Rum Truffles, 178
Chocolate Walnut Bars, 160
Chocolate Walnut Date Loaf, 143
Cinnamon Nut Coffee Cake, 145
Circassian Chicken with Walnuts
(Turkey), 91
Cream of Almond Soup
(Scotland), 25
Endive, Orange, and Walnut Salad
(Belgium), 41
Florentines, 160
Ginger Cream Cheese Ball, 12
Guinness Cake (Ireland), 154
Lamb-Stuffed Chicken, 84
Hawaiian Chicken Ono-Ono, 86
Indian Cashews (India), 10
Kadaifi (Greece), 161
Mandelbrot (Germany), 162
Nutty Currant Cheesecake
Squares, 159
Orange Nut Cake, 154
Orange Pecan Loaf Cake, 154
Party Nuts, 15
Pasta con Pesto, 118
Peanut Butter Balls, 144
Peanut Chutney Spread, 18
Peanut Streusel Pie, 149
Pecan Chicken (China), 82

Pineapple Delight, 174
Popcorn-Nut Crunch, 19
Nut Truffles, 179
Shrimp with Cashews (China), 103
Spiced Pecans, 18
Stuffed Quail, 93
Walnut Wonder Cake, 156
Zucchini Nut Muffins, 147
Nut Truffles, 179
Nutty Currant Cheesecake Squares, 159

O

Oignons à la Monegasque (France), 132
Old English Drunken Pudding
(England), 170
Old Fashioned Apple Dumplings, 166
Olives
Canard en Civet aux Olives Noires
(France), 92
Chicken and Cheese Enchiladas
(Mexico), 87
Chicken Cacciatore, 80
One-of-Each Soup, 36
Onions
Family Style Onion Soup
Metropole, 28
Oignons à la Monegasque
(France), 132
Onion Custard Pie, 111
Peasant's Chicken in a Pot
(France), 86
Plantation Onions, 132
Potato-Onion Soup, 34
Oranges
Aranci Orientali (Italy), 173
Endive, Orange, and Walnut Salad
(Belgium), 41
Orange Flan (Mexico), 172
Orange Nut Cake, 154
Orange Pecan Loaf Cake, 154
Orange Waffles, 144
Oranges L'Indienne, 173
Oriental Chicken Sprout Salad, 39
Ossobuco (Italy), 72
Oysters Mosca, 101

P

Paella (Spain), 104
Pancakes, Puffy German, 144
Pancit Cuisado (Philippines), 67
Paprika Huhn (Germany), 90

Party Nuts, 15
Pasta con Pesto (Italy), 118
Pasta Salad with Sausage, 41
Pasta Sauce with Beef and Mushrooms
(Italy), 119
Pastel de Choclo (Chile), 82
Pastitsio (Greece), 52
Pastry, Short Crust, 150
Pâté aux Champignons (France), 16
Pâté de Campagne (France), 16
Paxemadia (Greece), 162
Peaches
Blueberry-Peach Batter Cake, 151
Peach Chutney (Africa), 49
Peach Strudel (Germany), 146
Peanut Butter Balls, 144
Peanut Chutney Spread, 18
Peanut Streusel Pie, 149
Peas
Picnic Pasta Salad, 41
Piselli in Sugo Proprio con Prosciutto
(Italy), 133
Pears
Poached Pears with Crème Anglaise
(France), 173
Poires au Vin Rouge (France), 174
Peasant's Chicken in a Pot (France), 86
Pecan Chicken (China), 82
Peking Duck (China), 92
Pennsylvania Dutch Chicken Rivel
Soup, 27
Pepperkakor (Sweden), 163
Persian Leg of Lamb (Iran), 59
Pescado al Horno (Spain), 93
Pete's Guacamole, 13
Philippine Pork Stew
(Philippines), 77
Picadillo, 54
Piccata di Vitello (Italy), 72
Picnic Pasta Salad, 41
Pies
Black and White Ice Cream Pie, 147
Brown Sugar Apple Pie, 148
Butter Tarts (Canada), 148
Cinnamon Apple Tart (Ireland), 147
Damson Plum Pie, 148
Frozen Lemon Meringue Pie, 148
German Chocolate Pie, 148
Grasshopper Pie, 149
Mom's Lemon Pie, 149
Peanut Streusel Pie, 149

Short Crust Pastry, 150
Pineapple
    Cranberry Marble Mold, 39
    Hawaiian Chicken Ono-Ono, 86
    Pineapple Delight, 174
    Pineapple Flan (Mexico), 174
    Pineapple Salad Dressing, 44
Pirozhki (Russia), 19
Piselli in Sugo Proprio con Prosciutto
    (Italy), 133
Plantation Onions, 132
Plum Pudding (England), 175
Poached Pears with Crème Anglaise
    (France), 173
Poires au Vin Rouge (France), 174
Pollo alla Margherita (Italy), 81
Pastel de Choclo (Chile), 82
Pommes Anna (France), 134
Popcorn-Nut Crunch, 19
Pork
*(Following cross-references are in
addition to Pork recipes found in the
Meats section.)*
    Barbecued Spareribs, 21
    Burgoo, 26
Pork and Watercress (Africa), 65
Pork, Shrimp, and Mushroom Loo Mein
    (China), 66
Pork Vindalho (India), 66
Potatoes
    Aberdeen Carrot Puff (Scotland), 127
    Ajiaco (Colombia), 25
    Clapshot (Scotland), 133
    Chocolate Potato Torte, 143
    Colcannon (Ireland), 133
    Double Duty Potatoes, 134
    Dublin Coddle (Ireland), 67
    Feathery Potato Casserole, 135
    Frosted Zucchini or Potato
    Rounds, 139
    Greek Potato Salad (Greece), 42
    Peasant's Chicken in a Pot
      (France), 86
    Pescado al Horno (Spain), 93
    Pommes Anna (France), 134
    Potato Cakes (Ireland), 134
    Potato Dumplings, 133
    Potato Kugel (Germany), 134
    Potato-Onion Soup, 34
    Rösti Nach Zürcherart
      (Switzerland), 132

Sillsalad (Sweden), 42
Sweet and Sour Potato Salad, 42
Tortilla de Patata (Spain), 107
Potted Herrings (Ireland), 94
Poulet Dijonnais (France), 89
Pretzel Suppe, 34
Princess Chicken (China), 82
Puerto Rican Paella (Puerto Rico), 90
Puffy German Pancakes, 144

Q

Queen Stroganoff, 55
Quenelles de Poisson avec Sauce
    Normande (France), 101
Quiche Lorraine (France), 110
Quick Breads
    English Muffin Bread, 141
    Irish Soda Bread (Ireland), 142
    Mexican Corn Bread, 142
    New England Blueberry Spice
      Bread, 144
    Zucchini Nut Muffins, 147

R

Rabbit
    Sauté de Lapin au Vin
      (France), 76
Rainbow Pasta Salad, 42
Raisin Bread, 142
Raspberries,
    Cold Raspberry Soup, 33
    Raspberry Champagne Cocktails
      (Germany), 23
    Raspberry Fluff, 175
    Red Snapper with Raspberry Beurre
      Blanc, 98
Red Beans and Rice, 112
Red Hot Spicy Tofu (China), 58
Red Pottage, 35
Red Snapper with Raspberry Beurr
    Blanc, 98
Rhubarb Chutney, 45
Rice
*(Following cross-references are in
addition to Rice recipes in the Eggs,
Cheese, Rice, and Pasta section.)*
    Arroz Mexicana, 114
    Basmati Rice (India), 112
    Broccoli Rice Casserole, 113
    Red Beans and Rice, 112
    Rice Pilaf (Middle East), 115

Stir-Fried Shrimp and Ham Rice
    (China), 105
Stuffed Quail, 93
Ris de Veau, Madeira (France), 78
Risotto alla Milanese (Italy), 115
Riz au Four (France), 115
Roast Leg of Lamb (Greece), 61
Roast Veal Dijon (France), 70
Rösti nach Zürcherart
    (Switzerland), 132
Rotkohl mit Äpfeln (Germany), 126
Russian Cabbage Borscht (Russia), 29
Russia
    Johanna's Red Cabbage, 126
    Pirozhki, 19
    Russian Cabbage Borscht, 29

S

Salade des Lentilles (France), 41
Salade Elégante (France), 40
Salade Mignonne (Belgium), 83
Salade Tiede de St. Jacques
    (France), 103
Salmon Poached in Foil, 96
Samosas (India), 18
Sangria (Spain), 23
Sartu di Riso alla Napoletana (Italy), 114
Sauerbraten (Germany), 52
Sauerbraten Meat Balls with
    Gingersnap Gravy (Germany), 21
Sauerkraut Balls (Germany), 21
Saumon Grillé, Flambé au Fenouil
    (France), 96
Sausage
    Brandied Braunschweiger, 9
    Cervelat Salad (France), 38
    Conchiglie e Luganega (Italy), 119
    Dublin Coddle (Ireland), 67
    Lentil Soup, 32
    New Year's Day Sauerkraut
      (Germany), 67
    New Year's Stew, 74
    Nona Sauce for Pasta (Italy), 87
    Pasta Salad with Sausage, 41
    Pretzel Suppe, 34
    Red Beans and Rice, 112
    Sartu di Riso alla Napoletana
      (Itàly), 114
    Sausage and Cheese Casserole, 68
    Sausage 'n' Egg Casserole, 107
    Sausage Pinwheels, 19

Sausage Scrapple, 109
Spinach and Sausage Casserole
   (Italy), 69
Swiss Sausage Casserole, 69
Toad-in-the-Hole (England), 69
Weisswurst (Germany), 73
Sauté de Lapin au Vin (France), 76
Savarin (France), 176
Scalloped Chicken and Oysters, 102
Scallops
(See also Poultry and Seafood section.)
   Navarin de Coquilles St. Jacques
      (France), 15
Scallopini of Veal with Lemon Zest
   (Italy), 72
Scandinavian Sampler Loaves, 143
Schnitzel Beans, 124
Schwadenmagen (Germany), 21
Seafood Dressing, 105
Seafood Tartlets, 22
Seed Cake (Scotland), 154
Serundeng (Indonesia), 58
Sesame Chicken Salad, 39
Sesame Green Beans, 124
Sesame Seed Twists (Greece), 164
Short Crust Pastry, 150
Shortbread (Scotland), 164
Shortbread Fingers (Scotland), 164
Shrimp
(See also Poultry and Seafood section.)
   Camaron Rebosado (Philippines), 9
   Chinese Prawn and Bean Sprout
      Omelette (China), 107
   Longboat Key Salad, 40
   Pancit Cuisado (Philippines), 67
   Pork, Shrimp, and Mushroom Loo
      Mein (China), 66
   Puerto Rican Paella (Puerto Rico), 90
   Shrimp and Snow Pea Pods
      (China), 106
   Shrimp Fu Yung (China), 104
   Shrimp Toast, 106
   Shrimp with Cashews (China), 103
   Spicy Cajun Shrimp Remoulade, 104
   Stir-Fried Shrimp and Ham Rice
      (China), 105
   Sunomono (Japan), 44
Sillsalad (Sweden), 42
Skewered Chicken (Turkey), 84
Smoored Pullets (Scotland), 91
Snaffles Mousse (England), 15

Snow Peas
   Les Tomates Françaises, 136
   Shrimp and Snow Pea Pods
      (China), 106
Sole Florentine, 98
Souffles aux Fruits Frais (France), 171
Soupe de Choux Fleur et Poireaux
   (France), 28
Sour Cream Chocolate Cake, 152
Sour Cream Sauce, 45
Spaetzle, German, 121
Spaghetti alla Bolognese (Italy), 118
Spaghetti alla Carbonara (Italy), 118
Spaghetti alle Vongole (Italy), 100
Spain
   Arroz con Leche, 176
   Chuletas de Cerdo a la Madrileña, 64
   Espinacas Catalan, 136
   Gazpacho el Bodegon, 30
   Gazpacho Malaca, 31
   Hake à la Cazuela, 93
   Paella, 104
   Pescado al Horno, 93
   Sangria, 23
   Tortilla de Patata, 107
Spanakopita (Greece), 108
Spiced Beef (Ireland), 50
Spiced Beef with Fresh Asparagus
   (China), 54
Spiced Pecans, 18
Spicy Cajun Shrimp Remoulade, 104
Spinach
   Chicken Stuffed with Pork, Spinach,
      and Pine Nuts, 89
   Espinacas Catalan (Spain), 136
   Gnocchi di Spinaci (Italy), 117
   Picnic Pasta Salad, 41
   Sole Florentine, 98
   Spanakopita (Greece), 108
   Spinach and Sausage Casserole
      (Italy), 69
   Spinach Artichoke Casserole, 136
   Spinach Borscht, 35
   Spinach Souffle, 135
   Spinach Strata Supreme, 135
   Veal Florentine with Sauce Choron
      (France), 70
Spirited Angel Food Cake, 151
Spoonbread, 128
Spring Into Summer Salad, 43
Squash Casserole, 139

Stewed Tomatoes, Beans, and
   Artichokes (Greece), 136
Stifado (Greece), 77
Stir-Fried Shrimp and Ham Rice
   (China), 105
St. Nicholas French Stew, 75
Straw and Grass Pasta alla Edwards, 119
Strawberries
   Charlotte aux Fraises (France), 177
   Strawberries Elizabeth Nourse, 176
   Strawberry Cloud, 176
   Strawberry Mousse, 177
   Strawberry Sabayon, 177
   Strawberry Souffle, 178
Streusel Napfkuchen, 146
Stuffed Cabbage, 57
Stuffed Cabbage Roll with
   Sauerkraut, 56
Stuffed Mushrooms (England), 15
Stuffed Mushrooms with Bechamel
   Sauce, 130
Stuffed Pork Loin (Germany), 65
Stuffed Quail, 93
Sukiyaki (Japan), 57
Sultan Reshat Pilavi (Turkey), 63
Sun-Dried Tomatoes with Pasta, 118
Sunomono (Japan), 44
Sweden
   Baked Fish Mousse with Lobster
      Sauce, 94
   Pepperkakor, 163
   Scandinavian Sampler Loaves, 143
   Sillsalad, 42
Sweet and Sour Potato Salad, 42
Sweetbreads
   Ris de Veau, Madeira (France), 78
   Sweetbreads and Ham, 78
Swiss Sausage Casserole, 69
Switzerland
   Cheese Fondue, 116
   Rösti nach Zürcherart, 132
   Zürich Cherries Jubilee, 168

T

Tabbouleh Salad, 43
Taft Fruit Cake, 152
Tagliarini con Carne (Italy), 122
Tamale Pie (Mexico), 68
Tangy Cheese Bread, 11
Taramosalata (Greece), 22
Teriyaki Roast Tenderloin (Japan), 56

Terrine de Canard aux Raisins
(France), 23
Tiropita (Greece), 23
Toad-in-the-Hole (England), 69
Tomatoes
Aunt Dannie's Baked Tomatoes and
Artichoke Hearts, 137
Crustless Vegetable Pie, 140
Greek Summer Salad (Greece), 39
Green Beans in Olive Oil
(Middle East), 125
Les Tomates Françaises
(France), 136
Mystras Style Greek Vegetable
Casserole, 140
Nona Sauce for Pasta (Italy), 87
Pasta Sauce with Beef and
Mushrooms (Italy), 119
Pescado al Horno (Spain), 93
Picnic Pasta Salad, 41
Puerto Rican Paella (Puerto Rico), 90
Skewered Chicken, 84
Stewed Tomatoes, Beans, and
Artichokes (Greece), 136
Sun-Dried Tomatoes with Pasta, 119
Tomato Pudding, 137
Tomato Soup au Gratin, 35
Tortilla de Patata (Spain), 107
Tortillas, Flour (Mexico), 142
Tostadas de Carne (Mexico), 22
Trout and Bacon (Wales), 97
Turkish Coffee (Turkey), 24
Turkish Lamb Kabobs (Turkey), 61
Turnips
Clapshot (Scotland), 133
Navets à l'Orange (France), 137
Tzatziki (Greece), 24

U

Unheated Relish, 46

V

Veal
Ossobuco (Italy), 72
Veal Florentine with Sauce Choron
(France), 70
Veal Morels (France), 71
Veal Patties with Mushroom Cream
Gravy, 72
Veal Scallopini with Mushrooms
(Italy), 73

Veal Scallopini with Roquefort Sauce
(France), 73
Veal Stew, 77
Vitello alla Fiorentina (Italy), 70
Wiener Schnitzel (Austria), 74
Velvet Sweet Corn Soup (China), 29
Vichy Carrot Salad, 38
Vitello alla Fiorentina (Italy), 70

W

Waffles, Orange, 144
Walnut Wonder Cake, 156
Weisswurst (Germany), 73
West Indies Chicken Pilau, 90
Western Style Baked Lima Beans, 123
Wheat Bread, Whole or Cracked, 141
Whole Wheat Bread, 143
Wiener Schnitzel (Austria), 74
Wild Rice Soup, 36

Y

Yakitori (Japan), 87
Yeast Breads
Coffee Kuchen, 145
English Muffin Bread, 141
French or Italian Bread, 142
Herb Bread, 142
Honey Yeast Bread, 141
Raisin Bread, 142
Scandinavian Sampler Loaves
(Sweden), 143
Whole or Cracked Wheat Bread, 141
Whole Wheat Bread, 143
Yorkshire Pudding (England), 122
Yorkshire Pudding, Individual
(England), 122

Z

Zucchini
Courgettes à la Creme (France), 139
Crustless Vegetable Pie, 140
Frosted Zucchini or Potato
Rounds, 139
Marinated Mixed Vegetables, 140
Mystras Style Greek Vegetable
Casserole, 140
Parmesan Zucchini (Italy), 138
Squash Casserole, 139
Zucchini and Cucumber Salad
(Africa), 43
Zucchini Casserole, 137

Zucchini Nut Muffins, 147
Zucchini Parmesan, 138
Zucchini Puffs (Turkey), 138
Zucchini Ripiene (Italy), 138
Zucchini Stew (Italy), 77
Zürich Cherries Jubilee
(Switzerland), 168

From Palette to Palate

Order Form
Return to: Publications Department, Cincinnati Art Museum, Eden Park, Cincinnati, Ohio 45202

I would like to order . . . . . copies of **From Palette to Palate** *at $15.95 each plus $2.50 shipping. Shipping for each additional copy is $1.00. I wish to pay by ☐ check or money order enclosed and made payable to the Cincinnati Art Museum; ☐ Visa; ☐ MasterCard; ☐ American Express.*

Signature . . . .

Expiration date . . . . *Account number* . . . .

Send cookbook(s) to: Name . . . .

Address . . . .

City, State, Zip . . . .

Telephone . . . .

. . . . *cookbooks at $15.95 each, Ohio residents add state sales tax of 88¢ per cookbook* $ . . . .

Shipping charges ($2.50 for one cookbook and $1.00 per each additional copy) $ . . . .

Total enclosed $ . . . .

Office use only: rec'd . . . . *comp* . . . .

Proceeds from the sale of the cookbook will benefit the general operations of the Cincinnati Art Museum.

Order Form
Return to: Publications Department, Cincinnati Art Museum, Eden Park, Cincinnati, Ohio 45202

I would like to order . . . . . copies of **From Palette to Palate** *at $15.95 each plus $2.50 shipping. Shipping for each additional copy is $1.00. I wish to pay by ☐ check or money order enclosed and made payable to the Cincinnati Art Museum; ☐ Visa; ☐ MasterCard; ☐ American Express.*

Signature . . . .

Expiration date . . . . *Account number* . . . .

Send cookbook(s) to: Name . . . .

Address . . . .

City, State, Zip . . . .

Telephone . . . .

. . . . *cookbooks at $15.95 each, Ohio residents add state sales tax of 88¢ per cookbook* $ . . . .

Shipping charges ($2.50 for one cookbook and $1.00 per each additional copy) $ . . . .

Total enclosed $ . . . .

Office use only: rec'd . . . . *comp* . . . .

Proceeds from the sale of the cookbook will benefit the general operations of the Cincinnati Art Museum.